Whiting Up

Whiting Up

Whiteface Minstrels & Stage Europeans in African American Performance

Marvin McAllister

The University of North Carolina Press *Chapel Hill*

Designed and set in Miller and TheSerif by Rebecca Evans

Manufactured in the United States of America

The paper in this book meets the guidelines for permanence and durability of the Committee on Production Guidelines for Book Longevity of the Council on Library Resources.

The University of North Carolina Press has been a member of the Green Press Initiative since 2003.

Library of Congress Cataloging-in-Publication Data
McAllister, Marvin Edward, 1969–
Whiting up : whiteface minstrels and stage Europeans in African American performance / by Marvin McAllister.
p. cm.
Includes bibliographical references and index.
ISBN 978-0-8078-3508-1 (cloth : alk. paper)
ISBN 978-1-4696-1880-7 (pbk. : alk. paper)
1. Minstrel shows—United States—History. 2. African Americans in the performing arts—History. I. Title.
PN1969.M5M33 2011 791.43′652996073—dc23 2011020426

cloth 15 14 13 12 11 5 4 3 2 1
paper 18 17 16 15 14 5 4 3 2 1

THIS BOOK WAS DIGITALLY PRINTED.

to Maya A.

who is already making her books

Contents

Illustrations

Acknowledgments

I first encountered whiteface minstrelsy in an advanced placement U.S. history course during my senior year of high school, but I did not fully appreciate what I had been exposed to until several years later. In one especially memorable class session, a fellow student delivered a curious oral report on slavery in the antebellum South. Temporally, his presentation concentrated on the late eighteenth and early nineteenth centuries; geographically, he focused on the once major seaport town of Charleston, South Carolina. The presentation left an enduring impression on me because after extensive research, my classmate tried to inform us that some Charleston slaves earned their own money, occasionally lived apart from their masters, and even strolled down the city's main thoroughfares sporting ornate walking sticks, waistcoats, parasols, silk handkerchiefs, and fine dresses.

We were shocked and confused. Economic privilege and resplendent apparel did not square with the image of slavery most of us had learned in previous history courses or absorbed by watching Alex Haley's *Roots*; in fact, my classmate's report seemed like a cruel misrepresentation of a national tragedy. But he did have evidence. He read passages from slave narratives, travel journals by European visitors, and slaveholder diaries, all minutely detailing what the most fashionable enslaved Africans were wearing in the South. Despite those primary documents, my fellow students and I were still embarrassed for this kid but not empathetic enough to refrain from laughing at him. Regrettably, we were cruel to this young, revisionist historian, and our teacher even lectured him on the problematic representations of human bondage in his florid report. He took his seat, amidst giggles and odd looks, a bit confused and probably angry because he had done so much work on this stupid presentation.

It would take me years to fully understand what my former classmate was attempting to revise about our understanding of American history and slavery. Once I immersed myself in the same travel journals and master narratives he had consulted, I realized why his historically accurate report went horribly awry. He erred by asking the wrong question about slavery, wrong for our late-1980s understanding of that evil institution. He asked, Can any individual pleasure or personal freedom ever be found in human bondage? Slavery decimated families, perpetrated cultural and physical genocide, and inflicted heinous corporeal and psychic damage, but somehow this young historian unearthed pleasure in the midst of degradation, located a level of agency and self-esteem thought impossible for an enslaved population. After researching, writing about, and teaching the performance tradition of whiting up for several years, I now appreciate how and why African Americans can create insightful and spectacular performances of whiteness even in extreme moments of subjugation.

The seed, the potential for such appreciation, was planted by my former high school classmate, but the research and writing of this project was made possible through generous financial and intellectual support from various universities, research centers, and students. Mostly notably, I want to acknowledge the University of California–Berkeley's Chancellor's Postdoctoral Fellowship for Academic Diversity, the English department at the University of South Carolina–Columbia, and finally the Moorland-Spingarn Research Center and Channing Pollock Theatre Collection, both housed at Howard University. I especially want to thank Adia B. Coleman, research technician at Howard University's Founders Library, for helping me find the whiteface image that appears on the cover of this book.

As for conceptualizing whiting up, several university theater departments and their students have helped me define and clarify this tradition. At the Catholic University of America, I taught my first whiting up course to intellectually swift undergraduates who willingly ventured into unknown territory as we wrestled with various incarnations of whiteface minstrels and stage Europeans. At the University of California–Berkeley and the City University of New York's Graduate Center, I worked with undergraduate and graduate students who were generally open to analyzing race and representation but at times were understandably skeptical of this alleged performance tradition. I want to express my sincere gratitude to two CUNY graduate students, Patricia Herrera and Carmelina Cartei, who both were committed to illuminating this tradition and produced independent research projects that contributed significantly to this study.

I should also recognize and thank the many black artists I appropriate to define this tradition, from iconic celebrities like Whoopi Goldberg to theatrical footnotes like Harry Gillam. Most of these gifted innovators probably never realized they were contributing to a centuries-old Afro-Diasporic tradition of performed whiteness, but as a cultural historian and dramaturg, I am drawn to moments where courageous artists engage in potentially divisive yet ultimately transgressive cross-racial play. Offstage, onstage, on film, and on television, African American artists are creatively exploring and actively reconstructing whiteness, so consequently, friends, colleagues, and family members are constantly informing me of the latest whiting up act they witnessed. Of course this relatively brief study does not pretend to catalog every stage European or whiteface minstrel ever created or brought to my attention. There are still many more whiting up acts to research and analyze, because as Eddie Murphy warns at the end of his 1985 short film *White Like Me*, "We are out there and we have lots of makeup."

Whiting Up

Introduction

Whiting Up Work

This book is about a dual Afro-Diasporic tradition of whiteface minstrels and stage Europeans that has operated for centuries just beneath America's representational radar. From their earliest days in the New World, enslaved Africans and free blacks have carefully studied and re-created Euro-American culture in semiprivate social gatherings, illegal late-night cabals, and conventional theatrical spaces. I define whiteface minstrelsy as extra-theatrical, social performance in which people of African descent appropriate white-identified gestures, vocabulary, dialects, dress, or social entitlements. Attuned to class as much as race, whiteface minstrels often satirize, parody, and interrogate privileged or authoritative representations of whiteness. Stage Europeans can be defined as black actors appropriating white dramatic characters crafted initially by white dramatists and, later, by black playwrights.[1] Rooted in conventional theatrical practice, this component emphasizes physical and vocal manifestations of whiteness, often relying on visual effects such as white face paint and blonde wigs.

During the past two decades, a handful of scholars have produced historically grounded and theoretically rich work on performed whiteness, and this study builds on their scholarship.[2] However, whiting up has never been systematically analyzed as a coherent and sustained performance tradition until now. Ideally, this academic study will contextualize and popularize a unique brand of cross-racial performance with the potential to rehabilitate racial cross-dressing in American theater and expand representational opportunities for artists of all colors. Beyond historicizing an underappreciated African American tradition, this history harbors an ulterior motive, an ambitious, perhaps quixotic desire to influence the present and future of live performance.

Throughout the 1960s, minority actors saw a significant spike in theatrical opportunities, as institutions such as Joseph Papp's New York Shakespeare Festival embraced and advanced color-blind and nontraditional casting practices.[3] In an important 1996 speech to the Theatre Communication Group's national conference, playwright August Wilson equated color-blind casting with assimilation and encouraged black Americans to reject both ideas. Wilson took specific aim at stage Europeans when he declared, "To mount an all black production of *Death of A Salesman* or any other play conceived for white actors as an investigation of the human condition through the specific of white culture is to deny us our own humanity, our own history, and the need to make our own investigations from the cultural ground on which we stand as black Americans."[4] I fully appreciate Wilson's argument, and his call for historically and culturally grounded black theatrical production echoes the opinion of many African American theatrical artists and critics who came before him. Like Wilson, I also question the cultural agenda and even the plausibility of color-blind casting. Yet this book reconsiders and expands the cultural ground on which African American artists have worked and can continue to work. Our performance history has always involved black actors, writers, and social performers appropriating and investigating whiteness as a vehicle for communal and individual definition.

In terms of professional development, black actors have embraced but questioned the progress of nontraditional casting in American theater. In a 1991 interview, veteran African American actor Earle Hyman explained that "theater is illusion. . . . It is not a reality, however much it may seem so at times."[5] For Hyman, strict fidelity to social and biological categories such as race or gender was hardly a prerequisite for this representational medium. Solo performer and documentary theater artist Anna Deavere Smith has taken a similar position, arguing that if American writers, directors, producers, and casting agents insist only men can perform men and only whites can perform whites, then we are inhibiting "the spirit of the theater."[6] Both Hyman and Smith draw important distinctions between lived experience and the spirit or illusion of theatrical practice; more importantly, they explicitly challenge future generations to embrace race, gender, and other identities as fluid rather than fixed, as performable by everyone.

An impatient Earle Hyman also remarked, "I am 65 years old, and I'm still saying that all roles should be available to all actors of talent, regardless of race. Why should I be deprived of seeing a great black actress play

Hedda Gabler?" But the veteran actor only had to wait four years to witness television and stage actress CCH Pounder tackle Henrik Ibsen's Hedda in a 1995 production at San Diego's Old Globe, staged by African American director and color-blind casting advocate Sheldon Epps.[7] Unlike recent twenty-first-century revivals of Arthur Miller's *Death of a Salesman* or Tennessee Williams's *Cat on a Hot Tin Roof*, in which white family dramas were transformed into all-black family dramas, Pounder played the singular Norwegian heroine without transposing Ibsen's original narrative to a more easily identifiable black cultural context.[8] Although August Wilson might have objected to this bold casting decision, Pounder's Hedda represents an increasingly common example of what can happen when roles are made available to skilled actors regardless of race. As far as the ground on which she stood, Pounder's representational triumph was made possible by a host of earlier whiting up acts.

One such act was crafted by musical theater pioneer Robert Allen Cole Jr., known onstage as Bob Cole. In the early 1890s, this gifted young comedian and writer joined an innovative colored road show known as the Black Patti Troubadours, led by the opera diva Matilda Sissieretta Jones, or "Black Patti." As a featured performer for the Black Patti company, Cole developed a red-bearded tramp named Willie Wayside, a dispossessed, lovable loser perpetually down on his luck. Following a messy divorce from the white-owned Black Patti venture, Cole kept tinkering with and transforming his tramp into the white hobo who graces the cover of this book. Cole's agenda was to master allegedly white artistic forms, such as comedic specialties, in order to convince theatrical owners, producers, and managers that black artists could be as versatile as white talent. To elevate the status of Negro artists and, by extension, all of Afro-America, Cole took deadly aim at the nation's signature popular entertainment, blackface minstrelsy.[9]

For nearly eight decades, minstrel caricatures like Zip Coon and Jim Crow had inflicted serious and potentially irreversible damage on black American imagery. In the wake of blackface's commercial dominance, Negro performers like Matilda Jones, Bert Williams, and Bob Cole were limited in the roles they could assume. Matilda Jones managed to expand her professional prospects by mastering opera, and Cole attempted a similar feat through his red-bearded, whiteface (or mauve-face) stage European Willie Wayside. With blackface performance still very much alive, Cole reversed the minstrel mask and developed his white hobo as the central figure in an independently produced black musical, *A Trip to*

Coontown (1897). Following two Broadway runs and domestic and international tours, Cole's lovable loser became so recognizable that his image was used in an advertising campaign for laundry detergent and plastered on billboards across the nation.[10]

By definition, an artistic tradition presumes a long-standing set of styles, rules, codes, or modes that are passed on to subsequent generations of artists. Whiting up qualifies as a tradition because nearly a century after Cole trumped blackface with whiteface, African American hip hop innovator Busta Rhymes, along with director Hype Williams, crafted a pair of whiteface characters for the video of Rhymes's 1997 single "Dangerous." This music video features Rhymes trading his signature dreadlocks for a mop of stringy blonde hair to parody Mel Gibson's suicidal and exceedingly dangerous cop from the *Lethal Weapon* franchise. Also in the video, a member of Rhymes's "flip-mode squad," his creative entourage, applies white makeup and a bowl-cut blonde wig to embody an equally unhinged white supercriminal, played by Gary Busey in the original *Lethal Weapon*. Not done with these "flip-mode" theatrics, Busta Rhymes would later parlay his dangerous whiteface creation into something more marketable, a hyperkinetic white "skate rat" in a national Mountain Dew commercial.[11]

At the turn of two different centuries, musical pioneer Bob Cole and hip hop legend Busta Rhymes crisscrossed W. E. B. DuBois's "color line" with comedic, highly commercial appropriations of whiteness. On racial and performative levels, their cross-racial theatrics trespassed on representational terrain long thought to be the exclusive domain of white performers. In her work on popular entertainment, Daphne Brooks theorizes the notion of "performance as property," specifically how white cultural producers were determined to control racial representation and define black imagery for as long as possible.[12] Writing about "doing" blackness, E. Patrick Johnson queries if popular cross-racial appropriations, such as blackface minstrelsy, have to be rooted in subjugation. Johnson also asks if there are moments when the colonized have used the "colonizer's forms as an act of resistance" and if the colonizer has ever been "humanized by the presence of the colonized."[13] By whiting up, black artists like Bob Cole and Busta Rhymes have transformed "white" forms into resistant acts, humanized white America, and proven that cross-racial theatrics do not have to denigrate or exclude.

Whiting up operates in two closely related performance modes, whiteface minstrels and stage Europeans, and the primary difference between the two manifestations is context: extra-theatrical whiteface minstrels in less controlled public spaces versus more structured stage Europeans in conventional dramatic genres and theatrical contexts. Whiteface minstrelsy includes historical forms like plantation cakewalks or leisurely Sunday strolls along major city thoroughfares, as well as modern social performance such as the "white people be like" routines performed by black stand-up comics in interracial venues. Typically, stage Europeans appear in lighter theatrical genres like musicals and comedies, but over the decades, black artists have explored whiteness in serious theatrical modes, especially tragedy and expressionistic drama. The two halves of this tradition also reflect our predominant conceptions of culture: culture as a standard of excellence rooted in aesthetic forms like opera and drama, and culture as a particular way of life expressing specific meanings and values. Stage Europeans allow black artists to master what Matthew Arnold once called "the best that has been thought and said in the world," while whiteface minstrels reach beyond traditional artistic practices to play with or subvert white ways and cultural meanings.[14] Afro-America's dualistic, studied cross-racial play represents a form of symbolic inversion that unleashes chaotic, potentially dangerous energy without being particularly threatening, in most cases. This performance tradition exposes the ordering principles of America's racial and cultural hierarchies, while questioning the absolutism of these structures.[15]

This study of theatrical and extra-theatrical performed whiteness has been shaped by two sets of interrelated questions: First, who are these black artists turned cultural critics and why are they crafting cross-racial acts? Second, for whom are these artists performing, for whose benefit, and what are the multiple audience reactions at various historical moments?[16] In her work on postsoul comedy, Bambi Haggins embraces the term "persona" to theorize how artists project performative identities in relation to personal, professional, and political histories. As for an artist's persona and personal history, I am only interested in those biographical details that directly contribute to an artist's constructed onstage or offstage identities.[17] With each whiting up act, black artists engage in a subtle intercultural negotiation between three distinct identity streams: the black performer's sense of his or her own professional and cultural positions, which may be fluid or somewhat fixed; contemporaneous audience perceptions of whiteness and blackness, which can be historically grounded, stereotypic, mythic, and even archetypal; and finally, forward-projecting reconsiderations or reconstructions of what whiteness and blackness, as well as other identity markers such as class and gender, can potentially signify for artist and audience. Some of the personae featured in this history understand and fully embrace identities as dynamic, open-ended cultural products and use this knowledge to advance their careers and undermine audience assumptions. Conversely, other whiting up artists exploit essential notions of whiteness and blackness to expose white supremacy, affirm audience perceptions, and advance political or social agendas well beyond the performance moment.[18]

As for how audiences read and react to these intercultural negotiations, in her analysis of "Creole beauties" in nineteenth-century black musical revues, Jayna Brown approaches her female subject as a "performed social position, as a sign" operating in a specific cultural context.[19] The signs and significations of mixed-race female performers in popular musicals or black actors playing white roles on the American stage only have meaning in relation to the rigid and shifting perceptions of their audiences. With this in mind, I treat whiteness and blackness as performed social positions rooted in specific historical moments, not as lived experiences or racial absolutes. I am guided by historian Matthew Jacobson's succinct admonition that "race resides not in nature but in politics and culture."[20] Therefore, to truly appreciate how black artists have imaginatively reconstructed whiteness, we first need to understand how powerful political, legal, and social constructs have transformed whiteness into highly valued property. We also need to recognize the important distinctions between a dual performance tradition like whiting up and other social engagements with whiteness.

Whiteness as Property: Passing and "Acting White"

Whiting up is the product of a complex history of racial, cultural, and political stratification predicated on the inferiority of nonwhites in the United States. Yet even as the Euro-American majority declared racial minorities deficient, cultural critic Anne Cheng found that these racial others were still "assimilated" or, more specifically, "uneasily digested by American nationality."[21] In fact, this nation-state instituted racial domination even while trumpeting the ideals of American inclusion and unlimited opportunities in the New World. The United States has always been a contradictory multiracial, polyethnic, intercultural republic where even the most disempowered could exert cultural and psychic influence on the national imagination. But at its core, this nation has consistently viewed too much diversity as detrimental to a more perfect union, and especially troubling was a persistent "Negro problem": how to integrate and acculturate a significant population of African peoples.[22]

To order its problematic ethnic and racial plurality, the majority culture developed political, racial, and legal hierarchies that solidified a privileged whiteness on top and a debased blackness on the bottom. I intentionally use the term "hierarchy" rather than "binary" because a binary assumes a horizontal relationship between two poles of relatively equal weight, but this has never been the case for blackness and whiteness in the United States. A color-coded, vertical hierarchy first emerged with America's race-based slavery in the early seventeenth century, and by the 1680s, the first slave codes officially aligned racial identity with legal status, effectively marking "black" as enslaved and "white" as free. In 1790, a young U.S. Congress formally institutionalized a race-based political and legal hierarchy when it declared that "free white persons," no other races, "shall be entitled to the rights of citizenship." Thus, at the outset of this fledgling nation, American citizenship, and its attendant legal rights, was defined in racial terms.[23]

After emancipation, black codes and sharecropping further reinforced racial, economic, and legal hierarchies by criminalizing and virtually reenslaving black workers in the South; in addition, Jim Crow segregation officially divided black, white, yellow, and brown Americans in public spaces.[24] For decades, this ongoing process of racial stratification has defined the aspirations and prospects of American citizens, potential citizens, and even international visitors. European immigrants, Native Americans, New World Latinos, Asian immigrants, and African Americans have toiled, competed, and strategized to secure better positions within this country's racial, legal, and political structures. At certain key moments in U.S. history, rebellious Native Americans, resistant Mexicans, lower-class Irishmen, and Chinese "coolie" laborers have all been relegated to the "blackened" basement of our national hierarchies. Conversely, at other historical stages, Hispanic assimilationists and "model" Asian minorities have progressed up the racial and economic ladders. Waves of potentially white Americans, including late nineteenth-century Irish immigrants, early twentieth-century Italian arrivals, and even visitors from modern-day Israel, have all been introduced to a color-coded power structure that expects them to identify with a socially and legally privileged whiteness.[25]

The theoretical field of whiteness studies offers useful tools for understanding the relationships between whiteness, hierarchies, and cultural property.[26] According to Richard Dyer, the fundamental goals of whiteness studies are to expose whiteness as a culturally constructed race and to end the false assumptions that equate white with human. Historians George Lipsitz and David Roediger have traced the impact of a "possessive investment in whiteness" on white and black Americans. Especially enlightening is Roediger's concept of "herrenvolk republicanism," a racialized understanding of politics wherein white working-class groups are encouraged to align politically with privileged whiteness, often against their own economic interests.[27] Expanding on this idea, legal theorist Cheryl Harris reveals how, in a "society structured on racial subordination," whiteness has become property that can be used, enjoyed, and even denied to others. In America's racial hierarchy, whiteness has developed an autonomous, all-embracing quality, seemingly independent of the system of racial subordination that produced it.[28] For Dyer, Harris, and these other scholars, their intellectual activism attempts to undo or counteract this all-embracing, universalized notion of whiteness.

Given that whiteness has become a prized possession in America, one could potentially read whiting up as black theatrical and extra-theatrical artists strategically investing in whiteness and attempting to progress up the racial ladder toward opportunity, wealth, and prestige. Anthropologist Melville Herskovits claims enslaved Africans came to identify whiteness with a better way of life because whites rested atop the colonial and national power structures.[29] Similarly, from his postcolonial position, psychiatrist-turned-revolutionary Frantz Fanon offered this dire prognosis for the Negro: "However painful it may be for me to accept this conclusion, I am obliged to state it: For the black man there is only one destiny. And it is white."[30] It is true that when confronted with a dominant group's insistence on acculturation to a set of values, subordinate groups will often embrace the most appealing aspects of the ruling culture. But literary critic Hortense Spillers warns that we should be careful how we use oft-quoted sources like Fanon and Herskovits. Spillers contends "African-American culture is open, by definition," which means the black American psyche and personality is "situated in the crossroads of conflicting motivations so entangled that it is not always easy to designate what is 'black' and 'white.'"[31] With this notion of openness and crossroads as a guide, I hope to build more nuanced readings of Afro-America's acculturative processes.

For some African Americans, racial passing offered a stealth strategy for moving up the blackness/whiteness hierarchy, a strategy that implicitly endorsed the notion of whiteness as property. Passing is a social and cultural deception practiced by legally defined black citizens who visually appear white and take advantage of their biology to assimilate into the majority-white culture.[32] In slave and postemancipation contexts, many black Americans used passing as an avenue for material advancement, and as a rule, they were expected to perform an exact replica of whiteness. After all, remaining undetected marks the successful racial passer. Yet, there has always been a subversive dynamic to this racial cross-dressing. Feminist theorist Valerie Smith explains how a passing body simultaneously invokes and transgresses "the boundaries between the races and the sexes that structure the American social hierarchy." Passing reveals "a contradiction between appearance and 'essential' racial identity within a system of racial distinctions based upon differences presumed to be visible."[33] For centuries, racial passers have silently proven that what you see is not what you get, thus exposing the unreliability of racial and legal categories predicated on drops of blood. However, the key word here is "silently," because a racial passer can never openly announce the contradictions and fallacies he or she has revealed in America's visually based, color-coded hierarchy.

Another product of this insidious racial hierarchy is the "acting white" taunt. This historically rooted social pathology first emerged in response to enslaved Africans and free blacks who attempted to acculturate and improve their positions. They were accused by blacks and whites of striving to be white, and behind this name-calling was a damaging false consciousness that assumed certain tools of advancement, like ambition or erudition, were the exclusive properties of Euro-Americans.[34] Today, accusations of "acting white" still circulate in corporate America and in classrooms where high-achieving minorities working to progress professionally or educationally are deemed "white" by their peers. Working with a sample of 90,000 young students, Harvard economics professor Roland G. Fryer concluded that taunts of "acting white" are about personal performance in public settings and who dictates the parameters of these performances. The name-calling assumes "educated" looks, acts, and sounds a certain way and demands whites and nonwhites behave accordingly and not assume "borrowed robes."[35] Consistent with the concept of whiteness as exclusive property, this peer pressure is predicated on the assumption that minority students can never fully own allegedly white habits and aspirations.

Fryer closes his study of "acting white" by calling for new identity models to inspire minority students, but his exceptional analysis stops short of outlining what those new identities might look or sound like. Although this project does not purport to help students of color navigate everyday issues of whiteness, aspiration, and personal identity, it does demonstrate how artistic negotiations of whiteness and blackness, over several centuries, have placed a different face on achievement. Whiting up, not to be confused with the stealth practice of passing or the proprietary accusation of "acting white," was never about becoming white or sanctioning the nationally endorsed notion of whiteness as property. Unlike racial passers, stage Europeans and whiteface minstrels openly exploit the fissures and inconsistencies in America's hierarchies. From the late 1700s through the early twenty-first century, in multiple performance modes, black artists have challenged cultural and racial assumptions by transferring supposed markers of whiteness, like grace and universal humanity, to black bodies.

Whiting Up Work

The primary functional difference between whiting up and passing is best exemplified by an early whiteface minstrel act: Homer Plessy's subversive Louisiana train ride in 1892. Plessy, a mulatto with an especially fair complexion, decided to pass on an all-white train car to contest an 1890 Louisiana state law that mandated separate accommodations on public conveyances. Plessy casually assumed a seat in the white car but later announced his nonwhiteness, got arrested, and then pressed his legal suit all the way to the U.S. Supreme Court. Through an imaginative reading of the 1896 *Plessy v. Ferguson* case, performance theorist Joseph Roach arrived at the first definition of whiteface minstrelsy: "stereotypical behaviors such as white folks' sometime comically obsessive habits of claiming for themselves ever more fanciful forms of property, ingenious entitlements under the law, and exclusivity in the use of public spaces and facilities."[36] Roach identifies the all-white train car as an excellent example of "fanciful" white privilege, and I contend Plessy's social performance was a whiteface minstrel assault that appropriated and exposed this "ingenious entitlement." Unlike a racial passer, Plessy never planned to steal an undisturbed ride on a Louisiana train; rather, his expropriation of white advantage was designed to challenge the validity and enforceability of laws governing separate accommodations.[37] As part of his nineteenth-century whiteface political action, Plessy fully accessed whiteness, as legal and performative property, to reveal its loopholes, its constructed nature, and even its terror. This is the cultural work of whiting up.

The title of this study respectfully signifies on Robert Toll's influential blackface minstrel history *Blacking Up* (1974). Building on Toll's work, minstrel revisionists from Alexander Saxton to Eric Lott have expanded the conversation on blackface minstrelsy to include aversion/attraction dualities, class identity formation, political dissent, and even gender transgressions.[38] Responding to these important revisions, cultural historian Saidiya Hartman warns that "the seeming transgression of the color line and the identification forged with the blackface mask through aversion and/or desire ultimately served only to reinforce relations of mastery and servitude." While not completely denying some cross-racial identifications, Hartman emphasizes the white supremacy embedded in this popular theatrical form and its reinscription of a one-sided Manichaean competition between the races.[39] From behind a borrowed black mask and through a counterfeit black body, whites may have articulated class tensions, but ultimately America's racial hierarchy remained unchallenged. According to historian Kevin Gaines, the "most insidious" aspect of blackface minstrelsy was its mockery of African American aspiration as "a futile desire to be white."[40] This implied derision of ambitious black talent like Bert Williams, Bob Cole, and George Walker echoes the insidious "acting white" taunt, that crippling social pathology predicated on the idea of whiteness as desirable but never fully accessible performative property.

Far from aspiring toward whiteness, whiting up has always been about inserting black performers into this uniquely American conversation on race, class, and representation. When Bob Cole reversed the minstrel mask to create his down-and-out, whiteface Willie Wayside, he combined a satirical treatment of racial difference with a legitimate respect for the humanity of his lower-class white subject. As Saidiya Hartman and Kevin Gaines suggest, blackface failed to reach its full cultural and political potential because this entertainment was predicated on a privileged whiteness and a debased blackness. In stark contrast, the earliest whiteface minstrels and stage Europeans offered an alternative brand of cross-racial play generally devoid of the need to denigrate white bodies.

When I look at the cover image of Bob Cole as Willie Wayside, I am struck by the realism and specificity in this publicity illustration. In vibrant color, we can see how Cole's pinkish mauve complexion was nothing like the identity-effacing blackface mask of burnt cork or black greasepaint. Unlike the nondescript circus clowns in their whiteface makeup, this red-bearded stage European was brimming with personality and humanity. Instead of creating caricatured cross-racial performances to exact revenge on counterfeit Euro-American blackface minstrels, Bob Cole and other whiting up artists respectfully redeployed whiteness to stage their own liberation. The revisionists have written extensively about how the white originators of blackface minstrelsy experienced representational freedom from behind the mask, a sense of liberation that allowed them to move without inhibition and celebrate disorder in public spaces.[41] Similarly, through their whiteface masks or borrowed stage Europeans, African American artists experienced a license denied them in everyday life, as they could now say and do the socially forbidden, experiment with new black identities, and redefine their roles in American society.

In terms of where whiting up works, this dual tradition is by no means limited to specific artistic forms or mediums; whiteface minstrels and stage Europeans have appeared in theater, film, television, radio, and literature. One of the most well-known stage European acts is captured in Eddie Murphy's satiric short film *White Like Me*, broadcast on *Saturday Night Live* in 1985. Murphy and his writing partner Andy Breckman created a fantastical, passing scenario wherein Murphy applies whiteface makeup and a blonde wig, trains in white physical and linguistic mannerisms, and then infiltrates behind "enemy lines."[42] Without question Murphy and Breckman's stage European creation fully demonstrates the mainstream popularity of this dual performance tradition. However, after teaching university seminars that featured whiting up acts from film, television, and theater, I realized a comprehensive exploration of performed whiteness in multiple artistic media and over several geographic locations would require several volumes by a handful of qualified scholars.[43] Therefore, I made the calculated decisions to limit this project to one Afro-Diasporic location and to concentrate on live performance. As a theater historian and dramaturg, I am most comfortable and conversant with this material, so my study concentrates on social performance, solo performance, theatrical production, and stand-up comedy in the United States. Yet to recover the cultural work and audience dynamics of whiting up, I do rely on what Philip Auslander calls "mediatized performance," specifically solo performance videos and stand-up comedy albums based in "technologies of reproduction."[44]

As for how whiting up works, I have identified four cultural and political functions of whiteface minstrels and stage Europeans in African American performance. Although I am disaggregating this dual tradition into four distinct modes, any single act of performed whiteness can exhibit several of these functions simultaneously. The first function involves subtle and occasionally aggressive satires and parodies of whiteness, with the ultimate goal of undermining racial hierarchies. This mode is about seizing representational control and hitting satiric targets; more specifically, it addresses basic questions such as what do black artists want their audiences looking and laughing at, and why? In Chapter 1 I analyze a series of satiric and parodic whiteface minstrel acts—cakewalks, country dances, and weekly fashionable promenades—in and around Charleston, South Carolina, during the colonial and antebellum periods. I contend that white privilege was the immediate target of these social performances; however, as enslaved Africans and free blacks openly mocked or gently parodied European dance, dress, and pretension, their motivated signifying did not rest at mere derision.

In Chapters 3 and 5 I historicize and analyze satiric and parodic stage Europeans crafted by African American writers and performers. Chapter 3 catalogs a menagerie of stage Europeans from Bob Cole and Billy Johnson's *A Trip to Coontown*, a groundbreaking black musical written, produced, and performed solely by African Americans. While Cole and company produced mild parodies of white lower-class, working-class, and middle-class subjects, Douglas Turner Ward's whiteface fantasy *Day of Absence* (1965) engages in sharp and potentially divisive satire. Ward's reverse minstrel show targets and derides an anachronistic, "confederate" southern whiteness while speaking directly and compellingly to racial and occupational stratification in 1960s America. Finally, in Chapter 6, we return to whiteface minstrelsy and satire as we examine stand-up comedy and solo performance in the twentieth and twenty-first centuries. For decades, black stand-up comics have exploited, with varying degrees of success, a brand of "white people be like" humor rooted in white and black signs of cultural difference. In Chapter 6 I analyze how comics such as Jackie "Moms" Mabley, Dick Gregory, Richard Pryor, and Dave Chappelle, as well as solo performance artists like Whoopi Goldberg, Anna Deavere Smith, and Sarah Jones, target racial assumptions and challenge hierarchies during the civil rights, Black Power, and postsoul historical moments.

The second whiting up function consists of imitation or emulation of whiteness with the objectives of building personal, professional, and perhaps political identifications with white aesthetic practices, artists, and histories. This function openly acknowledges, even celebrates, how European cultures and specific white role models have influenced and enriched African American artistry. In Chapter 2 I focus on the stage Europeans produced by nineteenth-century Negro theater manager William

Brown, with particular attention to his lead attraction, James Hewlett. The earliest rising theatrical stars in Europe and America developed auras of "celebrity" through imitation of more established actors and through close identification with certain well-known roles.[45] Hewlett would blaze a similar trail as he strategically appropriated European theatrical icons, from English nobility to Scottish rebels. However, while advancing a career and crafting his onstage persona, Hewlett also worked to redefine and reenergize the future prospects of his Afro–New Yorker community. Similarly, in Chapter 3 I examine an ambitious collection of black artists, united around Bob Cole's aesthetic agenda: prove black talent could excel in presumably white artistic forms, especially opera and comedic impersonations.

My analysis of performed whiteness and black professional development continues in Chapter 4 and is guided by an editorial written by drama and social critic Abram L. Harris for the *Messenger*, an important African American literary magazine. Harris, in a 1923 article titled "The Ethiopian Art Players and the Nordic Complex," directly challenges the notion of white representational property. In this piece, Harris argues that Shakespeare and Molière are not the sacred or exclusive property of "Nordics," and Negro artists should feel empowered to "trespass" on this European material whenever they please.[46] Chapter 4 concentrates on two "trespassing" stage European presentations on Broadway: Evelyn Preer's 1923 performance of Oscar Wilde's *Salomé* (1894/1896) and Canada Lee's 1946 appearance in John Webster's *The Duchess of Malfi* (1614). Both productions sparked intense media debates over whether it was culturally, politically, and professionally productive for Negro actors to perform white roles on the American stage. Working with theatrical criticism and audience responses, I assess how Preer and Lee used "Nordic" drama to sharpen their skills, create stage opportunities for themselves and other actors, and reposition blackness. Black actors from James Hewlett to Bob Cole to Evelyn Preer to Canada Lee appropriated white roles to advance their careers but also to reconfigure, based on their integrationist professional and political desires, what it meant to be a citizen-artist in the United States.

The third and most dramatic mode of performed whiteness seeks to expose systematic white terror in order to warn and potentially transform Afro-America. The personification of a terrifying whiteness was articulated by nineteenth-century Negro intellectuals such as David Walker and Alexander Cromwell. Responding to the racist assumptions of ethnology, the science of racial differences, Walker and Cromwell countered claims of Negro inferiority by casting Europeans as overly aggressive, "Gothic barbarians" or "Angry Saxons" bent on conquest and destruction.[47] To interpret these images of marauding whiteness crafted by black artists, I draw on Bertolt Brecht's "estrangement-effect," a theatrical technique that involves making familiar situations strange so audiences will look at their quotidian circumstances with fresh eyes. More specific to black cultural production, I draw on Daphne Brooks's "Afro-alienation acts," which she defines as representational strategies wherein black artists convert "the horrific historical memory" of slavery and other degradations into critically enlightened performance.[48]

Black drama of the 1960s was very much rooted in theatrical practices of alienation and estrangement, as stage Europeans experienced a significant shift from white characters created by white playwrights to intensely dramatic white images constructed by black playwrights. This turn to white dramatic figures was partly inspired by the electric 1961 American debut of French playwright Jean Genet's postcolonial, absurdist drama *The Blacks: A Clown Show*. Genet's dualistic, metaphoric exploration of whiteness and colonial power provided a template for black theatrical artists to use in constructing their unique stage Europeans. In Chapter 5 I explore how Adrienne Kennedy's expressionistic *Funnyhouse of a Negro* (1964) and LeRoi Jones's revolutionary ritual *A Black Mass* (1966) staged the impact of whiteness on the African American psyche. I contend that their very different Afro-alienation acts moved black audiences to personal or political action, be it long-term psychic healing or figurative nationalist jihads.

In terms of artists, audiences, and political agency, I attempt to avoid a narrative of progress that historicizes this dual tradition as growing more resistant or subversive over time. In fact, the finely attired Negro promenaders in nineteenth-century South Carolina, covered in Chapter 1, were probably the most socially and legally defiant actors in this study. As outlets for substantive political activism became more available to black artists and audiences, the most strident aspects of whiteface minstrelsy were diminished, and the dialogical, cross-racial conversation was channeled into semiprivate, interracial comedy clubs. Furthermore, in her work on racial melancholia, Anne Cheng questions the overreliance of ethnic studies on advocacy and poses this significant question: "What can political agency mean for someone operating in a symbolic, cultural economy that has already pre-assigned them as a deficit?"[49] Cheng recommends that before considering the possibility of political agency, we first examine the psychic impacts produced by feelings of deficiency received from the dominant culture. To avoid an overly simplified narrative of social and political progress, we must locate each artist within his or her medium, historical moment, and psychological condition. From stand-up innovators like Richard Pryor to experimental dramatists like Adrienne Kennedy, whiting up acts have consistently explored how African Americans contend with dominant cultural projections and assumptions.

The fourth whiting up agenda identifies both with and against the majority culture as black artists disassociate and transfer presumably white traits and practices to black bodies. José Muñoz offers a theory of disidentification that describes how performers of color operate within the dominant culture but eschew assigned roles to forge contradictory combinations that produce new possibilities and identities.[50] As Paul McDonald suggests in his work on stardom, it may be productive to think of artists as "social agents" who do not necessarily determine "structures of representation or power" yet still manage to negotiate and restructure their identities within given hierarchies.[51] In South Carolina, at master-sponsored parties and dance competitions, multitalented enslaved Africans and free blacks produced cakewalks and weekly promenades that celebrated and transformed the face of American fashion and leisure. I argue that these public and semiprivate whiteface spectacles were less about ridiculing whiteness and more about using the trappings of white privilege to rehearse new African American identities and establish black style.

Yet the transference of racial markers works both ways. At the center of Bob Cole's commercially viable, disidentifying Broadway musical *A Trip to Coontown* is a tour-de-force reversal of blackface minstrelsy, Willie Wayside. Cole's whiteface creation simultaneously identifies with and against the majority culture, as this white hobo and other musically inclined stage Europeans disconnect racial and class-marked "cooning" attributes from blackness and displace them onto whiteness. Finally, to fully investigate this whiting up tendency to work with and against majority culture, I approach Chapter 6's stand-up comics and solo performers as ethnographers conducting "fieldwork" in the worlds of whiteness and blackness. As transracial informants they gather information and observations and report their "findings" through dialogical performances with an interracial public.

Returning to the issue of live performance, the dialogic, community-building potential of theater and social performance is the primary reason why I concentrate on live acts of performed whiteness rather than on "mediatized performance" like film and television, or literary forms like novels and short stories. Theater often tries to distinguish itself from other representational media based on its ability to build immediacy and community either between the spectators in attendance or between the artists and their audiences. Yet performance theorist Philip Auslander claims that the only communal bond uniting a live theater audience is the shared consumption of a cultural product. He also doubts true connections ever develop between performer and spectator because performance is predicated "on difference, on separation and fragmentation, not unity." Building on the audience theories of Herbert Blau, Auslander explains how performance assumes a gap between performer and spectator, an unbridgeable divide that can never produce real community but only a sense of failure to connect actors and audiences.[52] In the case of social performance—for example, the immaculately dressed promenaders on the streets of Charleston, South Carolina—the lines were definitely blurred between artist and audience, spectators and spectacles. Additionally, the solo performers in Chapter 6 contest this idea of an inevitable performer-public fragmentation. Richard Pryor's comedy of racial difference was designed to divide his audience, triangulate his position, and ultimately reunite his interracial public. All the live performances covered in these pages represent interventions into America's ongoing dialogue on race and representation, interventions that resonate and ripple well beyond one fleeting performance.

To close this study of performed whiteness, I briefly entertain the idea that in our twenty-first-century, allegedly postracial moment, whiting up may have outlived its usefulness or lost its relevance. Then I consider the potential benefits of performed whiteness, specifically how this tradition can redeem cross-racial performance in the twenty-first century. I have two different and perhaps contradictory motivations for defining and popularizing this centuries-old performance tradition. First, I want to see more producers and directors pushing cultural boundaries, taking chances, like casting Idris Elba, a black actor, in a Marvel Studios production of *Thor* (2011). I hope this book leads to more racially transcendent casting decisions that force audiences to operate on multiple and sometimes conflicting levels. Second, I would love to see a spike in racially deconstructive productions that allow artists of all colors to create satiric, imitative, terrifying, and disidentifying performances of whiteness, blackness, brownness, and yellowness. Although many Americans are committed to chasing the illusion of a color-blind society, I believe it is perfectly acceptable to see, celebrate, and perform difference in our national theater. We still have room for perceptive appropriations and deconstructions of whiteness, we still need actors of color "putting on" a changing normative culture, but we also need more skilled yet respectful white actors joining them in some seriously subversive cross-racial play.

Chapter 1 **Liberatory Whiteness**

Early Whiteface Minstrels, Enslaved and Free

On Saturday evenings and Sunday afternoons in the early nineteenth century, major thoroughfares such as Broadway in New York City or Meeting Street in Charleston, South Carolina, overflowed with impeccably dressed and remarkably audacious African Americans out for a leisurely stroll. In a letter to the editor of the *New York Evening Post*, one concerned citizen reported on this social ritual: "These people were all well drest, and very much better than the whites. The men almost without exception, wore broadcloth coats, very many of them boots, fashionable Cossack pantaloons, and white hats; watches and canes. The latter article was observed to be flourished with inimitable grace, to the annoyance of all the passengers."[1] "These people" refers to stylish Negro promenaders who, alongside white citizens, participated in a common leisure pursuit that was less expensive than attending the theater and less morally compromised than consuming spirits at the local beer or pleasure garden. As this open letter intimates, well-heeled Negroes often dominated these crowded public spaces and were the indisputable stars of this social performance; in fact, this concerned citizen counted nearly 1,500 black bodies on this particular afternoon. Throughout the 1820s, whiteface minstrelsy, the Afro-Diasporic practice of assuming and performing white privilege, was taking New York by storm, and for some, the swank and swaggering black fashionistas were more annoyances than attractions. The cane-wielding colored gentry was commanding city streets with elitist attitudes and physically terrorizing decent citizens.

In a July 1822 editorial titled "Blacks," Manual Mordecai Noah, editor of New York's *National Advocate*, further exposed the Negro insolence displayed during these public promenades:

We are among those who are for giving every protection of person, property, and civil and religious rights to the blacks; but it is not to be denied, that in this city they are becoming intolerable.

On Sunday, a strapping black was about chastising a genteel well behaved young white man, because he took the wall of him; and in their walks in Broadway, there is no enduring their insolence. A lady passing by St. Paul's Church, was met by 3 sable colored women, tricked out in the height of the fashion; one of them gave way for the other lady, while another exclaimed, loud enough to be heard by the passers-by—"Louisa, why did you give the wall to that white woman."[2]

Noah's editorial confirms that a struggle over urban space was being waged between white citizens and excessively fashionable "Blacks." "Giving the wall" meant a pedestrian allowed another passerby to walk closer to the buildings on a street, while the giver, in turn, moved out to the street. Custom dictated that Negroes, enslaved or free, "give the wall" to a white person, but in 1822, the racial hierarchy was under siege. Noah respected the rights of Afro–New Yorkers, but like many whites, he believed their stylish impudence had gone too far and needed to be contained.

New Yorkers were witnessing what political scientist and anthropologist James Scott would call a collision of public and private transcripts. According to Scott's theories on cultural resistance, subaltern groups often develop a critique of the dominant culture offstage, away from public, onstage transcripts, which are primarily defined and monitored by masters or colonizers. To prepare and perform their offstage commentaries on public life, subalterns typically borrow gestures, practices, speech patterns, and other cultural material from the dominant group.[3] But in the 1800s, fashionable Negroes in New York City and Charleston were not satisfied with performing private transcripts offstage or backstage. These early whiting up artists brought their kid gloves, broadcloth coats, parasols, and prodigious attitudes onto the main stages of Broadway and Meeting Street.

This chapter traces whiteface minstrelsy in private, semiprivate, and public spaces in the areas surrounding Charleston, South Carolina, during the colonial and antebellum periods. I contend that early African American whiteface spectacles were less about ridiculing whiteness and more about showcasing black style, forging communal identity, asserting representational freedom, and training American Negroes for emancipation. We begin with private, clandestine "country dances" popular in the Charleston area during the late 1700s and then transition to semiprivate cakewalk performances initially designed by and for the dominant class. These master-financed but slave-dominated parties and cakewalk competitions would lead to liberating Afro-Diasporic reinterpretations of European dance. Finally, I close this conversation on whiteface minstrelsy in South Carolina with a most jarring collision of private and public transcripts instigated by impeccably adorned enslaved and free persons of color promenading through the streets of Charleston. I am interested in what all three whiting up acts signified for the Negro participants, especially how the secretive country dances, cakewalks, and Sunday promenades appropriated yet altered white style, prestige, and privilege. But to appreciate the agency and creativity of these early African American artists, we first need to understand the incredibly complex world of bondage in colonial and antebellum South Carolina.

Slavery was the medium or performance context for the earliest whiteface minstrel acts, and this world was very different depending on one's position in the racial hierarchy. Writing about the American South from the master's perspective, historian Eugene Genovese identifies an often contradictory form of paternalism rooted in a system of mutual obligations between slave and master. As they cultivated a seemingly comfortable position atop the region's racial and class hierarchies, southern masters acknowledged certain duties to their slaves. The most patriarchic owners, especially in cosmopolitan cities like Charleston, treated their property as extensions of themselves and even cultivated specific slave talents. By acknowledging the skills, humanity, and free will of their property, paternalistic masters and mistresses provided enslaved Africans with the wherewithal to forge somewhat independent identities.[4]

In postemancipation interviews collected by the federal government's Works Progress Administration (WPA), former enslaved Africans revealed the impact of these master-defined racial and class hierarchies. They recalled with nostalgia how white folks were especially "proud of dey niggers" and displayed their prized possessions when company arrived. Conditioned by the master's paternalist self-image, enslaved Africans were encouraged to identify with upper-class whites more than with fellow slaves or lower-class whites. Demonstrating a surprising degree of familial bonding, former enslaved Africans from urban and rural plantations nostalgically referred to their former owners as "my white people" or "my white folks" and took pride in being owned by kind, genteel people, as opposed to "poor white trash" or "white free niggers."[5]

However, when we take a closer look at the enslaved perspective, a very different slaveholding world emerges. After working carefully and critically through the WPA interviews, historian Mia Bay concluded that the majority of former enslaved Africans did not experience the paternalism imagined by American slave owners. In their most honest and forthright moments, they did not remember themselves as dependent children or prized possessions. Instead, they overwhelmingly recalled how they were treated as beasts to be used and often abused by their masters. In fact, when they were treated well, meaning as human beings, ex-slaves often claimed they were treated "like white people."[6] Here we see the impact of racial hierarchy on an enslaved consciousness, as the former bondmen and bondwomen consistently drew powerful connections between whiteness, humanity, and humane treatment. Ultimately, Bay believes that the WPA interviews reveal an enslaved world at odds with the master's perception of reality, and if American slaves, north or south, urban or rural, did develop any sense of agency or autonomy, they did so despite the paternalistic attitudes of their masters.

As for the acculturation of New World Africans, historian Michael Gomez offers a dualistic model that resonates with James Scott's theory of private and public transcripts. Consistent with this incredible notion that only white people received or deserved kindness, Gomez argues that enslaved Africans were shaped by a "culture of coercion," a system of imposed cultural codes and norms dictated by the white "host society." Yet this coercive acculturative process was balanced by a "culture of volition" in which enslaved communities, often away from the gaze of whites, selected material from the dominant culture and whenever necessary adapted those cultural elements to their specific social settings and needs.[7] These two varieties of acculturation made it possible for African American social performers to appropriate white privilege, develop culturally distinct identities, and contest Euro-American supremacy.

Colonial South Carolina, where various whiting up acts first emerged, was carved from a North American territory originally inhabited by nearly thirty different Native American nations, with the Catawba, Yemassee, and Santee among the most prominent tribes.[8] In the 1660s, Spanish and English colonists arrived in the region and decimated the native population, and by 1670, the English had established a politically and economically dominant British crown colony of South Carolina. By 1720, there were sparse pockets of Native Americans, roughly 12,000 Africans, and only 5,048 whites in this royal possession. Given the majority-black population, economic cooperation between Europeans and New World Africans was a necessity, and this economic fact played a major role in the acculturation and identity formation of enslaved Africans and free blacks in the colony. In order to cultivate crops in the humid, tropical South Carolina climate, English planters depended on the hearty bodies and agricultural expertise of imported Congo-Angolans and Senegambians. Thanks, in large part, to a resourceful African population, this crown colony grew into an enormously successful venture responsible for producing massive amounts of rice, a significant staple crop for the British Empire. Additionally, South Carolina's dependency on skilled Africans placed this enslaved population in a prime position to negotiate certain economic privileges.[9] For example, on large plantations, enslaved Africans labored for their masters six days a week and worked for themselves one day a week on small plots of "their" land.

Charleston, in the late 1700s, was a major seaport with the largest enslaved population of any city in North America, and by 1820, the municipal census reported 12,652 slaves, 1,475 free blacks, and 10,653 whites.[10] As the majority in an international, even cosmopolitan city, members of Charleston's enslaved population were mildly "liberated," with unique relationships to their masters, other whites, and a significant free black population. Free persons of color gravitated to this port city because it was the safest and most lucrative harbor in South Carolina, if not the entire United States. Charleston offered free as well as enslaved Africans the widest range of economic opportunities. Within the city's complex economy, blacks were employed in skilled and unskilled occupations, including factory workers, shoemakers, stevedores, blacksmiths, leather craftsmen, bricklayers, and even firemen. Urban slaveowners profited greatly from such a diversified Negro labor pool, which thus allowed Charleston slaves to negotiate more entitlements, like the liberating practices of "hiring out" and "living out."

Hiring out was a fascinating economic arrangement popular in a few southern cities. Under this practice, skilled slaves were allowed to arrange wages and hours with employers, collect their wages, give a specified sum to their master each month, and retain the rest for themselves.[11] Here we have a clear example of enslaved Africans, in specific market conditions, attaining a level of economic autonomy based on their marketable talents. On face value, it would seem that if an enslaved individual was earning an income and pocketing a portion of his or her salary, the term "slave" might no longer apply. A South Carolina committee studying hiring out recognized an inherent danger in this economic practice specifically because "slaves are permitted to go at large, exercising all the privileges of free persons, making contracts, doing work and in every way being and conducting themselves as if they were not slaves."[12] To reinforce or remind Africans of their enslaved status, Charleston's city council, in the early 1800s, instituted a system for monitoring hired out slaves. This system included badges to identify the type of employment, specific areas to transact hiring contracts, limits on the numbers of enslaved Africans that could be hired by one employer, and even salary caps.[13]

As for living out, in major southern cities such as New Orleans and Charleston, most enslaved Africans resided in quarters adjacent to the master's house, but some bondservants were allowed to occupy homes completely apart from their owners.[14] Unlike hiring out, living out was never officially sanctioned or supervised by law. As early as 1740, so many Charleston slaves were living apart from their masters that local authorities officially forbade enslaved Africans from sleeping away from their master's compound. This colonial era ban on living out was never strictly enforced because wealthy slave owners did not support the municipal ordinance. Therefore, Charleston slaves continued to live out and even began renting rundown shanties in a suburb just outside Charleston; this area, known as "the Neck," became Charleston's first black neighborhood. Although quarters on the master's estate were quite commodious compared with Neck shacks, enslaved Charlestonians often preferred the latter. One white Charleston woman observed "that even if they receive wages, besides their old privileges, they are not free as long as they are with their old masters, and you see them leaving their comfortable homes and living in miserable shanties."[15] Residing with their master was a constant reminder of bondage, and many enslaved Africans were committed to escaping that reality, even if it meant sacrificing comfort and flouting the law.

For urban enslaved populations, social and economic autonomy clearly became priorities, and according to historian Richard Wade, "as cities grew, they produced conditions which first strained, then undermined, the regime of bondage in the South's metropolises."[16] With their aspirations fixed on liberation, Charleston slaves gradually redefined their social realities through shrewdly negotiated privileges like hiring out and living out. These economic practices also complicated the acculturation process in late eighteenth- and early nineteenth-century Charleston. Hiring out provided enslaved Africans with disposable incomes, and living out created private, slave residences; these unique social and economic conditions led to the development of black leisure. Thus the stage was set for multiple forms of whiteface minstrelsy to emerge and for enslaved South Carolinians to inch closer to some semblance of emancipation.

Semiprivate Whiteface: The Country Dance

Throughout the colonial and antebellum American South, enslaved Africans cultivated private, often illegal gatherings where they could "steal" time away from forced labor and white surveillance to indulge in various forms of pleasure. Saidiya Hartman characterizes slaves "stealing away" as "unlicensed movement, collective assembly, and an abrogation of the terms of subjection in acts as simple as sneaking off to laugh and talk with friends or making nocturnal visits to loved ones."[17] In antebellum Richmond, Virginia, traveler and historian Frederick Law Olmsted uncovered "Champaign Suppers" where urban bondservants would congregate apart from their masters to socialize. Former enslaved Africans from rural and urban South Carolina recalled how they would gather "mos' ev'ry Sa'day night for our li'l mite o' fun from de white folks hearin'."[18] In colonial Charleston, enslaved and free blacks routinely congregated around the city in social events euphemistically called country dances. These semiprivate acts of unsanctioned leisure represent the earliest recorded examples of whiteface minstrelsy in America. Often centered around parodic performance, these offstage transcripts afforded black South Carolinians space to construct and develop resistant commentaries on the dominant culture.

I use the term "semiprivate" because we only have a record of this unique event because a white informant, a European visitor writing under the pen name "The Stranger," reported on a country dance he allegedly witnessed. In August 1772, The Stranger began sending letters to editor T. Powell of the *South Carolina Gazette*, all intended to convince South Carolinians to enforce their languishing General Assembly laws and protect the "health and security" of their fair colony.[19] One vigilante letter, published in late August 1772, focused on what he perceived to be a serious social nuisance plaguing Charleston: insolent Negroes.[20] The Stranger found Charleston slaves to be notably more rude and uncontrollable than country or rural slaves. In his opinion, black Charlestonians were especially prone to gaming, drunkenness, and other lewd behaviors, and he was most offended by the city's remarkably well-dressed and incredibly haughty female slaves. We shall return to this particular nuisance shortly.

The Stranger is our principal witness to one of the earliest examples of whiting up in America, but what does it mean to rely on hegemonic journalism to reconstruct Afro-Diasporic culture? Having worked with similar primary sources written by "hostile and confused white spectators," both Daphne Brooks and Saidiya Hartman suggest we first acknowledge the limits of these biased sources. Next we need to accept the potential risk of "reinforcing the authority of these documents" as we use this indispensable material to recover enslaved and free black experiences.[21] I find it helpful to approach The Stranger like a powerful theatrical critic who arrives at a production with certain aesthetic and cultural presumptions. This European visitor and other white critics cited throughout this study carried deeply entrenched ideas about the performative and political presence of black bodies; some of their prejudiced assumptions prove useful or informative, but many are simply counterproductive. Much like Mia Bay critically decodes a slave master's paternalistic assessment of his property, I read through and around the bias in these vital sources to recover specific moments of performed whiteness.

To be of service to his adopted Charleston, The Stranger devised a plan to disguise himself as an inconspicuous indigent citizen, walk the streets of the city and its surrounding suburbs, and report on what he witnessed. On the front page of its September 17, 1772, edition, the *South Carolina Gazette* published The Stranger's exposé of a secretive, nocturnal gathering of enslaved and free Negroes just outside the city. The disguised Stranger supposedly hid himself in a nearby run-down hut to eavesdrop and had "an opportunity of seeing a Country-Dance, Rout, or Cabal of Negroes, within 5 miles distance of this town on Saturday night."[22] The Stranger's unique position as an uninvited, secret guest deserves some commentary. Our European visitor was essentially trespassing on a clandestine fete hardly designed for white consumption. If any participants had become aware of his concealed presence, the dance would have ended immediately, and under slightly different circumstances, the revelers would have surely tailored their performances to accommodate a white spectator.

In what they assumed to be an unobserved, hidden affair, colored Charlestonians parodied white social graces, drank and ate to their heart's content, gambled with intensity, and if The Stranger is to be believed, plotted social disruptions. He describes how this particular country dance hosted roughly sixty people, but he also remarks that "such assemblies *have been* very common, and that the company has sometimes amounted to 200 persons." According to The Stranger's local sources, "intriguing meetings of this sort *are* frequent even in Town, either at the houses of *free Negroes*, apartments *hired to slaves*." Here The Stranger takes direct aim at the unsanctioned practice of living out by stressing how country dances often occur in houses rented to enslaved persons.

Based on The Stranger's description, multiple groups—enslaved, free, rural, and urban—commingled at these late-night, illegal cabals. According to Saidiya Hartman, much of the pleasure associated with such "surreptitious gatherings" was rooted in the potential "empowerment derived from collective action" but also in the "precariousness and fragility" of unsanctioned activity.[23] Later in his article, The Stranger quotes a 1740 act passed by the South Carolina General Assembly in response to the 1739 Stono Rebellion, a Congo-led enslaved uprising that claimed over eighty lives. This legislation proclaimed that a slave "found out of the limits of the town or plantation to which he or she belongs, without a ticket, letter, or some white person in company" would be subject to "corporeal punishment," which typically meant twenty lashes on a bare back. In his whistle-blowing report, The Stranger clearly establishes the fact that this particular dance convened five miles outside Charleston.

His September 1772 letter describes a variety of entertainments, beginning with a culinary explosion of rum, assorted meats ranging from beef to ham to goose, and edible luxuries like "sweetmeats." The Stranger then explains how the "dancers" procured such luxuries. True or fictive, he claims the attendees freely admitted that they stole the items using keys made by an expert Negro key maker "who could make any Key, whenever the impression of the true one was brought to him in wax." Similar to sounding the alarm against living out, The Stranger was now linking this illegal entertainment to skilled black craftsmen who probably hired themselves out.

As for social performance, the party featured parodies of upper-class manners. The Stranger writes how "the entertainment was opened by the men copying (or *taking off*) the manners of their masters, and the women those of their mistresses, and relating some highly curious anecdotes, to the inexpressible diversion of that company. Then they *danced, betted, gamed, swore, quarreled, fought,* and did *everything* that most *modern* accomplished gentlemen are not ashamed of." By using the term "*taking off*," The Stranger suggests the enslaved country dancers were not simply imitating masters and mistresses but commenting on the foibles of their owners. Their performance exhibited the first cultural function of whiting up, satire or parody designed to create representational room. Linda

Hutcheon, writing about parody, argues that this mode of performative critique embodies both conservative and revolutionary energies. Parody repeats and conserves its original target, and in the case of these whiteface minstrels, the targets were white manners and white gossip. Yet parody replicates with a critical and ironic distance, which, according to Hutcheon, could range from "scornful ridicule to reverential homage."[24] Based on The Stranger's reconnaissance, I sense the dancers' cultural critique was slightly more reverential than ridiculing, designed more to freely partake of the privileges of liberated men and women rather than to derisively mock them. The cabalistic performers were armed with the gestures, practices, and stories of the powerful, which they took time to study and reproduce.

With nearly sixty black Charlestonians devoting their "stolen" time to parodying whites, the gathered revelers surely harbored a complex fascination with the ways of "their white folk." In truth, the country dancers could be dismissed as enslaved Africans exhibiting an unhealthy preoccupation with life atop the racial hierarchy. Yet notice how the full range of their whiteface performances subverted high/low distinctions and embraced dancing, gossiping, gaming, and even fighting, all leisure pursuits enjoyed across class and racial lines. As a break from the quotidian, an alternative to the daily public transcript, free blacks and enslaved Africans displaced white folks and creatively recast Negroes as the "*modern* accomplished gentlemen" free to do what they pleased. Paul Gilroy has noted how New World Africans achieved "significant everyday triumphs by mimicking, and in a sense mastering, their rulers and conquerors, masters and mistresses."[25] The country dance exemplified such a triumph by allowing enslaved social performers to test-drive emancipated attitudes denied them in their daily lives.

Beyond cross-racial play, there was a more sinister component to these cabalistic activities. The Stranger allegedly witnessed an ominous "secret council" meeting:

> They had also their private committees; whose deliberations were carried on in too low a voice, and with so much caution, as not to be overheard by the others; much less by the Stranger, who was concealed in a deserted adjacent hut. . . . The members of this secret council, had much of the appearance of Doctors, in deep and solemn consultation upon life or death; which indeed might have been the scope of their meditations at that time. Not less than 12 fugitives joined this respectable com-

> pany before midnight, 8 of whom were mounted on good horses, these, after delivering a good quantity of Mutton, Lamb, and Veal, which they brought with them, directly associated with one or other of the private consultators; and went off about an hour before day, being supplied with liquor, &c. and perhaps having also received some instructions.

Although not explicitly performative or "staged," the huddled, solemn deliberations of this private committee infused an otherwise festive event with serious overtones. The secret council seemed to operate as a political parallel to the playful *taking off* of the other revelers. Although this hidden affair was primarily devoted to drink, debauchery, and dice, the cabal within the cabal instantly marked this country dance as a fertile training ground for potential disruptions in the public sphere. The Stranger's report raises immediate concerns and questions, such as what were the instructions delivered to the fugitives with the "good horses," and could this clandestine party lead to full-scale insurrections or more self-emancipated Africans? But this detailed description of the secret council also raises questions about The Stranger's reconnaissance. How would he have remained undetected, in a hut, until the break of day? And how was he able to identify certain participants as escapees, especially when he found it difficult to hear their deliberations? Whether faithful or embellished, a published account of free blacks illegally commingling with fugitives and enslaved Africans would surely disquiet white South Carolinians. If any white reader was unsure of the secret council's intentions, The Stranger closed his exposé with this question: "May it not be concluded, that their deliberations are never intended for the advantage of the white people?"

Country dances and similar unsanctioned gatherings had been political problems since the early eighteenth century, and in the aftermath of the Stono Rebellion, the General Assembly understandably legislated against such activities. Unfortunately, colonial statutes were difficult to enforce, especially after South Carolina achieved statehood in 1788. On a local level, in 1800 and 1806, the Charleston City Council addressed illegal black assemblies by passing ordinances declaring that "assemblages of slaves, even with white persons, in a confined or secret place, and assemblages after dark are unlawful."[26] However, Saidiya Hartman poses an important question on the political threat of the country dance and other whiteface acts: "How does one make any claims about the politics of performance without risking the absurd when discussing the resistances staged by unauthorized dance in the face of the everyday workings of fear, subjugation, and violence?"[27] The implication here is that even in stolen moments of pleasure and parody, true liberation was still beyond the physically enslaved country dancers. Fleeting performative escape could not counteract the deep impacts of a dehumanizing institution, and when weekend parties wound down, the human chattel returned to their bestial routines.

On the relationship between performance and politics, performance scholar Tavia Nyong'o takes the position that "social action is organized around symbols, gestures, effigies, and dramatic narratives"; therefore, politics originates in the symbolic realm where individuals and collectives imagine what is possible beyond their given circumstances.[28] Historian George Lipsitz further explicates these connections between culture, politics, performance, and rehearsal. He writes that "culture can seem like a substitute for politics, a way of posing only imaginary solutions to real problems, but under other circumstances culture can become a rehearsal for politics, trying out values and beliefs permissible in art but forbidden in social life. Most often, however, culture exists as a form of politics, as a means of reshaping individual and collective practice for specified interests, and as long as individuals perceive their interests as unfilled, culture retains an oppositional potential."[29] Lipsitz appreciates the oppositional quality and transgressive potential of social performance, but he stops short of treating cultural production as equivalent to real political action. At best, these early whiteface minstrel acts function as rehearsals for future political action and as forums for clarifying important issues and unfulfilled desires in Afro-America. Despite the passage of colonial statutes and municipal ordinances, late-night whiteface sessions of flattering parody and ominous deliberation remained a part of urban enslaved culture, and it was only a matter of time before these private rehearsals for liberation surfaced in public.

Master-Sponsored Whiteface: The Cakewalk

A culture of coercion, that system of imposed cultural codes and norms, instilled potentially debilitating notions of inferiority and superiority in the minds of enslaved Africans and their masters. That said, there is a crucial difference between recognizing white prestige and accepting Europeans as incontrovertibly superior. Most early whiteface minstrel acts exhibited a delicate balance between acknowledging that Euro-Americans rested atop the power structure and aggressively separating various symbols of privilege—elite fashion, polished manners, physical grace, and humanity—from whiteness. Where better to execute this complex disidentification with the dominant culture than in public, master-sponsored parties and cakewalking competitions.

In the colonial and early national South, on plantations and in urban compounds, masters financed parties at Christmas, on the Fourth of July, and even on random Saturday nights.[30] Slave owners provided parties for a variety of reasons. For some, the fetes were part of an owner's paternalistic responsibilities to their property, and in funding the events, masters confirmed their commitment to stewardship. For other masters, a well-executed soiree served as a means of social control, far more effective than beatings or other physical discipline. Incentives like annual, monthly, or weekly celebrations could keep enslaved Africans in line as they learned to accept the demands and indignities of bondage. Finally, the laws designed to punish slaves for "stealing away" were ineffective, so shrewd owners realized that a well-placed celebration could keep their property at home and reduce the threat of unsupervised and potentially nefarious gatherings.

At these plantation parties, whiskey flowed, barbecued meats were in ample supply, and songs and dances were the primary forms of entertainment. Although masters and mistresses sponsored the events and participated in some of the frivolity, enslaved South Carolinians generally preferred to be left alone in their merriments. They especially resented when younger whites would try to dominate "de fairs of slave 'musements."[31] From the enslaved perspective, master-sponsored celebrations were no different than hiring out or living out, and they grew to expect these entitlements. Enslaved Africans would often count on Christmastime festivities, which customarily spanned several days, as opportunities to visit family on other plantations. Only harsh or incompetent masters denied their property such privileges, and owners who revoked festival rights were typically stigmatized by their servants and other slaveholders.

Not all enslaved Africans embraced plantation fetes. Frederick Douglass, the former-slave-turned-abolitionist, voiced his objections to the social control behind master-sponsored parties. He considered plantation soirees "among the most effective means in the hands of the slaveholders of keeping down the spirit of insurrection among the slaves." They were "safety valves to carry off the explosive elements inseparable from the human mind when reduced to the condition of slavery." If not for the whiskey-driven and hog-infested bacchanals, bondage would have been too severe for these human beings and enslaved Africans would have surely revolted. Douglass also claimed excessive drinking and gorging trapped bondservants in a cycle of "triviality and self-degradation." The master's plan was to "party" enslaved Africans into an amnesiac stupor until they were so disgusted with "freedom" they were happy to return to the relative "safety" of bondage.[32]

I agree with Douglass that slavers probably devised periodic debaucheries to control their enslaved population, but one of the more complicated whiteface minstrel acts, the cakewalk, emerged from this world of master-sponsored saturnalia. Also known as the "prize walk" or "chalk-line dance," the cakewalk was crafted by enslaved performers to parody and transform European minuets and marches.[33] Here is how one former slave from Georgia described a cakewalking event: "Cakewalkin' wuz a lot of fun durin' slavery time. Dey swept de yards real clean and set benches for de party. Banjos wuz used for music makin'. De womens wor long, ruffled dresses wid hoops in 'em and de mens had on high hats, long split-tailed coats, and some of 'em used walkin' sticks. De couple dat danced best got a prize. Sometimes de slave owners come to dese parties 'cause dey enjoyed watchin' de dance, and dey 'cided who danced de best."[34] Apparently masters were not always in attendance at cakewalking affairs, but when they were, slave owners were acknowledged as the ultimate arbiters of a proper cakewalk. In fact, slaveholders were primarily responsible for interjecting a competitive element into these social events, as they developed cakewalking teams that traveled to other plantations to compete with other enslaved dancers. The more confident owners even gambled on the prowess of their best cakewalkers. As for costuming, the former Georgia slave recalled festive finery, from canes to hoopskirts to high hats. Much of this attire was hand-me-down items supplied by masters, so again we see paternalism in action, with the bondservant reflecting directly on his or her affluent owner. Masters and mistresses were extremely proud of their enslaved talent and often provided more than secondhand clothing to outfit their property. As for the prizes, cakes or new clothing were typical rewards for the best dancers.

In the nineteenth-century South, the cakewalk functioned as a specific kind of parody ultimately designed to transfer style, grace, and privilege from masters and mistresses to enslaved African artists. Similar to portions of the country dance, cakewalking involved *taking off* certain signifiers of upper-class whiteness, but this whiting up act also developed a simultaneously sympathetic and critical relationship to the majority culture. By identifying with and against their parodic object, in this case a European dance, New World Africans creatively transformed the original. Dance scholar Jane Desmond, writing about cakewalk and hybridity, explains how African Americans transferred source material from white to black bodies, with "a little bit extra."[35] From the shadows, enslaved Africans would watch and study the elaborate balls and other elegant affairs thrown by their masters, the very best of European culture and courtship. The Georgia cakewalk description stresses the male-female dynamics of this derivative dance, a heterosexually charged performance rooted in mannered codes and flirtation. The cakewalk was directly inspired by a specific European couples dance called the "Grand March," an epilogue promenade traditionally performed after an especially dignified and courtly minuet. At cultured white parties, the ladies and gentlemen would first separate, then come together again at the center of the room, and finally march arm-in-arm throughout the space. For the plantation cakewalk, the enslaved couples would move in a procession around the room, stopping every three bars so each couple could showcase their talents; they would revolve for about four beats, and then the procession would resume.

Within the cakewalk, Negro dancers replicated the affected manners and aristocratic comportment of courtly white dancers but not their exact steps. Adding that "little bit extra" to the original European minuet and march, enslaved dancers exhibited highly individualized dance skills. In musical breaks, the slave couple would launch into separate twists, shuffles, and high kicks. On the feet of black dancers, the cakewalk became a grand promenade with unlimited improvisational potential, and audiences even interjected themselves into this incredibly fluid artistry by shouting out suggestions for movements that were sure to impress the judges.[36] The most distinctive features of the cakewalk would become the improvisational high-bounding maneuvers executed in the musical breaks. These impromptu, athletic moves became so emblematic that the best jumpers often took home the top prize.

This element of "extra" also materialized through what performance scholars Robert Farris Thompson and Brenda Dixon Gottschild identify as the Africanist aesthetics of "cool" and "contrariety."[37] A composed and perhaps overly restrained upper body was already a common component of European social dance, a key marker of the elegance on display in the original Grand March. Yet in African American performance, cakewalkers tended to exaggerate that upright carriage, perhaps as parodic commentary on the excessive propriety and gentility of the master class. Theorist

Margaret Rose explains a subtle yet significant difference between parody and satire. In revising and commenting on an original form, parody remains sympathetic to or friendly toward its target; in contrast, satire tends to "take no prisoners" in ridiculing the original. Rose also makes the important point that parody diverges from mimicry because it ultimately establishes a "comic discrepancy or incongruity" between the original and the new parodic creation.[38]

To foster this sense of incongruity, or what Brenda Dixon Gottschild calls contrariety, cakewalkers complemented or contrasted hypererect upper bodies and cool heads with incredibly mobile, "hot" lower limbs executing improvised leaps. Writing about Yoruba dance and the aesthetic of cool, noted Black Atlantic art historian Robert Farris Thompson describes how a West African performer dances a "bound motion" around the head, "a coolness" marked by control and symmetry, while her torso and arms exhibit the "most confounding expression of raw energy and force."[39] Cakewalkers extended their raw energy to the legs to cultivate a productive tension between restrained and liberated movement, a dynamic performance more indicative of West African than European dance.

The cakewalk, a new parodic and contrarian creation, amounted to an amicable collision of seeming opposites—blackness and whiteness, African and European, hot and cool—all inscribed on moving black bodies. But before their masters' eyes, Negro social performers were not only transforming a highly mannered white dance into an African American dance tradition; they were also actively forging and promoting black identities. In her analysis of the cakewalk in the early twentieth-century musical *In Dahomey* (1902), cultural historian Daphne Brooks argues that "one might read the dance as not merely an expressive act but one which is, in part, *constitutive* of African American identity." Brooks found in this dance a "formulation of an identity constantly in contestation with itself" or, phrased another way, a dance grappling with "the 'twoness' of DuBois's new-century of 'blackness.'"[40] Although focused on later, emancipated cakewalkers, Brooks speaks to the enslaved originators who worked to resolve this tension between perceived black and white cultural styles.

In an 1861 edition of *Harper's Weekly*, artist Winslow Homer published a compilation illustration titled *American Home Scenes* (fig. 1). His work does not depict a cakewalk but does capture the dual cultural styles cakewalkers effectively combined and perhaps resolved. The centerpieces of Homer's collage are two contrasting scenes of dance and leisure. In the upper image, labeled "The Dance," we have a finely attired white couple

Figure 1 *American Home Scenes*, by Winslow Homer.
Published in *Harper's Weekly*, April 13, 1861.

with a male dancer working his slight legs and feet in a light jig. Beneath that image is a vignette titled "The Breakdown," which features a Negro couple dancing in a cabin. Again, a male dancer draws visual focus, and in this case a somewhat stout black dancer pounds the earth with his large feet and legs. Featured in the foreground of both illustrations, these two male images encapsulate the predominant nineteenth-century conceptions of white and black dance traditions, light versus heavy, gravity-defying versus earthbound. As for the background of these two dance scenes, the Negro couple is surrounded by images evocative of plantation life, including a banjo, while the white couple is flanked by elegant couples engaged in conversation and shadowy figures simply observing the proceedings.

The cakewalk actively contested Winslow Homer's vision of diametrically opposed black and white cultures on two different levels. First, the dance's originating narrative undermines the notion that truly separate black and white "home" scenes existed in the South. The shadowy onlookers depicted in the back row of "The Dance" vignette read as Negro house servants watching the fashionable, domestic dance of "their white folks." These enslaved witnesses-turned-performers would re-create what they saw and blend "The Dance" and "The Breakdown" into the cakewalk. But while cultural hybridity assumes an amalgamation of black and white, the cakewalk was less about mixture and more attuned to what José Muñoz calls "disidentification," which brings us to the second level or layer of contestation.[41] Cakewalkers refused to accept their prescribed identities as dancing extensions of paternalistic owners and, instead, unveiled a new and unexpected product at the master-sponsored events. By appropriating and transforming the aristocratic Grand March, cakewalkers produced an elegant black identity that was both rough and refined, heavy and light, hardly reducible to the easy divisions featured in Homer's illustration. In full view of the planter class, cakewalkers proved that cool or restrained posturing did not belong to African or European cultures.

The fusion of white and black cultural identities, a seemingly resolved DuBoisian duality in action, was best illustrated in another nineteenth-century image, an earlier painting by German artist Christian Friedrich Mayr (fig. 2). This oil on canvas, titled *Kitchen Ball at White Sulphur Springs, Virginia* (1838), features a group of house servants celebrating at a wedding reception, probably financed by their owners. In this semi-private moment, supposedly witnessed by the white artist Mayr, enslaved celebrants imitated the grand dances and fine manners of their masters, but more importantly, they exhibited a sense of style, grace, and fashion rarely associated with African Americans in the mid-nineteenth-century American imagination. Notice how Homer's "Breakdown" scene caricatures his black subjects while also generalizing them. They all share the same thickly exaggerated noses, lips, and cheeks; in fact, the men look very much like the women. A closer look at the earlier Mayr painting reveals much greater variety in African American physiognomy, from facial features to skin complexions. Also, Mayr depicts more diversity in the activities of his Negro subjects, including couples engaged in conversation while others dance, and all are entertained by a fiddler and a flautist. Mayr effectively re-creates what country dances, Saturday night parties, and cakewalking competitions may have looked like, with splendidly dressed black bodies exhibiting elegance and carriage thought to be beyond them. Amidst the rapid rise of blackface minstrelsy, onstage and in the popular press, this kind of whiteface minstrelsy, skilled emulation of allegedly white cultural practices, was transpiring throughout the southern and northern United States.

Did self-indulgent, perhaps self-deluding masters even register this unanticipated production of black identity within the plantation cakewalk? Slaveholder accounts suggest whites understood that their formal dances were being mimicked, but the typical master reaction to whiteface minstrel dances was amusement or mild derision. Far from recognizing a complex resolution of opposites, many owners simply enjoyed the cakewalk as yet another failed attempt by New World Africans to imitate white culture.[42] Enslaved recollections of the cakewalk suggest that the allegedly inferior Negroes were one step ahead of the master class. The often-quoted anonymous slave girl from 1840s Beaufort, South Carolina, suggests whites may have missed the critical and resistant intent of the cakewalk: "Us slaves watched the white folks' parties . . . then we'd do it, too, but we used to mock 'em, every step. Sometimes the white folks noticed it but they seemed to like it. I guess they thought we couldn't dance any better."[43]

This slave girl believed whites came away from this collision of public and private transcripts oblivious to the mildly parodic commentary and heartened by a reinforced sense of their own superiority. But I suspect many slavers realized something was stirring down below. Eugene Genovese and other historians argue that most planters sensed that their enslaved charges were constantly up to something; in fact, it was the master's responsibility to detect any duplicity or ridicule.[44] However, if masters

Figure 2 *Kitchen Ball at White Sulphur Springs, Virginia* (1838), oil painting by Christian Friedrich Mayr. Courtesy of the collection of the North Carolina Museum of Art.

did notice some slight in a particular cakewalk performance, they would have to proceed with caution. If they openly reprimanded the dancer, they would be effectively recognizing an autonomous African American identity and publicly acknowledging that a blow against white supremacy had actually landed. By refusing to concede the cakewalk's representational threat, masters could pretend that all was well and that their patriarchy was fully functional.

If planters used cakewalking competitions to police and control their presumably obedient bondservants, it makes sense that enslaved Africans used the same shared events to advance their agendas. The cakewalk became yet another way for black Charlestonians to capitalize on the master caste's personal investment in its property. Even if their owners failed to recognize the African American identity formation at work, enslaved Africans still promoted an undeniably black cultural product that elevated the European Grand March to new and unexpected levels. Again, the mere suggestion of slave agency and artistic production sounds strange, given the violence and coercion of this devastating institution. Perhaps we can never remove the specter of domination from any moment of enslaved "fun and frolic," but unlike the illegal and dangerous country dance, the cakewalk was born from an affable combination of coercive and voluntary acculturation. Masters thrust their prized possessions into the center of plantation spectacles where black artists made highly selective choices about how and what they appropriated from elite European culture. Despite constant surveillance in this partly private, partly public performative context, cakewalkers used social dance to experience and express representational and literal freedom.

Public Whiteface: Promenading along Meeting Street

Nattily attired and physically dexterous cakewalk teams brought prestige to their owners; they were what Monica Miller terms "black luxury slaves," essentially ornaments displaying plantation wealth and reinforcing white supremacy.[45] Unlike the sponsored cakewalkers, our final whiteface minstrel act, well-dressed Meeting Street promenaders, were independent Negro artists intent on becoming "self styling subjects."[46] Their public performances were less about the fine garments they appropriated and redeployed and more about the liberated and autonomous attitudes they integrated into an evolving black style. Since the colonial era, fashion-conscious free and enslaved Negroes have been strolling and commanding urban catwalks in Charleston, New York, and Philadelphia. Back in August 1772, The Stranger noticed how different urban and rural Negroes were in terms of dress and deportment, with urban blacks exhibiting "insolent" and "shameless" behavior while their country cousins were comparatively more docile. The Stranger also noted how urban female slaves were "more elegantly dressed" than most white women strolling through "Charles-Town." A friend of The Stranger, someone more familiar with local customs, explained that Charleston was flush with impeccably dressed enslaved women because wealthy white men often cohabited with these ladies, "treating them as wives even in public." Based on his own observations, The Stranger directly implicated hiring out because it allowed black women to sell goods "on their own accounts" and purchase their own finery.[47]

Still serving as a whistle-blower, The Stranger reminded white Charlestonians of the Negro Act of 1735, which clearly stated that, except for "liverymen and waiting boys," enslaved Negroes were not allowed to wear apparel finer or greater in value than "negro cloth, duffils, kerseys, osanburgs, blue linen, checkt linen, coarse garlix, coarse callicoes, check cottons or scotch plaids."[48] Allowable slave textiles were cheap, coarse fabrics rarely used in the construction of fine attire. Colonial authorities believed Negroes who wore "clothes much above the condition of slaves" generally acquired those items through "sinister methods," and they did not wish to encourage criminal activity. Any enslaved person caught wearing valuable, "superfine" cloth could be immediately stripped and physically punished, and in certain parts of South Carolina, this law was enforced to the letter. Former slaves on St. Helena Island and in Marion, South Carolina, recalled that masters made the slaves' wardrobes strictly from calico.[49] This 1735 act was designed to reinforce, through apparel, social and political distinctions between whites and blacks. Monica Miller uses the phrase "crime of fashion" to describe the "racial and class cross-dressing that was, as practiced by blacks, a symbol of self-conscious manipulation of authority."[50] So when Charleston's enslaved strollers brazenly dressed and promenaded above their station, they were literally committing crimes against colonial, municipal, and state authorities.

On Sunday afternoons and some Saturday evenings in postcolonial and early national Charleston, well-heeled enslaved and free blacks dominated public spaces like Meeting Street, a bustling avenue filled with churches, stately homes, commerce, and leisure. Saturday evenings offered a prime promenading window because work typically ended early, and there were always parties, master- or slave-sponsored, to dress for and attend. Sunday afternoon was the best time to see and be seen because it was the only day of complete rest and relaxation for enslaved Africans, free blacks, and whites. After religious observances, African Americans wearing the latest fashions lounged slowly along the city's major thoroughfares. A significant record of Charleston's Negro promenaders comes to us from another concerned white citizen, writing under the nom de plume "Rusticus."

In September 1822, Rusticus was so overwhelmed by the "black dandies of Charleston" that he decided it was his duty to stroke a letter to Robert Howard, editor of the *Southern Patriot and Commercial Advertiser*. After a long and disturbing walk along Meeting Street, Rusticus wrote, "I saw as I conceived, the figure of an old acquaintance walking in front of me; his manner of walk and dress were apparently the same, I therefore quickened my pace, came up, and slapt him on the shoulders, but to my no small surprize (and equally so no doubt to buck blacky) a sable Dandy stared me in the face!!"[51] Just like The Stranger, Rusticus had ample issues with race, with the plethora of "buck blackies" dominating Charleston; nevertheless, we can still learn a great deal about this weekly whiteface ritual from his prejudiced report. Rusticus was completely fooled by this promenader, hoodwinked by the empowered strut of a "sable Dandy" whose carriage and dress reminded Rusticus of a free white citizen, a man as privileged and self-assured as himself. To complete his whiteface minstrel act, this impudent social performer had the nerve to do the unthinkable: stare a white man directly in the face like an equal.

Not soon after this first unsettling encounter, Rusticus was again duped by two finely dressed Negro "Ladies" with more of this liberated attitude:

> When I overtook a couple of well dressed Ladies, as I thought, for both were dressed in the modern large and costly *Leghorn*, "trimmed off quite in style"—one, in a black Canton Crape, flounced with Silk, black Silk Stockings (we country people are great observers when we come to town) and a fashionable pair of high heeled shoes to correspond, a fashionable half handkerchief trimmed with lace, adorned the neck, a parasol and bag (reticule) occupied the hands; her companion was no less fine, the only difference consisted in a white muslin frock in the same dashing style, with corresponding "accompaniment"—pretty faces must be under such bonnets, I thought, but lo! one was jet black and the other copper coloured! I thought to myself, *how much* could either *of you do* in a Cotton or Rice field?

Rusticus claims to be from the country, but for a "bumpkin" he is incredibly conversant with European fashion. His descriptions of the ladies' ensembles are quite detailed, from their expensive leghorn-style hats to their muslin and crepe dresses, even down to their matching handbags and umbrellas. With every layer of fashion, Rusticus attempts to make his derisive case that these two ladies were ridiculous, overly dressed for a leisurely stroll. Furthermore, after mistaking them for white women worthy of "pretty faces," he was highly displeased to find colored women so far removed from their "natural" element, the fields.

Rusticus agreed with the Negro Act of 1735: this conspicuous display of resplendent vestments encouraged "many vices" among Charleston's enslaved population. In his open letter, he directly questioned whether the high-priced items worn by black males and females were secured by "honest industry," intimating that "the guard would make a 'fine haul' by disrobing these modern fine gentry (no doubt of many a *borrowed* plume)." Basically, if city authorities confiscated the clothing of most promenaders, they would discover that most of their apparel was contraband. As for how enslaved Charlestonians actually acquired their fine attire, a legitimate resource would have been generous masters who were intent on displaying their property in nothing but the best. One former slave, Charleston's Elijah Green, explained how as the servant of a lieutenant in the South Carolina Company Regiment, he got "all his cas' off clothes." Green was especially proud of a pair of "brogan that had brass on the toe," and when he wore his handed-down brogans, you could not "tell 'em he wasn't dress' to death."[52] Traditionally, the more paternalistic Charleston slavers were pleased to pass on castoff clothing to their bondservants, even for weekly promenades, but according to the Negro Act of 1735, Green's master illegally passed this item on to his servant.

Enslaved Carolinians did find legal ways to build their exquisite ensembles. During the late eighteenth and early nineteenth centuries, most garments and fine cloths sold in America were imported from abroad, with local newspapers advertising shipments of "superfine fashionable broad cloths with trimmings, suitable for Gentlemen's summer wear" and "fashionable silks for ladies wear."[53] With funds earned from hiring out, some South Carolina slaves purchased superfine and coarse textiles to manufacture their own apparel. Historians Shane White and Graham White found that enslaved Africans used various kinds of cloth to make wraps and long frocks that were more African than European in design. Also, when hoopskirts became the rage in the mid-1850s, resourceful Negro designers fashioned their hoops out of grapevines.[54]

More than how enslaved and free African Americans acquired or constructed their fashions, white Charlestonians were concerned with the impact of aristocratic dress and ostentatious promenades on the psyches of urban blacks. This social performance was inherently dangerous because black Charlestonians treated their weekly strolls as rehearsals for freedom. An irate and disoriented Rusticus lamented how proper boundaries between enslaved and free, black and white, were being ignored: "As there is *now* no distinction (further than that of Blacks and Yellows being in appearance finer and more costly) made in dress particularly on a Sunday, I would beg leave to ask of the '*knowing ones*' how I shall distinguish our coloured Dandies and Dandresses from a Gentleman or Lady." During these Negro-dominated social rituals and liberatory training sessions, Rusticus and other disoriented white citizens needed to know how to discriminate between the races, between different classes of Carolinians. The only difference he now saw was that colored participants, the "Blacks and Yellows," were decked out in more expensive finery than other Charlestonians. At the close of his letter to the *Southern Patriot*, Rusticus claimed that "a line of distinction in *every respect* should be drawn." To save himself and other whites from that next embarrassment, Rusticus half-jokingly called for a specific law requiring fashionable Negroes to wear badges, so citizens could "distinguish their false colours 'front and rear.'"

In October 1822, just a month after the Rusticus letter went to press, the Charleston City Council convened a special grand jury and called on state legislation to regulate, or re-regulate, slave fashion and behavior. Echoing Rusticus, the council recognized a dangerous trend in black comportment and declared expensive dress was "subversive of that subordination which policy requires to be enforced."[55] However, the special grand jury arrived at an inescapable conclusion: laws against these "crimes of fashion" would never be sufficiently enforced because the prime enablers were overly solicitous masters. Black Charlestonians would be "allowed" to continue their racially confusing and caste-defying performances on the Sabbath thanks in large part to paternalistic masters.

But what were the full designs and demands of this increasingly autonomous and selectively acculturating colored gentry on public space? Along Charleston's Meeting Street and Broad Street, promenaders introduced an innovative and sometimes disconcerting expressive product, a public performance that separated refinement from "whiteness" and inserted black bodies into the center of civic life. Contrary to masters who believed well-dressed servants were exhibiting pride in their owners, enslaved Africans were using this social ritual to express pride in themselves. As the Negro Act of 1735 and the 1822 Charleston City Council feared, clothing and leisure were literally creating self-possessed, dignified Negro men and women. As black fashionistas altered hemlines, widened pantaloon bottoms, brandished ornate canes, and introduced colorful headdresses, their star turns on major thoroughfares were turning heads and reversing cultural polarities. According to cultural historian Monica Miller, "Black dandyism in the Atlantic diaspora is the story of how and why black people became arbiters of style and how they use clothing and dress to define their identity in different and changing political and cultural contexts."[56] By asserting their presence through fashion, black promenaders contested the "social death" of slavery, and in a seismic shift in hemispheric popular culture, black bodies now defined not just a racial subculture but many aspects of urban fashion.[57]

According to Dick Hebdige, subcultural style typically interrupts the "process of normalization," and it functions as a "symbolic violation of the social order."[58] His take on subculture partially describes Charleston's Negro promenaders and their whiting up work. Black subcultural style was considered a threat to the natural order because, as Rusticus painfully reveals, the wrong bodies were wearing the silk dresses and displaying airs of unchecked freedom. But enslaved and free black fashionistas represented a community no longer content with being subaltern or marginal. Their "symbolic violations" or expropriations of fashions and attitudes associated with the majority were never designed to assimilate urban blacks into the dominant culture, as if that were truly possible. Their ultimate agenda was to dominate public space. Hebdige theorizes that all "spectacular subcultures" produce a style that engages in "intentional communication" with the dominant culture, and by "repositioning and recontextualizing commodities" they open up material culture, like fashion, to "new and covertly oppositional meanings."[59] Yet far from settling for covert, Charleston promenaders loudly communicated that a new and audacious black style had moved from margin to center.

Secretive country dancers and master-subsidized cakewalkers offered critical and parodic representations of European manners and Grand Marches in private and semiprivate contexts, but the stylistic communication of fashion-forward Negro promenaders was openly aggressive. If the visual spectacle of Saturday and Sunday strollers was not imposing enough, black Charlestonians used this weekly social ritual to physically and forcefully establish black style. Henry Louis Gates's theory of "motivated signifying" offers a valuable tool for understanding the assertive energy behind this whiteface minstrelsy. Gates argues that parodies and revisions of an original text can redress a power imbalance by creating rhetorical room for new relationships and new perspectives.[60] Replacing literary texts with bodies as texts, Charleston's emboldened colored gentry created rhetorical room through their brazenly liberated and occasionally belligerent attitudes. As I mentioned at the beginning of this chapter, when enjoying the streets of Charleston or Manhattan, "giving the wall" was a common courtesy. Per the rules of this polite practice, one pedestrian would allow another to walk closer to the buildings, or give the wall, while the person giving the wall, in turn, moved out closer to the road. Traditionally, men would give the wall to women, so the fairer sex would not be exposed to the perils of urban traffic or muddy streets. Rusticus alerted Charleston to a turf war between whites and blacks over who would walk where. On Sunday, he noticed the "appearance, impudence, and bold effrontery" of Negroes and how quick they were to "take the wall."[61] Rusticus even described a "respectable old merchant" who was forced to use his walking cane against two black dandies who tried to force him to the "narrow edge of the pavement." Traditionally, Negroes would give the wall to whites, but that social pact was now null and void as black Charlestonians exerted themselves during a weekly ritual turned public showdown.

For some black Charlestonians, arrogance and aggression were integral parts of their "genteel" public displays of leisure and liberation. Joseph Roach defines whiteface minstrelsy as creating fanciful, even excessive entitlements, so we should not be surprised by the racial and class animus manifested by certain Negro promenaders. They were operating on the idea of whiteness as usable property, a reality rooted in America's conjoined racial and legal systems. Legal theorist Cheryl Harris explains how the "state's official recognition both of a racial identity that subordinated blacks and of privileged rights in property based on race, elevated whiteness from a passive attribute to an object of law and a resource deployable at the social, political, and institutional level to maintain control."[62] Black Charleston's weekly expropriations of white legal, material, and spatial privilege were designed to seize control of the public transcript, and that process required a level of physical and psychological domination that could become unpleasant.

As colored sartorial agents worked to command public space, an especially negative by-product was personal attacks on the most vulnerable white citizens. One visitor to Charleston, unfamiliar with the city's "dandified negroes," was shocked to hear enslaved and free blacks openly making sport of "poor and tattered crackers."[63] Such verbal cruelty suggests that many black promenaders believed they were better, more human, and perhaps "whiter" than the poor, propertyless whites they ridiculed. Part of this aggression was undoubtedly "payback" for the repression enslaved Africans endured under wealthy planters and comparatively poorer white overseers. If Charleston slaves could extort economic and social privileges like hiring out and living out from the most powerful Euro-Americans, there was nothing to stop them, during their public performances, from demeaning "poor white trash," a target closer to the bottom of racial and class hierarchies.[64]

Meeting Street witnessed a power struggle, a collision of offstage and onstage transcripts, that had been brewing for some time. It began with the unsanctioned country dance, where, offstage, black Charlestonians crafted parodic takes on white property and privilege. But then with the sanctioned cakewalk, African Americans moved their critical reinterpretations of the dominant culture onstage, into full view of generally supportive masters and mistresses. Finally, on Saturdays and Sundays in the colonial and early national periods, Negro promenaders broadcast whiting up as a mainstream display of motivated signifying designed to make room for liberated black bodies onstage. As The Stranger and Rusticus warned, the combined impact of all three whiteface minstrel acts was potentially devastating for America's whiteness/blackness hierarchy. The twice-fooled Rusticus loudly lamented how tangible distinctions between white and colored were rapidly disappearing. With so many self-possessed, modish, and occasionally surly black bodies, essential linkages equating whiteness with supremacy and blackness with subservience were under attack. With each promenade, who could say where exhibitions of couture French whiteness ended and representations of New World blackness began?

However, depending on one's perspective, Monica Miller argues, this kind of urban black dandyism could be interpreted as racial fixity and could be used to reinscribe cultural stereotypes. In response to Manhattan's and Charleston's fashionable promenaders, blackface minstrel artists constructed demeaning dandy caricatures such as Long-Tailed Blue and Zip Coon. This white-generated blackface minstrel imagery, onstage and in print, worked to denigrate and dismiss black fashionistas as ridiculous and ineffective white imitations ultimately unfit for social equality. Largely shaped by itinerant white performers, low men on the racial pecking order, this blackface reaction to whiteface minstrelsy amounted to a secondary "crime of fashion."[65]

Returning to the antebellum politics of whiting up, Saidiya Hartman's question still lingers: What was the impact of everyday subjugation on the leisure of the enslaved and on their potential for resistance? Building on Frederick Douglass's "decrial of slave holidays," Hartman argues that the pleasures and performances enjoyed under slavery frustrated "the emergence of an oppositional consciousness" so necessary to contesting if not ending this evil institution. Instead of innocuous plantation barbecues and coded cakewalks, Douglass was waiting for truly "dangerous music and dangerous thought."[66] So did whiteface minstrelsy in antebellum South Carolina ever amount to dangerous performance?

For an answer, we should consider the Denmark Vesey conspiracy, a planned insurrection with the ominous and immediate goals of freeing all enslaved persons in the Charleston area and killing all whites. The insurrection never materialized because authorities uncovered the plot in late May 1822 when a loyal servant informed his master that he had been recruited to join the plot.[67] However, the Vesey conspiracy did alert white Charlestonians to the dangerous relationships cultivated between enslaved Africans, free blacks, and maritime workers.

As residents of a cosmopolitan seaport, Charleston's enslaved population was exposed to interracial sailors and stewards from around the world. A young Denmark Vesey worked as a steward aboard a transatlantic slave ship, and during his international travels, he was introduced to radical ideologies like abolition, democracy, and revolution. After educating himself and purchasing his freedom with lottery winnings, Vesey established himself in Charleston as a respected carpenter and a lay preacher in the African Methodist Episcopal Church. To win converts to his insurrectionary cause, Vesey combined scripture with the Declaration of Independence and French Revolution rhetoric.[68] In addition, the Vesey court trial record reveals that this visionary and resourceful leader planned to use performed whiteness to attack slavery in Charleston.

In order to launch their planned June 1822 insurrection, Vesey and his conspirators first had to eliminate the sentinel at the city's guardhouse and seize munitions from a nearby arsenal.[69] To generate an element of surprise, Vesey hired a local white barber/hairdresser to craft wigs and false whiskers for him and his insurgents. According to court testimony from the white barber, "With the assistance of these, and by painting their faces, they hoped in the darkness of the night and in the confusion to be mistaken for white men." When confronted with the wig and whiskers in the courtroom, Vesey admitted his plan to use the "mask of whiteness."[70]

Vastly different from the cakewalkers and promenaders who playfully commandeered finer aspects of white culture, Vesey and his followers recognized a strategic and potentially deadly advantage to cross-racial deception. Vesey's approach was consistent with Cheryl Harris's theory of whiteness as property, as he planned to use this powerful social resource to create freedom of movement on the night of his insurrection. More than a fixation on privileged whiteness, their planned whiteface masquerade was an imaginative plan to "pass" momentarily as the dominant class to bring down the dominant class. Historian Natalie Zemon Davis has written instructively about a very different yet related masking and cross-dressing tradition in early modern Europe, where lower-class men concealed themselves behind blackface and women's clothing during riots, saturnalia, and other acts of subversion.[71] Unlike the men in those European moments of "misrule," in which masks of the disempowered were deployed, Vesey and his conspirators intended to expropriate the face of unquestioned authority to conceal their identities and camouflage their insurrectionary intentions.

All of the whiteface minstrel performances covered in this chapter, planned or executed, representational or tactical, were dangerous products of America's racial and cultural hierarchies with the resistant potential to destabilize daily power relations. Following the discovery of the 1822 Vesey plot, Charleston officials recognized this reality and debated various proposals to control the movement of free blacks, especially black maritime workers. The city council also discussed curtailing hiring out and completely prohibiting living out, two social and economic practices that directly contributed to whiteface minstrelsy and its liberatory possibilities. Much of the proposed legislation never reached the ordinance books, but free Negroes were assessed a $10 fee and forced to carry registration papers. Post-Vesey, all enslaved South Carolinians had to carry passes or "walkin' tickets" whenever they traveled apart from their masters. In an especially ironic and herrenvolk move, "poor white trash" were hired as slave patrols with the specific duties of checking passes and monitoring enslaved movement.[72]

Charleston's city council understood the eminent danger in the "thought and music" of their Negro population, enslaved and free. They realized that cross-racial masquerades could create representational room, psychic freedom, and perhaps substantive political transformations for black Charlestonians. Yet even in the hypervigilant aftermath of the Vesey conspiracy, some slaveholders refused to view their skilled and trusted property as significant threats to their well-being or white supremacy.[73] Here we see the incredibly dangerous contradiction inherent in the paternalistic, somewhat delusional brand of slavery practiced in Charleston and other parts of the South.

Writing about nineteenth-century performance and politics, Daphne Brooks concludes that black American artists "mastered the art of spectacle, (representational) excess, and duality," and that they "signified on the politics of racial imitation" to reinvent "the transatlantic cultural playing field."[74] To construct this broad playing field in the Charleston area, enslaved Africans, self-emancipated fugitives, and free blacks illegally gathered in the homes of absent masters, in houses rented by black South Carolinians, or in the woods just outside the city. Exhibiting the first function of whiting up, these country dancers playfully mocked and rehearsed a life of carefree leisure denied them the rest of the week, but in the midst of this parodic yet flattering "copying" of white privilege, certain ominous celebrants appeared to concoct plans for literal liberation. One wonders if Vesey's planned insurrection was devised by a secret council hidden within a late-night country dance. As the stars of master-sponsored cakewalks, Negro dancers transformed European lightness and African earthiness into a performative fusion of Euro-Afro cool and African hotness, while also forging a multifaceted African American identity situated in the crossroads. Finally, along Meeting Street and Broad Street, whiteface minstrel promenaders changed urban style forever by refuting racial assumptions that relegated blackness to an inferior position and claimed only whiteness could cut the figure of refinement, elegance, and even abusive power.

Chapter 2 Imitation Whiteness

James Hewlett's Stage Europeans

During the War of 1812, from roughly 1813 to 1815, British forces housed nearly 1,000 captive African American seamen and close to 5,000 French, Irish, and Euro-American prisoners at Dartmoor Prison, a facility located in the village of Princetown, Devon. In Number Four, a segregated section of Dartmoor, African American inmates devised stage European performances to entertain themselves. I define stage Europeans, theatrical cousins to whiteface minstrels, as black actors exploring whiteness through conventional white dramatic characters. Borrowing sets, makeup, properties, and costumes from French inmates, Dartmoor's black acting troupe mounted one- to two-week runs of popular European dramas such as the Reverend John Home's Scottish tragedy *Douglas* and Shakespeare's *Romeo and Juliet*. The admission price was four to six pence for these novel productions, which were enthusiastically supported by white and black detainees. According to maritime historian Jeffrey Bolster, one white sailor recalled attending a memorable Number Four production of *Romeo and Juliet*, where he "witnessed a tall strapping negro, over six feet high, painted white, murdering the part of Juliet to the Romeo of another tall dark-skin."[1] Whether or not they spoke their speeches "trippingly on the tongue," the sheer incongruity of gender-crossing combined with the spectacle of whiteface paint applied to dark bodies was surely worth the price of admission.

As a graduate student, I started using the term "stage European" as a way to explain the spectacle of black bodies assuming white roles, and as a way to integrate black actors into the popular American preoccupation with theatrical crossovers, most notably stage Indians and stage Africans. Throughout the nineteenth century, white playwrights, composers, and choreographers crafted their versions of Indianness or Africanness for the leisurely consumption of paying audiences eager to interface with strange and occasionally savage "others" from a safe, theatrically mediated distance. To create the most effective and fascinating staged others, white actors applied various shades of black or brown makeup, donned woolly wigs, and severely mangled the English language. Not surprisingly, in this same historical moment, black actors like the Dartmoor inmates whitened or rouged their faces, resorted to various wigs and beards, and elevated their speech to impersonate whiteness.

In conventional theatrical spaces all over the world, professional and amateur black actors made conspicuous spectacles of themselves as stage Europeans. Scotland in the 1770s witnessed a young black actress starring in John Gay's *Beggar's Opera* and Shakespeare's *Romeo and Juliet.* In the nineteenth century, Ira Aldridge built a career in Britain and Eastern Europe, in part by whiting up to execute characters like Dirk Hatteraick in Sir Walter Scott's *Guy Mannering* and Shylock in Shakespeare's *Merchant of Venice.*[2] In 1820s Manhattan, black theatrical entrepreneur William Brown and his predominantly Negro acting company staged an impressive range of whiteness, from Irish soldiers to Scottish rebels to Spanish Lotharios to English royalty.

For his lead actress, Brown featured a chambermaid-turned-actress named Miss S. Welsh, who tackled male and female stage Europeans in her inimitable style. Playing opposite Miss Welsh were two equally interesting and ambitious black leading men, two oversized personalities who relished appropriating a certain Shakespearean "bad boy." The first leading man was a freed slave named Charles Taft, alias Charles Beers, who harbored a sincere and eventually criminal fondness for the Duke of Gloucester from *Richard III*. Taft's passion to perform Richard led him to steal costume pieces, which eventually landed him in jail.[3] He was swiftly replaced by Brown's second leading man, James Hewlett, a multitalented young performer committed to crafting musical, comedic, and dramatic stage Europeans. The key difference between Welsh's, Taft's, and Hewlett's stage Europeans versus Euro-America's equally spectacular stage Africans and stage Indians was that those white actors were cross-racially executing dramatic roles written expressly for them. In the early 1600s, Shakespeare created a stage African figure like Othello with the white actor/manager Richard Burbage firmly in mind; likewise, John Augustus Stone wrote the stage Indian drama *Metamora* in the late 1820s to be performed by white actor/producer Edwin Forrest. In contrast, Brown's Negro actors assumed white roles never imagined, written, or intended for them.

This lack of official license invested Welsh's and Hewlett's whiting up acts with a level of performative subversion and political resonance unmatched by the stage Africans or stage Indians created by white artists. This chapter examines the aesthetics and politics of specific nineteenth-century stage Europeans crafted by James Hewlett, William Brown's most documented and celebrated company member. As one of Afro-America's earliest leading men, Hewlett was celebrated for his imitative appropriations of English stars, including Edmund Kean and Charles Mathews, as well as for his engagement with Scottish performance material, most notably Robert Burns's national ballad "Scots, wha hae wi' Wallace bled." I contend that two distinct varieties of cross-cultural identification were at work in Hewlett's stage Europeans. The first was rooted in professional aspiration, as Hewlett emulated European musical, dramatic, and comedic stars with an eye on matching or surpassing his celebrated models. The second cross-cultural connection was political in nature, as Hewlett and his black audiences used relatable white historical and theatrical figures to identify, articulate, and advance communal aspirations. Before exploring Hewlett's racial crossovers and the second whiting up function, we should briefly discuss the dynamics of imitation, emulation, and mimicry in nineteenth-century transatlantic theatrical performance.

Imitation, Emulation, and Mimicry

Transcendental philosopher Ralph Waldo Emerson famously wrote in an 1841 essay titled "Self-Reliance" that "there is a time in every man's education when he arrives at the conviction that envy is ignorance; that imitation is suicide."[4] Yet on both sides of the Atlantic Ocean, in the early nineteenth century, theatrical audiences respected a young artist's imitative abilities, especially when a novice performer used imitation to display signs of genius. To demonstrate and develop their talents, aspiring actors diligently studied the scenes, songs, and stage business most associated with more well-known artists and then publicly announced their imitations of established theatrical luminaries.

Here is part of a typical advertisement for a young actor in 1821 New York City: "In act one, Mr. Brown will give his Imitations of the following celebrated Actors: Mr. Kemble as Penruddock; Mr. Cooke as Sir Pertinax McSycophant; Mr. Phillips as Count Belino, in the song of 'Behold in his soft expressive face'; Mr. Munden as Capt. Bertram; Mr. Cooper as Othello; and Mr. Kean in the characters of Richard and Sir Giles Overreach."[5] As a newcomer to the Manhattan theater scene, Mr. Brown understood the invaluable publicity gained by linking his name with respected theatrical figures such as John Philip Kemble, George Frederick Cooke, Thomas Cooper, Henry Phillips, and Edmund Kean. Mr. Brown also realized that by selecting the roles and romantic ballads most suited to his natural talents, he could fine tune his skills as a balladeer, tragic actor, and comedian. In fact, for an aspiring performer, identifying the appropriate roles to imitate may have been more important to career-building than establishing a media association with Cooke or Kean.

Richard Dyer, building on Elizabeth Burns's work on theatricality, explains how the earliest transatlantic theatrical stars, such as David Garrick and Edmund Kean, used famous roles like Hamlet or Richard to achieve the very embodiment of "triumphant individualism." In other words, they were able to build personal prestige on the existing celebrity or notoriety of specific dramatic characters. Aligning oneself with a leading theatrical figure may have gotten one's foot in the proverbial door, but nineteenth-century actors took the next step to true stardom by dominating a well-known Shakespearean character and establishing that crucial connection between their public persona and that special role.[6] An actor would have attained this "triumphant individualism" when a theatrical manager could advertise his performance as "Kean's Richard III" and draw a respectable house.

However, even after one studied the masters and graduated from ambitious young unknown to featured theatrical attraction, imitation was not necessarily a performance mode one outgrew. Such was the case with English solo performance artist Charles Mathews, who proudly proclaimed himself an imitator and went so far as to identify imitation as "the very soul of the profession of an actor."[7] Reflecting on his craft, Mathews claimed his mimetic work was similar to that of a natural scientist; he closely observed and notated human behavior, gesture, and physiognomy in order to effectively reproduce the subtle details of various personalities. Mathews, a versatile English low comedian, singer, dancer, and ventriloquist, was famous throughout Europe for his solo performances called "at homes." To develop these one-person specialties, Mathews traveled throughout selected countries, observed the locals, and devised monologues, songs, and dances to stage nationally emblematic characters. Mathews was by no means the originator of solo entertainments in Europe. There were precursors such as Samuel Foote and Jack Bannister, but Mathews's "at homes" staged an unmatched range of ethnic, racial, class, gendered, and generational identities.

Along with his broad repertoire of national imitations, Mathews was also known for staging reproductions of his fellow actors in their most iconic roles, such as George Frederick Cooke as Richard III. According to theater historian Jim Davis, Mathews believed his re-creations of established performers transmitted "their unique qualities to future generations." Even in the late 1820s, when imitation, Emerson's idea of career suicide, was coming under critical attack, Mathews defended his craft by asserting that imitation "can perpetuate both the art and artist."[8] As an unapologetic imitator and theatrical luminary, Mathews embraced his role as a breathing performative archive personally responsible for preserving the art of nineteenth-century acting.

Writing about imitation and invention, rhetorician John Muckelbauer suggests we approach imitation not by focusing separately on the model, the English star actor, or on the imitator, the career-building young actor. Instead, we should concentrate on "the relation that exists between the model and the copy." By examining this affirmative relationship, we can appreciate "the dynamics of repetition and variation that circulate through any given practice of imitation." To help us appreciate the dynamic relationships between models and copies, Muckelbauer identifies three different imitative rhythms. Although all three rhythms can and often do exist in the same imitative act or practice, Muckelbauer disentangles them as "repetition of the same," "repetition of difference," and "difference and inspiration."[9] "Repetition of the same" is probably the most conventional imitative rhythm. This relationship is demonstrated in the work of a young actor like Mr. Brown, who delivered faithful replicas of Edmund Kean or George Frederick Cooke to advance his career. The last two imitative rhythms are more complex and can help us analyze the model-copy relationships behind James Hewlett's stage Europeans, as well as certain whiting up acts in subsequent centuries.

Imitation as "repetition of difference" repeats the model but also offers clear variations. The imitator, the young actor with a touch of genius, respectfully approaches the model as pregnant with multiple possibilities, and he or she realizes those potentials while also altering or transforming the original. The cakewalkers described in Chapter 1 could serve as excellent examples of this particular imitative rhythm. Exhibiting more emulation than imitation, those enslaved dancers expanded on and surpassed the European marches and minuets, and as we shall see shortly, this same rhythm aptly describes Hewlett's relationship to his white models.

Most British and American star actors built their careers by emulating rather than strictly imitating established performers, meaning the most talented thespians matched, challenged, and then surpassed their role models en route to becoming truly original performers. An excellent example of this emulative-relationship-turned-rivalry happened with George Frederick Cooke and Edmund Kean. In the early 1800s, throughout the United Kingdom, actors, critics, and audiences universally acknowledged Cooke's conception of Richard III as the model for all future performers attempting this role. Around 1810, Cooke made a memorable U.S. debut as the infamous Duke of Gloucester, performing America's favorite Shakespearean history at Manhattan's prestigious Park Theatre. A decade later, in November 1820, a promising upstart named Edmund Kean made his American debut also playing the Duke of Gloucester at the Park. Earlier in his career, Kean may have honed his acting talents by reproducing certain aspects of Cooke's restrained and classical Richard, but Kean would escape Cooke's shadow by advancing his own highly emotional interpretation of the role.[10] Through his innovative romantic acting style, Kean became the universally acknowledged leader of the pack, and other English and American actors now viewed him as the template.

In the United States, Junius Brutus Booth was the first American actor to imitate and then challenge Kean for representational supremacy. Most critics and theater patrons knew that the younger Booth copied "peculiarities" from the more seasoned Kean. Here is how one writer explained the relationship between model Kean and copy Booth: "It is true, in all plays there are some parts which all actors do alike, and two or three instances of particular resemblance are too apt to influence a general opinion, that an actor is a copyist. The fact is Mr. Booth has made all the great actors models and has doubtless caught many of the peculiarities of 'Kean' and gives them with great effect, but this by no means makes him liable to the charge of being an imitator."[11] For this critic, "copyist" and "imitator" were both deadly charges to level at any actor, yet he makes the subtle concession that modeling Kean or several other stellar actors did not render Booth a suicidal, derivative amateur. The young American actor reproduced aspects of Kean with "great effect"; in other words, Booth was talented enough to display his unique genius through this signature role, Richard III, and any temporary association with a respected model did not compromise his career.

With Muckelbauer's third and final imitative relationship, "difference and inspiration," the model can transmit inspiration to the copying artist; in other words, the person imitating is encouraged or induced to lose "oneself in the response to the model" and, in the process, become "something other than oneself."[12] The legendary nineteenth-century East African performer Totte Maze offers an intriguing example of "difference and inspiration" in action. In 1817, *American Monthly Magazine* published an article chronicling this Abyssinian actor who amazed spectators with his eerily accurate impersonations. As a court performer for the Ras, or prince, of Abyssinia (later Ethiopia), Maze displayed his "ingenuity upon persons of every description, without regard to rank or station."[13] Maze embodied everyone and everything, including the Abyssinian prince, a cowardly chief in battle, a courtier visiting a superior, a coquettish woman, and even "the sound of horns at a distance." The magazine reporter commented on how "the tones of his voice were so perfectly adapted to the different characters, and his action so thoroughly appropriate that it gave me a very unexpected gratification." Totte Maze seemed overcome or possessed by whatever he imitated, but perhaps his greatest talent was the ability to stare into an individual's face and compel that person to mimic the contortions of his own face. Here we see the third imitative rhythm reversed as the famed Abyssinian imitator transmitted inspiration to his model. Maze's induced or projected ventriloquism was an impressive feat, one to keep in mind as we examine Hewlett's cross-cultural tango with Charles Mathews. Also, as we shall see in Chapter 6, this particular rhythm, "difference and inspiration," was practiced by contemporary solo performers like Richard Pryor and Anna Deavere Smith.

Like most young nineteenth-century performers, James Hewlett was inspired to copy and potentially transform white dramatic roles and white role models. After all, there were no black actors to emulate, and most stage Africans were demeaning, low-comedy roles. When we consider the Negro acculturation process, cultural anthropologist Melville Herskovits would argue that African American actors were drawn to European theatrical material because Euro-Americans rested atop the nation's racial hierarchy, and therefore, their elite culture was most worthy of emulation.[14] However, white nineteenth-century cultural critics like M. M. Noah, editor of New York's *National Advocate*, characterized the relationship between Negro emulators and European models as nothing more than pathetic mimicry. Noah specifically described William Brown's colored entertainments, featuring James Hewlett, as another sad attempt by a social-climbing colored gentry to "ape their masters and mistresses in everything." Early nineteenth-century English literary critic and journalist Leigh Hunt used similar language to denigrate mimicry in general as nothing more than the unlearned, superficial antics of "an accomplished ape."[15]

Despite dismissive language from critics like Noah and Hunt, mimicry did serve as a legitimate representational outlet for Afro-Diasporic artists like Totte Maze and James Hewlett. Drawing on her anthropological background, the perceptive and multitalented writer Zora Neale Hurston has argued that "the Negro, the world over, is famous as a mimic," and that blacks mimic whites not based on feelings of inferiority but purely for the love of this challenging art form. For Hurston, mimicry hardly compromises the Negro's standing as an original; to the contrary, the average Negro artist does not "slavishly" imitate presumably superior white models but, rather, creates fresh reproductions of his or her subjects with a sense of difference and commentary.[16] Hurston salvaged mimicry for black artists by liberating this practice from racially coded language—"aping," "slavish"—and by placing African American actors in conversation with world performance. Her alternative perspective on mimicry was confirmed by the many Abyssinians who respected Totte Maze's talents and held him in the highest regard as a mimic, thus proving this much-maligned performative mode could foster originality. Today, we can appreciate world-class mimicry through solo performers like Sarah Jones and Anna Deavere Smith, but in 1820s Manhattan, the physically facile, emulative artist to watch was James Hewlett.

Crossover Hewlett: Emulating Kean and Mathews

As the lead singer, actor, dancer, and choreographer for a unique Negro acting company, James Hewlett was on the fast track to regional, if not national, notoriety. In part, his rapid ascent depended on visually associating himself with both Edmund Kean, the leading English actor, and Junius Brutus Booth, the rising American heir to the theatrical throne. Figures 3, 4, and 5 show three publicity images: a November 1821 engraving of Edmund Kean as the Duke of Gloucester, a May 1817 engraving of Junius Brutus Booth in *Richard III*, and an undated 1820s engraving of James Hewlett as Richard. The caption for Hewlett's advertising image reads, "Mr. Hewlett as Richard the Third in imitation of Mr. Kean"; thus the Negro leading man openly and proudly attached himself to the luminary both he and Booth were modeling. All three actors marketed the romantic Richard that Edmund Kean first popularized, a dashing, swashbuckling Duke of Gloucester noticeably free of the hunchbacked deformity Shake-

Figure 3 Engraving of Edmund Kean as Richard III (1821). By permission of the Folger Shakespeare Library.

Figure 4 Engraving of Junius Brutus Booth as Richard III (1817). By permission of the Folger Shakespeare Library.

Figure 5 Engraving of James Hewlett as Richard III (undated 1820s). Brander Matthews Dramatic Museum Portraits, Rare Book and Manuscript Library, Columbia University.

speare calls for in his original text.[17] As you can see, all three seductive Richards share dark, curly locks, a healthy mustache, and an ornate long coat with excessively puffy yet manly epaulets designed for battle. To further spotlight the "peacock" nature of these heartthrob Richards, Booth's and Hewlett's engravings added plumed headgear.

Hewlett's professional challenge was to develop into a singular artist who could ultimately advertise "Hewlett's Richard III" and not "in imitation of Mr. Kean." Yet his path to "triumphant individualism" was somewhat different from that of his white contemporaries, because as a Negro actor Hewlett first had to confront the idea of Shakespeare as white theatrical property. He attacked this cultural assumption by stressing similarity. Like the Booth and Kean visuals, Hewlett's publicity image accentuates fine, sharply anglicized features, but with a hint of swarthiness. This particular biracial projection is consistent with Hewlett's other promotional material, such as an 1825 biographical article, originally published in the *Brooklyn Star*, that promoted this Long Island native as "of lighter colour than ordinary mulattoes."[18] Apparently Hewlett could have passed for Caucasian, but instead he elected to promote a racially ambiguous, slightly "sun-bathed" Richard, just like publicity images of Kean and Booth.

Beyond exploiting biological or visual similarities, Hewlett also strategically placed his stage persona in the line of great actors past and present. The 1825 biography claimed that "his histrionic education took place under those celebrated masters Cooke and Cooper, whom he followed as a servant boy, and stole their actions and attitudes in moments of recreation or recitation." Veracity was not of paramount importance in nineteenth-century theatrical publicity, so whether or not Hewlett actually studied under George Frederick Cooke or Thomas Cooper is irrelevant. Such details were merely promotional carrots designed to attract crowds and critics, who would hopefully judge Hewlett on his merits and not on his alleged associations. While paying all due homage to an "old lion" like Cooke, Hewlett also billed himself as "Shakespeare's proud representative," with a special nod to Kean as his primary role model. For his recitations, Hewlett typically played Richard's act 1, scene 1, soliloquy ("Now is the winter of our discontent") and the act 5, scene 8, final battle at Bosworth Field, both in imitation of Kean, the 1820s theatrical leader.[19]

As for Hewlett's merits as a performer, the writer of the 1825 biographical article appeared sufficiently impressed: "Hewlett, however, must have had a natural talent for theatrical performances, and an excellent voice withal, or he never could have surmounted his early difficulties. His songs were excellent, and his style, taste, voice, and action such as would have done credit to any stage. His imitations of Kean, Mathews, Phillips and others were recognized as correct, and evincing a nice discrimination and peculiar tact on his part, which ought to recommend him to every lover of pure acting." The writer never explained what Hewlett's "early difficulties" may have been—educational, financial, or legal—but he did acknowledge that Hewlett had arrived as a performer. His imitations were accurate, and like Junius Brutus Booth, he was discriminating enough to realize what "Kean elements" were worthy of replication and which details were best left behind.

It is interesting how this generally favorable article claims that Hewlett "stole" onstage and offstage "actions and attitudes" from veteran actors like Cooke, which brings us back to the issue of whiteness and performative property. Although Hewlett's biographer may have harbored only the kindest intentions, his mere suggestion of theft highlights a lack of official license with regard to stage Europeans. The implication here is that white actors like Kean had a right to imitate Cooke, but when a mulatto "servant boy" borrows Cooke's signature business, criminal terms like "stole" creep in and resonate in disturbing ways. In Chapter 4, I return to this concept of Negro actors trespassing on European dramatic territory. But as part of a dual whiting up tradition, extra-theatrical African American social performers had been studying and appropriating white "attitudes and actions" for several decades, and Hewlett was simply bringing this Afro-Diasporic imitative mode into a conventional theatrical context. And ultimately, like every other young actor, Hewlett was co-opting the best of Cooke, Cooper, Kean, and Mathews to advance his theatrical career.

Much of early American theatrical production was predicated on cross-racial performance with the possibility of cross-cultural identification, rooted in a desire to consume and perform all available "others"; hence the emergence of stage Indians, stage Africans, stage Europeans, whiteface minstrelsy, and eventually blackface minstrelsy.[20] Blackface minstrel shows were the first national entertainments, fueled by the frenzy and fetish of cross-racial traffic, to gain widespread popularity across racial, gender, and class lines. Yet, as Saidiya Hartman argues, blackface minstrelsy failed to reach its full potential as a vehicle for cross-cultural identification because it was "predicated on chattel slavery" and could not transcend its inherent master-slave dichotomies.[21] However, there was an alternative tradition of cross-racial play. Even before working-class white blackface artists reached down the racial ladder to exploit a counterfeit blackness,

William Brown's colored company reached up the hierarchy for the mask of whiteness. While their white counterparts failed to produce respectful stage Africans, these Negro actors used stage Europeans to acquire certain "actions and attitudes" of the dominant culture and to transcend racial difference as an affirmation of shared humanity.[22]

William Brown's whiting up experiments went well beyond comparatively highbrow Shakespearean productions like *Richard III*. After his Negro company was literally arrested for performing Shakespeare—for trespassing on white dramatic property—in January 1822, the resourceful Brown turned almost exclusively to "minor" theatrical material and even temporarily renamed his enterprise the Minor Theatre.[23] With this self-identified Minor Theatre, Brown launched a series of entertainments that would allow Hewlett and company to cultivate multiple stage European flavors. In August 1822, Brown featured the triple-threat Hewlett—singer, actor, dancer—in John O'Keeffe's *Poor Soldier* (1782), a musical set in the Irish countryside about a simple soldier who returns home after fighting in the American war. On the same bill, Brown premiered his company's first production of William Blake's *Don Juan; or the Libertine Destroyed* (1795), a dramatic pantomime about the famous Spanish "bad boy."[24] Perhaps the most productive consequence of Brown's coerced embrace of minor stage Europeans was Hewlett's exploration of multiethnic solo performance in imitation of his other theatrical role model: Charles Mathews.

On March 24, 1823, before embarking on a solo tour of the American South, Hewlett staged a farewell performance that included a monopolylogue—a short play in which one actor plays several characters—titled "La Diligence."[25] This monopolylogue came from the concluding section of Charles Mathews's "at home" *A Trip to Paris* (1819), and in this piece, Mathews reintroduced all the characters presented over the course of the evening. Mathews's "at homes" and monopolylogues were solo works that fused song, dance, and ventriloquism into an incredible comedic confluence of simultaneous impersonation.[26] At the invitation of Park Theatre manager Stephen Price, in September 1822 Mathews toured America with the dual goals of popularizing his comedic specialties in the States and collecting material for a new "at home" about this young republic.[27] For his Manhattan debut, Mathews abstained from regular comedies and exclusively performed "at homes," but regrettably, most New Yorkers were unprepared for and underwhelmed by his unique entertainments. Some critics dismissed this master impersonator as a mimic, but ventriloquism scholar Steven Connor argues that those critics did not understand how difficult it was to balance ventriloquism or "dead mimicry" with a living, polyvocal presence.[28]

"La Diligence" features an assortment of French and English characters traveling from France to London in a *diligence,* a large, enclosed French stagecoach.[29] Here is the character lineup for Hewlett's March 1823 version of the Mathews monopolylogue:

Mr. Hewlett at Home
in
La Diligence

Jemmy, an English Boots	Mr. Hewlett.
Monsieur Peremptoir, a traveling Tutor	Mr. Hewlett.
Master Tommy Tarragon, his Infant Pupil	Mr. Hewlett.
Samuel Starch, Esq., a tailor made him	Mr. Hewlett.
Hezekiah Hulk, a great Attorney of Size Lane	Mr. Hewlett.
Miss Evelina Evergreen, an Old Maid	Mr. Hewlett.
Monsieur Poudre Meneur, a French Postillion	Mr. Hewlett.[30]

English characters dominate this list of national figures, thus providing Hewlett with opportunities to cross-culturally identify with a veritable menagerie of British whiteness. First there is Jemmy, the ostler who cares for the horses, takes the fares, and supplies an earthy and decidedly "republican" running commentary on the upper-crust English and French passengers. He is especially critical of the French, who strike him as especially "funny fellows." With his proletarian, "salt-of-the-earth" mentality, Jemmy would have connected well with early national Americans north and south. Next is Samuel Starch, a strutting parody of the fashion-focused dandy, a character which Manhattan had its fair share of, in both black and white varieties. Starch provided Hewlett with an opportunity for physical comedy, because during one particularly frustrating bit this dandy tries to put on his boots in spite of his excessively "starched" garments. Offering even more physical comedy, Hezekiah Hulk is a painfully oversized English attorney—perhaps a reference to the material excess or voracity of the lawyer class—who is so enormous he has to be hoisted into the conveyance by Jemmy. The sole female figure in this polyphonic piece is Miss Evelina Evergreen, an English "old maid." According to the notes accompanying "La Diligence," she is dressed in the "highest absurdity of fashion," thus providing Mathews, and later Hewlett, with an "excellent opportunity for the display of his great mimic talent" in performing the fairer sex.

Mathews's monopolylogue also demanded that Hewlett develop his ventriloquist skills. In the text, the fashionable Evelina Evergreen travels with two beloved animals, her parrot and a pug dog named Puggy. To stage her two prized pets, Mathews and Hewlett had to "throw" their best bird and canine voices into a basket that the old maid totes around. The final English character, a young tutee named Tommy Tarragon, also required ventriloquism. Tommy, a ventriloquist's dummy, travels in a "fiddle case" under the supervision of his French tutor, Monsieur Peremptoir. The script lists Peremptoir as "dressed French cockney," an interesting nation-class composite that suggests more London vernacular than Parisian formality, but this character is later described as "completely French, as to astonish every spectator."

With the pairing of Peremptoir and Tarragon, Mathews showcased age-old animosities between England and France, with France initially gaining the upper hand thanks to the quick-witted, sharp-tongued Monsieur Peremptoir. This character's name is a play on the French adjective *péremptoire*, meaning "excessively arrogant," which aptly describes Monsieur Peremptoir's superior and disparaging attitude toward his English fellow travelers. In their ventriloquist routine, Peremptoir pulls Tommy from the fiddle case, and the two engage in a fierce battle of comedic wit. Imagine Mathews or Hewlett assuming the role of Peremptoir and attempting to teach his willful young charge multiplication tables. As a ventriloquist's dummy, the English pupil was completely under his French master's control, so it would appear France would maintain an advantage in this particular showdown. However, the exasperating Tommy so thoroughly befuddles his tutor that Monsieur Peremptoir has to shove the puppet back into the case to regain his sanity. Finally, Hewlett's version of "La Diligence" closes with a French song of departure performed by Monsieur Poudre Meneur, a postilion or driver with the scatological name, who guides "La Diligence" on its journey.

Hewlett accomplished two important goals with this panoply of French and English stage Europeans. First, his mastery of multiethnic, multiclass, and cross-gendered characters demonstrated that the performed whiteness offered in William Brown's theater was by no means monolithic or predictable. Second, Hewlett proved that an African American performer could excel in this physical and verbal comedic universe typically populated by white characters and not stage Africans. As that prototypical aspiring performer, Hewlett expanded his comedic and vocal range by filling the considerable shoes of an innovative solo performer. Working within the second whiting up mode, Hewlett celebrated and mastered all of Mathews's special talents, including throwing his voice into baskets, cross-dressing as an English old maid, and singing parodic melodies in French. By modeling both Mathews and Kean, Hewlett declared his professional ambition to become the most versatile performer possible, but his crossover efforts went beyond trading on the renown of established performers.

James Hewlett elevated himself to that next original level by placing his unique performative persona within a Mathews "at home." For a January 19, 1824, benefit, Hewlett advertised that his "performance will commence with imitations of *Mathews at Home*." Typically on benefit nights, a performer showcased his or her best material, hoping to draw and please the largest number of patrons. To stage his latest homage to Mathews, Hewlett combined characters from various "at homes," including a stage Irishman named Daniel O'Rourke, who worked aboard passenger packet lines as a singing ship's steward, and a stage Frenchman named Monsieur Zephyr, who was a respected ballet master.[31] Hidden among this differentiated whiteness, Hewlett also interjected a hint of swarthiness with a curious character named "Hewlett."

Although we have no record of the specific songs, dances, or monologues Hewlett used for "Hewlett," I suspect this original character opened with a soliloquy from *Richard III*, maybe followed by a performance of Burns's ballad "Scots, wha hae wi' Wallace bled," and concluded with a Hewlett favorite, the popular romantic melody "Is There a Heart That Ever Loved," from Samuel Arnold's *Devil's Bridge* (1817). Conceivably, this "Hewlett" character could have been autobiographical, providing a very personal narrative of a young man from Long Island who became a ship's steward, then a tailor, eventually a heartthrob singer and swashbuckling actor, and finally an artist who could perform the full measure of humanity.[32] Hewlett emerged as a "triumphant individual," first by strategically cultivating the right roles and models and then by boldly showcasing Hewlett performing Mathews performing "Hewlett." Similar to Maze's facial ventriloquism, which displaced physical tics onto a spectator, Hewlett effectively transformed his model, an English comedic innovator, into his very own singular Afro–New Yorker persona.

Black-Scottish: Rehearsal for Revolution at Bannockburn

In early October 1821, manager William Brown transferred his theatrical operations from a second-floor private residence at Thomas Street on Manhattan's West Side to a larger venue on Mercer Street in Greenwich Village. Hewlett christened this brand-new space with a special benefit performance in which he showcased the rich tradition of Scottish folk music, specifically Robert Burns's historical ballad "Scots, wha hae wi' Wallace bled."[33] A couple years later, Brown and company further explored Scottish culture when they staged the Reverend John Home's groundbreaking tragedy *Douglas* (1754/1771).[34] Both Burns's lyrical rumination on colonial resistance and Home's declaration of Scottish dramatic independence allowed Hewlett, Brown, and their Negro patrons to experience rousing fight scenes, contemplate Afro–New York's most pressing issue, slavery, and assess this community's commitment to full American citizenship.

Brown and Hewlett were not the first theater practitioners to recognize and build on cultural commonalities between Africans and Scots. On multiple occasions in the early 1820s, the Park Theatre, Manhattan's premiere theatrical institution, merged Scottish and stage African musical material. As standard practice, the Park interjected popular songs into established dramatic pieces, most often between acts but occasionally within the natural flow of a dramatic narrative. In June 1821, Park managers inserted the stage African melody "Pity the Slave" from Thomas Morton's sentimental musical *The Slave* (1816) into the middle of a contemporary Scottish-flavored musical drama, *Rob Roy Macgregor; or, Au'd Lang Syne* (1818), composed by John Davy and Henry Bishop and based on the Sir Walter Scott novel. The Park's black-Scottish cross-cultural fusions flowed in the opposite direction as well. Two weeks after mounting their intertextual *Rob Roy*, the Park announced a production of Morton's *The Slave* with two Scottish melodies mixed in: "A Highland Laddie Heard of War" and "My Highland Home When Tempests Blow."[35] In advertisements for this production, Park managers announced that an actor named Mr. Moreland would sing the interpolated songs as a character named Captain Malcolm, a respectable Scottish lad in love with a quadroon named Zelinda. However, in Morton's original musical, there is no Scottish Captain Malcolm, only a Dutch Captain Clifton, but to justify interjecting Highland songs into *The Slave*, the Park's creative team opted to change names and nationalities.

The Park probably blended Scottish songs with stage African musicals, and vice versa, because they sensed some musical affinity between these two cultural groups. An 1825 article published in the *African Repository and Colonial Journal* titled "Specimens of African Genius" noted striking similarities between Scottish clans and the Solima people of Sierra Leone. One core commonality was how musical artists from both cultures composed ballads chronicling the legendary exploits of their heroes.[36] Additionally, musicologist Charles Hamm found that when composers like Thomas Morton crafted stage African musicals, they did not study West or East African tonal structures. Instead, they reached for more familiar Scottish folk songs to achieve the desired "primitive" musical effect.[37] Yet I doubt Hewlett and Brown were drawn to a Scottish heroic ballad like "Scots, wha hae wi' Wallace bled" or Home's *Douglas* because they viewed Scottish culture as uncultivated or primitive. During his "forced" Minor Theatre phase, Brown was searching for high-quality, non-Shakespearean dramatic material to showcase, and Home's *Douglas*, a rousing, action-packed symbol of Scottish literary independence, presented the perfect vehicle.

Rooted in Scottish folklore and Douglas clan history, Home's tragedy dramatizes an intricate confluence of long-standing interclan conflicts. To compose the piece, Home drew literary inspiration from *Gil Morice*, or *Child Maurice*, a well-known national ballad about an orphaned youth from a noble family. In the original tale, Morice is beheaded by his mother's jealous second husband, but Home eliminated that macabre detail to make his *Douglas* more palatable for theatrical audiences. Home's other major alteration was to replace the name Morice with that of another fabled Scottish lad, a youth named Norval from the Douglas clan of the Celtic lowlands. In Home's tragedy, this salt-of-the-earth farmer boy saves the noble Lady Randolph from a band of rogues, and in return she takes the youth under her wing. Her decision to adopt a strapping young commoner does not sit well with her second husband, Lord Randolph. And as ironic backstory, it turns out this young Norval is the long-lost son of Lady Randolph and her first husband, a presumed-dead nobleman named Douglas—hence the play's title.[38]

Sometime between January and May 1823, Peter Nielsen, a Scottish visitor to Manhattan, noticed Brown's colored company was mounting Home's complicated clan saga. The proud Scotsman conceded that a Negro theater was a novel idea, and he could probably tolerate a black *Othello*; but when he witnessed Brown's production, he remarked that "a black Douglas, with a kilt, makes a most preposterous appearance."[39] Nielsen was disturbed that Negroes would dare expropriate his cultural heritage, but the offended Scotsman probably did not realize Negro productions of *Douglas* were popular throughout the Americas. As mentioned at the beginning of this chapter, Dartmoor's African American inmates staged the Scottish tragedy for their captive fans. In 1816, European traveler Matthew Gregory Lewis reported roving Negro actors, or "Actor Boys," performing the climactic battle scene from Home's tragedy on the streets of Kingston, as part of Jamaica's annual Jonkonnu festivities.[40]

So why was *Douglas* the tragedy of choice for three different communities of New World Africans? Perhaps more than Shakespeare's privileged "bad boy" Richard, an orphaned Scotsman like Norval may have resonated with similarly marginalized Afro-Diasporic artists and audiences. On a purely theatrical level, the physical action in *Douglas* is particularly attractive. In Home's climactic scene, the presumed-dead Douglas returns to claim his wife, his son, and his inheritance, but he is viciously attacked by Lord Randolph and his henchmen. Douglas manages to dispatch all of his attackers except Lord Randolph, who stabs the title character in the back. Such a visceral combat scene would have understandably stirred both the blood and the emotions of Africans throughout the Americas.

Beyond emotional affinities and thrilling battles, there was a significant political dimension to this transnational black-Scottish connection. Since the late eighteenth century, Scottish intellectuals and dramatists had boldly broadcast their opposition to slavery. According to theater historian Richard Gale, when the British Empire first reconsidered its involvement in slavery and the transatlantic slave trade, Scottish Enlightenment writers like Francis Hutcheson assumed leadership roles in the early antislavery movement. Hutcheson, along with his students Adam Smith and William Robertson, propagated abolitionist sentiments across Europe and helped launch the abolitionist movement in the United States.[41] So it was no coincidence that Brown, Hewlett, and other black artists discovered a political undertone in John Home's *Douglas*, and even more so in Robert Burns's anticolonial ballad "Scots, wha hae wi' Wallace bled."

Alternatively titled "Bruce's Address to His Army" or "Robert Bruce's March to Bannockburn," this heroic ode immortalizes two Scottish national heroes, William Wallace and Robert Bruce. In 1793, after visiting

Bannockburn, the site of Scotland's most celebrated military victory over England, Robert Burns was inspired to write a song commemorating this early fourteenth-century battle. Composing in the Scots dialect and to the tune of the popular air "Hey tuttie taitie," Burns creatively reimagined what Robert Bruce might have said to his troops before this legendary confrontation. After its publication in 1794, Burns's poetic address became an anthem for the ongoing Scottish independence struggle within the United Kingdom, and it was even selected as the official song of the Scottish National Party.[42]

The nationalistic ballad allowed Hewlett and his largely black audiences to identify with Scots on two levels: first, as colonial subjects and, second, as would-be revolutionaries. To open the ballad Burns foregrounds two icons of Scottish independence, the martyred renegade Wallace and the Scottish clan leader Bruce:

> Scots, wha hae wi' Wallace bled,
> Scots wham Bruce has aften led:
> Welcome to your gory bed,
> Or to victory.[43]

In the late thirteenth century, William Wallace inadvertently joined Scotland's liberation struggle when he began plundering English travelers as a politically conscious highwayman.[44] Impressed with his lucrative guerilla tactics, Scottish noblemen like Robert Bruce recognized Wallace as "a guardian of the kingdom," a proletarian leader of an unofficial resistance campaign. Upon hearing of Wallace's insurgent banditry, England's Edward I, infamously known as "the hammer of Scots," dispatched forces to defeat Wallace and the traitorous Scottish nobles. Out of political expediency, some noblemen, including Robert Bruce, reconsidered their support of Wallace and switched allegiances back to Mother England, thus sacrificing the soon-to-be martyred bandit.

Wallace's grassroots insurrection was based on the same desire for self-rule that ignited New World revolutions in North America, South America, and the West Indies. The relatively recent uprising in the American colonies would have been fresh in the minds of most supporters attending Hewlett's 1821 benefit performance. Scotland's history of oppression under the English crown, especially the tyrannical Edward I, mirrored American colonial struggles with George III in the 1770s. More specifically, the options of "gory bed" or "victory" presented in Burns's opening stanza evoke Patrick Henry's famed "liberty or death" speech. In March

1775, Henry, a habitual rabble-rouser, delivered an impassioned address to a group of delegates gathered in Richmond, Virginia, on whether to defy British tyranny and chose revolution. He warned, "There is no retreat but in submission and slavery! Our chains are forged. Their clanking may be heard on the plains of Boston! The war is inevitable—and let it come!!" Henry then closed by dramatically stating his resolute position: "Give me liberty, or give me death."[45]

Similar to Henry's reference to forged and clanking chains, Burns's fictional address deploys chains and the cowardly stain of slavery to rouse his fellow Scotsmen. The next stanza of this anthem brings us to Bannockburn, where, in June 1314, England faced Scotland on the battlefield. Burns imagines a fully recommitted Bruce, who challenges and questions his men:

> Now's the day and now's the hour
> See the front o' battle lour;
> See approach proud Edward's power
>   Chains and slavery!
> Wha will be a traitor knave?
> Wha can fill a coward's grave?
> Wha sae base as be a slave?
>   Let him turn and flee!

Burns's "proud Edward" serves as the detestable symbol of English despotism, an unambiguous enemy who would have definitely elicited boos and hisses from the patriotic New Yorkers attending Hewlett's performances. The approaching Edward, and his army, evokes an equally arrogant George III, with his economically repressive taxation without representation. Both unjust colonial rulers were synonymous with "chains and slavery."[46] Then the clarifying questions: Who were the traitors, cowards, or base slaves in their ranks? If any man fit these descriptors, this battle was not for him. This national ballad was about never submitting or surrendering; therefore, when Burns writes "Wha sae base as be a slave?" he is far from sympathizing with enslaved persons in late eighteenth-century Jamaica or nineteenth-century America. According to Burns biographer Robert Crawford, Burns believed strongly in "the man of the independent mind," so his imagined Bruce was scorning and deriding any man who allowed his independence to be taken away.[47]

However, when Hewlett, a free Negro from Long Island, sang the question "Wha sae base as be a slave?" to a largely black audience, he transformed Burns's rhetorical exercise. Enslaved Africans were frequent patrons at William Brown's entertainments and loyal fans of Afro-America's first theatrical star, James Hewlett.[48] New York's bondmen and bondwomen were already "base," or degraded, in the minds of many and seemingly accustomed to shackles, so for this public, Hewlett intoned Bruce's address to decry oppression right here at home, not miles across the Atlantic Ocean or centuries in the past. In a powerful convergence of insurgent histories, Hewlett's rendition of "Scots, wha hae wi' Wallace bled" fused Patrick Henry and Robert Burns to create a painfully real and immediate reflection on the current condition of enslaved Afro–New Yorkers.

Oppression was only half of Bruce's, Burns's, Henry's, and Hewlett's message. After questioning his men and exhorting all cowards, traitors, and slaves to bow out, Bruce emboldened his would-be revolutionaries with freedom talk:

> Wha for Scotland's king and law
> Freedom's sword will strongly draw,
> Free-man stand, or Free-man fa'
>   Let him follow me!
> By oppression's woes and pains!
> By your sons in servile chains!
> We will drain our dearest veins!
>   But they shall be free!

The liberation rhetoric in this verse, rooted in struggle and sacrifice, provided Hewlett with the imaginative language to redirect his subjugated community toward the future. The sense of generational sacrifice here is palpable, as Bruce's soldiers prepare to shed their blood so future Scots will only know freedom. By singing such obligation to future generations, to prevent "your sons in servile chains," Hewlett spoke directly for Afro–New Yorkers who anticipated complete emancipation in the coming years. Back in 1817, the New York state legislature passed a gradual emancipation bill, which decreed that after a period of measured manumission, slavery would be completely abolished throughout the state on July 4, 1827.[49] Burns's freedom talk intensified Afro–New Yorkers' expectation of and desire for full emancipation, not just for themselves but for their sons, daughters, and grandchildren.

With oppression and freedom now clearly defined for Scotsmen, Americans, and Afro–New Yorkers, Burns's final verse calls for decisive action and perhaps the ultimate sacrifice:

Lay the proud usurpers low!
Tyrants fall in every foe!
And Liberty's in every blow!
Let us do or die!

In this verse, Burns takes us back to Bannockburn, where roughly 6,000 Scottish soldiers risked their lives against a much larger English army of nearly 20,000. The Scots miraculously emerged victorious, and in 1328, King Edward III signed a treaty at Edinburgh that formally recognized Scotland as an independent kingdom. England also accepted Robert Bruce as a sovereign monarch and acknowledged Scots as free men and women. From a marauding Wallace who was sacrificed to a redeemed royal Bruce who led, the Scots chose freedom over repression and committed mind, body, and soul to national liberation.

Scotland's revolutionary tradition inspired Hewlett and his fellow Afro–New Yorkers to reassess their commitment to liberty and citizenship: How long could they wait for gradual emancipation? Yet Hewlett and Burns's notions of citizenship were very much gendered concepts. Writing about citizenship and masculinity in early nineteenth-century America, historian Mia Bay reveals that white males often excluded black males from the polity because whites believed Negroes did not posses "all the qualities of men." Such exclusion struck a chord with nineteenth-century African American intellectuals like David Walker. When he wrote his famous *Appeal to Colored Citizens of the World* (1829), Walker appealed directly to the manhood of his black brethren, urging them not to be "submissive to a gang of men, whom we cannot tell whether they are as good as ourselves."[50] Burns's version of Robert Bruce similarly questions the manhood of Scottish soldiers in 1314 and, by extension, Burns's countrymen in 1790s Scotland. Likewise, in 1821 Manhattan, Hewlett's present-centered, cross-cultural rendition of "Scots, wha hae wi' Wallace bled" challenged male Afro–New Yorkers to submit no longer to the whims of white men whose moral superiority was clearly in question.

After watching Hewlett channel "Bruce's Address," did a brigade of enslaved and free Afro–New Yorkers, male or female, march out of William Brown's theater and initiate a glorious rebellion against Euro-American oppression? As far as we know, Hewlett's passionate performance of this Scottish ballad failed to ignite a Bannockburn on the island of Manhattan, but we should return to historian George Lipsitz to understand the political potential and limitations of Hewlett's Scottish stage Europeans.

As I mentioned in Chapter 1, Lipsitz claims cultural production can be "a rehearsal for politics" but never "a substitute for politics."[51] Hewlett's transnational, transhistorical identifications with Wallace and Bruce served as a training session for Afro–New Yorkers yearning for freedom and citizenship. This musical homage and imaginative reenactment of revolution was designed to simulate and envision, not deliver, substantive political change. Scottish liberation rhetoric reminded African Americans that their emancipation was incomplete, and therefore, free and enslaved Negroes needed to remain vigilant and oppositional.

The imitative and emulative function of whiting up seeks to foster professional and political identifications between black artists, white cultural production, and white histories. Hewlett's strategic identification, in print and performance, with Kean, Booth, and Mathews greatly enhanced his theatrical development and professional opportunities. Furthermore, as a rehearsal for Afro–New York's imminent liberation, Hewlett's black-Scottish performances ignored "primitive" musical assumptions, married revolutionary histories, and metaphorically removed the chains, all to clarify the struggles ahead on a long road to full African American participation in American society.

Chapter 3 Low-Down Whiteness

A Trip to Coontown

In November 1897, comedian and dancer Harry Gillam made a major career decision: he parted ways with Richard and Pringle's Georgia Minstrels and turned his proverbial back on blackface minstrelsy. As a free agent, Gillam bounced between stage-managing colored road shows and developing an acrobatic dance routine with his younger sister Bessie Gillam, who marketed herself as the "only colored lady doing ballet." Their act consisted of "Little Bessie" dancing on point for nearly five minutes while big brother Harry spun on his head. During this break from blackface, Gillam also cultivated a solo specialty act in which he embodied Jewishness through costume, gestures, banter, song, and acrobatic dance. By 1898, Gillam was touring North American cities from Winnipeg, Manitoba, to St. Paul, Minnesota, billing himself as "A Negro by Race, A Hebrew by Profession" who offered the "exact imitation of the Israelite."[1] To promote and develop this new stage Israelite, Gillam joined a more innovative minstrel outfit, George and Hart's Up-to-Date Minstrels, a company that employed nearly thirty-five black performers, with some appearing in blackface and others completely free of greasepaint. Primarily touring in the Midwest and Pacific Northwest, with its new take on blackface minstrelsy, George and Hart's company was one of the most popular road shows in the United States. On several tours, Gillam was the featured artist, nightly appearing in his "original creation," a stage European known as "The Acrobatic Hebrew."[2]

Truly independent, self-defining Negro artists such as Harry Gillam were anomalies. They tended to work slightly outside American mainstream touring circuits and theatrical traditions, only to be eventually sucked back into the relative economic security and representational limitations of blackface minstrelsy. Briefly, the blackface minstrel monster was born in the late 1820s in major cities like New York, Philadelphia, and Boston, and it was initially shaped by working-class Irish American performers. This variety of cross-racial play first emerged as individual acts of counterfeit blackness at the circus or between the acts of conventional comedies and dramas staged at working-class theaters. In the 1840s, this rising national sensation evolved into evening-long entertainments that infiltrated elite upper-class houses, such as the Park Theatre, and minstrel troupes began touring throughout North America, Europe, and Africa as ambassadors of American cultural production. Blackface became this nation's first youth-culture mania, driven by the creative energies of talented Euro-American and, eventually, African American artists. This uniquely national form, Americans performing available "others," left little representational room for William Brown's and James Hewlett's stage Europeans. American audiences were moving on from the older cross-racial novelty of black actors performing Shakespeare to the latest sensation, white actors pretending to be plantation Negroes.

Over the first half of the nineteenth century, blackface minstrelsy essentially absorbed most of the stage Europeans, stage Africans, and stage Indians produced by early national performance. Historian David Roediger noted an "astonishing ethnic diversity"—Irish dances, Scottish melodies, Negro humor, and Yankee defiance—all submerged within the blackface mask. Yet he writes that "this extreme cultural pluralism was at the same time a liquidation of ethnic and regional cultures into blackface, and ultimately into a largely empty whiteness." By "empty whiteness" Roediger refers to the collapse of European national and ethnic particularities into a homogenized whiteness. Legal theorist Patricia J. Williams concurs that whiteness emerged as its "own form of nationalism" by conflating various white ethnic identities into a monolith. Even novelist Toni Morrison has argued that black literary figures and blackface minstrelsy helped invent "whiteness" and enabled whites to reflect on their humanity.[3]

This chapter is about exploring that "empty whiteness" and recovering the humanity; it is about examining the race, class, and gendered contours of late nineteenth-century cross-racial play from the perspective of black performers. It is about Bob Cole, Billy Johnson, and a collection of ambitious artists who decided to confront the minstrel monster not from the margins like Harry Gillam, but on Broadway, the epicenter of American entertainment. After performing in blackface minstrel companies, vaudeville houses, and colored road shows controlled by white producers, most Negro artists had a definite idea of what America's class- and race-coded theatrical industry had to offer them. In the 1890s, Cole and Johnson would introduce something legitimately new and different. Despite opposition from white producers, they launched a revolutionary theatrical venture, *A Trip to Coontown*, which would become the first Broadway musical written, produced, and performed solely by African American artists.

This upstart company's declaration of economic and artistic independence from blackface and its collateral damage was predicated on mastering "white" artistic forms like Bessie Gillam's classical ballet or Harry Gillam's "Acrobatic Hebrew." As musical theater pioneers, Cole and Johnson were determined to prove African American performers could excel in all forms of expression, not just cakewalks or blackface minstrel shows. In the process, *Coontown*'s stage Europeans would expand the possibilities for an increasingly versatile Negro talent pool and reposition blackness on Broadway and beyond. Through their appropriations of allegedly white forms, such as opera and ethnic impersonation, this simultaneously defiant and complicit company would subvert the notion of whiteness as the measure of culture and refinement.

The fictitious little hamlet at the heart of *A Trip to Coontown* is populated by accomplished, middle-class African Americans who support their very own opera company. Yet the undeniable star of this groundbreaking musical is Bob Cole's dispossessed whiteface, or mauve-face, hobo Willie Wayside. This highly conspicuous stage European slides up and down the racial hierarchy, signifies across economic and social identities, and constantly challenges the fixity of all these relative positions. On a nightly basis, Cole's whiting up specialty act disconnected "cooning," with its multiple lower-class connotations, from blackness and attached some of those attributes to lower-class and middle-class whiteness. Beyond a low-down Willie Wayside, I also examine the company's other class-marked operatic specialties, ethnically distinct impersonations, and gender-specific comedy routines. With their multiple acts of performed whiteness, this disidentifying *Coontown* Company produced conservative and potentially transgressive reconstructions rooted in race, ethnicity, class, and gender. Thus they bring us to an important question: Did these Negro artists ultimately reinscribe whiteness as an incredibly fluid measure of humanity? Before exploring many stage Europeans, we should first locate African American artists in turn-of-the-century racial politics and an evolving American entertainment industry.

Blackface Minstrelsy, Vaudeville, and Colored Road Shows

At the turn of the nineteenth century, African Americans actually experienced an erosion of political and economic progress. The interracial politics of Reconstruction, which saw Negro senators and representatives elected to Capitol Hill, was a thing of the past by the 1890s. Early efforts at interracial union organizing were all but dead when the founder of the American Federation of Labor, Samuel Gompers, declared that black workers did not need union protection because they had no understanding of human rights. The two railroad industry–induced panics of 1873 and 1893 weakened the economic prospects of all Americans, but especially Negro labor. The Panic of 1893 sunk the United States into four years of depression and produced armies of unemployed, dispossessed Americans. In such troubled economic times, job competition, real or imagined, was a major concern, a concern exacerbated by the spike in black migration into northern and southern cities. Along with black migrants, major cities also experienced a significant influx of Jewish, Irish, and Italian immigrants searching for economic, social, political, and artistic opportunities.[4]

Negro migration coupled with European immigration precipitated some disturbing developments in America's racial and ethnic politics. Increased ethnic immigration produced a nativist movement intent on restricting new arrivals through national legislation. The 1890s also saw the early stages of an American eugenics movement, which cataloged racial and national characteristics and even considered the possibilities of biological engineering. These adverse national responses to racial and ethnic diversity were further intensified by America's involvement in the Spanish-American War of 1898, a war which resulted in the acquisition of the Philippines and the expansion of a U.S. imperialist presence in the world. According to historian Matthew Jacobson, when America was confronted with new colored "barbarians" in the Pacific, "undigested" Native Americans in the plains, and an unresolved "Negro problem" migrating into urban centers, the nation's racial solution was "the manufacture and maintenance of 'Caucasian' whiteness."[5] In other words, the majority culture created the monolithic, nationalized whiteness described by David Roediger, Patricia J. Williams, and Toni Morrison. Additionally, in response to "colored threats" at home and abroad, the U.S. Supreme Court decision in *Plessy v. Ferguson* (1896) officially sanctioned "separate-but-equal" public accommodations for blacks and whites throughout the United States.[6]

In the incredibly turbulent and polarized 1890s, American entertainment, especially a newly emergent vaudeville, actually worked to ease immigrant paranoia by rediscovering and celebrating the nation's ethnic plenitude. Historians Rudi Blesh and Harriet Janis have characterized late nineteenth-century vaudeville as "a general spoofing of the Irish and the Dutch, of pig-tailed Chinese, of Negro and of Jew." Although much of this entertainment may have been crude, Blesh and Janis argue that it was "productive of a certain intentional camaraderie" and a "recognition of the natural differences that exist between peoples."[7] Vaudeville was guilty of capitalizing on stereotypic humor, but this was neither the first nor the last American entertainment to exploit difference. However, unlike blackface minstrelsy, vaudeville cultivated camaraderie between performers and patrons by communicating a healthy respect for the presumed differences "spoofed" onstage. In short, vaudeville marketed ethnic diversity as a national strength, not a weakness.

Other vaudeville historians tell a more complex story of the relationship between ethnic performance, European immigrants, and the American assimilation/acculturation process.[8] Initially, vaudeville houses celebrated ethnic variety, but as major circuits emerged in the early twentieth century, this industry shifted to downplaying ethnic difference. Albert McLean found that many immigrant groups were fully committed to assimilating into their new environs and resented any ethnic caricatures that marked them as separate or indigestible into the body politic. As numbers of European immigrants increased in major American cities, vaudeville's ethnic focus softened or disappeared entirely; in fact, this performance outlet did its part to foster an ethnically unmarked and culturally "melted" America. Historian Robert Snyder contends that white vaudeville houses became acculturating avenues for immigrants, as vaudeville pioneers such as Tony Pastor used this middle-class entertainment to unite a nation across gender, class, and ethnic divides.

Cultural theorist Richard Dyer provides an interesting perspective on ethnicity, whiteness, and representation. Dyer claims that "ethnic representation for instance is based not on inevitable categories pre-existing human consciousness but on the organization of perception." For him, "ethnicity is in the eye of the culture," and the illustrative example Dyer provides speaks to race just as much as ethnicity. He cites how a light-skinned black person might be treated or perceived as white when visiting an African country. Similarly, whiteness in turn-of-the-century America was often less about skin color and more about access, as evidenced by the fact that some Jewish Americans were gradually allowed to claim a manufactured, national whiteness.[9] Writing about blackface in the twentieth century, Michael Rogin explains how Jewish vaudeville entertainers like Al Jolson used commodified blackface to divest themselves of their ethnic distinctiveness and acculturate toward Caucasian. From behind a powerful minstrel mask, itinerant Jewish American performers became respected white entertainers, basically by contrasting a monolithic and inherently privileged whiteness against degraded coons, sambos, and mammies.[10]

As for demystifying and deconstructing this racial monolith, cultural critic Michael Eric Dyson endorses the splintering of whiteness into Irishness and Jewishness as a positive development. For Dyson, one clear benefit of various "ethnographies of white cultures, practices, and identities is that we begin to get a fuller picture of differentiated whiteness. The fissuring and fracturing of whiteness, especially along axes of class and gender, gives us a greater insight into how white cultures have adapted, survived, and struggled in conditions where their dominance was modified or muted."[11] *Coontown* staged several varieties of white ethnicity, some dominant, some dispossessed, but the most dynamic fracturing of whiteness happened along class lines, especially with Bob Cole's complex whiteface creation Willie Wayside.

During economically depressed and racially divided times, American Negro artists were looking to reposition themselves professionally and culturally; some did so with more success than others. Following the Civil War, when Negro talent was welcomed into the national explosion of commodified blackness, blackface minstrelsy became the most lucrative avenue for African American performers. As willing participants, they planned to advance their professional careers as rapidly as those of their white counterparts, but the cost for black blackface artists was a profound lack of representational freedom. Blackface minstrelsy was white performative property; most colored performers did not control minstrel iconography or the troupes they traveled with, let alone the theaters in which they entertained. They could not undo or reimagine the Zip Coon and Jim Crow minstrel prototypes spawned by white artists and audiences, so these and other caricatures dominated the minstrel stage from the late 1820s into the twentieth century. As for vaudeville, which was an alternative to the minstrel monster, Jayna Brown argues that Cole and Johnson launched *Coontown* as an explicit critique of vaudeville managers and booking agencies, "which excluded most black acts from its circuits and exploited the black performers it did use."[12] Spurred by vaudeville's exclusionary policies, Cole and company were on a mission to prove Negro artists could excel at ethnic impersonation and assimilate into mainstream American entertainment.

While white vaudeville failed to fully embrace black performers, independent white producers used Negro artists to generate yet another alternative to blackface minstrelsy, specifically colored road shows and revues. These touring productions became a major outlet for black artists interested in cultivating nonminstrel material and developing a comedic tradition that was racially grounded but not riddled with stereotyping.[13] In 1890, Sam T. Jack, a white theater owner and producer, created a burlesque revue titled *The Creole Show*, which capitalized on the current vogue for magnificently attired and physically attractive fair-skinned Negro women. Jack's "Creole beauties" exploited highly sensual, colonial, and orientalist fantasies and offered what Jayna Brown calls a "malleable interchange between different racial delineations—mulatto, South Asian, North African, Filipina, Hawaiian."[14] Jack's racially ambiguous chorus girls operated on two levels. First, on a historical level, they recalled a slave past where mixed-race women were bought and sold as eroticized commodities. Second, on a performative level, the visual fluidity of these colored female bodies, morphing from one geographic location to the next, exposed colonial fantasies as nothing more than constructions.

Beyond the visuals and the fantasies, Jack's innovative company showcased the multiple talents of his sixteen beauties by featuring them as comedians, singers, and dancers performing specialty acts in a minstrel-style semicircle. Jack even cast his interlocutor, a mediating role usually performed by a white male, with a black woman named Florence Hines, who was well known for male impersonation. Finally, Jack's road show shifted the focus of colored entertainments from the plantation past to the urban present.[15] At a time when minstrelsy was predominantly male and focused on allegedly southern Negro culture, Jack urbanized his musical entertainments and introduced novel ways to use colored female talent.

Hoping to launch the next big trend, Sam T. Jack and other white producers trafficked in modern, transnational colored exotica, and whether they knew it or not, they also fed a growing desire among young African American artists for representational control and political progress.

Historian Karen Sotiropoulos characterizes turn-of-the-century black musical performers as ambitious men and women who grew up in "relative privilege" and migrated from smaller cities and towns in the West and South to the mecca of theatrical possibility, New York City.[16] Confronted with the limitations of commercial theater, especially blackface and vaudeville, promising talents like Bert Williams, George Walker, Aida Overton Walker, and Bob Cole integrated cultural and political agendas into their work. They poured themselves into racist minstrel remnants to reveal that "Two Real Coons" were merely roles and not true representatives of black communities. In the process, modern black entertainers advanced their careers while building a cadre of artistic "race" men and women well positioned to advocate for Afro-America.

Within the ranks of Afro-America's politically attuned and professionally shrewd artists, two musical pioneers, Will Marion Cook and Bob Cole, held divergent views on how best to use the stage to advance the race. Cook advised black artists to avoid "white patterns" and look to their roots to create musicals that would celebrate Negro culture and articulate the souls of black folks. One black cultural form on which Cook and Cole fiercely disagreed was the cakewalk. Cook embraced this plantation-derived form, while Cole opposed this popular dance because he felt it had been degraded by white appropriation. The cakewalk offers a powerful example of how a whiteface minstrel act can change over time. This dance emerged from a mixture of subjugation, paternalistic pride, and slave autonomy, yet it later devolved into a physically exaggerated dance parody featured at the close of blackface minstrel shows and colored road shows. Jazz pianist Terry Waldo believed the cakewalk changed forever when white blackface artists started using and abusing the form. In the 1890s, black performers like Cook attempted to reclaim the minstrel-tinged version, and thus, according to Waldo, the cakewalk gradually became a dance about "blacks imitating whites who were imitating blacks who were imitating whites."[17]

Bob Cole wanted nothing to do with this cakewalking hall of mirrors and advocated that black artists advance the race by competing with their Euro-American counterparts in all areas of artistic production. Cole's obituary from the *New York Age* claimed his "dominant thought was to elevate the race to which he belonged. He was ambitious to exhibit on the stage the real life of the progressive, cultured Negro of today with minute accuracy."[18] Cook and Cole may have disagreed on methods, but they were both committed to one particular goal: the greater visibility of cultured Negroes and their artistry. With respect to visibility, I agree with Jayna

Brown that the incredible range of ethnic diversity featured in *A Trip to Coontown* was a performative answer to white vaudeville's virtual exclusion of black artists from this minstrel alternative. Cole's artistic agenda was largely about asserting professional competency with a hint of political commentary. Similar to the motivated signifying of Charleston's black promenaders and the theatrical mutability of Sam T. Jack's "Creole beauties," Cole and Johnson's *Coontown* Company worked hard to give refinement and comedic versatility new faces and fresh bodies.

The Long Road to *Coontown*

A Trip to Coontown's production history reads like an epic tale of legal, racial, and representational struggle as a collective of intrepid black artists bypassed white producers to mount the first musical produced, written, directed, and performed by African Americans on Broadway. The groundwork for this artistic revolution was laid in the spring of 1892 when New York's Madison Square Garden hosted a series of performances titled "Jubilee Spectacle and Cake-Walk." This incredible event featured competitive cakewalking and an operatic showdown to crown the "greatest black prima donna." The primary contenders for the "prima donna" title were Matilda Sissieretta Jones, Marie Selika, and Flora Batson Bergen, and after several days of stiff competition, Jones was declared the undisputed black "Queen of Song." Following Jones's musical triumph, the New York press allegedly dubbed her "Black Patti," a reference to the Spanish-born, Bronx-raised opera star Adelina Patti.[19] After white theatrical producers Rudolph Voelckel and John J. Nolan heard Matilda Jones's impressive voice at the Madison Square Garden competition, they decided to exploit those comparisons to the popular white star Adelina Patti. They created a cutting-edge colored road show, the Black Patti Troubadours, which opened with comedic material, mixed in some gorgeous chorus girls, and closed with Black Patti featured in a finale of arias from noted operas like *Faust* and *Carmen*. At a time when most productions closed with an elaborate cakewalk, Matilda Jones and her operatic entourage proved nightly that audiences could accept black singers in a high-class, "white" form.

Both Bob Cole and Billy Johnson were musically inclined sons of the South, Cole from Athens, Georgia, and Johnson from Charleston, South Carolina. As for education, Cole pursued a degree at Atlanta University and Johnson nearly earned his diploma from Augusta High School in Charleston, but these two restless artists elected to abandon their studies and search out musical vocations.[20] Following the typical career path for black entertainers, Cole and Johnson developed their performative and writing skills touring with blackface minstrel outfits such as Charles B. Hicks's Hicks-Sawyer Minstrels or the Colored Georgia Minstrels. They later transitioned to Sam T. Jack's innovative Creole Burlesque Company, and by 1896, Bob Cole was the featured comedian and writer for Voelckel and Nolan's Black Patti Troubadours and Billy Johnson was his comedic partner.

Cole's primary responsibility was to script the Troubadours' opening one-act farce "At Gay Coon-ey Island," which was a playfully "blackened" appropriation of an 1896 white musical, *At Gay Coney Island*. Within this white-owned touring company, Cole blossomed as a performer and producer and first realized his vision of appropriating "white forms" to showcase black brilliance. In the opening comedic sketch, Cole started experimenting with an eccentric clown act that would eventually develop into Willie Wayside. Cole's initial Willie Wayside character was a red-bearded tramp with no face paint to speak of, white or black, the kind of eccentric comic specialty act typically reserved for white comedians.[21] Over time, Willie Wayside would evolve into the "whitened" figure featured on the cover of this book, a mauve-face mask of broadly comical, yet endearing humanity.

After touring with Black Patti and her company, Cole was convinced a mix of highbrow operas and eccentric comedy could successfully showcase the cultural advancement of the race. But during the 1890s, the cultural politics of racial uplift involved a complex alchemy of constructing and publicizing productive black identities in a deeply divided, white supremacist country. Sociologist E. Franklin Frazier characterizes black middle-class racial uplift at the turn of the nineteenth century as constantly knocking on the door of the dominant culture without ever gaining full entrée. Educated and striving Negroes wanted recognition and acceptance from the majority culture, so they adopted white cultural and moral values. Regrettably, their absolute commitment to assimilation only instilled a deeper sense of inferiority in the black middle and upper classes. The more whites personally rejected or legally segregated blacks, the more educated, progressive Negroes clung to their intimate knowledge of Shakespeare and opera as indications of refinement and class.[22] Historian Kevin Gaines offers a less caustic reading of racial uplift; he claims "race" men and women were committed to transforming the wounded attachment of race into a "source of dignity and self-affirmation," with the hope that some whites would one day acknowledge the "humanity of middle-class African Americans."[23] This deeply embedded desire to prove the race's worth to white audiences, critics, and theater managers would at times complicate and compromise the meanings of *A Trip to Coontown*—but more on the potential pitfalls of racial uplift later.

Cole did not last long with the Black Patti Troubadours because he was frustrated by his low salary, poor working conditions, and a copyright dispute with the white owners of the company. While Cole was performing with the Troubadours at Proctor's Pleasure Palace on Broadway, Voelckel and Nolan had him arrested and charged with larceny. They alleged Cole stole music and other material from "At Gay Coon-ey Island," but Cole counterclaimed that the material he created for the production was his intellectual property. In June 1897, a grand jury refused to charge Cole with anything, and more importantly, a court upheld Cole's authorship claim, a legal victory that allowed Cole to continue developing Willie Wayside.[24] After the legal ruling, Voelckel and Nolan labeled Cole a troublemaker and effectively blackballed him from all other colored road shows.

Blackballed but legally vindicated, Cole announced his own production company with an official-sounding "Colored Actor's Declaration of Independence." In this statement, a defiant Cole proclaimed, "We are going to have our own shows. We are going to write them ourselves, we are going to have our own stage manager, our own orchestra leader and our own manager out front to count up. No divided houses—our race must be seated from the boxes back."[25] In time, Cole would deliver the shows produced, written, and performed by African Americans, but the integrated houses would be much tougher to achieve. Inspired by Charles Hoyt's successful, exotic, and Asian-inflicted musical revue *A Trip to Chinatown* (1891), Cole imagined *A Trip to Coontown* as a series of vaudeville specialty acts, completely free of blackface and arranged around a simple plot. Cole recruited a cadre of eighteen Negro artists, including Billy Johnson, Lloyd Gibbs, and Tom Brown, all plucked from the Black Patti Troubadours. The first theater manager to show interest was Frederick Francis Proctor, who opened his Twenty-third Street variety/vaudeville house to Cole and Johnson in early July 1897. The *Freeman*, a Negro theatrical magazine out of Indianapolis, reported this premiere performance as a big hit but neglected to say whether it was a full production or a pared-down revue.[26]

Voelckel and Nolan were not thrilled to lose talent to a renegade Negro production, so when Cole and Johnson planned to debut *Coontown* on Broadway in the fall of 1897, the vindictive white managers successfully barred their musical from all of the major houses in New York City. But in September 1897, the *New York Clipper*, New York's premiere theatrical journal, announced the *Coontown* Company would appear as a variety act at Proctor's Theatre, with Cole, Johnson, Tom Brown, Camille Casselle, and other artists performing songs and scenes from the new farce *A Trip to Coontown*.[27] In a March 1898 open letter to the *Clipper*, Cole and Johnson explained how "untiring efforts were made by some traveling managers to stop the bookings of this attraction. But the merits of the organization has [*sic*] made it much sought after by managers all over the country."[28]

Apparently, the September 1897 variety run at Proctor's Theatre did generate significant out-of-town interest. Momentarily barred from New York, *Coontown* embarked on a maturation tour. The first stop was Philadelphia, where the new musical played six nights; it then moved on to Patterson, New Jersey, and Boston, Massachusetts. Eventually the company ventured across the border to Canada, starting with Montreal in January 1898, then Ottawa and London, Ontario. By early March 1898, the *Coontown* touring company was migrating back south into upstate New York and inching ever closer to Broadway. Based on reviews and audience reactions, J. Harry Jackson, cultural and theatrical critic for the *Freeman*, proclaimed *Coontown* was "unanimously indorsed [*sic*] by the press and public as being the most artistic combination of colored talent ever organized."[29] Thanks to Voelckel and Nolan, the extended tryouts in Canada and the northeastern United States only made the production stronger, more visible, and more marketable. By circumventing white managerial control, avoiding most blackface remnants, and eschewing the cakewalk, Cole and company were poised to introduce a most innovative black musical into American popular entertainment.

On April 4, 1898, *A Trip to Coontown* finally and fully arrived on Broadway, playing at the Third Avenue Theatre to packed and enthusiastic houses for six nights. After this brief run, Cole and Johnson returned to the road, booking a summer tour through Canada. The company returned to Manhattan in September for a second Broadway engagement, but this time *Coontown* played to full houses at Broadway's higher-end Grand Opera House. This was a major achievement because for the first time a colored road show graced the stage of one of the most prestigious Broadway houses.[30] James Weldon Johnson, musical theater lyricist and future field secretary for the National Association for the Advancement of Colored People (NAACP), declared *Coontown* "the first to make a complete break from the minstrel pattern . . . the first to be written with continuity and to have a cast of characters working out the story of a plot from beginning to end." Henry T. Sampson, in his work on early Negro entertainment, wrote that the "success of Bob Cole's show *A Trip to Coontown* in 1898 was the spark that fully ignited the development of black theatricals."[31]

An extant copy of the musical has never been discovered, but we do know *A Trip to Coontown*'s story unfolds in the comfortable, middle-class community of Coontown, where the whiteface hobo Willie Wayside rescues Silas Green, a black retiree with a $5,000 pension, from the stratagems of a cunning black con man named Jim Flimflammer, portrayed by Billy Johnson. A *New York Sun* critic claimed this plot was originally concocted by poet and lyricist Paul Laurence Dunbar, but Cole and Johnson beat him to the productive punch. The *Sun* reviewer also declared the fully realized musical at the Third Avenue Theatre "one of the most artistic farce comedy shows that New York has seen in a long time."[32]

Before a single lyric was sung, the spectacle of a tattered white hobo contrasted against Coontown's affluence contradicted long-held racial and class presumptions.[33] When the post-Broadway *Coontown* tour reached Indiana in October 1900, a reviewer from the *Freeman* raved about how the production "beautifully staged" the parlor of Silas Green, "the grand old man of Coontown."[34] By all accounts, this imagined Coontown was a segregated yet prosperous community blessed with lovely homes, stable families, lively social engagements, and substantial retirement funds. The musical's most visible class conflict centered on Willie, a dispossessed white drifter, versus Jim Flimflammer, a cultured black adversary in finely tailored clothing. A *Freeman* review highlighted this striking pair: "Mr. Johnson as Jim Flimflammer, the bunco, is also a rare professional, and handles the 'straight' of the play in masterly style. While he is strictly business in his role, he combines business with pleasures, making the whole affair funnier and perplexing for his partner, the tramp, who produces the fun in the plot."[35] Typically, blackface minstrel shows featured a dapper white interlocutor who interacted humorously with Tambo and Bones, a pair of tattered, comical black end-men. Cole and Johnson reversed that convention by crafting an outwardly respectable black con artist who plays the serious or "straight" role and instigates the major scheme driving the plot, while the broad comedy or "the fun" was supplied by Cole's low-down stage European clown.

The *Freeman* magazine visually re-created Cole and Johnson's inversion by publishing publicity illustrations of the bedraggled Wayside and the dapper Flimflammer (figs. 6 and 7). Cole's Willie Wayside costume consists of a ragged overcoat, flimsy scarf, and scruffy beard, creating a down-on-his-luck yet laughable figure. In contrast, Billy Johnson's Flimflammer, in a dashing top hat, tailored suit, and stylish cravat, projects a most refined image. David Krasner has argued that black musical pioneers like Cole and Johnson, as well as Williams and Walker, retired the "darky" figures inherited from blackface by staging this more dignified imagery of an emergent "New Negro."[36] Johnson's stylish Flimflammer was new and modern yet also reminiscent of Charleston's Meeting Street promenaders and their audacious command of public space. In an upscale Coontown, Cole and Johnson's cultured turn-of-the-century Negroes were defined not just by their clothing but also by their command of European art forms, especially opera.

"White" Forms: From Opera to Ethnic Impersonation

Italian opera first arrived in the United States in 1825 when Manual Garcia and his family took up residence at New York's prestigious Park Theatre. In their U.S. debut, the operatic family experienced modest success with works like Gioachino Rossini's *Otello*, but initially American audiences were unsure how to behave or dress for this new and strange entertainment. According to opera historian John Dizikes, there was great disagreement over whether this aristocratic European form would ever gain a foothold in the United States.[37] Some believed America lacked the necessary landed aristocracy and was far too democratic to support opera, while others believed the mercantile climate of urban America would generate a "fashion" around this novel diversion. One clear indication that European high culture could survive, even flourish, in the United States surfaced in the early 1880s when the Metropolitan Opera House opened its doors in Manhattan. This magnificent edifice was funded by an unapologetically wealthy merchant class. The box holders controlling this brand-new opera house demanded that fine jewelry be conspicuously displayed by patrons in the boxes, European stars be featured onstage, and arias be sung in French, Italian, or German.

In the late nineteenth century, the Met hosted world-famous divas such as French soprano Emma Calvé and Australian soprano Dame Nellie Melba, but the main attraction was Polish tenor and matinee idol Jean

Figure 6 Publicity image of Bob Cole as Willie Wayside, from *A Trip to Coontown*. Published in the *Indianapolis Freeman*, October 20, 1900.

Figure 7 Publicity image of Billy Johnson as Jim Flimflammer, from *A Trip to Coontown*. Published in the *Indianapolis Freeman*, October 20, 1900.

de Reszke. Over several Met seasons in the 1890s, de Reszke was the lead tenor and dominant presence in the opera company, with starring roles in *Faust* and *Romeo and Juliet*. One *Coontown* star spirited away from Voelckel and Nolan's Troubadours was Lloyd G. Gibbs, an African American tenor who billed himself as "The Black de Reszke." Much like James Hewlett, Negro operatic talents such as Matilda Jones and Lloyd Gibbs marketed themselves through associations with European stars. But more than merely advertising Gibbs as emulating de Reszke, *Coontown* publicity materials proclaimed Gibbs "The Greatest Living Black Tenor."[38]

Although Gibbs received top billing in *Coontown* productions, most of the company's featured opera singers were female. Historian Daphne Brooks has uncovered a long line of Negro sopranos, from Elizabeth Taylor Greenfield to Matilda Jones, who strategically infiltrated the world of classical music. Brooks claims black women embraced "highbrow" cultural expression to achieve a level of "representational propriety denied their foremothers in slavery." For black sopranos, opera offered access to a level of class and social privilege denied most Negro women, access these singers used to "rewrite black female iconography in the cultural imaginary."[39] Such was the case with Edna Alexander, a Chicago "society belle" and leading Negro soprano noted for her "remarkable voice and culture." As early as 1896, Alexander was appearing in romantic operas with the Afro-American Opera Company. In 1898 she joined the *Coontown* venture, where she was prominently featured in touring advertisements alongside Cole and Johnson.[40] Her marketing illustration (fig. 8) presents an extremely light, nearly white image of Alexander. By promoting Alexander as a mulatto-looking female, Cole and Johnson adopted the Sam T. Jack "Creole beauty" strategy. However, the significant difference was that the Negro producers featured a visually malleable mixed-race body with legitimate soprano ability.

According to playbills for the Canadian tours, this imaginary Coontown was a thriving Negro community supporting not only individual opera singers like Gibbs and Alexander but its very own Coontown Opera Company. In fact, the entire second act of the musical takes place in Silas Green's elegant parlor, where the sounds of live opera predominate. On one program, the high culture specialties commenced with another soprano diva, Camille Casselle, performing an original aria titled the "Creole Calve."[41] Similar to Gibbs's emulative relationship with de Reszke, Casselle exploited a connection with French soprano Emma Calvé. During the 1896–97 opera season, the real Calvé sang several roles at the Met

Figure 8 Publicity image of Edna Alexander, featured soprano, from *A Trip to Coontown*. Published in the *Indianapolis Freeman*, October 20, 1900.

and, with her title performance in Bizet's *Carmen*, nearly wrested company dominance away from Jean de Reszke.[42] Following Caselle's "Creole Calve," Gibbs filled Green's home with a collection of his favorite arias, including a selection from Verdi's *Attila*, an opera about the legendary king of the marauding, nomadic Huns. Cole learned from touring with Matilda Jones that he could legitimately send audiences home with Verdi and Puccini ringing in their ears rather than cakewalks pulsating through their limbs. So each night at the end of *Coontown*, the entire Coontown Opera Company closed with a chorus of "popular operatic successes."

Perhaps due to the popularity of the Black Patti Troubadours, a reviewer for the *New York Sun* expected these "inevitable operatic selections" to conclude the evening. But he was disappointed that the Coontown Opera Company did not deliver a supremely talented "dusky De Reszke or ebonied Melba," a reference to Dame Nellie Melba, who had recently thrilled audiences at the Met. According to the *Sun* review, Caselle's, Alexander's, and Gibbs's operatic efforts were underwhelming and "not altogether happy."[43] Despite this poor critical reception, members of the Coontown Opera Company exhibited the second function of whiting up by emulating European luminaries to celebrate a white aesthetic tradition and advance their careers. We should also think about these aspiring Negro opera stars in terms of the imitative rhythms generated between white model/form and black artist. Gibbs and Caselle may have been limited by marketing personae like "The Black de Reszke" or the "Creole Calve," but commodified signs of difference were ultimately beyond an artist's control and part of the price of doing business. Yet Gibbs, Caselle, and Alexander were not content with simply associating themselves with the best and brightest of European high art. By venturing into an artistic arena once considered untenable for Negro performers, they expanded professional options for themselves and future generations of black musical talent.

Operatic specialties helped establish *Coontown*, the musical and the fictional community, as a collection of cultured and perhaps even privileged African Americans, but Cole's plan to master white forms extended well beyond elite representations. The diverse stage Europeans featured in this groundbreaking musical allowed the ensemble to inhabit multiple white ethnic, class, and gender identities. Tom Brown was a versatile character actor in the *Coontown* Company who appeared as detective Billy Binkerton, a role that required transformations into "an Italian, a Hebrew, a Chinaman, and a Rube." His ethnic shape-shifting harkened back to the

French, English, Irish, and Scottish stage Europeans executed by James Hewlett in the 1820s, but unlike Hewlett, who borrowed material from white artists such as Charles Mathews, Brown's ethnic impersonations were written specifically for him. In reviews of the Broadway premiere, Brown was singled out for his ability to juggle many disguises. The *New York Clipper* mentioned how his "dago"—more precisely Italian—song earned him several encores from a supportive public.[44] A *New York Sun* review also lauded Brown for his Italian act, claiming that "there are many white comedians who could set at the feet of these Negro actors and learn a thing or two."[45] Cole's mission was clearly realized as he, Brown, and other company members joined white artists as creators, practitioners, and now models of cross-racial performance.

Brown's Italian and Hebrew transformations were contemporaneous with many other white immigrant representations appearing not just in vaudeville houses but in Yiddish, Italian-language, and other ethnic enclave theaters. As mentioned earlier in this chapter, Harry Gillam developed his solo "Acrobatic Hebrew," which involved joking, singing, and spinning on his head as a Jewish character. Figures 9 and 10 show publicity photos for Gillam's "Acrobatic Hebrew." These before-and-after images, which originally appeared in the 1899 Christmas edition of the *Freeman*, are designed to underscore the extreme transformation Gillam underwent to embody his version of Jewishness. The heavily costumed Gillam creates a bearded, bedraggled, seemingly dispossessed Hebrew, similar in appearance to Bob Cole's Willie Wayside. Gillam's humpbacked and noticeably pigeon-toed Jewish creation does not appear the least bit capable of spinning on his head, but perhaps Gillam used these curious physical attributes to surprise his public. Initially upon seeing this Jewish caricature, an audience might expect certain Yiddish songs and jokes, which Gillam reportedly delivered, but he could then shatter expectations by launching into a hyperkinetic, head-spinning dance routine.

Admittedly, Gillam's slightly deformed Hebrew may offend twenty-first-century sensibilities, but he and Brown were not the only black artists indulging in such exaggerated Jewish impersonations. In his history of Negro humor, William Schechter recalls the vaudeville team of George Cooper and Bill "Bojangles" Robinson, who created a comic routine featuring "burlesqued" and highly stereotypic Jewish characters.[46] As vaudeville historians Blesh and Janis have suggested, when ethnic imagery reemerged after decades of blackface minstrelsy, racial and ethnic caricature did not disappear immediately. Brown and Gillam's Italian and Jewish

Figure 9 Harry Gillam publicity image for his performance as the "Acrobatic Hebrew." Published in the *Indianapolis Freeman*, December 30, 1899.

Figure 10 Harry Gillam as the "Acrobatic Hebrew." Published in the *Indianapolis Freeman*, December 30, 1899.

impersonations represented the kind of unassimilated otherness some immigrant groups and vaudeville managers wanted to downplay. But out of an incredible sense of camaraderie and shared license, white and black musical and comedic artists staged ethnically and racially insensitive "coons," "chinks," "dagos," "shylocks," and "patties." Following the blueprint of successful productions like *A Trip to Chinatown* and *The Creole Show*, Cole and company catered to an increased interest in and perhaps paranoia with orientalism and otherness. One would like to think that a modern and politically savvy theatrical artist like Bob Cole would not approach cross-racial play and this popular fascination with exotica uncritically. In fact, Cole wrote a play titled *Tolosa*, which was set in the Philippines and critiqued America's involvement in the Spanish-American War.[47] That said, Tom Brown's cross-cultural Hebrew, Italian, and "Chinaman" delineations were all part of a spectacular exploration of faraway locations and curious populations, with America's expanded imperialist presence serving as an important backdrop or context. Closer to home, the *Coontown* Company also discovered a uniquely thrilling and equally exotic working-class whiteness on the streets of New York.

Gender, Class, and Racial Uplift

Beginning in January 1900 with performances in London, Ontario, the *Coontown* Company added two new performers: comedian Barrington Carter, who replaced Tom Brown, and comedienne Jennie Hillman. Carter and Hillman were featured in the North American tour as the "Bowery Spielers."[48] In Irving Lewis Allen's dictionary of urban slang, "spielers" were working-class young ladies who performed a whirling, high-flying couples dance typically in dance halls. Also, "spiel" comes from the German word *spielen*, meaning "to play."[49] As for the "Bowery" descriptor, this refers to the vibrant youth culture of Bowery B'hoys and Gals that emerged on Manhattan's Lower East Side in the early 1800s. The Bowery B'hoy was a street tough who by day toiled as an apprentice carpenter or butcher's assistant and by night roamed the Lower East Side looking for a good time and the occasional fight. He was a working-class, popular culture hero, the antithesis of the high-class gentlemen of Old New York, but the Bowery B'hoy was also a protective figure who showed "rubes" from upstate New York how to adjust to city life.[50] The Bowery Gal was a white female domestic who worked in the elegant homes of wealthy New Yorkers. Although Bowery B'hoys were fiercely protective of "their" women, the typical Bowery Gal did not need protecting. According to historian Christine Stansell, these young women "contributed to a cultural imagery betokening a prideful working-class female independence distinct from the imagery of female virtue produced by bourgeois culture."[51] Unlike her middle-class counterparts, the Bowery Gal was less concerned with gendered expectations and much more interested in establishing her place in the Bowery and perhaps beyond. This independent Bowery Gal and her Bowery B'hoy took their leisure spieling in dance halls or "walking out" along Broadway. Their Saturday evening or Sunday afternoon promenades were part of an elaborate courting ritual that allowed these young working-class New Yorkers to escape the direct surveillance of families, neighbors, and employers.[52]

While writing for the Black Patti Troubadours in the 1890s, Bob Cole not only developed his Willie Wayside character, but he also teamed up with his wife Stella Wiley to create a stage European character named Lize Leary. Wiley's Lize was a "brassy Irish working-girl" specialty lifted straight out of Bowery youth culture, and she even had her own geographically specific signature song, "The Belle of Avenue A." But well before Cole and Wiley's creation, in 1848, the Bowery B'hoy and Gal first appeared onstage in a play titled *A Glance at New York*, written by Francis S. Chanfrau and Benjamin A. Baker. Chanfrau also starred in this comedy, which was about a Bowery hero named Mose who was a butcher by trade and "fireboy" or street tough by inclination. Mose was joined in his dramatic exploits by his loyal lady Lize, a shopgirl with a penchant for street slang and a secret passion for blackface minstrel melodies. Mose and Lize's adventures began with *A Glance in New York* and continued over seven more Mose and Lize plays. These lowbrow comedies played to huge crowds in Manhattan and on the road, and by the close of the nineteenth century, Mose and Lize were inspiring specialty acts like the stage European Lize Leary.[53]

Stella Wiley earned respect and notoriety for her faithful rendition of this working-class Irish "tough girl," an homage to migrant and immigrant women toiling in factories and domestic situations. Physically, Wiley was a light-skinned black performer, mutable enough to "pass" as an Irish American female. And she did so, ironically enough, at a time when the Irish were transitioning from despised immigrant outsiders to acculturated, white Americans.[54] Also, instead of staging and promoting refined black middle-class womanhood, the preferred image for racial uplift, Wiley and Cole projected to interracial audiences, across classes, what Christine Stansell calls a "prideful working-class female." Around the time Cole parted ways with the Troubadours, his marriage to Wiley also dissolved, but Cole eventually found a new comedienne to embody this tough, streetwise stage European. Singer, actress, and dancer Jennie Hillman joined the *Coontown* cast as Dudina, one of the residents of a respectable Coontown boardinghouse owned and operated by a black woman named Widow Brown. As previously mentioned, Hillman's new theatrical partner, Barrington Carter, replaced Tom Brown in the role of Billy Binkerton, a detective and master of disguise.

To execute their eccentric comic specialty, the Bowery Spielers, both Carter and Hillman, momentarily stepped away from their narrative roles and perhaps their social responsibilities to uplift the race. One reviewer witnessed *A Trip to Coontown* at the Grand Opera House in Boston and offered this assessment: "The Africans do not often bring forward the women in the fun-making. But this troupe had Carter and Hillman, the lady in which firm mimicked the typical Bowery girl with gum and a jersey. Her partner sang an irresistible new 'tough' ditty with rhymes so strong that he could jerk out every syllable hard and fierce. During this the ferocious pair pursued strong men and police, who fled at their threatened approach."[55] This reviewer's observation on the paucity of black comediennes was somewhat accurate, although as mentioned earlier, Sam T. Jack's *Creole Show* did attempt to showcase black female comics.[56]

Offering far more than "fun-making," Carter's muscular rhymes and Hillman's ferocious female presence were aggressive and intimidating. Consistent with Cole's agenda to master and transform "white" theatrical forms, Hillman did more than mimic the original Bowery Gal; she introduced a significant modification.[57] In the Mose and Lize plays, when it was time to brawl or menace, a somewhat passive Lize was content to hold Mose's coat.[58] By contrast, Hillman's gal joined Carter's b'hoy as an equally intimidating partner in municipal mayhem. Carter and Hillman faithfully re-created the rough speech and probably reproduced the liberated spieling, with Carter twirling Hillman high into the air. But when the chips were down, Hillman's Bowery lass was far from docile. Vocally and visually, the fearless, antiauthoritarian defiance of these stage Europeans recall the arrogant whiteface minstrel promenaders who once dominated Charleston's Meeting Street.

Blackface minstrel revisionists have highlighted the class politics in the production and reception of blackface performance, and Carter's and Hillman's tough white kids offer a significant contribution to this conversation on class and cross-racial play. When Hillman shifted from respectable Negro boarder Dudina to raging Bowery Spieler, she sacrificed the Victorian ideal of feminine virtue propagated by middle-class white America and the black bourgeoisie. Much like Stella Wiley explored white working-class female imagery instead of black middle-class respectability, Hillman used the Bowery subculture to momentarily rebel against classed and gendered notions of decorum and propriety. According to blackface minstrel revisionists, the black mask freed white artists to speak the unspeakable, perform the unexpected, and articulate working-class desires.[59] The Bowery Spielers offered Hillman and Carter a similar kind of license to spew combative rhymes and dance morally loose spiels, both atypical behaviors for the morally upright African Americans populating an imagined Coontown and real black communities.

Ultimately, the freeing mask of unruly whiteness was less about rebelling against middle-class values and more about showcasing the comedic talents and professional possibilities of this dynamic duo. Racial uplift was undoubtedly part of *A Trip to Coontown*'s long-range plan, but with this particular stage European, Hillman chose to advance her career rather than her race. The aspiring comedienne focused on impressing white and black patrons unaccustomed to seeing black women excel in comedy. Hillman imitated and expanded on the Bowery Gal to prove no specialty act was beyond African American performers, male or female. On an ironic level, Carter and Hillman's low-down stage Europeans were based on a Bowery youth culture shaped by blackface minstrel shows popular in working-class venues like the Bowery Theatre. Essentially, these two modern Negro artists were embodying white working-class kids who were embodying blackface artists who were allegedly embodying Negro folk culture. The seemingly endless racial and class crisscrossing grows even more complicated when Cole's Willie Wayside joins the performative conversation.

Willie: Whiteface "Coon," Middle-Class Farmer, Hobo-Hero, Jim Crow Enforcer

If the visual imagery of a dispossessed Willie Wayside and a dapper Jim Flimflammer was not divergent enough, their signature songs further highlighted their class and racial differences. In a line from his song "I Hope These Few Lines Find You Well," Flimflammer boasts how "a damn swell coon" can bilk money from any unsuspecting mark.[60] By invoking the phrase "swell coon," Cole and Johnson placed the boastful Flimflammer in a representational tradition that dates back to the eighteenth century.

The earliest stage "coon" appears in Andrew Barton's comedy *The Disappointment; or, the Force of Credulity* (1767), which features a hapless but wealthy free black character named Raccoon, or "Coony," who functions as the unsuspecting mark of a confidence scheme. In 1835, white composer and minstrel performer George Washington Dixon perfected a blackface specialty act titled "Zip Coon" about an overly adorned, socially ambitious black dandy prone to malapropism. Around the time Cole and Johnson were developing *A Trip to Coontown*, Euro-American caricaturist Edward Windsor Kemble produced an entire book of vicious "coon" cartoons, with Negro dialect captions, titled *Coontown's 400* (1899). Finally, in the 1890s, black composer and performer Ernest Hogan elevated "coon" caricatures to international prominence with his hit song "All Coons Look Alike to Me." Throughout the nineteenth and early twentieth centuries, Hogan's "coon" songs could be heard throughout England, France, and the United States.[61] Hogan also factored into *Coontown*'s production history because he was installed as Cole's replacement in the Black Patti Troubadours. Voelckel and Nolan ignored the court ruling in Cole's favor and continued to open with "At Gay Coon-ey Island," with songs and sketches now devised by Hogan. The *Freeman* reprinted a review from an unnamed Chicago daily that declared if anyone was interested in authentic "coon" comedy, they needed to see Hogan with the Black Patti Troubadours.[62]

Theater historian David Krasner, in his excellent analysis of *Coontown*, concedes that artists like Hogan, Cole, and Johnson "reflected racial humor of the time by portraying the stereotyped 'darky' character." Yet even as they capitulated to minstrel humor, Krasner argues, Cole and company self-reflexively produced a contradictory, "hybrid aesthetic" that married accommodation with resistance.[63] This contrarian aesthetic makes sense given Cole's biography. In his history of African American comedy, Mel Watkins characterizes Cole as a somewhat college-educated young musician from an affluent, well-connected Atlanta family. As an educated, well-read composer working in low comedy, Cole was never fully constrained by "standard coon humor," with its ludicrously exaggerated Negro dialect, scurrilous black caricatures, and hyperbolic situations.[64] Even more contrarian, the musical's title, setting, and lyrics are all riddled with the offensive "c" word, but the population of this imaginary Coontown consists of middle-class, upstanding, law-abiding citizens. Apparently, Cole and Johnson appropriated this pejorative term to refashion its meanings. In this new universe, cultured "coons" rest comfortably atop economic and cultural hierarchies, and the lone white character is an itinerant clown/hobo. Furthermore, unlike Barton's gullible Coony, who functions as the "mark" in an eighteenth-century comedy, Flimflammer's modernist "swell coon" is a polished, cunning antagonist devising a financial scheme.

In assessing Cole's hybrid, contrarian aesthetic and this significant shift from hapless and hopeless to cultured and cunning "coons," Krasner concludes that "a reversal of racial mimicry" was a hard sell in late nineteenth-century commercial theater. He claims few critics at the time were "aware of the revolutionary trope initiated by Cole's appearance in whiteface."[65] I partially agree with Krasner; Cole's low-down stage European immersed in Negro affluence was revolutionary in many respects and did slip underneath most critical radars, but Cole did not initiate the trope of whiting up. The *Coontown* production was drawing on a theatrical and extra-theatrical performance tradition that emerged more than a century earlier. Krasner also claims Cole's whiteface creation "reverses the implications of racial signs used to reify and perpetuate bigoted images." A complete reversal was probably too ambitious for this production, but sharing signifiers across racial lines was entirely possible. After contemplating *Coontown*'s bigoted racial signs and imagery, Krasner poses a crucial question for analyzing Cole's stage European: If Cole, a black actor, is performing "coon" songs in whiteface, "who then is 'the coon'?"[66]

I maintain Cole's true revolution was in creating a whiteface character that could read as simultaneously black and white, thus potentially altering how we interpret the relationships between race and class onstage. Mel Watkins claims Cole's Willie Wayside managed to shift "the emphasis from the character's ethnic background to a conspicuous social problem," specifically the tramps and hobos created by two economic panics at the close of the nineteenth century.[67] Through a series of racially marked "coon" melodies, Cole partially disconnected "darky" stereotypes from African Americans and shared certain characteristics, specifically financial dispossession and an obsession with chickens, with multiple white identities across class lines. In effect, the central character, Willie Wayside, at times shifted the musical's focus from cultured "coons" to the comic possibilities of being down and out. After a close reading of Cole's Willie Wayside, we can reassess how much "cooning" was actually displaced, how much of the "c" word was really refashioned, and ultimately who were the real "coons."

Various *Coontown* playbills show that the musical's song roster changed frequently, but the one constant was chicken odes. Black musical historian Thomas L. Riis has recovered two chicken songs once featured in this musical: "All I Wants Is Ma Chickens" (1899), by Laurence Deas and Jack Wilson, and "Chicken" (189?), by Bob Cole, Billy Johnson, and Willie Accooe.[68] Chicken odes traditionally focused on lower-class, black chicken thieves, but the songs were so popular, most accomplished black composers included a chicken composition in their repertoire. The writing team of Paul Laurence Dunbar and Will Marion Cook authored the popular song "Who Dat Say Chicken in Dis Crowd" (1898). Laurence Deas and Jack Wilson, two respected colored road show veterans, introduced their popular tune "All I Wants Is Ma Chickens" in the 1898 tour of John W. Isham's Tenderloin Coon Company.[69]

According to Thomas L. Riis, Cole's Willie Wayside performed a version of Deas and Wilson's "All I Wants Is Ma Chickens" in act 1, and he performed it as a one-man, tri-vocal harmony of various chicken lovers. In the first verse, Willie embodies a white farmer named Jasper Smith who raises prize Shanghai chickens and vows to protect his valuable livestock from any chicken thief. The second verse introduces another poultry devotee, an esteemed black academic named 'Fessor Kidney who attends a "coon" picnic where he wins two prize hens in a hotly contested chicken race. Following the picnic, the professor and his wife encounter some trouble:

> To the boat he quickly went and for home he did start
> Four miles from home the boat went down, his wife sank with a groan;
> In a half-drowned state they picked him up, and he began to moan:
> All I wants is ma chickens, dem lubly chickens, ma feathered pickens!
> Now don't mind ma wife, but save my chickens![70]

Clearly 'Fessor Kidney values his lovely hens more than his lovely wife, and in the next verse, he even calls for divers to recover his poultry. For the final verse, Cole/Willie finally represents a stereotypic "coon" named Razor Jake; he is the prototypical shiftless chicken thief, the kind of resourceful bandit who keeps Jasper Smith vigilant. Sadly, Razor Jake has fallen ill and lies on his deathbed; with his last words, he requests "roasted chicken with gravy drippings" for his trip to the great beyond.

From behind the whiteface mask, Cole uses this poultry opus to signify across race, social class, death, and matrimony. Among the selected chicken fanatics, 'Fessor Kidney is identified racially by the "coon" picnic he attends and his occasional slippages into Negro dialect, with words like "dem" and "ma." He is a respectable, educated, married Negro, the very embodiment of a solid "race" man, yet he is also overly invested in his poultry. As the more conventional "coon," Razor Jack is marked by even heavier doses of Negro dialect, and his name immediately triggers stereotypical associations between black skin, knife fights, and livestock larceny. Additionally, his name suggests that he is thoroughly Negro and quite dangerous, but his severe illness diminishes that threat and generates some empathy for Jack's insatiable quest for chicken. With these two wildly divergent components of Willie's tripartite chicken ode, we see how Cole's conception of "coon" was actually not bound by class; African Americans from college professors to chicken thieves could qualify as "coons" and attend "coon" picnics. In terms of audience reception, it remains to be seen whether this new catchall "coon" registered as a familiar product of white supremacy or a successful redirection of a derogatory term.

Cole's more complicated feat would be transferring "coon" characteristics across racial lines. Farmer Jasper Smith, with his economic position and proprietary attitude, reads as the privileged white gatekeeper. However, Smith sings in a southern dialect similar to Razor Jake's, signified by words like "ma" and "wid." Also, over three verses of "All I Wants Is Ma Chickens," Cole's whiteface creation unites this white chicken farmer with a black professional and an ailing black chicken thief by finding a commonality that transcends racial perceptions. That shared value was an obsession with chickens, as all three men "prize" chickens for either their beauty or their delectability, precisely the kind of commonality vaudeville looked to cultivate in its experiments with ethnic and racial performance. By representing all three figures through one malleable Willie Wayside, Cole revealed that college professors could be "coons," and he also explored how "coonish" whiteness could be.

This process of attaching "coon" signifiers to whiteness continues in two other chicken melodies, "Chicken" (189?) and "Pickin' on a Chicken Bone" (1900), as both songs chronicle the exploits of a chicken devotee named Eph Jackson. In "Chicken," Jackson is a black valet embarking on a world tour with his wealthy white employer. He is treated very "white"—meaning humanely—by his millionaire boss, entertained by sultans, and exposed to foreign lands and their delicacies. Yet he still declares his unwavering allegiance to chicken, with this refrain:

> Chicken, kase its best to eat
> Chicken, kase it's good and sweet
> Chicken, kase it can't be beat.[71]

As Cole, in whiteface and red beard, sings this impassioned hook, his tripled cross-racial connection, between black comedian Cole, stage European Willie, and Negro character Eph Jackson, transfers "coon" signifiers like servility and a limited worldview to lower-class whiteness.

With "Pickin' on a Chicken Bone," Cole performs a similar racial transference with even more interesting class implications. This tune, composed by Bob Cole and Rosmand Johnson, features Eph Jackson singing about his two life aspirations: earning a spot in the Coontown orchestra and winning the affections of a lovely Coontown "society girl."[72] Sadly, Jackson fails to win a spot in the orchestra because he cannot play a violin, mandolin, xylophone, or trombone; all he can do is "pick a chicken bone." He also loses the society girl to a cadre of more musically inclined and genteel suitors. Unlike "All I Wants Is Ma Chickens" and its conflation of "coon" with college professors, this "Pickin'" melody suggests that parochial, chicken-obsessed "coons" like Jackson are social pariahs in a middle-class community like Coontown, where opera is preferred over cakewalking and strumming bones. Through his synthesis of Willie Wayside and Eph Jackson, Cole displaces more "coon" imagery, like playing chicken bones, onto Willie's whiteness, while the snooty, "un-coon-like" black citizens of Coontown are content with their mandolins.

This second Eph Jackson chicken melody also exudes a level of elitism reminiscent of the Meeting Street promenaders and their verbal abuse of poor whites mentioned in Chapter 1. In another "coon" melody, "Mr. Coon You're All Right in Your Place," cowritten by Bob Cole and Billy Johnson, Coontown's rejection of typical "coons" takes an even uglier turn. This song is about a "pretty yaller gal" from Coontown's "swell society" who is accosted twice by a dark, burly "common coon." Noted sociologist E. Franklin Frazier explains how the turn-of-the-century black bourgeoisie were taught, at home and at school, to differentiate themselves from "common" Negroes through their discourse, deportment, and morality.[73] At their initial encounter, the "coon" politely approaches the lady and offers to escort her to church, but she harshly rebuffs his overture and warns this ill-matched paramour not to hang around her door. In the next encounter, the "common coon" grabs the "yaller gal" on the street, and she is so emotionally wounded by his impertinent advance, her family hunts him down and hangs him from a tree.[74]

By composing such a disturbing song, were Cole and Johnson offering political commentary on lynching? The 1890s did see an increase in lynching, so perhaps the team was using this horrific image, albeit at the hands of the black middle class, to publicize an upsurge in this barbaric practice.[75] Several reviews described *Coontown* as a farce, so maybe the writing team was hyperbolizing and burlesquing colorism and classism in Afro-America. Kevin Gaines proffers a more serious and historically grounded explanation. He explains that part of racial uplift ideology "assented to the racist formulation of 'the Negro problem' by projecting onto other blacks dominant images of racialized pathology." Gaines even singles out "coon songs" as prime culprits because of their tendency to divide Negro communities and undermine black aspirations by exploiting urban, lower-class images onstage. In "Mr. Coon You're All Right in Your Place," Coontown society ruthlessly denigrates the dark, burly "common coon" with multiple pathologies before deciding he has stepped out of his place and must pay with his life. Echoing E. Franklin Frazier, Gaines claims the strategy of these "bourgeois agents of civilization" was to distinguish themselves from the underdeveloped Negro masses, but in the end, the black middle class simply "replicated the dehumanizing logic of racism."[76]

Could fairly successful late nineteenth-century composers like Bob Cole, Billy Johnson, and Ernest Hogan be guilty of sacrificing or exploiting less-accomplished "coons" to advance their careers and uplift certain segments of Afro-America? It is difficult to envision how a song about wealthy Negroes lynching a lower-class Negro served any progressive function. Historian Jayna Brown reminds us that black artists at the turn of the century were working "within a particularly violent field of referents," and their shows were "multi-signifying, risibly glancing in many directions."[77] Brown's explanation speaks to the disidentifying fourth function of whiting up, as these composers and performers identified both with and against the dominant culture. In his work on whiteface minstrelsy and queer performers of color, Muñoz defines disidentification as "the survival strategies the minority subject practices in order to negotiate a phobic majoritarian public sphere that continuously elides or punishes the existence of subjects who do not conform to the phantasm of normative citizenship."[78] Most minority artists are forced to work within a public sphere largely defined by the majority; as a result, they tend to identify with and against normative racial, gender, sexual, and class codes. So in one direction, Cole and Johnson might confirm racist assumptions for the majority-white Broadway crowd, while in another direction, they might drop a wink of recognition to black audiences and fellow Negro artists, signaling their rejection of this violent racial and class imagery.

Yet as Coontown's black middle-class elites appeared to project coded pathologies onto lower-class Negroes, were any "coon" stereotypes actually sticking to Willie Wayside, Cole's stage European? In other words, was it possible to view Willie as a dispossessed, common "coon" who has forfeited the prestige and privilege commonly associated with whiteness? Film theorist Richard Dyer has found that in the pantheon of white filmic and stage representations, some white figures can and do fail to uphold certain ideals or standards of whiteness. In westerns, white bad guys who cavort in Mexican bars and sleep with native women are "blackened" figures who have fallen short of or abdicated a fully entitled whiteness.[79] Such underachieving whites are often labeled "white trash." Whiteness scholars Annalee Newitz and Matt Wray question these media representations, which "suggest that poor whites are trash who don't deserve the benefits of social welfare, sympathy, or national power." They explain that "such stereotypes maintain—in a contained, taxonomic sense—images and narratives about poor whites in order to provide something against which 'civilized' whites can measure themselves."[80] Like Eph Jackson or the burly "common coon," "white trash" Willie Wayside seems to represent a laughable, hard-luck loser, a character all self-respecting, industrious nineteenth-century Euro-Americans should never identity with. Cole's whiteface hobo may have indeed registered as a race failure because he appeared to be estranged from the benefits of white America and isolated on the margins of a dominant, African American oasis. In the racially reversed world of *Coontown*, Willie Wayside could read simultaneously as "white trash" and "coon."

Yet Newitz and Wray warn audiences, past and present, against this kind of racial absolutism when analyzing artistic constructions of whiteness and blackness. They maintain that "social problems like unequally distributed resources, class privilege, irrational prejudice, and tyrannical bureaucracy which we associate with whiteness are just that, associated with whiteness, particularly at this point in history. They are not essential to whiteness itself, any more than laziness and enslavement are essential to blackness."[81] Cole presented his version of an economic and social problem, a tattered, aimless, white tramp wandering through life and accidentally arriving in a prosperous Negro community. Willie Wayside represents an obvious lack of privilege, but his dispossession is not essential to his whiteness any more than Eph Jackson's chicken obsession is essential to his blackness. Newitz and Wray's representational and cultural truth explains why Cole could use dichotomous figures like Jasper Smith, 'Fessor Kidney, and Razor Jack to exchange racial and class stereotypes.

This truth also partially explains why Cole's low-down whiteness is never permanently marginalized. Within this world of cross-racial play, Cole displaced certain unflattering "coon" traits onto Willie Wayside, characteristics that were not necessarily accurate or representative of all white people.[82] The representational logic of Cole's whiting up was vastly different from the cultural work of blacking up, which permanently affixed derogatory characteristics to black bodies, regardless of class or social position. So even in this inverted world of nattily attired Negro con artists and multitalented black musical suitors, the lone stage European is allowed the fluidity to read as a low-down "coon" and later identify with white privilege and property.

Thomas L. Riis has published an arrangement of *Coontown*'s act 1 "grande finale," which consists of a four-song medley including reprises of Flimflammer's signature "I Hope These Few Lines Find You Well" and Wayside's tri-vocal "All I Wants Is Ma Chickens."[83] However, for the act 1 curtain, Cole's Willie Wayside no longer channels his inner "coon"; he does not sing the 'Fessor Kidney or Eph Jackson verses. He only repeats Jasper Smith's stern warning to chicken thieves: "I'll bet six bits I'll kill a coon if I don't get ma chickens." The "coon" in farmer Smith's threat specifically refers to black criminals like Razor Jack, but also to potential felons like the respectable 'Fessor Kidney, who, despite his education, remains an irredeemable chicken fanatic at heart. Here we witness the disturbing potential of cross-racial play to fix or affirm the dominant culture's racial absolutes concerning black bodies. Additionally, this curtain-closer visually associates farmer Jasper Smith and Willie Wayside with propertied white authority. The stage directions in the recovered sheet music call for Willie to exit and reenter with his coveted Shanghai chicken nestled under his arm.[84] Cole's originally cross-racial, multiclassed fugue is now collapsed, and the audience is left with the dominant image of a white chicken farmer securing his prize poultry from ravenous "coons." Yet the disidentifying ironies are still at work in this musical. As a character, Willie continues to vacillate between a white "coonish" outsider who undermines racial assumptions and a propertied white farmer who reinforces the very same assumptions. As a production, *Coontown*'s act 1 finale comically portrays white property as in need of protection from the black masses, but that message is delivered by Bob Cole, a versatile Negro comedian trespassing on white cultural and performative property.

Ultimately, Willie Wayside was not a race failure or a pariah for mainstream white audiences. Cole carefully designed this underdog character, complete with a real bulldog sidekick named Bo, to be embraced by the dominant culture. After all, who could reject a hobo and his loyal dog? Despite the hints of "coon" collecting around Willie Wayside, the predominantly white audiences were encouraged to identify with this black man playing a white man. Some patrons may have even connected without fully realizing Cole's race. The *New York Sun* reviewer reported the combination of white makeup and comedic skill made "it almost impossible to guess his particular tint."[85] All audiences, aware or unaware, black or white, were encouraged to root for this white outsider. According to a *Freeman* review, patrons could not resist the antics of this homeless free spirit and his dog, and the comic pair kept "the audience in one long, continuous roar of laughter."[86]

Cole's complex stage European was the centrifugal force in *Coontown* and the key component in his overall mission to reposition black theatrical artists. Yet the talented Bob Cole did not necessarily need whiteface to hook mainstream American audiences on this iconic, dispossessed tramp. Even when Willie Wayside was simply a red-bearded tramp in the Black Patti Troubadours, his image was used as part of a national advertisement campaign for the Kirk Soap Company. This tattered, lovable loser graced signboards and train stations all along the East Coast.[87] And beyond the imaginary worlds of Broadway and urban billboards, Cole's "white trash" hobo tapped directly into the late nineteenth-century problem of social and economic dislocation. In addition to selling soap to turn-of-the-century housewives, Cole's stage European resisted racial absolutes such as black poverty or white wealth to highlight financial instabilities felt across the racial divide. Given the economic hardships of the late 1890s, this drifting, singing, homeless figure represented an irresistible underclass everyman with whom many similarly challenged American audiences could sympathize. Not surprisingly, Cole's creation inspired imitators in colored road shows and other entertainments.[88] Soon after the early *Coontown* revue at Proctor's Theatre, the *Freeman* announced that John W. Vogel and Billy McClain's *Darkest America* production was featuring a tramp character. A black actor named Will Porter was playing a hobo hounded by the police, and he was "receiving curtain calls nightly."[89]

No matter how endearing and entertaining Willie Wayside and his dog Bo may have been, the spectacle of a whiteface hobo dominating the first all-black Broadway musical remains difficult to reconcile. If the act 1 finale is not re-inscriptive enough, the musical ends with a heroic Willie Wayside swooping in to rescue Silas Green and his substantial retirement funds from Jim Flimflammer. Given this nation's long history of class-rooted racial antagonisms, Willie Wayside's selfless act was decidedly ahistorical.

Riot historian Paul Gilje found that when blacks and whites engaged in class conflict in the nineteenth century, most often lower-class white mobs attacked middle-class black churches, schools, and fraternal orders.[90] In the real world, Silas Green would have been perceived as a challenge to "herrenvolk republicanism," a threat to Willie's position in America's racial, economic, and political hierarchies. Nevertheless, to conclude their unpredictable musical, Cole and Johnson call on a white homeless and jobless man to protect the financial security of an elderly black man. The larger interpretive problem here is not about historical accuracy, but the social and political message sent by having a penniless white vagabond save a vulnerable Negro from the schemes of a cunning black trickster. *Coontown* appears to endorse the belief held by the majority culture that African Americans were helpless and in need of white assistance, and that a cunning "swell coon" like Jim Flimflammer could never outsmart even the most underprivileged Euro-American. This intriguing narrative development and its concomitant issues become even more problematic when Cole and Johnson musically explore the issue of Jim Crow segregation.

Coontown debuted five years after Homer Plessy's 1892 appropriation of whiteness in protest of segregated Louisiana train cars, and a year after the 1896 *Plessy v. Ferguson* Supreme Court decision supported separate accommodations. The political "coon" melody "No Coons Allowed," written by Cole and Johnson and showcased in *A Trip to Coontown*, directly confronts the Jim Crow laws dividing "coloreds and whites."[91] The song is about a "swell gentleman of color," performed by Billy Johnson, who wants to take his girl to dinner at the finest restaurant in town. When the Negro couple arrives at the restaurant, they are greeted by a blunt placard reading, "No Coons Allowed," and this chorus explains the signage:

> No coons allowed
> No coons allowed
> This place is meant for white folks that's all
> We don't want no kinky-head kind
> So move on dark down the line
> No coons allow'd in here at all.[92]

As part of the headlining comic duo, Cole's Willie Wayside would have sung this rebuffing chorus to Flimflammer. Similar to his watchdog position as farmer Jasper Smith, Wayside was now called upon to represent the majority culture as a Jim Crow enforcer.

After being turned away from this fine restaurant, Billy Johnson's musical persona next secures a lawyer and seeks redress at the courthouse, only to be greeted by the same sign with a new explanatory chorus. The courthouse moment is especially powerful because Cole and Johnson's "coon" melody suggests Negroes in America, like Homer Plessy, should not bother seeking justice in the American legal system. The core message of "No Coons Allowed" is that in America, race still trumps class. Both the lyrics and the performances by white Wayside and black Flimflammer confirm an inescapable racial reality: if Wayside stumbled into a financial windfall, he could dine at the finest white restaurant, while the more refined yet darker Flimflammer, or any Coontown resident, would be denied on sight. The song reveals that Willie's whiteness, no matter how debased, still matters more than Silas Green's money or Jim Flimflammer's flare. Unwittingly, Cole and Johnson's anti–Jim Crow song exposed the limits of racial uplift predicated on the questionable strategy of color or class differentiation. Their composition made it clear that both a burly "common coon" and a well-mannered, immaculately dressed member of the black bourgeoisie were vulnerable to exclusion based on pigment.

To summarize Willie Wayside's compelling political resonances: this centrifugal stage European firmly identifies with a white poultry protector to close act 1; Cole's dispossessed white clown emerges as a black musical hero; and finally, this tattered white outsider emerges as the defender of Jim Crow segregation. If we heed Jayna Brown's recommendation to read nineteenth-century performances like *Coontown* as "multi-signifying," this summary is only half of the story. The other half involves José Muñoz's theory of disidentification, which helps us understand how *Coontown* could both reinscribe and rewire whiteness in America.

Cole's disidentifying practice began with his larger agenda of proving black brilliance through facility with allegedly white artistic forms. With a hint of contradiction or contrariety, Cole advocated embracing "white" art while also declaring artistic independence from powerful white producers; thus he was identifying both with and against America's mainstream entertainment industry. Next, Cole encouraged Negro artists to break away from traditional but degraded cakewalks, but he and his writing partner Johnson exploited the popular appetite for "coon" songs. Cole and Johnson contributed to a punitive majority culture by writing offensive material, yet at the same time, they diverged from artists like Ernest Hogan in their efforts to reinvent this loaded racial signifier. As far as their progress in reorienting "coon" significations, after experimenting with "coon" over several tours of *Coontown*, Cole decided to abandon the term altogether. Much like Richard Pryor vowed to remove the "n" word from his stand-up comedy in the 1980s, post-*Coontown*, Cole officially renounced the "c" word, vowed to crusade against its usage, and urged his fellow black artists to follow suit.[93] Cole's renunciation of "coon" sounds like an admission of failure in his efforts to redefine a troublesome signifier.

The disidentification concludes with Willie Wayside, a walking, talking, singing, and clowning negation of the assumed linkages between whiteness, political power, and economic prosperity. Cole's mauve-face hobo-turned-hero, this guardian of "herrenvolk republicanism," is the key to reorienting how Euro-Americans see themselves and African Americans. Complete with his adorable dog Bo, this stage European struck a chord with the majority culture, and so it is no coincidence that Willie Wayside became a commercially viable pitchman for Kirk Soap. Willie's low-down whiteness transcended class and race failure to shine as a relatable icon for mainstream America. Even if he obsessed over chicken, like the typical "coon," or experienced life as a minority outsider, like many African Americans, his identifying fans, white or black, took the journey with him. Coontown's elegant parlors and cultured opera company may have worked to undermine racial absolutes linking blackness and poverty, but the musical's lone white character functioned as the perfect pitchman capable of disrupting and defending centuries of racial division. As with any product of popular culture, *Coontown* leaves us with complex significations and unresolved issues. But why would we expect anything less from the first black-produced musical on the Great White Way?

Over a couple Broadway runs and several North American tours, Cole and Johnson cultivated an incredibly productive yet experimental environment in which artists of color could work through fixed and fluid conceptions of race, class, and gender. As for the company's primary agenda, proving black performers could excel in supposedly white artistic forms, *A Trip to Coontown* marked Cole's emergence as a first-rate comedian on par with the best American entertainers. *The Dramatic Mirror*, a national theatrical magazine, declared, "Bob Cole as a tramp was fully as good as any white comedian whose specialty is this style of eccentricity." In addition, a *New York Sun* review declared Cole was "capable of playing any white part far better than most Negro comedians play black ones."[94] Cole was by no means alone, as previously mentioned; Tom Brown's shape-shifting Billy Binkerton was equally lauded by critics.

Also, within Coontown's highly structured world of black middle-class comfort, where cakewalks were banned and opera reigned, Jennie Hillman and Barrington Carter still found space to channel a couple of Bowery "bad-asses." In particular, Hillman's Bowery Gal embraced a working-class female subculture and rejected the majority culture's Victorian propriety. In the end, this minstrel reversal worked: a strikingly relatable mauve-face hobo and a white working-class "bad girl" successfully trumped blackface minstrelsy and middle-class morality. However, the mission of the *Coontown* Company was never just about besting blackface or exploiting low-down whiteness; it was also about their public.

According to his obituary published in the *New York Age*, Bob Cole was deeply committed to elevating "the public to his own mental level rather than cater to the prevalent, although ofttimes unfair and inaccurate ideas existing with reference to all citizens of color."[95] The kind of audience elevation Cole envisioned involved moving forcefully yet strategically against the grain of American entertainment. To debunk "unfair and inaccurate ideas" about colored citizens, Cole and company had to confront the blackface minstrel monster, which had already obscured and compromised America's racial and ethnic multiplicity. *Coontown* allowed nineteenth-century audiences to truly experience national diversity, especially low-down whiteness and middle-class blackness, in new and progressive ways. Elevation also meant challenging a purportedly diversified vaudeville with a definitive message: white theater managers should stop excluding or limiting Negro artists. Bob Cole's all-star lineup promoted constructive cross-racial, multiethnic, and class-identified stage Europeans that could entertain and ultimately benefit artists and audiences of all colors.

Chapter 4 **Trespassing on Whiteness**

Negro Actors and the Nordic Complex

Act 1 of Langston Hughes's modern tragedy *Mulatto* (1927) features a scene in which the title mulatto, Robert Norwood, is confronted by his Negro mother, Cora, and his biracial brother William about his recent transgressions. Robert, the unacknowledged son of Colonel Thomas Norwood, has decided to walk through the front door of the colonel's house, like a white man, instead of through the back door, like a Negro. Cornered by a concerned family, Robert reveals his true feelings: "Back here in these woods maybe Sam and Livonia and you and mama and everybody's got their places fixed for 'em, but not me. (*seriously*). Nobody's gonna fix a place for me. I'm old man Norwood's son. Nobody fixed a place for him (*playfully again*) Look at me. I'm a 'fay boy. (*pretends to shake his hair back*) See these gray eyes? I got the right to everything everybody else has."[1] Robert Norwood covets fluidity; he craves the privilege of white skin, the freedom of movement and interracial association his white father has enjoyed and exploited for years. Hughes highlights Robert's desire for white privilege and mobility with a simple yet powerful gesture—shaking his hair back.

This racially marked gesture foregrounds Afro-America's estranged or disidentifying relationship to white cultural and biological ancestry. By shaking his imaginary hair and claiming his "'fay" or white-boy status, Robert identifies both with and against the dominant culture, as specifically embodied through his father.[2] He assumes the biological privilege of long tresses but critiques whiteness as vacuous and hypocritical, as exemplified by references to his white father's secretive relationships with black women and denials of paternity. Robert's hair-flipping, this sign of perceived white arrogance, would become a signature gesture in whiting up performance. Richard Pryor would use it repeatedly and perhaps idiosyncratically in his stand-up comedy, and in her solo work, Whoopi Goldberg would weave it into her impersonation of a white "Surfer Girl."

On the surface, Robert Norwood is a prototypical tragic mulatto in the postemancipation South, a place where his biracial slippage between white privilege and black militancy is isolating and eventually devastating. But Harry and Michele Elam argue that Robert "is not tragic, he is anarchic, he does not want to be white, he wants to indict the white status quo."[3] Throughout the drama, Robert tenaciously fights fixity by refusing to embrace any position in America's racial hierarchy, thus making him a natural enemy of the state. More specifically, the Elams claim that Robert wants to achieve a level of "realness" and secure the "privileges of masculinity" only available to white men in the South. Tragically, Robert's unambiguous possession of a biracial masculinity is tied to the destruction of his mendacious white father.

In his construction of this stage mulatto, Hughes was consciously playing with the performance of whiteness, dramaturgically commenting on white signifiers of supremacy. However, he was also building a three-dimensional Negro character, not a stage European. Hughes initially conceived of his multifaceted Robert as a part for a black actor, but in the play's 1935 Broadway debut, the role was performed by a white actor.[4] This cross-racial casting decision was standard practice in 1930s American theater. As blackface minstrelsy's popularity diminished in the early twentieth century, white actors discovered fresh and exciting performative territory in dramatic Negro impersonations. Commenting on this casting convention, Lester A. Walton, theater critic for the *New York Age*, noted that "the most prominent black face artists before the public today are white performers." Yet, in the same 1916 article, Walton also opined that it was "possible for colored performers to make up as white people as it is for white performers to make up as colored people."[5]

In this chapter, I examine colored actors who took up Walton's offhand challenge "to make up as white people." Whiting up in the early twentieth century underwent a significant shift as ambitious Negro actors reached beyond crude ethnic impersonations or humanely comedic whiteface hobos. They decided to conquer serious stage European roles never intended for them to play. This increased Negro interest in "Nordic" theatrical material was understandable, given the dearth of dramas featuring black characters and the common practice of casting whites in those scarce dramatic black roles. In order to achieve mainstream recognition and affirmation, professional black actors such as Anita Bush, Charles

Gilpin, Evelyn Preer, Fredi Washington, Canada Lee, and Paul Robeson had to rely on white dramatists, dead or alive, and white roles. The current discussion focuses on two specific moments in African American theater history: the Ethiopian Art Theatre's 1923 production of Oscar Wilde's *Salomé* (1894/96) starring Evelyn Preer in the title role and the 1946 Broadway production of John Webster's *Duchess of Malfi* (1614) featuring Canada Lee as a whiteface Bosola.

During the "New Negro" aesthetic explosion of the early 1920s, cultural critic Abram L. Harris defended Negro actors drawn to European drama by arguing that the works of Shakespeare and Molière were not "the indisputable heritage of the white man," and that Negro actors should feel free to "trespass" on this material whenever they pleased.[6] Similar to Bob Cole's embrace of elite white aesthetics, Harris accepted the qualitative differences between white and black dramas in the early 1920s, but he rejected the idea that certain white roles were beyond Negro artists. With the backing of some critics, Preer and Lee would attack and disentangle the connections between whiteness, universality, and virtuosity and, in the process, expand the range of what Negro actors could represent.

Not every theater critic or political commentator agreed with Lester A. Walton or Abram L. Harris on this question of what black actors could or should be performing. As Preer and Lee pursued their artistic and professional development by any means available, they were drawn into fierce debates over whether Negro actors should perfect their craft by performing white roles or concentrate on building a sustainable American Negro theater rooted in plays about Negro life. In reviews, editorials, articles, and public forums, the debate raged on, and ironically, neither Preer nor Lee truly "starred" in this multileveled conversation on the future of African American performance. The real stars were the architects of the debates, the white and black critics writing for Negro magazines like the *Messenger* or the *Crisis*, white dailies like the *New York Times* or the *Chicago Tribune*, or Communist newspapers like the *Daily Worker*. More than actors ever could, the media made this stealth tradition of whiting up visible, and the first American critic to seriously examine stage Europeans and strategic passing was *New York Age* critic Lester A. Walton.

Strategic Passing and the Nordic Complex

Anita Bush, a former singer and dancer with Bert Williams and George Walker's touring company, left the minstrel and vaudeville world to establish a Negro acting ensemble devoted to performing legitimate comedies and dramas.[7] The Anita Bush Stock Company debuted at Harlem's Lincoln Theatre in November 1915, but they were soon enticed to transfer to the rival Lafayette Theatre in December 1915. And after this relocation, Bush changed her company's name to the Lafayette Players. Before Bush's company moved in, the Lafayette Theatre typically employed white actors in shortened versions of Broadway hits. Such theatrical fare seemed to satisfy Harlemites, but the Lafayette management, which included Lester A. Walton, envisioned productions featuring Negro actors in white plays. In the *New York Age*, comanager Walton argued that this new casting direction was "an idea which is bound to take root, spread and redound to the great good of the Negro on the stage."[8]

Soon after Bush's company started performing at the Lafayette Theatre, Walton reported that the players were being criticized by Harlemites for ignoring Negro subjects in their theatrical entertainments. When Bush organized her ensemble, devoted to nonmusical theatrical material, there was a paucity of Negro dramas, by black or white writers. Nevertheless, the communal complaint inspired Bush and the Lafayette management to mount Dion Boucicault's *Octoroon* (1859), a melodrama about passing in the plantation South. In 1916, the Lafayette Players staged a condensed version of *Octoroon* with veteran Negro actor Charles Gilpin playing the role of Jacob McClosky, a white slave master. Walton remarked that Gilpin "so cleverly makes up that he resembles the slave owner of days gone by to a remarkable degree, investing this type with a certain distinction."[9] A newcomer to the company, Mrs. Charles H. Anderson, assumed the role of a young white maiden named Dora Sunshine. Anderson's performance prompted Walton to enthuse, "It is doubtful that the original portrayal of the role of *Dora Sunshine* was as pretty a 'Southern Belle' as Mrs. Anderson."

As for the overall impact of this stage European production, Walton called it "the most meritorious dramatic production ever presented by a cast made up entirely of colored actors." Understanding the potential of Negro actors in melodramatic whiteface, Walton remarked, "What was most intensely interesting to me was the fine sense of art shown by the actors in their makeup," and he confidently declared that "the colored performer has taken a long step forward in the realm of dramatic art." In subsequent productions, other Lafayette Players applied white face paint. Notably, veteran actor Clarence Muse, with the help of a German actor and friend, learned how to pull off white roles, complete with wigs, makeup, and a Nordic accent. One of Muse's most memorable Lafayette performances was playing the title roles in *Dr. Jekyll and Mr. Hyde.*[10]

Beyond the stage, as far as audience education, Walton maintained that the *Octoroon* was a timely production especially for Euro-Americans because it awakened them to "the fact that there are thousands of colored people throughout the country of Negro origin who are living in their respective communities as white people."[11] The theatrical and cultural ironies here are incredible: Negro actors like Charles Gilpin and Clarence Muse whiting up to educate white America about passing. On the subject of real-life cross-racial performance, Walton was one of the few critics openly discussing this social deception. In one article, Walton even suggested that a young, fair-skinned actor with the Lafayette Players named Andrew Bishop could and should pass to advance his career: "He has everything in his favor, even to joining the ranks of those who to-day are 'passing' and enjoying big reputations; that is, if his field of dramatic endeavor was limited."[12] Walton essentially lifted the veil by publicizing that many Negro artists were strategically passing for white in the American entertainment industry and enjoying lucrative careers. Far from decrying the practice, a Machiavellian Walton recommended that if this talented young actor encountered casting limitations, he should pursue the same deception. Based on the image Walton published with his article on the actor, Bishop was a fair-skinned Negro with matinee-idol looks, but one wonders if Walton realized he was racially "outing" this potential "crossover" star before he could even launch his passing career.

One famous Negro act that strategically passed as white, onstage and offstage, was the Whitman Sisters—Mabel, Alberta, Essie, and Alice. In her history of these vaudeville pioneers, Nadine George-Graves reveals that early in their career, the Whitman Sisters booked performances as a "white act."[13] They received their first big break because a talent agent heard the sisters singing and assumed they were white. Even after the agent officially met the sisters, his assumption remained unchanged. In addition to passing to secure performance opportunities, on the road, the sisters strategically passed to secure better services and accommodations.[14] But beyond exploiting their biology offstage, onstage the Whitman Sisters consciously constructed stage Europeans that challenged America's racial categories. George-Graves explains how the sisters intentionally crisscrossed representations of whiteness and blackness in their performances, making sure audiences noticed the "ease with which they could step in and out of racial identity."[15]

The Whitman Sisters present a compelling example of how both passing and whiting up function as performative practices mired in perception, speculation, and cultural hierarchy. Stage Europeans and racial passing both acknowledge the primacy of whiteness in America and view the dominant culture as a target for invasion, but the two traditions diverge profoundly in terms of the cross-racial performers' agendas. Stage Europeans are never fully invested in racial histories and absolutes, as evidenced by Bob Cole's dispossessed, disidentifying white hobo. Whiting up is a present-centered commodity that conforms to some rules while challenging others in order to create an entertaining and occasionally enlightening cross-racial product. In the hands of capable artists, stage Europeans reveal that racial identity is fixed and fluid, defined and definable. Although this particular character is not a stage European, Langston Hughes's Robert Norwood is an excellent example of performed whiteness at its most deconstructive, as this anarchic mulatto consistently highlights the cultural and social tensions between being white and being black.

Conversely, the racial passer works to dissolve those tensions by becoming essentially invisible within a rigid racial hierarchy. Cultural theorist Amy Robinson writes that "the social practice of passing is thoroughly invested in the logic of the system it attempts to subvert."[16] A legally defined Negro passing for white does not challenge the dominant culture's legal definition but instead consciously dissembles to enjoy the privileges and benefits of whiteness. Many African Americans, during slavery and post-emancipation, used passing as a vehicle for advancement. Thus passing could be read as subversive, but the ultimate agenda of the racial passer was remaining permanently undetected.

Taking a closer look at the business of passing, we see that for decades, Negro newspapers and their advertisements endorsed the creation of racial passers and a calculated co-option of white privilege. From the late nineteenth century well into the middle of the twentieth century, Negro media outlets ran various notices for whitening creams and hair relaxers. In the late 1890s, on the same page with a rave review of Bob Cole's whiteface triumph, the *Freeman*, a colored Indianapolis weekly, ran an advertisement for "black skin remover."[17] In this ad space, Thomas Beard, an entrepreneur based in Richmond, Virginia, promised the *Freeman*'s subscribers the ability to "no longer complain any longer about black skin." Beard claimed his product, if used properly, could "turn the skin of a black person four or five shades whiter, and that of mulattoes perfectly white." Even in the 1940s, the *New York Amsterdam News*, a conservative Negro weekly, continued to generate revenue with ads for skin-whitening and hair-straightening products. In a quarter-page advertisement running in nearly every issue of the *Amsterdam News*, an Atlanta company offered "Dr. Palmer's Skin Whitener." This cosmetic boasted a "special bleaching ingredient" that activated the minute it touched dark skin, and in just days, the Negro consumer could "expect to be thrilled and delighted with your lovelier lighter complexion!"[18]

Similar to Robert Norwood's anarchic thirst for fluidity, these advertisements exposed a Negro desire for the privileges, opportunities, and mobility that came with white or fair skin, as well as a deep-seated racial inferiority complex within Afro-America. Hubert Harrison, founder, editor, and cultural critic of the *Voice*, declared in 1917 "that color is the great social obsession among our Negroes." The West Indies–born Harrison observed that among American Negroes, "one's social value in this group is in direct ratio to one's lightness." Harrison specifically accused mulattoes of perpetuating vicious color prejudice in the United States with their constant references to "good hair" and "good color." Negroes of "good color" tended to demean their fellow blacks with terms like "black niggers" or "loads of coal."[19] As seen in Chapter 3, the same intraracial color prejudice was rife in "coon" songs composed by artists like Bob Cole and Billy Johnson. But Harrison was most upset with black leadership, with Fred R. Moore, editor of the *New York Age*, who claimed Negroes had to lighten their skin because white employers preferred fair Negroes. Harrison rejected Moore's "advancement" justification as untrue and damaging to the race.[20]

Writing about the politics of passing, Elaine K. Ginsberg explains how passing is "about specularity: the visible and the invisible, the seen and unseen."[21] Ginsberg argues that the very existence of passing individuals exposes the unreliability of racial categories predicated on visual markers, proving that what you see and assume is not always what you get. But she further explains how passing is "also about the boundaries established between identity categories and about the individual and cultural anxieties induced by boundary crossing." Racial passers recognize, even accept, a formidable divide between black and white, and their ability to transgress that boundary generates fears, preoccupations, and paranoia on both sides. Valerie Smith reaches a similar conclusion, specifically that "passing narratives do not provide an unproblematic way out of the discourse of racial essentialism. . . . Not only do bodies that pass function as markers of sexual and racial transgression, but they signal as well the inescapable class implications of crossing these boundaries."[22] Smith's "inescapable class implications" refer to the fact that given cultural, legal, and political hierarchies, it is often in the best social and economic interest of passers to transcend rather than challenge the boundaries.

In the early 1900s, racial passers were both endorsing and evading racial categorization on a daily basis, and anxiety over their undetected racial crossings was intensifying. Lester A. Walton, in an article titled "Passing for White," mentioned the recent case of Mrs. Frank Leslie, whose will was contested in a New York court because she was discovered to be a Negro passing as white. Walton believed most white Americans were completely oblivious to this social practice, but an event such as the scandalous Leslie case "forcibly brings to the minds of the white people that such conditions really exist and that the so-called color line is more mythical than real."[23] Walton understood that passing, as a social deception of last resort, could benefit Negro actors such as the Whitman Sisters, who strategically transcended the imposition of race to advance their careers. Yet at the same time, he praised productions like the Lafayette Players' *Octoroon*, where stage Europeans directly contested and demystified the color line, the defining issue of the twentieth century.

This theatrical and extra-theatrical conversation on black bodies, whiteness, passing, and performed whiteness was part of a broader public discourse on American racialism, which was the primary focus of the *Messenger*, an anti-racialist Negro monthly published by union organizer A. Philip Randolph. In his analysis of the *Messenger*'s cultural politics, George Hutchinson identifies the journal's mission as promoting the Americanness of Negroes to a black middle-class readership.[24] Randolph, his cofounder Chandler Owen, and the staff writers understood the United States as a mulatto nation marked by assimilation and amalgamation, a mixed-race republic where Anglo-Saxons were no longer the normative Americans. Like Lester A. Walton in his exposés on passing, J. A. Rogers, the *Messenger*'s specialist on politics and race relations, often wrote about the prevalence of passing and miscegenation in America.[25]

George Schuyler, iconoclastic satirist, essayist, dramatist and novelist, joined the *Messenger* staff in 1922, and as managing editor, he defined the journal's strident stance against any form of racialism, be it white supremacy or black cultural nationalism. Schuyler contended that black daily newspapers and their "racialistic seasonings" perpetuated the Negro's "inferiority complex," and he flatly dismissed the Harlem Renaissance and its cultural production as a "submission to the racial absurdities of white supremacy." As for so-called New Negro art, Schuyler rejected the entire notion as "hokum" and denied the emergence of a "black aesthetic" connected to Africa.[26] In Schuyler's opinion, middle-class black Americans had more in common with white Americans than with the most cultured Africans.

The *Messenger*'s first drama critic was the aforementioned Abram L. Harris, an insightful commentator on American culture. In July 1923, Harris wrote an article on critical reactions to Negro performances, especially the Ethiopian Art Theatre's production of Oscar Wilde's *Salomé*. He was particularly drawn to a "Nordic Complex," which often surfaced in this criticism. Harris argued that whenever Negro players "approached the beautiful fairness of the Nordic[, there] would linger in the critic's subconsciousness a mental parallelism of white art for white folk, and black art for black folk."[27] In the minds of most critics, white and black, there was a presumption that Negro actors should stay away from allegedly white theatrical material. Referencing American racialism, Harris explained that "because of our American heritage of color psychology it is more gratifying to our aesthetic whims to hear a Negro sing his own songs than to hear him sing those of the white man and to see him give a rendition of serious plays. It is needless to say that such a position puts the dramatic critic in the class with the compromising politician of the Harding ilk who admonishes the Negro to be 'the best Negro he can and never the best imitation of the white man.'" This "Harding ilk" comment refers to a 1921 speech in which President Warren G. Harding advised American Negroes to be themselves and not try to equal whites in economic, educational, political, or artistic pursuits.

As an outright repudiation of America's debilitating fascination with color, Harris made the *Messenger*'s antiracist position crystal clear: "We do not share the belief that playing drama is mimicking the white man."[28] This was the performative and broader cultural context Evelyn Preer and Canada Lee had to contend with as they attempted to star in serious white dramas playing serious white roles. The subsequent debates on whiteness, morality, cultural legibility, and political activism that swirled around these pioneering actors would bring whiting up into greater focus.

Evelyn Preer and the Ethiopian Art Theatre

As a student at Wendell Phillips High School in Chicago, Evelyn Preer discovered her natural affinity for musical comedy while performing with the

Chicago Ladies Amateur Minstrels.[29] Immediately after high school, Preer turned professional and toured the West Coast as a singer with Charley Johnson's vaudeville company. Upon her return to Chicago, Preer assisted her mother, Blanche Preer, who was an aspiring minister in the Black Apostolic Church. Mother Preer was a dynamic street preacher who schooled young Evelyn in the intensely dramatic art of winning souls for Christ, and although she developed into a dynamic and effective street preacher, Evelyn Preer was soon enticed to return to the entertainment industry. In 1918 she signed a contract to star in the films of Oscar Micheaux, an independent black filmmaker who migrated from Chicago to South Dakota, where he started writing, directing, and producing films based on his own novels. Based on her previous performance experience, Preer was most at home as a comedienne, but her feature film debut was as a dramatic actress in Micheaux's *The Homesteader* (1919), a silent film about interracial love in the Dakotas and the first film produced by an African American.

When she returned to the stage, with Anita Bush's Lafayette Players in Harlem, Preer rediscovered her niche playing female leads in comedies, precisely the kinds of roles most directors and critics thought suitable for Negro actors. But in 1922, Preer again stepped out of her comfort zone when she agreed to take a leave from the Lafayette Players to star in Oscar Wilde's symbolist drama *Salomé*. Preer decided to take this latest artistic risk as part of a larger mission to broaden acting prospects for Negro actors.

The bold experiment began in Preer's hometown of Chicago when a group of politicians, artists, activists, and investors, called the All-American Theatre Association, created an interracial theater collective. Originally conceived as the Negro Folk Theatre, this project consisted of an all-Negro acting company led by white director Raymond O'Neil.[30] The association believed an integrated cultural institution was necessary to help address the racial unrest that had plagued Chicago over the first two decades of the twentieth century. As the former head of the experimental Cleveland Playhouse, O'Neil was an ambitious and innovative young director heavily influenced by European art theatre, especially Konstantin Stanislavski's Moscow Art Theatre and the German director Max Reinhardt. Under O'Neil's leadership, Chicago's interracial theatrical experiment developed an eclectic repertoire; the two diametrically opposed core pieces would be Oscar Wilde's one-act symbolist drama *Salomé* and Willis Richardson's one-act Negro folk drama *The Chip Woman's Fortune*. The other plays slated for performance were Molière's *The Follies of Scapin*,

Shakespeare's *Taming of the Shrew* and *Comedy of Errors*, Hugo von Hofmannsthal's version of *Everyman*, D. B. Bowerfind's expressionist drama *George*, and Frank Wilson's Negro drama *A Train North*.

Even before rehearsals officially began, O'Neil scheduled a twelve-month training session for Preer and the other Negro actors to "develop the natural warmth and richness of their voices, their graceful and expressive movements." O'Neil explained that his intention was not "to train them in imitation of the more inhibited white actors, but to develop their peculiar racial characteristics—the freshness and vigor of their emotional responses, their spontaneity and intensity of mood, their freedom from intellectual and artistic obsessions." His approach involved matching the intellectual, artistic, and psychological passions of theatrical modernism—naturalism, surrealism, expressionism, symbolism—with the Negro's theatrical "gifts."[31] O'Neil believed black actors lacked the inhibitions of white American actors and that their gifts of spontaneity and heightened emotionalism would serve them well in experimental dramas. But the young director's first challenge was to convince his company they could "develop their peculiar racial characteristics" with European dramas like *Salomé*. Sidney Kirkpatrick, cast as Herod of Antipas, admitted he "did not think we could ever give a creditable performance of it." His wife Laura Bowman, who was to play Herodias, had toured internationally with the Williams and Walker Company, studied in Europe, and witnessed modern literary plays, but she "thought the mastery of such dramatic art would forever be far beyond my race."[32] Bowman entered O'Neil's training process with professed "fear and trembling," a testament to the depth of her own inferiority complex and to how closely Negro artists were identified with musicals and comedies.

On January 29, 1923, a fully trained and hopefully confident Negro Folk Theatre premiered *Salomé* and *Chip Woman's Fortune* before an invitation-only, thoroughly integrated audience at the Avenue Theatre on Chicago's South Side. The initial hometown response was overwhelmingly supportive. The *Chicago Tribune*, a white paper, remarked how ambitious this Negro company was to tackle *Salomé*. The *Chicago Defender*, a black weekly, reported on the classy, racially mixed crowd attending opening night. The white *Chicago Daily News* proclaimed the event a "great occasion" and that "few things more significant have come to Chicago's art life in recent years than this opening at the Avenue Theater."[33] After Chicago, a determined Negro Folk Theatre toured to Washington, D.C., for a brief run and then performed a few nights at Harlem's Lafayette Theatre.

Finally, on May 7, 1923, the experimental company, newly renamed the Ethiopian Art Theatre, arrived on Broadway, playing the Frazee Theatre.

Despite O'Neil's idealism and the effusive opening night media reception, critics and audiences in Chicago, D.C., and especially New York were not ready to enthusiastically embrace Negro actors in Wilde, Molière, or Shakespeare. O'Neil underestimated the Nordic Complex infecting black and white critics, many of whom expected and preferred "white art" from "real" Caucasians and "folksy" Negro dramas from black actors. Recognizing, understanding, and accepting stage Europeans would take time, but I am struck by how few reviews of the Ethiopian Art Theatre's *Salomé* truly appreciated the complicated aesthetic, racial, and gender dynamics at work in this unique production. As we will see shortly, many critics fixated on the commercial viability, racial incongruity, and questionable morality of this production choice. Yet how did whiteness read in Evelyn Preer's performance of Salome?

Salome and Whiteness

At its thematic and structural core, Oscar Wilde's *Salomé* is about aestheticism and the seductive power of whiteness. During his time at Oxford University in the 1870s, where he earned a degree in the classics, Wilde led his fellow students in an aesthetic movement focused on appearance, behavior, style, and artifice.[34] Their aestheticism was a way of life as much as a philosophy—a style radically at odds with the somber moods and moral codes of the Victorian era. *Salomé* was a product of Wilde's aggressive brand of aestheticism and a direct assault on the strict morality of his time. He originally composed *Salomé* in French in 1891, and it was translated into English by his lover Lord Alfred Douglas in 1894. While Wilde was serving a prison term for homosexuality, his *Salomé* premiered in 1896, produced by Aurélien-François-Marie Lugné-Poë at Théâtre de l'Oeuvre in Paris. With its vibrant masses of color, endless metaphors, and stylized movement, Wilde's drama helped launch the symbolist theatrical movement.

Although experimental in nature, *Salomé* dramatizes a familiar biblical figure. Salome was the child of Jewish princess Herodias and the stepdaughter of Herod of Antipas, the tetrarch of Judea and vassal to Rome. Wilde's multifaceted snapshot of ancient Judea features many racial and ethnic groups. The play opens with three slaves, a captured young Syrian, a Nubian, and a Cappadocian, all engaged in conversation with Judean soldiers about the lovely princess Salome and the new prisoner Jokanaan. We later learn that Judea's heterogeneity is a product of Roman imperial conquest and Herod of Antipas's military victories in Syria and Cappadocia, an Asia Minor province. When Salome joins the conversation between the soldiers and the slaves, near Jokanaan's cell, she expands on the play's racial and ethnic multiplicity by reporting that Herod is hosting a banquet attended by argumentative Jews from Jerusalem, overly painted Greeks from Smyrna, silent yet subtle Egyptians, and coarse Romans.[35]

Wilde's racially and politically rich representation of the Middle East and eastern Africa seemed like a perfect match for O'Neil's company. In an article published in the *Crisis*, the official magazine of the NAACP, O'Neil asserted that his Negro company "will not do the absurd thing of producing so-called 'Broadway Successes,' which, as you know, have no relation to the life of the Negro, his psychology, his hopes, and aspirations." Instead the ensemble would produce "dramatic pieces which have a universal appeal and are true for the colored people as for the white or yellow races."[36] The mention of "Broadway Successes" was a thinly veiled swipe at the Lafayette Players' practice of restaging condensed versions of commercially proven white dramas with Negro actors. Unlike Anita Bush, O'Neil was interested in dramas that were genuinely universal, not because they embodied European values, aesthetic principles, or psychologies, but because they legitimately spoke to and for all races. Among the plays in the Ethiopian Art Theatre's repertoire, a culturally diverse work like *Salomé* had the most potential to showcase "peculiar racial characteristics" as well as universality.

Within Wilde's symbolist drama, colors abound, with red, vermilion, opal, black, silver, and ivory dominating and metaphorically shaping the play's universe. But whiteness is the most powerful and deadly color, especially Salome's whiteness, and two characters incessantly stare at the princess with dire consequences. As the first victim, a young Syrian slave openly admires Salome's "white hands . . . like white butterflies." He is so obsessed he has to be repeatedly admonished by Herodias's page to stop looking because only bad things happen when he fixates on her whiteness. Inexplicably, the Syrian captive kills himself once Salome focuses her affections on Jokanaan. The other character lost in Salome's whiteness is Herod of Antipas, and he is chided by his wife Herodias for constantly gazing. Herodias warns that looking at Salome is like looking at the moon, and staring at the moon can drive men mad, which could explain the Syrian's suicide. Herod admits he looks at Salome too much and her beauty troubles him, but he makes this admission only after he promised her anything for a dance and she requested Jokanaan's head.[37]

Herein lies the central conflict of *Salomé*: Jokanaan, or John the Baptist, has condemned the union between Herod of Antipas and Herodias as an abomination before Jewish law because Herodias was formerly married to Herod II, the still-living brother of Herod of Antipas. Jokanaan's outspokenness has landed him in Herod's dungeon, and this is where Salome first encounters and falls in love with the incorruptible truth-teller. Apparently, Salome is not the only character emitting an intensely seductive and potentially destructive whiteness, as Jokanaan's whiteness has a magnetic, "moon-like" effect on Salome. She describes Jokanaan as a "thin ivory statue," as "the image of silver," or "as chaste as the moon is." Salome is fully aroused and amorous, as she describes his body as "white like the lilies of the field" or "white like the snows that lie on the mountains." She declares that "nothing in the world is so white as thy body," and the princess feels compelled to touch the imprisoned prophet. Salome is drawn to the purity and chastity of his whiteness, but Jokanaan spurns her advances, even rebukes this alluring princess. Once Salome is rejected, in her now vindictive mind, his white body becomes a "whitened sepulcher full of loathsome things," and his hair is suddenly "like a cluster of grapes, like the clusters of black grapes" or "like a knot of black serpents."[38] This immediate Manichaean shift in Jokanaan's imagery, from pure whiteness to serpentine blackness, speaks directly to Salome's instability, but also to the metaphoric power of color, lightness, and darkness.

In her *Salomé* publicity photos (figs. 11 and 12), Preer visually reads as a light source, a white celestial orb in the darkness. Her light skin was part of Evelyn Preer's physical and performative appeal, and a way for her to achieve the mythic or symbolic power this Salome role demanded. Although she was not white, a fact some critics would dispute, Preer projected the idea of whiteness as purity and luminescence so central to Wilde's text. This visual dynamic resonates with Richard Dyer's work on whiteness, femininity, luminosity, and purity in film representations. Dyer remarks how white leading ladies, such as the early film star Lillian Gish, were able to project themselves as morally and aesthetically superior by becoming the focus of the light. At times Gish was so suffused with light onscreen that she appeared to be the energy source from which beams were emanating.[39] In figure 12, Preer's light skin seems to produce significant lumens, as if she were indeed a source of morality and virtue.

Figure 11 Evelyn Preer in Oscar Wilde's *Salomé*. Courtesy of the Crisis Publishing Co., Inc., publisher of the magazine of the National Association for the Advancement of Colored People. This image was first published in the February 1924 issue of *Crisis Magazine*.

Figure 12 Two poses of Evelyn Preer in Oscar Wilde's *Salomé*. Courtesy of the Crisis Publishing Co., Inc., publisher of the magazine of the National Association for the Advancement of Colored People. This image was first published in the February 1924 issue of *Crisis Magazine*.

As for universality, Preer's luminescence also projected a multi-signifying Negro performer with the visual capacity to play any woman. For a black female in the early twentieth century this was quite an achievement, and Preer was creating a template for future universalizing black female performers such as Fredi Washington, Diana Sands, Anna Deavere Smith, and Sarah Jones. However, several white critics in 1923 New York expressed deep discomfort with the mutability and seeming racial counterfeit of Preer's stage European. John Corbin, critic for the *New York Times*, felt something was awry and expressed his consternation: "To begin with, those who expect the barbaric splendor of 'a rich jewel in an Ethiope's ear' will be disappointed. The complexions of the company run through the lighter shades of café au lait: several of the abler players might easily pass for white. . . . The mental testers have found that negro intelligence increases with the admixture of white blood, and the director of this theatre, Mr. Raymond O'Neil, seems to have come to the same conclusion with regard to artistic talent."[40] As an audience member, Corbin felt duped by the company's name, the Ethiopian Art Theatre, and he complained that "what is described as from darkest Africa is in reality of frosty Caucasus, almost imperceptibly *negroid*." Exhibiting a serious case of the Nordic Complex, Corbin accuses O'Neil of stacking his company with quadroons and octoroons to ensure a talented ensemble; this racist comment demeans the intelligence of Negro actors and ascribes any histrionic skill to percentages of white blood.

Intent on wading through the whiteness to find the African, Corbin singles out Sidney Kirkpatrick's Herod as "powerfully Ethiopian." Corbin praises his "torrential flood of words" as "deeply felt and justly phrased," and he claims that when Kirkpatrick "is stirred to the depths it is the spirit of the jungle that finds utterance." When confronted with the results of miscegenation in America and with a previously hidden tradition of performed whiteness, Corbin reached for racialist, pseudoscientific assumptions and stereotypic jungle utterances to find comfort and security. He was not alone in his reductive responses, as his fellow white critics also rejected Preer's Salome and the other stage Europeans in a similarly derisive fashion.

Alexander Woollcott's *New York Herald and Tribune* article, mockingly titled "Black Art," claimed that a "chance passerby [who] drifted into the theater a little too late to consult his program before the darkening of the house would sit all through 'Salome' without the faintest notion that these were negro or negroid players." Percy Hammond of the *New York Tribune* remarked that Preer "appeared to be as fair as most brunette players are, with no traces of African ancestry." Like Corbin, he "wondered why they would call her an Ethiopian actress" at all.[41] To reconcile Preer's performance, which he admits was impressive, with this visual dissonance, Hammond was forced to conclude that "her representation of Salome is that of a white actress rather than that of a negress; and so it is not the unusual stunt that it is alleged to be." O'Neil and Preer were hardly perpetrating a racially counterfeit "stunt" on the American public; Hammond, Corbin, and Woollcott were merely victims of the Nordic Complex. These white critics could not move beyond America's color psychology and applaud luminosity and universality in a nonwhite actress.

Returning to our biblical-turned-theatrical princess, how might Salome's whiteness, in relation to her Jewishness, read for American audiences in the 1920s? Historian David Roediger found that throughout the 1910s, a decade marked by race riots and hate crimes against Jews and Negroes, Jewish communities "at times identified with both the suffering and the aspirations of African Americans." Yet as the numbers of Jewish immigrants increased and their economic position improved in the United States, Roediger noticed a new "in-between" racial position for Jews. They were not "fully admitted to Anglo-whiteness but not racialized as definitely colored." Jews began to occupy a liminal space between whiteness and blackness, an "in-between consciousness" that assimilated somewhat but did not melt into a "full identification with whiteness" or sacrifice their "strong national/cultural identifications as Jews."[42] Similarly, Matthew Jacobson contends that we need to appreciate the "historical process of racial mutability" as it applies to European ethnic groups, understand this long and complicated progression of becoming Caucasian in the United States. Under the 1790 immigration restrictions, Jews may have been admitted to the country as "free white persons" and could be naturalized as citizens, but in the 1920s, Jews in America were still seen as both white and "other."[43]

Offering another perspective on whiteness and Jewishness, during a dialogue with Cornel West on black/Jewish conflicts and commonalities, Rabbi Michael Lerner explained that "to be 'white' is to fit into the social construct of the beneficiaries of European imperialism, whose relationship to the world has been one of conquest." According to Lerner, historically Jews have not been the beneficiaries of the privileges of white skin; in fact, Jews "have been socially and legally discriminated against, have been the subject of racism and genocide, and in those terms Jews are not white." He further claims that when Jews are called white, their history of oppression is effectively denied.[44]

In Wilde's re-created Judea, Salome's whiteness is seemingly disconnected from nation or religion. She never identifies with the Jewishness surrounding her, especially the argumentative Pharisees and Sadducees debating in her stepfather's court. In fact Salome, Herodias, and Herod of Antipas, all Jewish by lineage, seem to identify more with Roman imperial power and Judea's ancillary position of privilege. So by Rabbi Lerner's definition, Wilde's Salome would register as white, not because she is Jewish by birth, but because her privileged Judean family is directly benefiting from an imperial whiteness. Also on a highly visual yet morbid level, this princess of Jewish heritage is drawn to the vivid whiteness of the outspoken Jewish prophet Jokanaan, a "thin ivory statue" whose vermilion lips Salome just has to kiss, even after his death. She is drawn to his purity, his chastity, and his goodness, which is only rivaled by the moon in its stark whiteness. Metaphorically, Wilde's symbolist drama vacillates between an imperial, harsh, even sadistic whiteness and a purer, virtuous, spiritual whiteness of the incorruptible Jewish prophet. These are the varieties of whiteness Preer attempted to balance in her conception of Salome.

Chaste Virgin or Monstrous Seductress

In *Opportunity*, the official magazine of the National Urban League, journalist Esther Fulks Scott published a glowing article/interview on the Ethiopian Art Theatre's *Salomé*. In the piece, Preer explains her conception of the role and the infamous "Dance of the Seven Veils": "Salome was a religious fanatic and a virtuous girl who had given her heart to Jokanaan. She did not want to dance for Herod, nor did she want to attract him. Her dance then would necessarily be a chaste and restrained one. I felt that an impassioned dance would be entirely out of keeping with Salome's emotion at the time."[45] Some critics might dismiss Preer's "virtuous girl" gone horribly awry interpretation as a misread of Wilde's aesthetic attack on Victorian morality, but there is textual support for this approach. In the final moments, as Salome holds Jokanaan's head and is about to kiss his vermilion lips, she explains, "I was a princess, and thou didst scorn me. I was a virgin, and thou didst take my virginity from me. I was chaste, and thou didst fill my veins with fire."[46] Salome remembers herself, socially and sexually, as an unspoiled royal personage set apart, cloistered.

At their first encounter, Jokanaan obliterated that chaste self-image when he became the first man the Judean princess ever loved. Metaphorically, she became a woman when Jokanaan looked at her because her heart was filled with desire, but his rejection transformed her love into an irrational hatred. As for the infamous dance, Preer was sensitive to its objectionable reputation, but she believed that moment was not about seducing Herod; rather, it was about getting what she wanted, the head of the prophet who filled her heart with fire and then scorned her. Preer fully appreciated Salome's fragile emotional state as she danced to ensure the execution of the only man she ever loved, so an "impassioned dance" or an erotic performance would have been dramatically inappropriate.

An undeniable struggle between purity and depravity rages throughout Oscar Wilde's *Salomé*, and in early twentieth-century American performance, depravity appeared to dominate operatic, dramatic, and modern dance incarnations of this now infamous princess. German composer Richard Strauss devised an operatic version of Wilde's one-act drama, which debuted in Europe in 1905 and premiered at New York's Metropolitan Opera House in 1907. Strauss's staging featured an intensely sexual "Dance of the Seven Veils" and an excessively macabre final scene in which Salome caressed and kissed Jokanaan's severed head. After this stunningly provocative American debut, the Met banned Strauss's opera from their stage, yet the production generated enough national interest to warrant a multicity tour in 1909.

Feeding off the *Salomé* excitement in the early 1900s, roughly twenty-four different New York dancers, primarily in vaudeville houses, exploited Salome's "forbidden" "Dance of the Seven Veils" to advance their careers.[47] Within this "Salomania," the predominant conception of the Judean princess was as a monstrous, mesmerizing, all-consuming seductress, an image very much at odds with Preer's approach to the character. Salome's stage reputation was so notorious that when Raymond O'Neil attempted to arrange a Boston engagement for the Ethiopian Art Theatre's *Salomé*, he was denied. In October 1923, Boston mayor James Curley also banned Richard Strauss's operatic version from his city because he felt it "would in no way contribute to the purification of the moral atmosphere of our people."[48]

I presume O'Neil and Preer's *Salomé*, unlike Strauss's, never approximated necrophilia onstage because neither the Chicago nor the New York press mentioned that level of spectacle. In April 1923, the Negro Folk Theatre moved from Washington, D.C., to Harlem's Lafayette Theatre, and

Salome's signature dance again drew focus. The *New York Age* ran an introductory article to generate interest and assuage patrons who might object to the assumed immorality of *Salomé*. The Negro weekly announced that "the famous 'Dance of the Seven Veils' is reported to be marvelous in its beauty and yet entirely within the edicts of the most drastic censorship."[49] As a preemptive and protective move, the Lafayette Theatre managers shifted the focus of this notorious dance from death and decadence to aesthetic beauty and societal respectability.

The theater's shrewd publicity spin was legitimate given the fact that Preer's conception of the role was less sensationalized than that of her contemporaries. And among the many dancing, singing, and emoting Salomes circulating throughout the United States, there was already a precedent for a more reserved interpretation. African American modern dancer Aida Overton Walker was the first black woman to perform the "Dance of the Seven Veils." David Krasner and Daphne Brooks have situated Aida Walker, the onetime head choreographer for the Williams and Walker Company, in the context of black musicals, modern dance, and Salomania. In 1908, Walker first ventured into the world of modern dance by interpolating her modest version of Salome's dance into *Bandana Land*, a musical comedy created by Bert Williams and George Walker. Four years later, she developed a one-woman show around the much-discussed veil dance. Krasner stresses that Walker entered her modern dance project fully committed to "the social propriety and racial uplift" of the black middle class, which meant she would not sacrifice black female respectability for professional notoriety. Thus, her Salome strove to be "more dramatic and less erotic" than that of her white female contemporaries, who generally performed a hedonistic Judean princess on vaudeville and operatic stages.[50]

Daphne Brooks similarly reads Walker as a New Negro activist who used this infamous white female figure to reposition black women. Despite an assumed "deviant black female sexuality" and the mainstream media's desire to eroticize her performance, Brooks claims Walker presented the black female body as a source of "visceral, visible aesthetic agency and desire."[51] In publicity photos for Aida Overton Walker's Salome, she wears a sequined or bespangled robe and her neckline plunges to reveal a modicum of cleavage. Walker's agenda, according to Brooks, was to unleash the "unspeakable language of black female erotic energy" but to do so on her own terms.[52] When Preer interpreted Salome, she elected to perform in a similarly modest costume, showing no cleavage but baring her tantalizing shoulders (see figs. 11 and 12). Preer's interpretation of the "Dance of the Seven Veils" was less erotic than Walker's, but both performers emphasized Salome's emotional intensity and her desire, not the desire of male spectators.

Preer's atypical approach to this controversial role would become an issue in the critical debates over stage Europeans. Certain reviewers embraced her intense yet modest Salome. *Chicago Evening Post* critic Sam Putnam felt Preer's "Salome was a saint rather than a devil. Her dance was one of the most chaste exhibitions I have ever seen. It was almost austere."[53] Putnam further commented that "as one of the several Salomes to be encountered in Wilde's drama of decadent estheticism, it is a contribution to the theatre, and one which should remain." He not only applauded Preer's nearly austere conception of the part, but in comparing her to the many other Salomes, he declared that her "contribution to theatre" should be respected for its innovation and endorsed as a future model for the Judean princess. A reviewer named Metcalfe, writing for the *Wall Street Journal*, felt Preer's execution of the climactic dance wooden and underwhelming, and he claimed that Oscar Wilde probably would have objected to this stage European performance. Nevertheless, he conceded that no other production of *Salomé*, operatic, dramatic, or vaudevillian, demonstrated "more concentrated attention" to Wilde's original text.[54]

Unimpressed by textual fidelity or the Lafayette Theatre's claim of respectability, West Indian cultural critic Hubert Harrison strongly objected to the Ethiopian Art Theatre using prurient material like *Salomé* to showcase Negro talent. Following a dinner conversation about *Salomé* with literary luminaries Carl Van Vechten, H. L. Mencken, and Theodore Dreiser, Harrison wrote an essay titled "The Negro Actor on Broadway: A Critical Interpretation by a Negro Critic." In this piece, Harrison dismissed *Salomé* as a "hot-house product" and "a spiritual and artistic miasma" with no higher purpose than decadence. He marveled at Preer's voice but regretted that her talents were used to express a "perverted passion for John the Baptist."[55]

Like many male critics, Harrison was perhaps uncomfortable with Salome's potent sexuality and was looking for ways to diminish this feminine power.[56] In addition, like many New Negro cultural nationalists, Harrison linked racial progress to patriarchal gender roles whereby black women were protected, provided for, and praised for their beauty. Black bourgeois convention dictated that a black woman's power should stretch no further than her place in the home as a wife and a mother.[57] For Harrison, Preer's appropriation of a legendary seductress posed a problem for racial uplift and middle-class values because it failed to promote black women as venerated symbols of a controllable domesticity.

Harrison's racial, moral, and gendered objections were echoed by *New York Times* critic John Corbin. While conceding that the "idea behind the Ethiopian Art Theatre was psychologically sound and practically constructive," Corbin felt *Salomé* was the wrong vehicle to demonstrate racial progress. He wrote, "Whatever may be the artistic value of Oscar Wilde's sadistic vagaries, they are ill adapted to the purpose of affording an unfortunately suppressed people a wholesome outlet for their emotions."[58] Corbin also tried to contain or undermine Preer's agency by questioning her simultaneously chaste and fanatical conception of Salome. He understood that O'Neil's agenda was "to display the virtuosity of his company," and he considered the entire production "dignified and impressive"; but he found Preer's Salome merely "adequate." In his words, "She was quite without the distinction of great art, which alone can compensate for such an exhibition."[59] Corbin felt that if Preer had achieved unparalleled artistry, the inclusion of this morally objectionable play would have been justified; but regrettably, the star actress did not deliver. And Corbin blamed Preer's mere adequacy on her indecisiveness. He wrote that she was "reasonably well equipped for the physical demands of the role, but apparently uncertain, artistically, whether it were better to be bold and brazen or coy and hard to please." From his perspective, Preer's attempt to balance spiritual purity and sadistic fanaticism devolved into a muddled performance. Corbin felt she needed to choose one definitive idea of Salome and move confidently in that direction.

Corbin and Harrison failed to appreciate that Preer's dualistic approach was tied not just to her nuanced reading of Wilde's *Salomé* but to the expectations attached to this white role and black female sexuality. According to Daphne Brooks, the legendary, biblical Salome had been portrayed as merely seductive until Oscar Wilde's *Salomé* introduced a three-dimensional female character with a real psychology. Preer continued to flesh out her psychology, that third dimension, by developing an intensely spiritual young girl who sinks into depravity. Despite succumbing to moments of "murderous eroticism," Wilde, Brooks argues, managed to shift the dramatic focus from "heterosexual male desire" to an "open-ended sexual expressiveness rooted in the female performer's potential agency."[60] In the biblical and theatrical narratives, Salome is a powerful seductress who makes men do what she wants. Yet, referring back to

Preer's conception of the role, in the moment of seduction, she chose to play Salome not as dancing to be the object of Herod's desire but, rather, as pursuing her now perverted sense of pleasure and justice.

Writing about female blues and jazz singers, like Bessie Smith and Lena Horne, cultural critic Hortense Spillers characterizes these women as role models who redefined black female sexuality as the "physical expression of the highest self-regard."[61] I would add Preer and Aida Overton Walker to the list of redefining women who devised ways not merely to corroborate prevalent notions of black female sexuality but to stage their own unique senses of self and cultural power. Preer's virtuoso performance asserted female agency and filled the stage with a large mythic presence, while also externalizing Salome's troubled psyche. And as Preer expanded popular conceptions of Salome and black women, we should remember that she was "trespassing" on presumably white performative property, playing a role Oscar Wilde would never have expected a Negro to fill. Finally Preer was redefining white and black female imagery not on the margins but on Broadway, at the center of American entertainment. As Spillers points out, black women "do not live out their destiny on the periphery of American race and gender magic but in the center of its Manichaean darkness."[62] Again we return to a duality of lightness and darkness, with Preer attempting to function as a universalizing, cross-cultural beacon cutting through racial and gendered darkness.

Cultural Legibility

On the question of whether stage Europeans were aesthetically beneficial to black actors and culturally legible to American audiences, the original supporters of the Chicago-based social and aesthetic experiment enthusiastically endorsed Negro performers in white roles. In fact, the hometown press praised *Salomé*, often to the exclusion of other more culturally appropriate repertory pieces, such as Willis Richardson's folk drama *Chip Woman's Fortune*. White critic Sam Putnam, of the *Chicago Evening Post*, was pleasantly surprised by the Negro ensemble's "distinctive interpretation" of white theatrical material. Putnam also admitted he did not realize Negroes could deliver controlled, multidimensional performances: "[We] discovered that the Negro is capable of restraint as well as abandon, a quality which may not have been credited in the past."[63] Apparently, O'Neil's twelve-month training program produced a level of mastery and restraint rarely seen or acknowledged in black actors. Putnam probably anticipated an intensely emotional, highly physical performance, but he was open to leaving his Nordic Complex behind.

Ashton Stevens, of the *Chicago Herald and Examiner*, noted Preer's beauty and intelligence, a rare combination for critical commentary on black female performers. Stevens called her "a gorgeous creature, whose reading is even more thrilling than her person. Words just seem to breathe from her, with the impulsiveness of a bird; and there is behind her reading a high and very unbirdlike quality of intelligence."[64] Preer's person may have been impressive and appealing, but Stevens was clearly taken with her mastery of Wilde's language. She managed to strike a delicate balance between Salome's impulsiveness, or emotional instability, and a "very unbirdlike" or grounded understanding of the dark psyche she was interpreting. In the *Chicago Tribune*, white critic Sheppard Butler applauded the intelligence of the entire cast, writing, "These players give a thoughtful and imaginative performance of *Salomé*. There is reticence in it and intelligent feeling both for the poetry and the horror of the tale."[65] Butler's use of "reticence" echoes Sam Putnam's comment on the restraint displayed by the Negro players. Like Ashton Stevens, Butler stressed the dualities in the production, "the poetry and the horror," which is fully realized in the final moments when Salome reaches her lyrical heights during a most monstrous encounter with a severed head.

The New York media was far less supportive of an all-Negro *Salomé* yet still managed to praise certain elements of Preer's performance. But instead of mastery, restraint, or intelligence, the *New York Tribune*'s Percy Hammond emphasized more culturally stereotypic traits such as musicality and passion: "Miss Preer pictures Salome with a musical voice, an authentic stage manner, and a relentless abandon that make Miss Mary Garden's business-like impersonation seem a shrinking timidity."[66] For Hammond, Preer's musicality and emotional acting style registered her as culturally Negro and distinct from white performers. Mary Garden was a Scottish soprano considered the greatest singing actress of her generation. She starred in the 1905 premiere of Strauss's *Salomé* in Paris and reprised the title role in the 1909 U.S. tour.[67] Hammond interjected Garden to distinguish the emotionality of Negro versus white actors, a reductive contrast Raymond O'Neil had already drawn. Much like O'Neil tagged white actors as inhibited and black actors as expressively supple, Hammond reinforced this popular perception by comparing an unrestrained Preer and her "relentless abandon" with the "business-like" and restrained Garden.

Ironically, in Hammond's predictable comparison between black and white artists, Preer emerged as the more complete and compelling artist. Hammond was impressed with the versatility she displayed on Broadway, and he wrote that "Miss Preer, who is so complete as the gorgeous and abnormal voluptuary of 'Salome,' plays a sloppy negress in the 'Chip Woman's Fortune,' and she plays it perfectly. Though we are enthusiastic concerning the prowess of the current white actresses, we feel that few of them are able to do what this so-called colored lady does." On a nightly basis, Preer transformed from a "sloppy negress" in Willis Richardson's folk drama to a stunningly seductive yet abnormal stage European in Wilde's symbolist drama. Percy Hammond doubted any white actress in New York could match this feat, but then again, he also slyly questioned the racial credentials of Preer, a "so-called colored lady."

Although some New York critics commended Preer's work as Salome, most reviewers—black and white—agreed that Richardson's *Chip Woman's Fortune*, the first serious drama by a Negro on Broadway, was the more culturally legible and appropriate vehicle for African American talent.[68] Even Abram L. Harris, who encouraged Negro actors to appropriate Shakespeare and Molière, admitted he preferred *Chip Woman* over *Salomé*. John Corbin, in the *New York Times*, found it regrettable that the Ethiopian Art Theatre's productions "had no moments at all when it was Ethiopian."[69] The week after Corbin's review, O'Neil replaced *Salomé* with a jazzy version of *Comedy of Errors* at the Frazee, and the *New York Herald* declared this "blackened" version of *Comedy* was still not Negroid enough, despite the interjection of a Bert Williams song. It seems O'Neil was failing to draw out the Negro's "peculiar racial characteristics" with Wilde and Shakespeare, so the *New York Herald* suggested the black troupe retreat to Chicago and return when they had a repertoire of Negro plays.[70]

It would appear Preer and company's bold experiment was stalling in the second function of whiting up, building imitative or emulative stage Europeans to affect professional and political progress. Even black audiences seemed to reject *Salomé* and its serious, cross-racial play. Sheppard Butler's review of the Chicago debut noted how initially Negro audiences would "titter at the wrong moments" until they realized *Salomé* was a tragedy and then they sat "abashed" and not necessarily empowered. During the company's brief run at Harlem's Lafayette Theatre, W. E. Clark of the *New York Age* reported that "some did not realize that the play was not a comedy nor did they know that its plot was taken from a Biblical story. This lack of understanding by the audience made the acting extremely difficult."[71] In fact, Lafayette management was forced to remove unruly patrons who were unwilling or perhaps unprepared to sit through something other than a comedy or musical revue. Ignorance or resistance from their Negro public made a full realization of this experimental modern drama on the Lafayette Theatre stage nearly impossible for O'Neil, Preer, and company.

So why was *Salomé* not progressively resonant or culturally legible for some black patrons in Harlem and Chicago? Two possible political reasons have already been mentioned. First, Salome violated black middle-class aspirations for Victorian morality; the production was counterproductive for "race" men and women committed to racial uplift. Second, Salome was too powerful for a family-centered image of the New Negro woman. Preer may have failed to sell or fully realize her restrained yet fervent conception of Salome and was overpowered by the popular perception that this was, as Hubert Harrison suggests, a drama about perversion. But there were other possible explanations for why this material was unfit for Negro talent or incompatible with the current entertainment preferences of middle- and working-class black audiences.

Theophilus Lewis, an outspoken critic for the *Messenger*, identified the disconnection between the Ethiopian Art Theatre's stage European repertoire and Negro audiences. He explained how the "better classes" of Negroes were traditionally indifferent to Negro theatrical production, so the lower orders, or "dregs," largely determined what kind of Negro theater would prevail. Consequently, the most culturally legible or acceptable black theatrical productions were musicals and low comedies bereft of wit. Lewis went a step further and claimed that even when educated Negroes demanded a certain caliber of Negro entertainment, they insisted their Negro theater copy the "manners and conventions of the contemporary white American theatre, unaware that the white stage reflects the racial experience of a people whose cultural background has never resembled ours."[72]

The implication here is that Preer performing Salome was not in the best interest of the race or racial progress because whiting up tried to embrace a foreign and culturally inaccessible experience. Lewis distilled the long-term sustainability and desirability of stage Europeans down to this challenge: "whether a youthful people living in the midst of an old and moribund civilization shall die with or find themselves able to shake loose from its complexities and build their own culture on its ruins." Unlike *Messenger* critic Abram L. Harris, who recommended trespassing on "dead" white dramas, Lewis advocated that neophyte black theatrical artists build a fresh and vibrant culture on what remained of the old white ruins. Lewis believed there was ample talent among Negro performers, and "where considerable racial or national theatrical talent exits you quite naturally expect to find an indigenous theatre striving to interpret the group life and character." Sadly, for Lewis and other critics like Hubert Harrison, what inhibited the emergence of a vibrant Negro theater was an almost sycophantic dependency on white dramatic material and leadership.

With this attack on stage Europeans, Lewis was taking direct aim at Raymond O'Neil and his modernist project, but in other articles, he singled out the Lafayette Players as the one "adult effort" with a chance to forge a sustainable Negro company. However, unlike Lester A. Walton, who praised Anita Bush and her players for exploring stage Europeans, Lewis was not impressed with the second cultural function of whiting up. He claimed this derivative Negro company "has not attempted to achieve distinction by presenting anything novel or provocative of thought; it has not even kept pace with the white theatre it set out to imitate."[73] Lewis also lamented that Negro theaters lacked unique dramas about black life; therefore, performers such as Charles Gilpin and Paul Robeson were unable to develop as serious actors "at home" and had to build careers in white theaters. So at least the *Messenger* critic understood why Negro actors were gravitating toward white theaters, playwrights, and roles.

In his essay "The Negro Actor on Broadway," Hubert Harrison weighed in on this debate over cultural legibility, but with an emphasis on what Negro actors should be performing and what Broadway should be producing. Harrison declared that with Richardson's *Chip Woman's Fortune*, a folk play about a mother's love for her son, the Ethiopian Art Theatre "achieved as notable a success in this season as Charles Gilpin did in *The Emperor Jones*." By linking a young Negro playwright, Richardson, to an established white dramatist, Eugene O'Neill, Harrison anointed *Chip Woman's Fortune* as the future of Negro theater. He also shrewdly posed this rhetorical question to the Ethiopian Art Theatre: "What was the contribution, the new and unique thing, which these players contributed to Broadway?"[74] Harrison and white critics like John Corbin and Alexander Woollcott all arrived at the same answer: An average Broadway company could mount a competent production of *Salomé*, but few could stage creditable productions of *Chip Woman's Fortune*.[75] *Chip Woman* offered Broadway something unique: a Negro play by a Negro writer with Negro actors in a recognizably Negro situation.

Ultimately, contemporary black critics Harrison and Lewis concluded

Salomé was a poor fit for black audiences because the masses were unprepared for or indifferent to modernist experiments unrelated to the everyday aspirations of most African Americans. Theater historians Addell Austin Anderson and Jane Peterson similarly concluded that Raymond O'Neil badly miscalculated on his material, his actors, and his audience. He erred by selecting a repertory of predominantly European plays for a Negro company, by presenting his Negro actors before they were ready for Broadway, by marketing a peculiar combination of Negro actors and "high art" in the epicenter of American commercial theater, and finally by pushing stage Europeans before the national press was prepared to interpret what they saw. As for the press, Jane Peterson concluded that this "white repertory performed by a 'high yeller' cast and directed by a white proponent of art theatre" was ultimately "unable to fulfill the expectations of a press demanding images of Africa or at least 'the South which is the Negro's true background.'"[76] In other words, the Nordic Complex ultimately prevented black and white Americans from accepting anything other than "jungle utterances" or authentic Negroid art from black performers.

Obviously Raymond O'Neil and Evelyn Preer disagreed with the critics on their theatrical gamble. At a time when black musicals like *Shuffle Along* and *Runnin' Wild* virtually defined African American theater, Preer wanted to master a modernist drama so future generations of Negro actors could entertain more progressive options. Preer was committed to the second cultural function of whiting up, and she articulated her representational agenda in Esther Scott's article/interview. After the comedic actress and singer received extensive dramatic training under O'Neil, she was confident she had found her true theatrical calling. She was now inspired "to go higher," and her ambition was to continue performing dramatic roles. According to Scott's article, Preer's newfound mission was to contribute "her talents towards dramatic culture," and she believed the entire social and cultural movement launched by O'Neil and the Chicago association was "a wonderful opportunity for Negroes to demonstrate dramatic ability along more serious lines than musical comedy."[77]

Crisis editor W. E. B. DuBois, a strong and active supporter of Raymond O'Neil's stage European project, offered the best concluding assessment of the Ethiopian Art Theatre. In a July 1923 editorial, he wrote, "Financially the experiment was a failure; but dramatically and spiritually it was one of the greatest successes that this country has seen."[78] DuBois did not elaborate on this hyperbolic statement, but he probably considered this touring production a major dramatic and spiritual achievement because it brought the first serious Negro playwright to Broadway, paired an innovative white director with Negro performers, and fused black artists with European art theatre—all in a country thoroughly segregated in its most basic pursuits. He did explain that when "a black American does anything well there is immediate consternation," and he specifically singled out Preer, who "comes to Broadway and does Salome better than New York ever saw it done." According to DuBois, whenever a Negro does "it better than the white man, then it is dangerous to allow him to do it." This claim rings true, especially considering how disturbed certain white critics were with Preer's racial and performative transgressions. On the surface, they felt deceived by her visual image, but on a deeper level, they were disturbed that Preer exhibited beauty, power, intelligence, luminosity, and virtuosity—qualities traditionally reserved for universalized white actresses. One white critic, perhaps offering some indication of a qualified success, did shed his Nordic Complex long enough to extol Preer as a potential model for future Salomes.

Thanks in large part to Evelyn Preer's virtuoso sojourn into the Manichaean darkness, another actress, Fredi Washington, was able to break through important professional barriers. In 1926 Washington played the mulatto Edith Warren opposite Paul Robeson in *Black Boy* on Broadway, thus becoming the first Negro actress to portray a mulatto on the Great White Way. As mentioned earlier, such biracial roles were typically handled by white actors, despite objections from black dramatists like Langston Hughes. After this theatrical first, Washington was pressured to strategically pass, socially and artistically, to gain even better roles on Broadway and in Hollywood, but she refused. Her greatest film achievement would be playing the passing mulatto Peola Johnson in the 1934 film *Imitation of Life*. This was yet another significant moment for Negro actors because a black woman was finally being featured in a Hollywood film, and not as a strumpet or a servant.[79] Preer's dualistic, redefined Salome, which broadened how America viewed black female artists, made Washington's representational breakthroughs possible.

"A White Canada Lee": Gimmick or Breakthrough

One potential lesson learned from the Ethiopian Art Theatre's economic and perhaps cultural failure was that there had to be a more productive vehicle for merging Negro actors with European or Euro-American dramas. The trick was finding that middle ground where white dramatic material was "blackened" or made sufficiently "Negroid" to ease the sensory crises of white critics like John Corbin, Alexander Woollcott, and Percy Hammond. Raymond O'Neil experimented with a more culturally legible alternative when he replaced *Salomé*, for one week in May 1923, with a jazz-inflected version of Shakespeare's *Comedy of Errors*. In addition, the Ethiopian Art Theatre placed the medieval drama *Everyman* in a "black and tan" or integrated cabaret. John Corbin reviewed the swinging, all-Negro *Comedy of Errors*, and although he was unimpressed with the "various shades of café au lait and dissonances suggestive of the African Jungle," he loved the comedic work of an actor named Charles Olden. Olden performed both Dromios, and Corbin declared him "a genuine low-comedy figure" who possessed "a native instinct for clowning." He was especially impressed with Olden's rhythmical nature, his "waltzing as he speaks and speaking as he waltzes." If all of O'Neil's Negro actors had exhibited Olden's "grace and inspiration," Corbin might have declared their ambitious theatrical experiment a success.[80]

One compelling production that merged European form and historical content with Negro talent was Virgil Thomson and Gertrude Stein's highly experimental opera *Four Saints in Three Acts*. Conceived in the late 1920s and developed over several years in Paris and New York, *Four Saints* debuted on Broadway in February 1934 and became the longest-running opera in Broadway history. Thomson and Stein's plot-free production takes sixteenth-century Spanish saints as its vibrant subjects but features a musical score that sounds more religious and folkloric than operatic. The original opera showcased an all-Negro cast of singers and dancers under the choral direction of Eva Jessye and the stage direction of a young John Houseman. According to cultural historian Steven Watson, this project was a "self-consciously American" piece in which two American expatriates, Thomson and Stein, effectively merged Negro urban chic, high-art bohemia, the modern museum movement, and commercial theater. In terms of whiting up, Watson also declared *Four Saints* a "landmark event" for Negro artists because "never before had African Americans been cast in a work that did not depict black life."[81] More accurately, Thomson and Stein's modernist use of stage Europeans extended the work of Raymond O'Neil and Evelyn Preer's *Salomé*. Whether they realized it or not, Thomson and Stein were directly contributing to this Afro-Diasporic tradition of performed whiteness.

In subsequent years, other, more racially conscious mergers of black talent and white theatrical material produced major critical and commercial successes. First, in 1936, the Federal Theatre Project's (FTP) *Macbeth* successfully transplanted Shakespeare from Scotland to nineteenth-century Haiti. The Harlem Negro unit of the FTP, under the direction of another young white director, Orson Welles, staged this fascinating marriage of early modern drama and postcolonial black republic at the Lafayette Theatre. Then, in 1944, Abram Hill of the American Negro Theatre (ANT) convinced screenwriter Philip Yordan to allow him to transform Yordan's Polish family drama into a "dramedy" about an African American family. The ANT's *Anna Lucasta* debuted in Harlem and later transferred into a long Broadway run.[82] With both of these "blackened" commercial productions drawing significant audiences, when would another "straight" stage European production like *Salomé* or *Four Saints in Three Acts* get another chance on Broadway? In September 1946, in Boston, Negro actor and political activist Canada Lee would apply an experimental white face paint to play the Spanish role of Daniel de Bosola in John Webster's *Duchess of Malfi* (1614). Months before Lee's Boston debut, the New York press was dissecting this bold casting decision and anticipating a history-making Broadway premiere.

Leonard Lionel Cornelius Canegata was born in 1907 in Harlem, and after many artistic twists and athletic turns, he would become Canada Lee, Broadway star, Hollywood actor, and leftist activist.[83] Lee's personal history, marked by encounters with perceived and real racial barriers, explains why he would take on a role like Bosola and test the limits of what was possible for a Negro actor in the 1940s. Lee Canegata first showed artistic promise as a classically trained violinist when he made his concert debut at age eleven, but in an impulsive move, the prodigy abandoned classical music because he did not see a future for a black man in this profession. Instead, he ran away from home to learn to race thoroughbreds as an apprentice jockey at Saratoga Race Course in upstate New York. He was not the most skilled or motivated jockey, and visible, virulent racism forced Lee out of the horse racing industry.

After frustrating stints as a welterweight boxing contender and the owner of a small jazz club, in 1934, a jobless, penniless, and uneducated Canada Lee wandered into the Harlem YMCA and into a production of Frank Wilson's minstrel-tinged comedy *Brother Mose*. The production was part of a state-sponsored work-relief program for unemployed actors, and Lee's next major acting break would come through another publicly funded relief effort, the aforementioned 1936 FTP production of *Mac-*

beth. Lee played Banquo, a minor role, but when Welles introduced him to Shakespeare, Lee realized theater was where he belonged. He worked with Welles again, in 1941 on Broadway, when Lee created the role of Bigger Thomas in a stage adaptation of Richard Wright's *Native Son*. From there, Lee's theatrical star ascended. After a quick trip to Hollywood to struggle with a mildly stereotypic role in Alfred Hitchcock's 1943 *Lifeboat*, Lee returned to Broadway with a small role in the ANT remount of *Anna Lucasta*. After six weeks with that long-running hit, Lee jumped ship to play Caliban in Margaret Webster's production of *The Tempest*. Still energized by his first encounter with *Macbeth*, Lee was eager for another Shakespearean challenge, and more importantly, he was determined to not allow anything to limit his acting prospects.

The *New York Amsterdam News* and the *Pittsburgh Courier*, two black newspapers, openly criticized Lee's decision to play Caliban, claiming he would demean the race by portraying this monstrous character. According to biographer Mona Z. Smith, Lee understood their concerns, but he wanted to end the practice of classical roles going exclusively to white actors. Following Robeson's 1943 success with *Othello*, Lee wanted to become the second black actor to perform a classical role on Broadway. Lee's ambition was commendable, but it was historically impossible, because just two decades earlier, Raymond O'Neil's Ethiopian Art Theatre had featured Negro actors in Shakespeare's *Comedy of Errors* at Broadway's Frazee Theatre. But Lee did have a significant "first" in his future. After wrapping up his run in *The Tempest*, Lee turned to producing and starring in *On Whitman Avenue*, a new play by a white writer named Maxine Wood that dealt with housing discrimination in a middle-class white neighborhood. With the help of his friend Mark Marvin, Lee premiered *On Whitman Avenue* at the Cort Theatre in May 1946, becoming the first black producer of a drama on Broadway.

Lee's next and perhaps greatest challenge was a potentially game-changing stage European opportunity. While in rehearsals in Providence, Rhode Island, for a Broadway-bound production of W. H. Auden's adaptation of John Webster's *Duchess of Malfi*, starring Elizabeth Bergner and John Carradine, director George Rylands received some disturbing news. McKay Morris, who was cast in the critical role of Daniel de Bosola, was forced to leave the production for health reasons.[84] As producer Paul Czinner frantically searched for a replacement, he and his wife Elizabeth Bergner agreed that they needed a replacement with "real playing power." Both were familiar with Lee's work and felt they needed someone dynamic like him, "a white Canada Lee," but then Czinner and Bergner realized they should just ask Lee if he wanted the part.

After *On Whitman Avenue* closed, the *Duchess of Malfi* producers officially offered Lee the role; he accepted and immediately began rehearsing. Expert makeup artists were flown in to experiment with a special white paste for Lee's impersonation of the white villain Bosola. Lee missed the entire run in Providence and even delayed his debut in Boston because he did not want to "mess this up by a poor performance." Lee finally debuted as Bosola on September 25, 1946, in Boston, and according to Mona Smith, he became the "first actor of color to play a white character on the American stage."[85] Without question, Smith has written an excellent biography of Canada Lee, but her statement reveals how concealed and underappreciated whiting up has been. James Hewlett in the early nineteenth century, Bob Cole in the late nineteenth century, and Evelyn Preer, Charles Gilpin, and Clarence Muse in the early twentieth century had all performed white characters on various American stages. Lee's performance was simply the next chapter in a long history of stage Europeans, and this violinist-turned-boxer-turned-actor-turned-political-activist had a clear understanding of how significant his moment of performed whiteness could be.

In an article published in the *Daily Worker*, a Communist newspaper, Lee explained how playing Daniel de Bosola "can open up vast new fields to the Negro actor whose parts previously have been limited by color. Most of the time Negroes are relegated to funny parts that make fun of a whole race."[86] Lee wanted "to prove it is art that counts," and although he anticipated his work would receive intense scrutiny, he firmly believed this stage European could "open up all roads to the Negro actor." Though both Preer and Lee had a similar fundamental mission, to elevate black actors from the comedic to the dramatic, Lee's agenda included an additional dynamic. Personally, Lee saw this experiment as "a long step toward becoming 'actor Canada Lee,' not 'Canada Lee, Negro actor.'" Some might interpret this statement as Lee's repressed desire to be a white actor, but according to Mona Smith, he "had no desire to pretend to be white" in his real life.[87] He simply could not turn down this career-defining opportunity because, as reported in the *Daily Worker*, this was the "first time in theatrical history a producer had selected the man he considered the best actor for a role regardless of color."[88]

Czinner and Bergner's bold casting solution may have been the earliest example of color-blind casting in American theater, but color-blind performance reception was hardly a possibility in 1940s America, which is why the producers had to white up Lee. Critic Elliot Norton of the *Boston Post* fully endorsed casting Lee, explaining that "there is no reason why a colored actor should not play any role for which he is qualified, in the whole range of drama, regardless of color." Yet with regard to color, Norton accurately characterized this production as a major event because it was "the first time a colored man has had the opportunity to appear as a white man, to try his ability in what is really a classic, alongside of white players."[89] Lee's color was an undeniable obstacle for the *Duchess of Malfi* producers because in order for Lee to perform seamlessly "alongside of white players," he needed to appear in whiteface. Dramaturgically, the producers reasoned that Bosola was a Spaniard who had recently arrived in Italy; therefore he could play as "a man of swarthy complexion" with some African features, but not a full-blooded Negro. Bradford F. Swan of the *Providence Bulletin* reported that the producers "were careful to stress that although they were not changing the Bosola role from that of a white man to that of a Negro, the part did not call for the actor to look the way a white man would, for instance, in a drawing-room comedy."[90] There was flexibility in Bosola's whiteness, but the ultimate goal was to de-emphasize race, make it less visible, in order to focus on the dramatic narrative and Lee's talent.

Initial media reactions to the casting announcement and the early Boston reviews did focus squarely on race, specifically the novelty of Lee's whiteface. When Bill Chase of the *Amsterdam News* heard Lee was playing a white man, he wrote in his column "All Ears," "The recent news that Canada Lee opens in Providence tonight as a white man in 'The Duchess of Malfi' recalls the days of the WPA Theatre when one of the members of the all-Negro cast fell ill, and Orson Welles (then the director) donned dark grease paint and stepped into the role at the last minute."[91] It is ironic that Chase references this "blackened" *Macbeth*, a production that sparked Lee's interest in Shakespeare, but such comparisons to other cross-racial performances were understandable. Given the history of white actors "blacking up," who could blame critic Robert Garland, from the *New York Journal-American*, for quipping that Lee was "getting even" with Al Jolson.[92]

On a serious note, Chase agreed with Canada Lee that there was much at stake in his cross-racial play. After his initial blurb on whiteface versus blackface, Chase published an in-depth, front-page article on how Lee's racial impersonation brilliantly challenged "Jimcrow theater." Expanding on the second function of whiting up, performed whiteness designed for professional advancement, Chase heralded stage Europeans as a theatrical innovation that could redeem American theater and even attack the color line. He believed there was just one practical question to be resolved: "Could they successfully make him up to appear white, and not as some ghost-like monstrosity of myriad hues?"

To address this technical question, the Lydia O'Leary company sent a makeup expert to Providence. O'Leary was developing a special white paste that had never been used in the theater and was originally designed to mask burns and other "disfiguring marks."[93] This paste was waterproof and perspiration-proof and allowed Lee's skin to breathe. Accompanying his top-of-the-fold article on Lee's Boston debut and on the same page with advertisements for skin whitener, Bill Chase published behind-the-scenes photographs of Lee's "whitening" process. Chase reported that Lee "was pleased with the results of O'Leary grease paint, and felt doubly reassured he could do the role," and when Lee confidently stepped onstage, "he convinced a heretofore skeptical Boston audience that the color problem in the theatre can be licked." For Chase, Lee could "prove to be the pioneer in a venture which may well revolutionize the plight of the talented Negro whose traditional roles in the theater and movies have been relegated to the lot of buck-eyed buffoons and menial servants."[94] Yet the implication here is that O'Leary's experimental paste, not exceptional acting ability, would open unlimited opportunities for Negro actors.

Although he also featured pictures of Lee's extensive makeup process in his front-page article, *Boston Post* critic Elliot Norton focused more on how the whiteface erased race: "In profile, there was no hint of his race. When he faced the audience squarely, the flatness of his nose was strikingly apparent. As the afternoon wore on, however, you could forget about that. . . . Perhaps this was the most striking thing about the whole performance: there were some scenes in which you forgot entirely that he was a colored man in makeup."[95] The *New York Times*, which sent a reporter to cover the Boston debut, also marveled at how the makeup obscured Lee's race. The reporter wrote that "so effective was the make-up that it was difficult to tell that Mr. Lee was a Negro when he made his debut as the villainous Daniel de Bosola."[96] Norton and the *New York Times* suggest the "knowing" audience's willing submersion in the narrative was a testament to the makeup job and Lee's ability to deliver a creditable villain.

Disagreeing somewhat with Norton and the *Times* reporter, I believe race was made less visible without being erased or de-emphasized in Lee's performance of Bosola. Regarding his imitation whiteness, Lee was in-

Figure 13 Canada Lee (as Bosola) and John Carradine (as Ferdinand) in a scene from the 1946 Broadway production of John Webster's *Duchess of Malfi*. Wisconsin Center for Film and Theater Research.

tent on visually passing for white without fully misleading or deceiving his public. Figure 13 shows a scene between Lee and John Carradine, who played Ferdinand, the Duchess's deceitful brother. When I initially saw this image, I had a hard time distinguishing who was in whiteface, Lee or the pale Carradine. But then I was drawn to the difference in facial features which Elliot Norton mentioned in his article, and I noticed that Carradine is much sharper around the nose and lips. Markers of racial difference are still visible, but dramaturgically one could rationalize that the Spaniard Bosola has traces of North African blood, which would explain the flat nose. The hands also draw attention. Lee's are covered to conceal his dark skin and avoid hand makeup; but according to the story, Bosola is an assassin who sheds blood, hence the gloves, while Ferdinand is a nobleman who hires assassins to do his murderous work.

I read Lee's fully credible performance of villainous whiteness as continually referencing his blackness, rather than transcending race, by making Bosola's narrative a potentially African American story. Working through the second and fourth cultural modes of whiting up, imitation/emulation and disidentification, Lee's Bosola shared fixed and fluid cultural commonalities between a Negro actor and this Spanish outsider. We can start with the obvious intersection between Bosola's criminal past and blackness. Bosola is an acknowledged, even respected assassin, and his backstory reveals a seven-year stint in prison. Elliot Norton remarked that this penal servitude "hardened and embittered" the Spaniard, and Lee used this character's troubled past to create not only a "shocking villain" but "a credible one."[97] How hard would a 1940s Broadway audience have to work to accept a Negro actor as a hardened criminal? Thus Bosola's nefarious whiteness intersected with and traded on stereotypic notions of blackness.

Furthering this comparison, we could remove Bosola's criminality and insert several other characteristics that demonstrate cross-cultural commonality. For example, Bosola admits his belief in potions and charms; superstition is an attribute often associated with Negroes.[98] Also, Webster's text describes Bosola as carrying an edge of "out of fashion melancholy," a psychological malaise that might remind white and black audiences of the collective dysthymia, or low-grade chronic depression, exhibited by many American Negroes, especially in urban contexts.[99] Finally, like many pragmatic Negroes, Bosola is described as an ambitious, even "saucy slave" who is realistic enough to "look no higher than I can reach."[100] The same mind-set was drilled into mid-twentieth-century black Americans, as they were discouraged from aspiring or reaching too far, and this was precisely the mentality actor-activist Canada Lee worked to overcome with his performed whiteness.

Frankly, most of what Daniel de Bosola represents is disturbing, and over the course of *Duchess*, the hired assassin orders the strangulation of small children and murders several people himself. His schemes partly drive the psychological action of this tragedy, and only famous heavies like Shakespeare's Iago or Richard III are responsible for more mayhem. So my point is not to associate that level of depravity with blackness, but to make the case that Bosola's multifaceted and relatable villainy afforded Canada Lee a platinum opportunity to realize his full potential as an actor. From the start, Czinner and Bergner understood that this criminal, superstitious, melancholic, and cunning role required an electric stage presence, and the producers were confident Lee had the power and passion to make it work.

When *Duchess of Malfi* moved into Broadway's Ethel Barrymore Theater on October 15, 1946, the novelty of white paste had diminished, and most critics agreed the overall production was unbearable. Robert Garland, from the *New York Journal-American*, called it one of the "longest evenings I have ever spent on Broadway" and claimed "Webster's 'timeless nightmare' is badly acted." Yet he marveled at Lee, who "gives 'The Duchess of Malfi' such vim, vigor and vitality as it manages to achieve in its first professional showing in these United States. His makeup is something for the record."[101] *Duchess* had been limited to college productions, and now Garland understood why. Although the whiteface was vaguely historic, only Lee's "playing power" made the show less excruciating.

As further proof that Lee's whiteface gimmick was waning and perhaps unnecessary, the *New Yorker*'s Wolcott Gibbs and *New York Times* critic Brooks Atkinson both ridiculed Lee's makeup job while praising his acting. Gibbs wrote, "Canada Lee, in a putty nose and with the complexion of a bisque doll, is not altogether convincing as a white man, but he gives an honest and intelligent performance as the hired assassin." Atkinson flatly dismissed Lee's mask of whiteness: "Inside his make-up he counterfeits a white man about as successfully as a white man in burnt cork counterfeits a Negro—which is hardly at all."[102] Atkinson was clearly not a fan of cross-racial impersonations, but he went on to explain how he had not seen Lee perform in four years, and he could "only express delight over the way in which a good elemental actor has acquired a mastery of the stage." He dismissed the bisque-face as merely an "amusing detail" when compared "with the intelligence, ease and scope of Mr. Lee's acting as Bosola."

It would appear Lee had partly achieved his and the producers' goal of shifting focus from race to talent. But biographer Mona Smith suggests that, in retrospect, Lee may have regretted the decision to strategically "pass" as Bosola and submerge himself behind white paste. She writes, "For many Americans, Lee's principal claim to fame was his ability to successfully impersonate a white man," and "this was ironic and more than a little frustrating to Lee." Lee's original reason for accepting the Bosola role was to see more black actors performing classic parts. According to Smith, Lee "only permitted himself to be painted because, in 1946, that was the only way he could play a white man onstage."[103]

A color-blind society sounds like a wonderful utopia to aspire to, especially for Negro citizens long discriminated against on the basis of color, but at the end of the day, Canada Lee wanted Boston and Broadway audiences to recognize and accept the fact that a black actor was interpreting this white role. Theater is fundamentally a visual medium, so had he not worn white makeup, Broadway audiences would have been forced to see and then reconcile a dark-skinned Canada Lee with this European role. That bolder representational challenge is precisely what pioneering-black-actress-turned-journalist Fredi Washington would have preferred from Lee. In her weekly column for the militant Harlem weekly, the *People's Voice,* Washington reviewed *Duchess* and characterized Lee's Bosola as "a minor triumph despite the fact that he played the role in white makeup."[104] For Washington, the whiteface was an unnecessary gimmick and an unfortunate capitulation to American racialism.

Classical Whiteness Meets Radical Blackness

Canada Lee, critic Bill Chase from the *Amsterdam News*, and other members of the media understood that Lee's potentially innovative stage European was never about perspiration-proof makeup or winning plaudits on Broadway. Throughout his career, Lee used his talents and celebrity to reposition the Negro in American society. His political consciousness was first awakened while performing Bigger Thomas in *Native Son,* a production that Lee felt was "making history" by broadening the scope of how Negroes were portrayed in mainstream theater.[105] It may have been Bigger Thomas's story that activated Lee, or perhaps it was his interactions with writer Richard Wright; but in 1941, Lee started using his Broadway visibility to speak on behalf of important causes. While starring in *Native Son,* Lee appeared at a banquet for the International Defense League, a legal aid society for the Communist Party that represented the Scottsboro boys during their 1930s case. Lee's presence at the event attracted the attention of the House Un-American Activities Committee (HUAC), which started to amass a thick file on Lee's comings, goings, and associations. Texas congressman Martin Dies, the force behind HUAC, was investigating "communist penetration of the New Deal," and he was specifically interested in exposing any links between Communists and civil rights activities.[106]

Although Lee was never blacklisted, in the late 1940s finding work became increasingly difficult for him because of his social and political activism. It became so difficult that Lee felt compelled to tell the *New York Times*, in separate articles in June and July 1949, that he was not a Communist. Yet in the press, Lee asserted that he would continue to fight for Negro people and other minorities who were discriminated against, despite the labels affixed to his activism. He planned to support politically and socially relevant causes whether or not the Communist Party was involved. Lee's increasingly defiant attitude came to a head in July 1949 when he joined Paul Robeson, already blacklisted and under FBI surveillance, at a conference on discrimination in the radio and television industries. In a keynote speech, Lee charged American radio with a "lynch mentality" and urged all those assembled to fight against Jim Crow in the media. The speech, which was covered by the *New York Times*, resulted in Lee being banned from forty radio and television programs. Now most theater producers were more afraid to hire him.[107]

Artist-activists like Lee and Robeson were caught in a precarious position where radical politics both fueled and hindered their artistic aspirations. Dating back to the days of the WPA and the FTP, the Communist press was one of the biggest supporters of Negro artists working in theater, literature, music, and other arts. Politically and artistically, Communists and black radicals were often drawn to similar causes, so finding them together onstage, on film, in picket lines, or at protest rallies was inevitable. Historian Robin D. G. Kelley found that the Communist Party's "high visibility in antiracist causes drew more than a few black entertainment stars to their organized benefits," including major names like Count Basie, W. C. Handy, Lena Horne, and Canada Lee. Kelley concedes that many Communists "fetishized" black cultural production; however, some black artists "forced the white Left to see and hear differently" and to recognize that "the birth of a utopian future" would emerge from an "abyss of racism and oppression." Kelley contends that "no one played a more pivotal role in demonstrating the revolutionary potential of African American expressive culture than Paul Robeson."[108] I would add Canada Lee as a representative of this revolutionary potential because both he and Robeson were defining a utopian future where Negro actors were free to assume any dramatic role they chose.[109]

As for the ongoing critical debate on Negroes and white roles, in the case of Evelyn Preer and the Ethiopian Art Theatre, the press reduced the conversation to issues of cultural legibility and morality. Canada Lee, however, would find himself in the middle of a Left/Right ideological debate largely shaped by liberal and conservative theater critics from New York dailies. This early battle in America's "culture wars" would expose the possibilities and pitfalls of whiting up, but this political fray would also further jeopardize Lee's theatrical career.

One theatrical and cultural critic on the left who praised and politicized Negro performance was Samuel Sillen, a theater columnist for the *Daily Worker* and an educated, vocal proponent of Negro theater. Based on his writing and advocacy, Sillen was invited to take part in an important forum, "The Negro in American Theatre," which convened in October 1946 partly in response to Canada Lee's whiteface appearance on Broadway. This forum was organized by Stage for Action, a radical workers' theater linked to the Communist Party, and their involvement illustrated the interconnectedness of black and Communist causes. According to a report in the *Daily Worker*, W. E. B. DuBois chaired the forum, and leftist critic Samuel Sillen shared a panel with artists such as Abram Hill of the ANT; Maxine Wood, author of *On Whitman Avenue*; and Frederick O'Neal, star of a Negro version of *Romeo and Juliet*.[110]

In a September 1946 article preceding the Negro theater forum and following Lee's Boston debut, Samuel Sillen joined Bill Chase, from the *Amsterdam News*, in declaring this unique *Duchess of Malfi* a major blow against "Jimcrow" in American theater and "one of the most important announcements in the history of American theater." Sillen placed such importance on this casting decision partly because he saw it as an issue of worker's equity. Expanding on the story of how Lee got the role, Sillen wrote that "the deal was consummated through Jules Ziegler, newly appointed head of GAC's equity department."[111] GAC, or General Artists Corporation, was a talent agency committed to securing new opportunities for Negro talent, and one of its more important accomplishments was brokering this significant racial and professional breakthrough.

Sillen also attached great significance to Lee's stage European because seven months earlier, well before the casting announcement, Sillen had challenged American theater to be more egalitarian in its hiring practices. In February 1945, Sillen published an article titled "Should the Negro Actor Be Limited to Negro Roles?," a piece which acknowledged "progress had been made against Jimcrow on the stage" but argued more work had to be done. One remaining challenge was securing "the right of the Negro actor to perform in any part, Negro or white." To build his case, Sillen did his homework on whiting up and found an earlier precedent where Negro tragedian Ira Aldridge performed King Lear "made up as a white." Sillen continued: "To the extent that the Negro actor continues to be barred from a role merely on the basis of color, he is the victim of prejudice."[112] An outspoken Sillen believed American theater was predicated on white supremacy, and drastic measures, in theater and society, were necessary to dismantle the racial hierarchy.

Sillen did not mean to suggest that "the casting of Negro players in white roles is the primary need of the anti-Jimcrow theater today"; rather, he simply wanted American theater "to reexamine its prejudiced assumption that such casting is impossible in principle." In the larger picture, Sillen fully supported the development of plays by and about Negroes. Echoing the concerns of *Messenger* critic Theophilus Lewis, Sillen warned that if Abram Hill and the American Negro Theatre only performed plays by white playwrights, black theater would never come into its own. Nevertheless in September 1946, Sillen was gratified "to report the announcement that Canada Lee has been cast without reference to color in the revival of John Webster's famous 17th century play." I think Sillen should have qualified or revised the phrase "without reference to color" because color was everywhere in this casting decision. Color was referenced when Czinner and Bergner started looking for a "white Canada Lee," when Sillen launched his prescient campaign for racial equity in a white supremacist American theater, and finally when Lee accepted the role to begin repopulating classical performance with black actors.

The reaction on the Right to Lee's racial politics and cross-racial performance came from well-respected dramatic critic George Jean Nathan and syndicated conservative columnist Westbrook Pegler, both writing for William Randolph Hearst's *New York Journal-American*. Nathan never directly reviewed *Duchess of Malfi*; he left that chore to the reluctant Robert Garland. Instead Nathan responded to Sillen and Canada Lee with a scathing editorial on the highly improved status of the Negro actor in the American theater, a piece provocatively titled "Black Up, You-All, and Get a Job."[113] Nathan opened by decrying the "professional mourners" who attempt to solve the supposed plight of the Negro actor through worker's equity programs; this was a direct assault on Sam Sillen, who was campaigning for more Negro acting jobs as early as February 1945.

Nathan also castigated "actors doing speaking engagements," a remark aimed squarely at Canada Lee, who frequently lent his celebrity presence to various political causes. As for Lee playing Daniel de Bosola on Broadway, Nathan made the case that "the alleged limited opportunities are largely imaginary. The Negro today enjoys opportunities in the theatre relatively every bit as plentiful as his white brothers and sisters." Nathan assumed a level playing field and therefore did not see the need to continue promoting Lee's stage European model, Negro actors in white roles. Actually, Nathan feared the pendulum had already swung too far, and he listed some of the many "classic and semi-classic" plays Negroes had recently appeared in, including *The Duchess of Malfi*, *The Tempest*, *Othello*, and *Romeo and Juliet*. Nathan made the historically accurate statement that

Negroes were appearing "in all kinds of plays in which the roles in other days would have been confined strictly to whites or to whites in blackface." He alluded to Negroes taking significant roles in musicals by George and Ira Gershwin, Bizet, and Gilbert and Sullivan, as well as modern dramas by Eugene O'Neill, Elmer Rice, and Paul Green. American theater had indeed progressed, and this conservative critic waxed nostalgic for the "good old days" when white actors played stage mulattos like Robert Norwood.

Nathan's agenda was to silence the "professional mourners" by providing cold, hard evidence of the Negro's near-domination of modern American theater. Columnist Westbrook Pegler took a much different approach and focused on Lee's political persona, not because he believed the actor was engaged in important work, but because he was convinced Lee was a Communist puppet. In a May 1947 article, Pegler dismissed acting as "unimportant work" supported by "vain, frivolous, self-important people who have got out of hand since our politicians discovered they could draw crowds and adorn bad causes by presenting actors at their rallies."[114] Pegler believed Communists used the Negro as a propagandistic tool by putting him "on a spot while pretending to love him." The Communist Party's cynical plot was "not to improve the colored man's condition, but to create friction, strike sparks and cause commotions."

So by playing an "evil white man" on Broadway, Lee, as well as his Communist "masters," fomented racial discord in America. The intelligent, melancholic, yet aggressive Bosola was definitely a malevolent force in Webster's tragedy. Far from the manipulated stage African Othello, the Spaniard was more akin to the calculating Iago, an aggrieved insider with an axe to grind. Theatrically speaking, Pegler was offended that Lee played this European fire-starter in whiteface, because as he fondly recalled, when whites played comedic roles in blackface, there was "no malice or disparagement of the colored people in anything they did."

Not a theater historian by training, Westbrook Pegler clearly missed the representational damage wrought by blackface minstrelsy, but the columnist was highly skilled at red-baiting. In a second December 1947 editorial Pegler suggested Lee might be a "Red" because his name kept appearing in "the company of other names often cited by the Committee on Un-American Activities."[115] The conservative columnist also alleged that Communist papers typically lauded artists who agreed with their policies, and the *Daily Worker* had nothing but praise for Lee. Pegler's editorials were exactly the intense scrutiny Lee expected when he accepted the Bosola role, but he never anticipated that this calculated experiment in whiting up would contribute substantially to the end of a promising theatrical career.

After a qualified success with *Duchess*, Lee's next proposed stage European project was to star in *King Lear*, without white paste and surrounded by a mixed-race cast. Sadly, this production never materialized because Lee went to Hollywood instead to film *Body and Soul* (1947), with several actors who would later be blacklisted. Out West, Lee reportedly tried to create a fully integrated Shakespearean repertory company whose repertoire would feature *Macbeth* and *Othello*, with Lee performing both title characters. Interestingly, he planned to play the Scottish usurper in whiteface. According to industry gossip, Lee worked diligently to bring major stars into the project and secure financial backing from movie studios, but with Lee's hefty HUAC file and the Red Scare targeting lefties in Hollywood and Broadway, the film and stage star was too risky to green-light.[116]

Despite the ambitious projections of critics like Bill Chase and Sam Sillen, Lee's stage European failed to eradicate the color line or fully revolutionize Jim Crow theater in the 1940s. But the artistic and political debates that engulfed Evelyn Preer and Canada Lee did place whiting up on America's representational radar screen like never before. In passionate and sometimes perplexed reactions to these stage Europeans, white and black critics tried to figure out where this performance tradition came from or if it was indeed a tradition at all. Critics scrambled to identify which Negro actor performed the first white classical role or when the first whiteface character appeared onstage, and often their answers were off by a couple decades or even an entire century. On Broadway, the epicenter of American commercial theater, Preer and Lee followed in and transformed the footsteps of earlier African American actors like James Hewlett, Bob Cole, and the Whitman Sisters. Likewise, the all-black cast of Thomson and Stein's *Four Saints in Three Acts* replicated and revived the urban chic of fashionable whiteface promenaders from nineteenth-century Charleston and Manhattan, as well as the operatic exploits of Lloyd Gibbs and Edna Alexander from *A Trip to Coontown*.

From the 1920s through the 1940s, depending on their geographic, political, moral, or racial inclination, cultural and political commentators registered very different responses to this chapter's fundamental question: Should Negro actors be performing white roles? For most critics in the 1920s, even those taken with Preer's beauty, intelligence, and restraint, *Salomé* was inappropriate for Negro actors, and the future of black theater lay in another, more organic direction. By the 1940s, Canada Lee had paid his dues in classical roles, and critics could not deny his power as Daniel de Bosola; but some reviewers felt his whiting up erased race, while others mistrusted the whiteface gimmick and wondered what all the fuss was about. Yet forward-thinking critics like Lester A. Walton, Abram L. Harris, Bill Chase, Elliot Norton, and Sam Sillen understood that Preer and Lee were working for future generations of American actors. Although Lee was hardly perfect in his pioneering efforts, Boston critic Elliot Norton declared that the production made its historical point: "A colored actor can portray credibly a white character."[117] Norton believed "democracy should be made to work in theater," and he specifically defined this theatrical democracy as white actors playing Othello, black actors playing Daniel de Bosola, and both competent performances thrilling audiences.

Post–Canada Lee, black actors such as Diana Sands and Earle Hyman would realize Norton's theatrical democracy by continuing to trespass on white performative property, including Ibsen, Shakespeare, Webster, Wilde, and Shaw. As an actor Sands is perhaps best known for her stage and film performances as Beneatha in Lorraine Hansberry's *A Raisin in the Sun* (1959), but she also starred in various traditionally white roles. Most notably, in 1968 she assumed the title character in a production of George Bernard Shaw's *St. Joan* at New York's Lincoln Center, a performance which expanded the theatrical playing field for Sands and other black actors.[118] Theater historian Glenda E. Gill has written about the theatrical contributions of Earle Hyman, a seasoned, world-traveled veteran actor, probably most recognizable as jazzman Russell Huxtable, Cliff Huxtable's father on the 1980s situation comedy *The Cosby Show*.[119] Onstage, Hyman would build an impressive career playing Falstaff, Peer Gynt, and Cyrano in theaters all around the world, from England to Scandinavia. But his most significant American triumph in a white role, or what Gill calls a "non-traditional" role, came over a decade after Canada Lee's Bosola experiment. In 1957 Hyman played Antonio, the Duchess of Malfi's husband, in an off-Broadway revival of Webster's tragedy at the Phoenix Theatre. Most critics did not appreciate or embrace Hyman's break with tradition; one critic called his Antonio merely "decorative without being in any way compelling," and another complained that Hyman failed to master the language and could never find Webster's "resonant rhythms."[120]

Despite unfavorable reviews, Hyman succeeded in 1957 where Canada Lee had regrettably failed in 1946; the fair-skinned Hyman played Antonio, in a cast with white actors, completely free of whiteface makeup. Without sounding too progressive, earlier acts of performed whiteness, like James Hewlett's Scottish appropriations and Bob Cole's Willie Wayside, chipped away at racial hierarchies and cultural expectations, so Earle Hyman could play Antonio, free of gimmicks like the Lydia O'Leary company's white paste. In fact, with the representational advances of Sands and Hyman in the 1950s and 1960s, it may have seemed like whiting up was giving way to nontraditional, race-neutral opportunities where Negro actors could permanently transcend pigment to showcase their mimetic capacities. However, in the 1960s, black playwrights were just beginning to script a new generation of dynamic, explosive, racially incisive stage Europeans.

Chapter 5 Estranging Whiteness

Queens, Clowns, and Beasts in 1960s Black Drama

An actor once asked Jean Genet to write a play with an all-Negro cast, and the French writer mused, "But what exactly is a Negro? First of all what is his color?" Susan Taubes, in a 1963 article on *The Blacks*, answered Genet's philosophical queries: "Negro" would be his color because that is how imperial powers identified enslaved or colonized Africans.[1] In *The Blacks*, Genet constructs two competing worlds to explore his questions: an on-stage, metaphoric "ritual masque" and an offstage world dominated by a court trial and an ongoing revolution. He effectively divides his dramatic action into public and private transcripts to make the larger point that the "blackness" affixed to colonial bodies does not say anything true about the "real lives" of Africans. Conversely, "whiteness" does not capture the full import and power of the ghostly Queens, Judges, and Generals whom the Negroes impersonate with their grotesque white masks.

When *The Blacks* debuted at St. Mark's Playhouse in New York City in May 1961, this absurdist, raw, and dualistic drama was a sensation and instantly contributed to a representational firestorm offstage. A new tenor of black cultural production swept New York, Hollywood, and the rest of the United States as Genet's metaphoric "clown show," or reverse minstrel show, ran for three years off-Broadway. It showcased established and rising African American talent such as James Earl Jones, Roscoe Lee Browne, Cicely Tyson, Maya Angelou, Charles Gordone, Helen Martin, and Godfrey Cambridge.[2] Similar to Virgil Thomson and Gertrude Stein's *Four Saints in Three Acts* (1934), Genet's work offered black actors a professional challenge; it also spoke to the 1960s moment without being trapped by this much-discussed, much-debated decade. As proof of the play's timelessness, in 2003 the Classical Theatre of Harlem revived *The Blacks* and its revolutionary energy with a commercially successful and critically acclaimed production that captured a modern audience, especially the white spectators for whom Genet wrote this drama.[3]

Genet unapologetically wrote this play for white audiences and clearly states this intention in his brief introductory note to *The Blacks*. But as an artist and activist, Genet was fully committed to challenging the legacy of French colonial oppression and even wrote a second play on that subject, *The Screens* (1966). Genet obviously viewed himself as a white man, but he once described how politically he could see himself "only in the oppressed of the colored races, the oppressed who revolted against the whites. I am a black whose skin happens to be white, but I am definitely a black."[4] Despite his political blackness and the sensational American debut of *The Blacks*, Genet hardly considered himself an integral part of African American theatrical practice. In response to his complex absurdist drama, black critics in the 1960s questioned and debated what Genet was trying to say about the African Diaspora, colonialism, and postcolonial realities.[5] Although his play was crafted from some physical and cultural distance, Genet's white figures designed for black actors exerted an important influence on African American writers. Inspired, emboldened, and perhaps challenged by *The Blacks*, black dramatists began constructing their own stage Europeans to assess and potentially address the political, social, economic, cultural, and emotional well-being of Afro-America.

This chapter is partly about an indirect transatlantic dialogue between the politically "black" Genet and three very different African American playwrights: Adrienne Kennedy, Douglas Turner Ward, and LeRoi Jones (later Amiri Baraka in 1968). I am interested in how these theatrical artists extended or contested what Genet had to say about whiteness, blackness, estrangement, and decolonization in the African Diaspora, and how each artist estranged or denaturalized African American relationships to metaphoric and material whiteness. For the first time we have stage Europeans featured in extant plays scripted by black writers, so I will engage in extensive and hopefully illuminating dramatic analyses of 1960s black drama. Yet at the same time I want to emphasize that these whiting up playwrights created performance texts rooted in Brechtian estrangement or Afro-alienation acts and designed to captivate and potentially transform live black audiences.

Adrienne Kennedy's modern tragedy *Funnyhouse of a Negro* (1964) creates nightmarish stage Europeans to externalize the potentially debilitating effects of blackness and whiteness on the African American psyche. Activist and artist Douglas Turner Ward's *Day of Absence* (1965) plays with

Confederate whiteface clowns reminiscent of Bob Cole's Willie Wayside in a reverse minstrel show. Ward's satiric mission is to expose white economic and cultural dependency on African American labor, thus questioning the foundations of white supremacy. Similarly, LeRoi Jones created several stage Europeans to undermine America's white/black hierarchy onstage and beyond. His mythic, magical, ritualistic theater deployed white devils and effete white hipsters to dislodge the notion of whiteness as the measure of humanity and to move black people to the center of the universe. There are many Jones/Baraka plays with stage Europeans to choose from, but I focus on his metaphorically rich *A Black Mass* (1966), which stages how whiteness was created by an "anti-human" black magician.

Estranging Whiteness

Theorist Frederic Jameson offers the best explanation of German theatrical artist Bertolt Brecht's "estrangement-effect." Jameson explains how Brecht drew on Russian formalist filmmakers such as Sergei Eisenstein to create stage effects that forced audiences to look at familiar situations and circumstances with "new eyes."[6] Building on Brecht's estranging practices, Daphne Brooks further theorizes a more specific "Afro-alienation act" that refers to how black performers "defamiliarize the spectacle of blackness in transatlantic culture" to "awaken" audiences to horrific histories and produce "alternative racial and gender epistemologies."[7] For Brooks, Afro-alienation acts make blackness strange and liberated for black performers and their audiences, but I contend if we replace the spectacle of blackness with the spectacle of whiteness, the same practice can apply to the whiting up playwrights featured in this chapter.

To stage the dual and in some respects dueling worlds of *The Blacks*, Genet demanded that black bodies participate in the estrangement of whiteness and blackness, beginning with his requirement that all the masked and unmasked performers be Negroes.[8] Writing about various Genet dramas, Christopher Lane explains that in *The Blacks* Genet wanted to demonstrate the "effect of racism by partial familiarity with white people and partial self-strangeness." Using artificial, plastic white masks, Genet's Negro figures stage parodic yet distant versions of their European colonizers—hence the "partial familiarity with white people."[9] The idea of "partial self-strangeness" refers to the reality that colonized or enslaved Africans learned to see themselves through the eyes of the dominant culture and therefore are strangers to their core selves. Lane's interpretation of Genet's Negro subjects echoes W. E. B. DuBois's turn-of-the-century description of similarly colonized American Negroes who can only see themselves as whites see them and are, therefore, incapable of developing truly independent selves or identities.[10] So in terms of performed blackness, the black bodies in Genet's absurdist drama are asked to perform not faithful representations of themselves but the "racist fantasies" white colonizers imagined them to be.

Yet dramatic critic Geneviève Fabre argues that by the end of Genet's dualistic spectacle designed for white consumption, lead black characters like Village and Virtue do experience a breakthrough and discover their core selves as they "renounce the imitation of whites" to express true feelings.[11] The implication here is that when the colonized are not distracted by diversions, like the plantation parties Frederick Douglass decried or even parodic explorations of whiteness, their "true feelings" emerge and express a desire for revolution. In Genet's other universe just beyond the metaphoric stage, something politically tangible is happening to move the blacks toward full liberation, self-knowledge, and self-possession. Offstage, in a different kind of hidden transcript completely free of imitative whiteness, there is a black court judging and executing a traitor in order to keep an uprising against the white colonizers alive and moving forward.

In a 1983 interview, more than twenty years after *The Blacks* premiered in America, Genet explained that "revolution represents *one* image, among others, of society, and an *image*, among others—of revolution. In both cases it's only an *image* you see on stage."[12] Here Genet concedes the limits of any theatrical representation of revolution or capitulation; it is merely an act, a ritual spectacle that can never substitute for real political action or inaction. Of course, we should never underestimate the power of performance; as Tavia Nyong'o reminds us, "Its importance to politics cannot be ignored insofar as social action is organized around symbols, gesture, effigies, and dramatic narratives."[13] Genet interviewer Edward de Grazia recalled the intense energy surrounding the 1961 New York premiere of *The Blacks* and commented on how "powerful and frightening" it was, how it seemed to "make people want revolution." A seemingly disappointed Genet responded, "But it should have inspired a desire for revolution in blacks." Genet's agenda was to foment the kind of upheaval building offstage, in the alternate world of his dualistic play, and he appears to regret that a tangible black revolution never materialized in the United States.

Yet throughout the 1960s, isolated acts of rebellion did detonate in urban centers from Harlem to Milwaukee to Watts, community-crippling eruptions of violence, looting, and arson. President Lyndon Baines Johnson, in July 29, 1967, created a commission to investigate the civil and racial disorder involving primarily young black male urbanites. The Kerner Commission, named after Illinois governor Otto Kerner Jr., filed its report in March 1968 and arrived at this summary conclusion: "Our Nation is moving toward two societies, one black, one white—separate and unequal."[14] The commission partially blamed this dilemma of two emerging Americas on television and newspapers that presented a world to black audiences that was "totally white in both appearance and attitude." Years before the federal government acknowledged the media's impact on the black psyche, LeRoi Jones had declared American television "a steady deadly whiteness beaming forth."[15]

As for who was inciting and participating in the racial disorders and rebellions, President Johnson declared the rioters were "criminals" who had no connections to legitimate "civil rights protest."[16] The Kerner Commission disagreed with the president's assessment, and characterized the rioters as typically young African American males "informed about politics" but "highly distrustful of the political system." The commission also found the rioters were disaffected but not interested in completely destabilizing American society; they simply wanted "fuller participation in the social order and the material benefits enjoyed by the vast majority of American citizens."[17]

While the Kerner Commission warned of two Americas emerging, it ultimately identified greater integration as the only solution. Understandably, Black Power advocates like Stokely Carmichael and H. Rap Brown disagreed with the Kerner Commission's profile of the rioters and viewed the rebellious yet misdirected young black politicos as searching for radical alternatives to the current system and an increasingly complicit civil rights movement. Activist groups like Carmichael's Student National Coordinating Committee (SNCC) offered alternatives such as racial separatism and cultural nationalism. The *Kerner Report* actually conceded the appeal of Black Power for young black urbanites, in terms of engendering a "new mood" and replacing apathy with an activist racial pride. However, the report also argued that Black Power, by abdicating its role in the struggle for peaceful integration and preaching separatism, unconsciously functioned "as an accommodation to white racism."[18]

The *Kerner Report* also detailed how representational whiteness factored into urban unrest. The commission found that during the 1967 civil disorders and earlier riots, the aggressive participants tended to attack not white persons but "the symbols of white American society—authority and property."[19] In 1968, the year the *Kerner Report* was published, writer/theorist Larry Neal articulated a black aesthetic manifesto that also took deadly aim at symbols of white cultural authority. In an essay titled "The Black Arts Movement," Neal aligns Black Arts with Black Power by identifying a shared value: "the necessity for Black people to define the world in their own terms." In his oft-quoted summary of black cultural nationalism, Neal also explains what artists like LeRoi Jones/Amiri Baraka and Don L. Lee (later Haki Madhubuti) were already doing to develop a black aesthetic in this country. He explains that "currently, these writers are re-evaluating western aesthetics, the traditional role of the writer, and the social function of art. Implicit in this re-evaluation is the need to develop a 'black aesthetic.' It is the opinion of many Black writers, I among them, that the Western aesthetic has run its course: it is impossible to construct anything within its decaying structure."[20] For this black aesthetic to truly take root among artists and communities, whiteness, its values, and cultural structures had to be replaced. In the 1920s, Theophilus Lewis advocated building a new, vibrant Negro culture on the ruins of "Nordic Civilization," but in the 1960s, Neal radically rejected the "decaying structure" of white art.

As for black artistic production in the 1920s, Neal claimed the Harlem Renaissance or New Negro movement squandered an opportunity to create a transformative cultural nationalism for Afro-America because it was not supported by the black masses but by white audiences, publishers, and sponsors. He explains how that movement "failed to take roots, to link itself concretely to the struggles of that community, to become its voice and spirit."[21] In 1923, Negro critics like Theophilus Lewis and Hubert Harrison offered similar evaluations of the Ethiopian Art Theatre's stage Europeans. Both men rejected Wilde's decadent aestheticism as the future of Negro theater because it was not rooted in the real struggles of the Negro community. Expanding Lewis's earlier criticism of black dependence on white theatrical leadership, Larry Neal denounced Euro-American theater as an escapist, empty, sterile cultural product, and he even declared this deadly "Euro-American cultural sensibility" responsible for the oppression of Afro-America. He believed "anti-human" white cultural values were dominating "the psyches of most Black artists and intellectuals." This white cultural aesthetic had to "be destroyed before the Black creative artist can have a meaningful role in the transformation of society."[22]

Reassessing Black Arts nearly forty years after its emergence, cultural critics Lisa Gail Collins and Margo Natalie Crawford identified both openness and fixity in the cultural nationalism defined by Neal, Jones, Lee, and others. Artistically, Black Arts offered a highly experimental literary and performative field committed to change and fluidity; in addition, these new aesthetics were collaborative, boundary-defying endeavors that stretched across multiple artistic genres: music, dance, poetry, and theater. Ideologically, this potentially transformative aesthetic movement often promoted a monolithic conception of blackness that excoriated "non-revolutionary Negroes" and exhibited disturbing, unproductive signs of sexism and homophobia. Collins and Crawford claim that no other cultural movement has ever been so committed to purging internalized "anti-black ways of seeing and thinking" from the African American psyche. Ultimately and unfortunately, Black Arts would be defined by an essentialist "anti-white rhetoric" and an undeniable "obsession with images of pernicious whiteness."[23]

In her comparative work on the Harlem Renaissance and the Black Arts movement, Emily Bernard unpacks this preoccupation with purging white aesthetics and cultural values. First, Bernard asserts that "white support *and* corruption have been central to every episode in the evolution of African American creativity." Whiteness is "a crucial part of what makes African American art exactly what it is. In other words, there would be no black creativity without white influence." Bernard next explains how "the centrality of whiteness to black cultural *identity*" has always been balanced by "attendant anxieties about that centrality." In the 1960s, those anxieties surrounding white influence intensified and drove African American artists, activists, and rioters "to denounce and extinguish white presence from black life."[24] In short, whiteness, along with a desire to cleanse whiteness, would directly shape the stage Europeans of Kennedy, Ward, and Jones.

Biracial Terror: White Masks, Kinky Tresses

Funnyhouse of a Negro, Adrienne Kennedy's first and most-produced drama, is one of the more complex and thoroughly examined black plays to emerge out of the 1960s.[25] Kennedy first shared *Funnyhouse* with the public in 1962 as an overwhelmed, neophyte playwright in Edward Albee's playwriting workshop. Albee believed in Kennedy's one-act more than Kennedy initially did, and he produced a workshop version at Circle in the Square in 1963, with Diana Sands as Sarah. As a young writer, Kennedy was heavily influenced by Albee's absurdist, confrontational, and often violent explorations of personal alienation. With compact one-acts like *The Zoo Story* (1959/1960), Albee was moving American theater in a bold and sometimes terrifying new direction. Albee also arranged the first professional, fully mounted production of *Funnyhouse* in 1964 at New York's East End Theater. It was directed by Michael Kahn, with Billie Allen as Sarah, and the production won Kennedy an Obie Award for best new off-Broadway play.[26]

Kennedy's one-act takes us inside the consciousness of a biracial college student named Sarah, the Negro, who is deeply enamored with European culture, continually haunted and pursued by her African heritage, and suspended on the verge of suicide. This tragic narrative may sound esoteric or inaccessible, and perhaps because of Kennedy's association with Albee and white theaters, *Funnyhouse* has often been excluded from black aesthetic discussions. Unlike prominent Black Arts icons like Amiri Baraka, Kennedy's ritualistic interior journeys do not openly promote cultural nationalism or outline deliberate steps toward black liberation and wholeness. At a time when black ritual theater was defined as communal, political acts predicated on a constructive, healing relationship between performance and spectator, Kennedy was writing about a destabilizing identity crisis in Afro-America.[27] More than any dramatist in this chapter, Kennedy stages the damage done to the black psyche by America's racial hierarchy.

Kennedy fails or refuses to produce harmony or recognizable transcendence because at the heart of her work is a persistent and perhaps futile African American struggle to mediate between blackness and whiteness. Kennedy explains her writing process as "an outlet for inner psychological confusion and questions stemming from childhood. . . . You try to struggle with the material that is lodged in your unconscious, and try to bring it to the conscious level."[28] In performance, this outlet becomes "interiority," or an extremely vulnerable "public privacy" that, according to Fred Moten, represents its own radical black aesthetic tradition.[29] Moten arrived at this concept of interiority while analyzing the work of performance artist Adrian Piper, who places her body, her histories, and her representational tensions on full display as an "object of art." For black artists, who have traditionally been exploited by white art (think blackface minstrelsy), Piper and Kennedy's willingness to become spectacles or objects is fraught with danger.

Through her willing and radical interiority, Kennedy exposes black and white audiences to an unresolved mixed-race ancestry, an uneasy conglomeration of racial traditions and cultural myths. Much like Genet's philosophical queries on color, *Funnyhouse* asks, What is black? What is white? To answer or entertain such questions, Kennedy operates primarily inside Sarah's unconscious, where various "selves" or characters physically embody contradictory racial signs and signals. By challenging the very "idea of dramatic character," she opens up what Philip Kolin calls "a new world of postidentity, crossing and collapsing racial, gender, ethnic, political, and historical boundaries."[30] From this progressive perspective, Sarah's selves contest America's various hierarchies by operating betwixt and between blackness and whiteness, femaleness and maleness, even fiction and fact. According to Jacqueline Wood, Kennedy's interiority ultimately functions as "a dynamic and unwieldy third space," an alternative to the wreckage of racist constructions Negroes have internalized.[31]

Sarah's fluid yet admittedly fragile third space is populated by black, white, and yellow disaggregated aspects of her identity. She is divided into four selves. Three are essentially European: Queen Victoria, the Duchess of Hapsburg, and Jesus. The lone African self is Patrice Lumumba, a reference to the first prime minister of the Republic of Congo. To layer this interiority, the four selves are surrounded and tormented by other, external characters that represent Sarah's expressionistic projections. They are "funnyhouse" figures, such as a ghastly, light-skinned mother; a faceless black father carrying an ebony mask; a constantly laughing boyfriend; and an equally maniacal landlady. Kennedy's splintered selves produce multiple crossings, partly as a testament to the penetrability of supposedly inviolable identity categories, but also as proof of the impossibility of Sarah ever achieving stability within her dualistic inner struggle. Here we arrive at an ominous and perhaps more realistic perspective on Sarah's alternative third space—but more on this shortly.

As for how the splintering and multiple crossings play onstage, *Funnyhouse* uses a cross-racial ventriloquism similar to James Hewlett playing Mathews playing "Hewlett." Sarah's psyche produces a transracial, cross-gender madhouse where various selves speak and perform for her. For example, in a scene with Raymond, Sarah's Jewish boyfriend, the Duchess of Hapsburg physically inhabits Sarah's life while she watches. Also, the four selves, including Lumumba, re-voice, revise, and critique Sarah's history, feelings, and insights, which foregrounds her tragic splintering but also demonstrates her unique ability to remain self-reflexive even as her life unhinges. Claudia Barnett, in her work on *Funnyhouse*, notes how

Sarah projects her personal narrative onto prominent historical personalities like Queen Victoria and Patrice Lumumba rather than absorbing their specific histories uncritically.[32]

Onstage, Kennedy's interiority may not read as the transgressive, dynamic third space theorized by some literary and dramatic criticism. Responding to *Funnyhouse*'s 1964 debut, theatrical critics were universally at a loss for how to respond to Kennedy's cutting-edge one-act drama. Howard Taubman, of the *New York Times*, first tried to assess the play in conventional theatrical terms but concluded that nothing happens in the roughly fifty minutes of playing time. Yet putting convention aside, Taubman lauded Kennedy for venturing into "relatively unknown territory" and tapping into the "tortured mind of a Negro who cannot bear the burden of being a Negro."[33] Similarly, *Village Voice* critic Michael Smith admitted he did not how to evaluate this play "as art or craft" and ultimately conceded that Kennedy was operating on a level where "criticism is nearly irrelevant." However, Smith did recognize that "as an obsessive, cruelly honest statement of self it is extraordinary and devastating."[34]

In terms of theatrical setting, Sarah's splintered Euro-Afro identities work through multiple markers of racial difference and political power in a nightmarish world of deathly castles and wild jungles. As a textbook example of expressionism, this world is a projection of Sarah's truly devastated psyche. Sarah's selves and other expressionistic projections operate in two metaphoric spaces: first, sites of colonial power, like Queen Victoria's chamber/castle and the Duchess's chamber, and second, sites of colonization, like the jungle, the dangerous, dark spaces inhabited by black figures like Sarah's father and Patrice Lumumba.[35] As an undergraduate, I performed in a campus production of *Funnyhouse of a Negro* that transported the audience inside Sarah's "unwieldy third space" by re-creating her psyche around the patrons. To stage Sarah's last moments, the chambers of imperial power and the colonized jungle, all exhibits in her internal madhouse, were arranged in a circle engulfing the audience.[36]

In these spaces that Sarah's selves inhabit, Kennedy produces a series of Afro-alienation acts that exhibit the third function of whiting up, which seeks to expose and explore the terror of whiteness and blackness, both personally and historically. Sarah's potentially game-changing interiority, with its "post-identity" crossings, quickly dissolves into a nightmare, a mutually terrifying hall of mirrors where warring black and white selves fracture Sarah. On the sociological surface, Sarah, the Negro, embodies the "twoness" W. E. B. DuBois outlined in *Souls of Black Folk*: "two souls, two unreconciled strivings; two warring ideals in one dark body, whose dogged strength alone keeps it from being torn asunder."[37] Her white selves, Queen, Duchess, and Jesus, are cast as imperial and colonial aggressors, but they also struggle with an embedded blackness, represented by Lumumba, that questions and undermines their cultural purity. Within Sarah's dark body, the warring ideals are in some respects equally matched and exert comparable degrees of damage on Sarah's psyche. Her white selves suffer from biracialism, miscegenation, amalgamation, as they are all victims of an encroaching dark "jungle." Over time the young Negro's "dogged strength" is worn down, and constant siege is literally played out on the bodies of her selves, with white masks juxtaposed against kinky tresses that are always falling out.

Sarah's psychic decline begins well before her final suicidal moment. The mutual terror starts with the white imperialists who ventured around the world converting nonwhites to Christianity, capitalism, and a European worldview. In *The Blacks*, Genet creates a character named the Missionary who is part of a European court; he is a figure of religious authority and, of course, is realized by a black actor in a white mask. As a part of an elaborate ritual, the Missionary explains the worlds that Europeans constructed for their black, brown, and yellow colonial subjects. He describes how "for two thousand years God has been white. He eats on a white tablecloth. He wipes his white mouth with a white napkin. He picks at white meat with a white fork."[38] Genet establishes a very specific start date for the primacy of whiteness: Two thousand years ago with the birth of Jesus Christ, God anthropomorphized into a universal white human being—consistent with the idea of Jesus being God on earth—who enjoys the comforts of fine dining and an all-enveloping whiteness.

From the perspective of the colonial subject, Kennedy's Negro Sarah restates but particularizes Genet's normative whiteness: "It is my dream to live in rooms with European antiques and my Queen Victoria, photographs of Roman ruins, walls of books, a piano, oriental carpets and to eat my meals on a white glass table. I will visit my friends' apartments which will contain books, photographs of Roman ruins, pianos and oriental carpets. My friends will be white."[39] A couple of centuries after God became white and nearly a hundred years removed from Victorian imperialism, English major Sarah surrounds herself in whiteness, in layers of British Empire. The Roman ancestors and the "oriental" conquests are now reduced to carpets, and the white glass table coordinates well with her white friends. But Sarah admits that she needs these white friends "to keep me from reflecting too much upon the fact that I am a Negro." Also, during her prelude to death, Sarah describes the most dominant and defining figure of whiteness in her apartment, "a gigantic plaster statue of Queen Victoria who is my idol."[40] According to the published text, we have to wait until the very end of this one-act drama to catch a glimpse of this monument to empire, but in the original 1964 production of *Funnyhouse,* a huge white plaster statue of Queen Victoria "sat in state" for the entire show.[41]

To fully understand Sarah and Kennedy's identification with whiteness, specifically white female authority, we should consider the circumstances and influences surrounding the play's composition. Kennedy began writing *Funnyhouse* in 1960 while traveling through Africa and Europe, in particular Ghana, England, and Italy, with her family. Kennedy recalls how "the imagery in *Funnyhouse of a Negro* was born by seeing those places: Queen Victoria, the statue in front of Buckingham Palace."[42] She felt awe and admiration for this queen memorialized in front of England's royal palace, for Victoria, a woman who dominated and defined an age. Jacqueline Wood, in her work on *Funnyhouse,* identifies Queen Victoria Regina, Monarch of England, as the "icon of Western dominance" and describes how during her era, England annexed, settled, or colonized many countries, from Africa to the Pacific Islands to South Asia. This queen would become a major influence and revered figure for Kennedy, who initially identified with Victoria as an empowered woman and not as an imperialist.[43]

During her travels, Kennedy incorporated another image of white female power into her theatrical imagination, the Duchess of Hapsburg (or Habsburg). This Germanic royal first began working on the playwright when Kennedy saw Bette Davis play the mentally unstable Duchess Carlotta of Mexico in the film *Juarez* (1939). The real Duchess of Habsburg was born Marie Charlotte Amélie into a Belgian royal family, and in the 1850s, she married Archduke Maximilian of Austria, who would become the ill-fated emperor of Mexico. In the film *Juarez,* Duchess Carlotta initially exerts a powerful influence on her husband Maximilian, but after learning she cannot bear children and that Napoleon has rescinded his support of their reign in Mexico, the duchess slips into madness. While composing *Funnyhouse,* Kennedy realized that this Duchess would become "one of my character's most sympathetic alter egos or selves."[44]

Within Sarah's interiority, Victoria is a source of empowerment, and the clearly destabilized Duchess is her most connected and understanding self; but Kennedy uses both stage Europeans to identify with and against Western imperialism. When directly asked about Queen Victoria and the Duchess of Habsburg, two symbols of monarchy and colonial oppression, Kennedy admits she was always fascinated by royalty, like most people. However, the mental gymnastics of contemplating why they were indeed "royal" personages drove Kennedy "out of her mind." After her initial attraction to these imperial personages, Kennedy gradually grew to accept the full histories of her heroes, even conceding their legacies of oppression.[45] Both symbols of female power would transform into terrifying but clarifying Afro-alienation acts. In fact, *Funnyhouse* is defined by this colonized/colonizer tension, and Kennedy's unrelenting text never denies the devastating impact of white royals on people of color. Yet she refuses to indict whiteness and European conquest as the sole causes of Sarah's crowded and damaged consciousness.

Kennedy was also writing *Funnyhouse* and traveling just as the African continent was producing independent states free of overt European control. She fondly recalls "the savannahs in Ghana, the white frankopenny trees, the birth of Ghana newly freed from England, scenes of Nkrumah on cloth murals and posters." But she also remembers seeing "Patrice Lumumba on posters and small cards all over Ghana, murdered just after we arrived in Ghana, fall 1960." In colonial Congo, the Belgians were notorious for their brutal reign, and they were implicated in President Lumumba's assassination. By bringing this martyred African leader into contact with Sarah's splintered unconscious, Kennedy participated in what Nikhil Pal Singh calls "the geopolitics of images that linked decolonization and the struggles against U.S. racism."[46]

The Lumumba character placed Kennedy and African American audiences in a larger, contested conversation between American civil rights leadership and international Black Power politics. At the first Congress of Black Artists and Writers in Paris, in 1956, Aimé Césaire remarked that because of racial discrimination, American blacks "find themselves within a great modern nation in an artificial situation that can only be understood in reference to colonialism." Refusing this pan-African connection, American delegates at the conference deflected Césaire's claim with qualifications, such as American Negroes are not a colonized people or the issue of integration in the United States has nothing to do with colonialism.[47] Interestingly, Césaire's pan-African, Afro-Diasporic connection was precisely what Jean Genet had in mind when he introduced his plotting colonial subjects from *The Blacks* to potentially revolutionary American

Negro audiences. Kennedy, as a neophyte playwright, also embraced this transatlantic, pan-African commonality in her work.

Inside Sarah's "unwieldy third space," the powerful but less than imperialist Queen Victoria contends with the lurking, anticolonial Lumumba. In the text, Lumumba fights back against the colonial terror using Sarah's own ruminations on whiteness. Starting with Sarah's dream to live in rooms with Roman ruins, oriental carpets, and images of Queen Victoria, Kennedy projects this speech onto Lumumba, and when he possesses these sentiments, the African leader rearranges her words with outright, postcolonial disgust. Functioning as an Afro-alienation act, Lumumba forces the audience to look at Sarah's personal feelings from a different perspective. He calls her fantasy world "my nigger dream" and "my vile dream to live in rooms with European antiques and my statue of Queen Victoria."[48] In Lumumba's mouth, her desired immersion in whiteness and European high culture now reads as a servile aspiration fit for the most debased and thoroughly colonized African. Yet by having Lumumba comment on this desire and scream back at this horrific colonial history, Kennedy creates space, within Sarah, for a critical relationship to marauding, imperial whiteness.

Much earlier in the play, Sarah explains how she, as her Duchess alter ego, interacts with whiteness and colonial power: "When I am the Duchess of Hapsburg I sit opposite Victoria in my headpiece and we talk. The other time I wear the dress of a student, dark clothes and dark stockings. Victoria always wants me to tell her of whiteness. She wants me to tell her of a royal world where everything and everyone is white and there are no unfortunate black ones."[49] Sarah's description reveals that in becoming the Duchess, her Negro core identity agrees to a gradual yet complete immersion in whiteness and an erasure of blackness. The black college student who wears the stereotypically dark attire of an intellectual gives way to a strictly royal world where colonized Africans no longer exist or matter. The most clarifying detail in the description is that when Sarah becomes the Duchess, Victoria commands that she "tell her of whiteness." Queen Victoria's royal request could be read in a couple different ways. First, it could be interpreted as the colonial subject compelled to recite hard-learned lessons back to the seat of power. Alternately, we might read the Duchess/Sarah's "telling" of whiteness as a colonial subject reinterpreting the Queen, the European castles, and Roman ruins. If we combine both readings, when Sarah/Duchess discourses on whiteness, she is forced to inhabit a world that she did not create and cannot reconcile, yet within her fractured psyche, Sarah, the Duchess, and even Patrice Lumumba can and do rearrange this received world of white supremacy.

Speaking of rearrangement, Kennedy places the opposing forces of decolonization within Sarah, and therefore terrifying consequences await her stage European selves as well. White imperialist icons become the ironic "victims" of colonization, and the terror experienced by Queen Victoria, the Duchess, and Jesus begins with the most prominent markers of racial heritage: hair and skin color. Here is Kennedy's description of how Queen Victoria and the Duchess should look: "*Their headpieces are white and of a net that falls over their face. From beneath both their headpieces springs a headful of wild kinky hair. They look exactly alike and will wear masks or be made to appear a whitish yellow. It is an alabaster face, the skin drawn tightly over the high cheekbones, great dark eyes that seem gouged out of the head, a high forehead, a full red mouth and a head of frizzy hair.*"[50] Both powerful women were once admired symbols of whiteness in Sarah's active imagination, but now, in the moments before her suicide, the white figures have devolved into deathlike projections, estranged versions of a grotesque whiteness.

Let us start with the hair. As an African American woman, Kennedy has admitted to a preoccupation with hair, and she recalls that while writing *Funnyhouse*, "this was the first time in my life that it was impossible to keep my hair straightened. In Ghana and for the rest of the thirteen month trip I stopped straightening my hair."[51] It is difficult to tell whether thirteen months of frizzy hair empowered or transformed Kennedy, but in Sarah's world, kinky hair serves as an uncomfortable reminder of African ancestry and racial impurity. Negroid hair juxtaposed against "whitish yellow" alabaster faces destroys the European notion of beauty and undermines any claims of pure biological whiteness. With this persistent, highly visual Afro-alienation act, the white selves/subjects relive a personal and historical terror played out on their bodies.

These horrifying white royals are the victims of racial intermixture, as evidenced by their unruly combination of whiteface and frizzy hair. Again, the source of their contamination is Sarah's African ancestry, and the spread of this infectious blackness is symbolized by the persistent loss of those unruly, kinky tresses. Earlier in the drama, Sarah explains that her hair first fell out because she "wavered in my opinion of myself," and a few pages later Patrice Lumumba revises that claim with "If I did not despise myself then my hair would not have fallen."[52] Whether the cause is ontological doubt within Sarah or a viral self-hatred, this metaphoric contamination spreads quickly to Sarah's white selves.

The Queen and the Duchess are slowly robbed of their once flaxen, now frizzy locks over the course of the one-act, and soon this disease of amalgamation metastasizes and infects Jesus, an ethereal being. In a scene with the Duchess, Jesus and the German monarch commiserate over their follicle loss, and the stage directions describe how "*their hair is falling more now, they are both hideous.*"[53] Jesus and the Duchess are the most closely aligned selves in Sarah's tortured psyche, so the pair comforts each other as they comb the remaining locks back into place. But their shedding kinky hair is only part of the problem; there is also the issue of color.

Kennedy's nightmare of a devastated whiteness deepens when she provides a theatrical alternative to basic white masks: "*If the characters do not wear a mask then the face must be highly powdered and possess a hard expressionless quality and a stillness as in the face of death.*"[54] A version of this powdered option appears in figure 14, an image from a January 2006 Classical Theatre of Harlem production of *Funnyhouse*. In this photo, Sarah's white heroines are menacing, despite the rosy cheeks painted on the Duchess of Hapsburg. The dark, frizzy, stringy hairs creeping from underneath their headdresses resemble snakes or tangled vines. Escalating the terror, Kennedy's stage directions call for a still, deadly, expressionless whiteness, and the excessively powdered Queen Victoria and Duchess of Hapsburg evoke that sense of ruin and decay.

Unlike the undeniably white Queen Victoria Regina, the Duchess and Jesus struggle with color and even identify themselves as biracial products of miscegenation. Their yellowness functions as both a refuge and an aggrieved "third space." During a conversation with the Queen, in which they typically discuss whiteness, the Duchess, speaking as Sarah, tries to affirm her mother's near-whiteness, based on her straight hair and her resemblance to a white woman. And despite her father, whose parentage and blackness are undisputed, Sarah/Duchess takes solace in the fact that "at least I am yellow."[55] Also, in the scene with her boyfriend Raymond, the Duchess/Sarah is bombarded with questions about this Negro father, evidence that her strictly "white friends"—and we are reading Jewish Raymond as white—fail to provide an effective "embankment" from the fact that she is a Negro. The Duchess/Sarah laments, "I am in between. But my father is the darkest. My father is a nigger who drives me to misery. Any time spent with him evolves itself into suffering. He is a black man

Figure 14 Queen Victoria and the Duchess of Hapsburg terrorize Sarah, the Negro, in a scene from the 2006 Classical Theatre of Harlem production of Adrienne Kennedy's *Funnyhouse of a Negro*. From the *New York Times*, January 20, 2006.

and the wilderness."[56] The Duchess/Sarah defines her father's blackness as beyond racial, more like geographic. He embodies the wilderness, an utter lack of civilization, and the yellow Duchess/Sarah is marooned in between Victoria's palaces and the Negro father's jungle.

For Jesus, Sarah's other vulnerable European or biracial self, his yellowness proves devastating. Kennedy introduces a thoroughly unrecognizable and estranged Jesus with this description: "*a hunchback, yellow-skinned dwarf, dressed in white rags and sandals.*"[57] Sarah then starts to explain his unconventional appearance with an alternate history of the messiah's ancestry, but this is difficult because Sarah no longer trusts the relationships or histories between her selves; she declares them all lies. The "false" connection she finally articulates is that "Jesus is Victoria's son," but she leaves the identity of Christ's father in doubt. Later in a scene where Jesus and the Duchess hide from Sarah's father, who is constantly pursuing them, the paternity issue is resolved. The two characters speak in unison:

"My father isn't going to let us alone. (*knocking.*) Our father isn't going to let us alone, our father is the darkest of us all, my mother was the fairest, I am in between, but my father is the darkest of them all."[58] Notice how the lines begin with "my father" but transition into "our father" after the knocking, which gradually suggests the Duchess and Jesus share a father, and a black one. This Negro father, an untiring assailant who is both returning and abandoning, takes a devastating toll on the already unstable Duchess, pushing her to the brink. One day Jesus visits the Duchess in her chamber, and he "discovers" her body when the swinging and dead Duchess literally falls on him.[59]

Her suicide foreshadows Sarah's inevitable death, but more importantly, it enrages Jesus, estranges a Christian icon, and reactivates a white colonial terror. This vengeful, hunchbacked, biracial messiah provides an entirely different perspective on the son of God. Yet at the same time Kennedy's latest Afro-alienation act, this alternative projection of Christ, functions as an expression and validation of Sarah's personal history. Infuriated by the loss of his playmate to suicide, the hunchbacked Jesus transforms into a vengeful bounty hunter intent on heading to Africa to track down and kill Lumumba/Sarah's father. But this merciless Christ has an even more compelling motive: Jesus is also vengeful "because all my life I believed my Holy Father to be God, but now I know that my father is a black man."[60] Jesus is now officially trapped in the same liminal crisis that destroyed the Duchess and will soon exterminate Sarah. He and legions of followers assumed his father was God, but now he realizes his father was nothing more than a black man who abandoned his mother to become a missionary. Christ's story is now Sarah's story.

Although Patrice Lumumba, Queen Victoria, and the Germanic Duchess of Habsburg are historically the marquee combatants in the internecine colonial battle between whiteness and blackness, in the end of this drama, a higher power in the form of a yellow-skinned Jesus takes the lead in a crusade against Lumumba/Sarah's father.[61] With this act of estrangement or alienation, Kennedy reminds her audience of the horrific history of colonial oppression and biblically justified slavery by recasting the very embodiment of love and mercy as a literal "holy terror," a raging "Angry Saxon" intent on revenge. To complete the Afro-alienation of Jesus Christ, during a climatic showdown scene, in the jungle of "red sun, flying things, wild black grass," yellow Jesus enters, but "unlike previous scenes," he has a nimbus above his head.[62] The nimbus represents sainthood, meaning Jesus has died and returned as an apocalyptic ancestral spirit whose mission is not to give life, like a savior, but to destroy life. Yet Kennedy allows her audience to see Jesus Christ in this new light, as a lone avenging deity, for only a few moments. The climactic jungle showdown is further complicated by the appearance of Sarah's other three selves, including the African Lumumba, all wearing nimbuses above their heads. Now, in the text, all four of Sarah's selves are re-aggregated, speaking in unison, and taking great pleasure in their victory over a Negro father who left but keeps returning.

By the end of Kennedy's drama, a kinky-haired, rapidly balding, in-between whiteness appears to have conquered the father's contaminating blackness. Yet right before Sarah's suicide, Kennedy's final revelation undermines any sense of victory: "*Another wall drops. There is a white plaster statue of Queen Victoria which represents the Negro's room in the brownstone, the room appears near the staircase highlight lit and small. The main prop is the statue. . . . The figure of Victoria is a sitting figure, one of astonishing repulsive whiteness, suggested by dusty volumes of books and old yellowed walls.*"[63] With this last act of estrangement, the dramatic dropping of a wall, we finally see the statue Sarah admired for its "astonishing whiteness" from the start of this drama. Also earlier in the play, Sarah mentioned how her boyfriend Raymond described Queen Victoria's bust as "a thing of terror, possessing the quality of nightmares, suggesting large and probable deaths."[64] Raymond's assessment proves prophetic as Queen Victoria is finally revealed and her whiteness is not astonishing; it is repulsive, antiquated, and truly deadly. In her final moment on earth, Sarah, along with Kennedy's audience, sees this destructive white monarch with clear eyes.

We should remember that Sarah's psyche is the source of all these Afro-alienation acts: She projected an empowering ideal of Queen Victoria onto this decrepit, antique statue; she refashioned an unforgiving Yellow Jesus; and she generated a juxtaposed alabaster mask and frizzy hair for her white selves. Womanist theorist bell hooks can help us understand what these "things of terror" represent for Sarah and why she needed to possess this alabaster statue of the monarch. Hooks explains that "blacks who imitate whites (adopting their values, speech, habits of being, etc.) continue to regard whiteness with suspicion, fear, and even hatred. This contradictory longing to posses the reality of the Other, even though that reality is one that wounds and negates, is expressive of the desire to understand the mystery, to know intimately through imitation, as though such knowing worn like an amulet, a mask, will ward away the evil, the terror."[65] The bust of Victoria has wounded, negated, and deluded this young woman, but it is necessary for Kennedy, Sarah, and many African Americans to unlock its mystery, which is why Sarah has to possess her.

Responding to the horror and darkness at the heart of a 1995 revival of *Funnyhouse*, *New York Times* critic Margo Jefferson identifies a productive power emanating from Kennedy and her selves. She claims that in this funhouse, this madhouse, "horror has invented you and you are inventing it right back."[66] Jefferson clearly appreciated the demystifications happening throughout *Funnyhouse* and how Kennedy was reinventing or restaging the painful and terrifying history that instilled "warring ideals" in so many dark bodies. Thankfully Kennedy worked through her early trepidation in Albee's workshop and completed this messy black interiority indicative of the turbulent 1960s and centuries before. But as much as Kennedy possesses, unmasks, and estranges whiteness, one wonders if the evil and the terror are ever truly warded off. Kennedy never claimed to be as process-oriented as LeRoi Jones or Robert Macbeth, with their healing, communal rituals, so we should not expect victory or triumph from *Funnyhouse*. However, Kennedy's difficult expressionist drama is committed to a heightened self-awareness and potential purging of whiteness, if we are willing to wait.

At the close of *The Blacks*, Genet scripts a conversation between the Queen of the Court, a fading white monarch, and Felicity, a wise black matriarch. In this deadly yet friendly exchange, the ladies reveal how Kennedy and 1960s Afro-America might eventually triumph:

> *Felicity:* If you're death itself, then why, why do you reproach me for killing you?
>
> *The Queen:* And if I'm dead, why do you go on and on killing me, murdering me over and over in my color? Isn't my sublime corpse—which still moves—enough for you? Do you need the corpse of a corpse? (*Side by side, almost amicably, the two women move forward to the very front of the stage.*)
>
> *Felicity:* I shall have the corpse of your corpse's ghost. You are pale, but you're becoming transparent. Fog that drifts over my land, you will vanish utterly. . . .[67]

Right before this exchange, Felicity called the Queen "a ruin," and the mildly indignant Queen responded by embracing and aligning herself with death. Therefore, in this particular beat, the Queen cannot understand, if she is already decayed and dead, why the Negro performers feel compelled to continue enacting imitative rituals that end in the death and destruction of whiteness.

Kennedy's *Funnyhouse* provides an answer. Unlike other 1960s black playwrights, Kennedy developed a partly historical, partly autobiographical, and intensely ritualistic interiority that labored to break through dichotomous categories like white/black, male/female, civilized/savage, colonist/colonized. Unfortunately, those dualities were all determined from the top down, by white royals, like Genet's Queen, who designed these hierarchical relationships to withstand generations of contestation.[68] Felicity, Genet's black matriarch, acknowledges that the craftsmanship of the white colonizer is so imprinted on her land and in the minds of her people that they need the repetitive ritual murders to eradicate all vestiges of whiteness. Kennedy's *Funnyhouse* is about re-creating the horror and performing the original white architects of the terror, over and over, until they are completely exposed, transparent enough to "vanish utterly."

A Dependent South

Actor, producer, and playwright Douglas Turner Ward's *Day of Absence* was "conceived for performance by a black cast, a reverse minstrel show done in whiteface."[69] This one-act expands on Bob Cole's turn-of-the-century assault on blackface minstrelsy by relocating Willie Wayside from a fictional, black middle-class Coontown to the metaphoric heart of Dixie. Ward's satire is about a Confederate, oddly anachronistic small town in the "present-day" South, which suffers a major identity crisis when its "Nigras" mysteriously disappear. In 1965, Ward teamed up with actor/producer Robert Hooks to mount a twin bill at St. Mark's Playhouse in the East Village, pairing *Day of Absence* with another one-act by Ward called *Happy Ending*. The companion piece was an equally satirical but less fantastical comedy about manipulative black domestics working for a wealthy white family. Both Hooks and Ward starred in *Day of Absence*, with Ward assuming the lead role of Mayor Henry R. E. Lee, a whiteface Confederate clown saddled with saving his town from this mysterious "Nigra" absence. The double bill enjoyed a fourteen-month run, 504 performances, at St. Mark's. Ward would win a Vernon Rice Award for his playwriting and an Obie Award for his acting, and this Hooks-Ward collaboration would lead to the creation of the Negro Ensemble Company, which quickly became a powerhouse in 1960s black theater.[70]

Demonstrating the first function of whiting up, Ward's *Day of Absence* uses satiric cross-racial play to expose how white and black Americans are economically and culturally interdependent. It is regrettable that Douglas Turner Ward is rarely given credit for his enduring and nuanced reading of race, power, and economics in America. In 1965, critics agreed that the production's comedic style was too broad and Ward's white caricatures were antiquated, even condescending. In 1993, *New York Times* critic Alvin Klein dismissed Ward's one-act as an archaic sketch that reinforced the racist linkage between black workers and menial jobs.[71] To be accurate, this revival of *Day of Absence* did not reinforce racial assumptions but, rather, highlighted a disturbing economic reality: Thirty years after Ward's reverse minstrel show debuted, African Americans were still disproportionately represented, or trapped, in low-level service-economy jobs.

Samuel Hay is the one theater historian who has thoughtfully considered Ward's theatrical practice in light of his economic agenda and activist background.[72] As a student at the University of Michigan from 1947 to 1948, Douglas Turner Ward joined a campus organization with Communist leanings because this student group was interested in eradicating racism. His collegiate involvement in leftist causes allowed Ward to advocate for voiceless Americans on the margins of society, and many of these marginalized Americans were Negroes. Similar to labor organizer A. Philip Randolph and activist-actor Canada Lee, Ward believed the progress and futures of labor and American Negroes were interconnected. After college, in New York City, Ward became a leader of the Labor Youth League, an organization funded by the U.S. Communist Party to attract young workers. While he organized for the Left, Ward also attempted to build a life in the theater, but predictably, his artistic pursuits were hampered by his political activities. In 1951 Ward was convicted of draft evasion, probably due to his opposition to the Korean War and his involvement with the Labor Youth League. Fortunately, in 1953 the U.S. Supreme Court overturned his conviction, and Ward was free to resume his theatrical activities.

In a 1966 *New York Times* editorial titled "American Theater: For Whites Only?" Ward articulated his position as politico and artist, and he also diagnosed a major problem in our national theater. The leftist Ward characterized American theater as a bourgeois theater, more specifically a "pretentious theater elevating the narrow preoccupations of restricted class interests to inflated universal significance."[73] This exclusively middle-class identification rendered the current American theater "incapable of engaging the attention of anyone not so fortunate as to possess a college diploma or five-figure salary." Perhaps referring to recent productions by Jean Genet, Edward Albee, and Adrienne Kennedy, Ward identified much of New York theater as sheltered in a "lofty-modern niche" and locked into "a pseudo-absurdity and closet-avant daring" with no real communal connections or political consciousness. A couple years before Larry Neal's Black Arts manifesto condemned Western theater as empty and disconnected, Ward argued the very same point in the editorial section of the *New York Times*.

As an example of what a connected theater might look like, Hooks and Ward's 1965 twin bill purported to offer "works of satirical content written from an unapologetic Negro viewpoint." In terms of a public for his satire, ideally Ward wanted "a sufficient audience of other Negroes, better informed through commonly shared experience to readily understand, debate, confirm, or reject the truth or falsity" of his satiric product. Ward's pointed and connected work required spectators with an experiential foundation and an ability to critically assess the ideas presented. Back in the 1920s, in Chicago and New York, Evelyn Preer encountered Negro audiences and critics unprepared or unwilling to divest themselves of the Nordic Complex and accept Negroes outside low comedy. Although Ward envisioned a sophisticated black public who could appreciate his satirical wit, he did not want to exclude whites. In fact, Ward's *Day of Absence* targeted white America, challenging the majority culture to see itself with fresh eyes and develop a good, tension-releasing chuckle. Ward wanted to reach and teach whites, and he imagined that in a theater filled with Negroes responding wholeheartedly to a performance, "white spectators, congenitally uneasy in the presence of Negro satire, at least can't fail to get the message."

So what was Ward's message for interracial audiences in 1965, 1993, and the twenty-first century? This stage European fantasy reaches well beyond simply swapping whiteface for blackface for cheap laughs. In his satiric reverse minstrel show, Ward targeted an incredibly peculiar yet familiar slice of the American South; he staged a retrograde place deeply defined and fixed by the "Rebel Cause." However, he leaves it up to his audience to "understand, debate, confirm or reject the truth" of his imaginative re-creation of southern whiteness. Working within this artificial and satiric world, Ward's primary message is that white economic privilege in America is predicated on underappreciated Negro labor. Most of the black workers Ward references in *Day of Absence* are confined to backbreaking blue-collar jobs, but some "undercover" African Americans have infiltrated into other segments of this southern economy. This brings us to Ward's secondary message: Southern identity and culture are so thoroughly defined by blackness, it would be disastrous, apocalyptic, to separate black from white.

Ward claims the play takes place in the "now," 1965, but his unnamed southern town feels frozen in a bygone era. Reminders of the failed Confederacy are everywhere, in the town hospital, Confederate Memorial, and a regional social club named Daughters of the Confederate Rebellion, a clear play on the Daughters of the American Revolution. Even the town's political and spiritual leadership honors the "Rebel Cause" with names like the Reverend Reb Pious and Mayor Henry Robert E. Lee.[74] The most entertaining illustration of a town mired in the past occurs when a northern white reporter interviews Mayor Lee following the loss of the town's "Nigras." In front of a national television audience, Mayor Lee takes advantage of the local trauma to subjectively recount how Lincoln "temporarily" freed the slaves and how carpetbaggers forced elected "Nigra" officials on state and federal legislatures during Reconstruction.[75] Despite these vile fruits of the War of Northern Aggression, Mayor Lee confidently proclaims that "Southern courage, fortitude, chivalry and superiority always wins out." His boastful speech is glaringly ahistorical as it suggests the South somehow prevailed in the Civil War. But the sly comment on Lincoln's "temporary" emancipation is not so much revisionist as an allusion to the economic repression southern landowners implemented to replace slavery. In the face of crisis, Mayor Lee needs to adopt this overly confident posture; he has to reassure himself and the town that the "same chips-down blood courses through these Confederate gray veins of Henry Robert E. Lee."

Although New York critics generally panned *Day of Absence*, they singled out Ward's "Confederate gray" mayor as an amusing and impressive highlight; such praise probably earned Ward an Obie for his acting performance.[76] With this caricatured representation of southern small-town whiteness, performed in clownish whiteface, Ward suggests that these irredeemable rebels and white supremacists were asking to lose their "Nigras." This isolated little hamlet was targeted by some mysterious force because it is a retrograde emblem of the Old South, firmly resistant to progress and paralyzed by its adulation of a failed Confederate cause. For Ward's immediate East Village public in 1965, the implication was that "they," those southerners and not us northerners, must contend with a monumental identity crisis. Playing on regional difference, Ward effectively distances southern whiteness from the northern variety, thus allowing white patrons at St. Mark's Playhouse to feel superior to laughable targets like Mayor Lee. Apparently, Ward's pointed satire hit its targets and missed the "innocent." Much to his surprise, *Village Voice* critic Michael Smith reported that white and black patrons in the East Village audience "responded to the play with great enthusiasm."[77]

This comedy sends the message that northern, presumably more liberal whiteness is nothing like the whiteness of those backward southern Confederates. But there is a subtextual, economic threat lurking in *Day of Absence*: This could happen in New York if northern white leadership is not careful. Ward begins his economic cautionary tale at the very bottom of America's workforce but builds to a gradual reconsideration of how Negro labor fully impacts this southern economy and potentially beyond.

The satire opens with two clownish stage Europeans, Luke and Clem, lounging in front of their store. One man notices a disturbing absence of Negroes "sweeping sidewalks, cleaning stores, starting to shine shoes and wetting mops."[78] This is the "grunt" work often overlooked by a community until this labor is conspicuously absent. When Mayor Lee learns the town's Negroes have not reported for work, he automatically assumes he is dealing with "a bunch of lazy Nigras been out drunk and living it up all night!" Yet the Mayor's image of an indolent, undisciplined black workforce is contradicted when an industrialist, speaking on behalf of local factory owners, informs the Mayor that "seventy-five per cent of all production is paralyzed" because they are missing Negro workers.[79] Admittedly, the absent Negro employees were not the skilled labor operating machinery but, rather, the "menials" cleaning the machinery, sweeping floors, lifting crates, delivering equipment, and cleaning toilets. Some might misread the industrialist's distinction as stereotypic, but I read it as Ward highlighting an important caste division within blue-collar labor. In this southern town and northern cities, "Nigras" are limited to maintenance or support jobs, not directly involved in equipment operation, yet their hard labor is still integral to daily production.

Ward follows his argument about blue-collar stratification with ironic contrasts and revealing interdependencies between white-collar workers, blue-collar workers, and black domestics. Inside the home of a white couple, John and Mary awake after a "head splittin' blow-out last night" where Mary guzzled countless bourbons and John drank the "entire bar."[80] Ironically, the Mayor accuses the "Nigras" of being absent because they were out drinking, but apparently John and Mary needed this lecture on

Figure 15 A frightened John and Mary in a scene from the 2008 University of Virginia production of Douglas Turner Ward's *Day of Absence*. Photo ©2009 Michael Bailey.

work-night discipline. In figure 15 we see a distraught, hungover John and Mary from an October 2008 University of Virginia production of *Day of Absence*. After a rough night, this couple has been rudely aroused by a crying baby whom Mary cannot comfort because that job belongs to Lula, her black domestic—hence the terror on their faces. This domestic image of a frightened, helpless white couple embodies the southern family in decline without their black help. As a testament to how dependent southern white families had become on black domestics, a clubwoman in the town forecasts "advanced diaper chafings," "unsanitary household disasters," and "a complete breakdown in family unity" if the Negroes do not return soon.[81]

Beyond the home front, this whiteface, blonde-haired John represents the white-collar head of the southern household who pursues promotions so his stay-at-home spouse can enjoy a life of leisure. And what keeps it all together is the seemingly invisible labor of black housekeepers and child-care workers. He explains to his pampered and hopelessly undomesticated wife that while she sits on her "fanny," he has been "beating a frantic crew of nice young executives to the punch," getting to work earlier to engage in "the most brown-nosing you ever saw!"[82] John has been able to leave early because Lula has always had his breakfast, especially his coffee, ready, so in her absence, he demands that his wife step up and deliver.

The production image (fig. 15) visually underlines the dependence of white families on black bodies. But we should also note how the intentionally incomplete makeup job, especially the black hands of the two actors, highlights the simultaneous, interconnected performance of blackness and whiteness. This intentional revelation contrasts with Canada Lee's *Duchess of Malfi* photo (fig. 13), in which he covers his hands with gloves to conceal his blackness. In Ward's satiric *Day of Absence*, the duality of heavily powdered faces and dark hands foregrounds how intertwined black and white Americans are in this town and the entire country. The clownish white faces, red lips, and blonde wigs identify these stage Europeans with an absurd, excessive, and potentially destructive white privilege, while the dark hands signify the black maids, cooks, and nannies who make John and Mary's southern comfort and extreme leisure possible. In short, there is no white manager John without his black domestic Lula.

Initially, the "Nigras" in Ward's satire are glaringly and understandably absent from John's world of managers and executives, but this absence can be read as more commentary on occupational stratification. However, economic and social dynamics shift drastically when a Courier drops a bombshell on the Mayor and the town. Vice-Mayor Woodfence, the town's second-in-command, who also happens to be the Mayor's brother-in-law, has not reported for work, and the Mayor's worried sister has not seen her husband since last night. The Courier also reports that two City Council members, the chairman of the Junior Chamber of Commerce, and the chairlady of the Daughters of the Confederate Rebellion have all disappeared. The Mayor and the Courier arrive at the same inescapable conclusion: These prominent white citizens have been passing, infiltrating as "Secret Nigras." The implication here is that America's notorious one-drop laws, passed in many states to identify mixed-race citizens as Negroes, have failed miserably. Legally defined mulattos, quadroons, and octoroons have climbed into prominent and privileged positions in this highly Confederate town through conscious or unconscious racial deception.

Some critics might accuse Ward of suggesting that these "secret" Negroes attained their white-collar positions because of their white bloodlines, but here is yet another controversial idea for Ward's audience to debate and assess for its truth or falsity. Unequivocally, the revelation that some citizens were passing cuts to the core of this Confederate town's identity, but is Ward's satiric reverse minstrel show equipped to process the serious damage of this racial deception? As soon as Mayor Lee announces that Woodfence and other city officials have been passing, Ward's stage directions call for an assortment of "bedraggled" souls carrying signs in a picket line. Among them is a "woman dressed in widow-black"; this is Woodfence's wife, and she is a shattered figure carrying a sign that reads, "Why didn't you tell us—your defiled wife and two absent mongrels."[83]

This darkly comic sign expresses the disintegration of a family and the absolute destruction of a woman who thought she knew who she was. The same is true for Mr. Woodfence, who could have been spirited away by this mysterious Negro absence without ever knowing about his racial background. Like the three European selves in *Funnyhouse of a Negro*, Mrs. Woodfence believes her life has been "contaminated" and her whiteness compromised. This is no laughing matter, but the deeper truths Ward reveals are that Negroes have been part of white genealogies for generations and that the absurd laws and cultural conventions that once defined two mixed-race children as "mongrels" were the true tragedies. Southerners and northerners in the 1960s would not have been surprised by the bombshell of passing or the truth it exposed about American intermixture. Among Ward's immediate audience, an integrated New York public, his over-the-top treatment of passing could be interpreted as satire designed to wound real-life versions of Mrs. Woodfence.[84] Yet Ward's intended target was never specific white southerners, but the retrograde Confederate heritage and mentality that produced one-drop laws and prevented the American South from truly rising again.

This discovery of "secret Nigras" serves as a powerful fulcrum moment in Ward's one-act, setting up a series of broader, rapidly accumulating reversals that touch on white southern identity, Euro-American identity, and the popular image of urban blacks in the tumultuous 1960s. During his first interview with the northern reporter, Mayor Lee admits that "the South has always been glued together by the uninterrupted presence of its darkies. No telling how unstuck we might git if things keep on like they have."[85] Southerners could hardly deny the Mayor's admission, and as discussed in Chapter 1, white slave masters tried to cultivate a paternalistic slave system based on economic and social interdependence. There is ample evidence that this Confederate town is coming apart, and its white citizens need Negroes for salvation.

In a deliciously ironic speech, Mayor Lee decries the Supreme Court's efforts to desegregate schools and accuses this federally backed integration scheme of helping the "Nigra" to "put hisself everywhere."[86] One byproduct of desegregation across the United States was white flight from urban centers, as Euro-Americans rushed to get away from the "plague" of an elevated Negro presence. Paradoxically, in this southern town, where the black citizens have been mysteriously absent for less than twenty-four hours, townspeople have been "overtaken by anarchistic turmoil" and are "seeking haven elsewhere." They are fleeing their decimated town to locate a "soothing" black presence in other communities, but these particular white southerners are being turned away because other white towns believe the intruders are jinxed or cursed.[87] In an ingenious comic reversal, Ward stages unglued whites "flying" toward black contact, as the rest of the nation scrambles to protect their cities, and their Negroes, from suffering the same mysterious fate.

Ward does not stop with this one reversal and unleashes another sardonic twist. As the rapidly unraveling Confederate hamlet comes to "a strickened [*sic*] standstill" and the "industrial machinery clanks to a halt," the northern television announcer reports that "National Guardsmen and State Militia were impotent in quelling the fury of a town venting its frustration in an orgy of destruction—a frenzy of rioting, looting and all other aberration of a town gone beserk [*sic*]."[88] Playing on countless 1960s newscasts of blacks burning their communities, the same unrest studied by the Kerner Commission, Ward reverses this prevailing imagery of urban chaos in the minds of New York audiences. He takes the anger, frustration, and nihilism associated with urban blackness and attaches it to southern, small-town whiteness, a masterful displacement reminiscent of Bob Cole's work with whiteness and chicken.

As for a black satiric tradition, Ward's *Day of Absence* builds on the work of George Schuyler, the editor and columnist for the *Messenger* who spewed sardonic venom at countless targets in his weekly "Shafts and Darts" column. In 1931 Schuyler channeled his iconoclastic wit and style into a novel about American racialism titled *Black No More*, one of the best satirical investigations of race in American literature. The novel is about a black scientist, Dr. Junius Crookman, who creates a treatment that combines nutritional and glandular science to erase the "everlasting stain" of race. According to historian Jeffrey B. Ferguson, Schuyler's cultural agenda was to provoke all Americans to view race as a shifting "social category" that should be approached "practically and complexly" rather than dwelled on obsessively.[89] Crookman's first client is Max Disher, a black man who undergoes the treatment and begins his new life as white Matthew Fisher; he marries a white woman and rises through the ranks of a white supremacist organization similar to the Ku Klux Klan (KKK).[90]

In 1998, Arena Stage in Washington, D.C., produced playwright Syl Jones's stage adaptation of Schuyler's *Black No More*. One reviewer described Max Disher's "stage whiteness" as "entirely a matter of attitude and posture" and noted that the lone "white" costume item used was a "golden wig." The rest of the transformation was purely physical and vocal, as "the moment Max is ramrod straight, talking like a TV anchor, walking without a strut, and hankering for a game of golf, he's embraced by white society."[91] With the proper walk and privileged attitude, the new Matthew Fisher was on the road to whiteness and prosperity, and not surprisingly, masses of racialized African Americans in Schuyler's novel and Jones's adaptation follow Disher's lead and undergo the race-changing treatment.

Regrettably, Ward and company's 1960s performed whiteness was unfocused and failed to achieve the same satirical precision as Schuyler's (and Syl Jones's) *Black No More*. Master satirist George Schuyler understood that his shafts and darts hit their targets only when his comic constructions were carefully and accurately drawn. In 1965, *New York Times* critic Howard Taubman concluded that Douglas Turner Ward was learning Schuyler's craft but was not yet a "devastating satirist." Also, in staging Ward's broadly satirical *Day of Absence*, director Philip Meister miscalculated by encouraging his black actors to use an exaggerated "Negro diction." For Taubman, this racially specific sound was difficult to understand, and as result, the actors' satirical "shafts often go astray."[92] Southern regional dialects and "Negro diction" can be confused, especially in the ear of a New York critic, but this particular confusion may have indicated a more serious problem in Ward's stage European project.

Critic Howard Taubman experienced a crisis of recognition. He was seeing whiteface caricatures of white southerners onstage but hearing and barely understanding Negro speech; so in essence, the white characters were not reading as distinctly Caucasian. One generous explanation for this signification problem is that maybe Meister's production was intentionally conflating southern white and Negro sounds, similar to the intertwined blackness and whiteness depicted in figure 15. More likely, Meister, Ward, and the rest of the artistic team simply failed to make the necessary distinctions in the Negro actors' speech to re-create the "sound" of white privilege and authority. More fully delineated satirical targets, from Ward, and more racially distinct stage Europeans, from Meister and his actors, would have ensured that their pointed attacks landed and landed with greater force.

In terms of the cultural work of these satires, during his era, the 1920s and 1930s, Schuyler viewed Negroes as overly invested in the "race concept," as evidenced by racial passing and newspaper inducements to straighten and lighten. *Day of Absence* makes a similar albeit less strident case in the 1960s, but Ward is more focused on the economic impacts and cultural dynamics of a specific region. Schuyler also believed blacks needed to reject American racialism and the desire to pass. Instead, according to Jeffrey B. Ferguson, this model satirist wanted Afro-America to embrace the qualities that "made blacks resilient, one might say even triumphant under difficult environmental circumstances."[93] Ward does offer a similar message of black social and political empowerment as he attempts to explain the mysterious and increasingly complicated forces behind this "Nigra" disappearance.

Reminiscent of the hidden revolution running parallel to the "clown show" in Genet's *The Blacks*, Ward suggests a mystical yet politically motivated offstage universe in *Day of Absence*. Mayor Lee's assistant Jackson constantly updates the Mayor on the status of efforts to the save their town. He reports that the NAACP is denying any responsibility for the missing "Nigras," but they are being aggressively investigated by a Senate committee. But regrettably, certain black leaders who were expected to make appeals for the Negroes to return have "themselves mysteriously disappeared," which suggests that some yet-unnamed political force is behind this mass disappearance. Jackson announces that imprisoned Negroes being transported to the town revolted and escaped before reaching the city limits.[94] As a result, no fresh infusion of Negro comfort is allowed to rescue this beleaguered town, and like the white Court in *The Blacks*, the white citizens must be resigned to their fate. Of course, this being a comedy, once twenty-four hours are up, Ward lets this Confederate stronghold off the hook, as a lone Negro named Rastus reappears. The still-unexplained assault on the town seems to have subsided, but Rastus lets a "flicker of smile" play across his lips, a knowing gesture that suggests Afro-America's campaign for economic justice is not over.[95]

Returning to the critical reception of *Day of Absence*, although Ward's satire is perhaps too broad and imprecise, I think many theater and cultural critics assume they are always a few steps ahead of this deceptively simple comedy. Critic Jacqueline Wood, who has written insightfully on Adrienne Kennedy, argues that "*Day of Absence* does little more than suggest that things should or could be different. The actions and developments of the characters do not in any consistent way challenge the materiality of race but rather accentuate and protest the ludicrous inequities and assumptions of racist difference."[96] Wood misses an important function of Ward's satire, which is to expose the constructed nature of race. As we see in figure 15, this play demands a visual language where whiteness and blackness are performed on top of each other. In this forced, less than seamless blend of biological markers of difference, an audience is never allowed to lose sight of the fact that race is performative. And as for "assumptions of racist difference," Ward uses satire, rather than tragedy like Adrienne Kennedy, to challenge the notion of a pure or protected whiteness.

Wood is correct when she says Ward merely suggests things could be different, but by staging black economic and cultural presence through absence, Ward introduced a powerful method for protesting economic inequities. Writing about *Day of Absence*, Geneviève Fabre concedes Ward's one-act was more entertaining than threatening to white America; however, she believes the production invited black audiences to imagine "the possible consequences of such an absence" and essentially functioned as "an incitement to strike."[97] Ward's satire generated an activist statement about the value of black labor even while substantive economic protests were building beyond this East Village theater. Ironically, *Day of Absence* debuted in the midst of a subway strike, which initially reduced Ward's audiences but, more importantly, highlighted the capacity of black, white, and brown workers to plunge the city that never sleeps into a prolonged coma. Also, some Harlem militant groups, inspired by *Day of Absence*'s early performances, decided to institute an official "Day of Absence" to be observed every November 5.[98] The operating principle of this public protest was for all African Americans to stay home from work to demonstrate black economic power through absence. Since Douglas Turner Ward had a background in leftist politics and workers' rights, this kind of extra-theatrical demonstration must have been truly gratifying for him. Also, during his days as artistic director of the Negro Ensemble Company in the East Village, Ward made a concerted effort to attract working-class blacks, of course without excluding whites from his potential public.[99]

Another potential objection to *Day of Absence* is that Ward's seemingly archaic 1960s satire is irrelevant in the twenty-first century. Recently two black academics, Jackie M. Roberts and Brandi Wilkins Catanese, have written about teaching, producing, and processing black political dramas on majority-white campuses. Based on her work as an acting teacher, Roberts argues that the work we do in and out of the classroom should be "in dialogue with our students' immediate community and wrestle with some tension of our students' daily lives."[100] Surprisingly, Roberts found that plays from the 1960s—works by Baraka and Kennedy—tended to invest students with "a greater sense of cultural ownership," and those works accomplish this significant feat because of the racial complexity, the cultural specificity, and the "radically transformative political and emotional trajectory" of the characters.[101] Ward's *Day of Absence* has the same capacity to tap into personal and campus tensions around issues of class and race.

In a pedagogical article specifically on *Day of Absence*, Brandi Wilkins Catanese explains how teaching and directing this satire on a modern college campus is "an exercise in site-specificity." *Day of Absence* has been frequently produced on college campuses across the country, but for today's purportedly postracial students, the play may read like a distant rumination on racial assumptions that no longer exist. According to Catanese, one question an instructor should ask to effectively teach this material is "What are the racial demographics of my institution."[102] On majority-white college campuses, the racial disparity between faculty and support staff makes the central economic message of *Day of Absence* extremely relevant. Whenever I teach *Day of Absence*, I ask students to note the demographic discrepancy between the people who are "serving" them as instructors and professors in the classroom and those who are "serving" them in other campus contexts. The workers distributing food in the dining hall, cleaning buildings, landscaping the campus, and providing administrative support to departments tend to be disproportionately of color. Conversely, the faculty members advising, teaching, and conducting research on campus remain overwhelmingly white, even as the student populations on majority-white campuses become increasingly diversified.

This is precisely the kind of occupational discrimination Ward made comically apparent through the crisis of one small southern town bereft of its Negroes. He also used the mask of whiteness to challenge contemporary concerns like black urban unrest or white flight and to make a somewhat obvious case for the hidden "blackness" of southern families. Yet amidst such challenges and revelations, Ward incited his audiences to question the economic discrepancies and cultural assumptions in their everyday lives. In doing so, this reverse minstrel show reoriented where African Americans saw themselves in America's cultural, political, and economic hierarchies. A day of presence through absence moved blacks from the margins to the center and affirmed American dependence on a most significant labor force.

The White Beast

Radicalized by a trip to Cuba in 1960 and the death of Malcolm X in 1965, LeRoi Jones (later Amiri Baraka) abandoned his bohemian, Beat roots in Greenwich Village to inhabit a relatively new but already dynamic world of black cultural nationalism in Harlem.[103] Although a neophyte in this particular Afro-Diasporic universe, Jones was soon defining a new black aesthetic, and doing so with funding from the federal government. Before creating the Kerner Commission to investigate the causes of urban riots in the 1960s, President Lyndon Johnson tried the proactive step of pouring millions of dollars into Harlem Youth Opportunities Unlimited, the nation's first community-based antipoverty program, founded by noted psychologist Kenneth Clark in 1962. During the summer of 1965, Jones accessed some of this money and launched a multidisciplinary arts program that used trucks and portable stages to take art to the people.

Jones, backed by a volatile cadre of cultural nationalists, would eventually launch a revolutionary theater, Black Arts Repertory Theatre and School (BARTS), committed to creating plays that reoriented the worldview of Africans in the Americas and moved them to action. To facilitate personal and communal reeducation, the formerly middle-class and integrationist Jones constructed ritualistic, mythic, moralistic, yet still activist dramas featuring highly experimental stage Europeans. The primary function of Jones's whiting up dramas was to identify the white terror within, which often read as a troubled double consciousness or ambivalence, and eradicate that terror. Far from exploring, as did Kennedy or Ward, how interdependent or co-dependent whiteness and blackness were in the 1960s, Jones staged whiteness as a most destructive enemy.

His earliest stage Europeans appeared in *Experimental Death Unit #1* (1965), a one-act about two absurd and sexually ambivalent white hipsters searching for the "heat" of a black prostitute. The white characters Duff and Loco resemble the comic pairs in Samuel Beckett's *Waiting for Godot*, and their language harkens back to the aesthetics and attitudes of Jones's Beat Generation days. The two hipsters create a pointless, absurd couple; the black prostitute is a lost Negro soul; and all three are exterminated by a roving band of black revolutionaries who choose action over metaphors and euphemisms.[104] *Experimental Death Unit #1* debuted in March

1965 at St. Mark's Playhouse. The audience was largely white, perhaps the wrong community for Jones's experimental reeducation, but this specific production was part of an ambitious fund-raising campaign to renovate a Harlem brownstone to house BARTS. For the premiere of *Experimental Death Unit #1,* white actors played Duff and Loco, and in the original text there is no specification that the two characters have to be played by black actors. However, in a subsequent remount at a 1972 Imamu Amiri Baraka theater festival at Harlem's Afro-American Studio, a more militant Baraka cast the two white roles with black actors performing in whiteface.[105]

Jones also explored performed whiteness in *Madheart,* a morality play composed in 1966 and first performed at San Francisco State College in 1967. *Madheart* is about a white Devil Lady, a "vampire-like" white temptress in an "elaborately carved white devil mask" who, through television and sentimental movies, exerts tremendous influence on two black females, Mother and Sister.[106] Like Sarah and her obsession with whiteness in Kennedy's *Funnyhouse,* these two women exhibit an intense desire for and fear of whiteness, with Mother even revering whites as gods. After the drama's revolutionary hero, Black Man, drives a stake through the Devil Lady's heart, Sister mourns her role model, calling the dying Devil Lady "my dead sister reflection." In an attempt to restore her "beautiful self," Sister insists on wearing a blonde wig and transforms into a "mad raving creature." Black Man, with the assistance of the enlightened female character Black Woman, tries to "redeem" Sister and Mother, but Black Man ultimately has to turn a water hose on these lost souls until they lapse into unconsciousness. Jones's usage of a water hose, which references images of black protesters doused with water during civil rights demonstrations, is a disturbing and surely calculated choice.

Jones constructed *Madheart* and *Experimental Death Unit #1* on the premise that black females are more vulnerable to European notions of beauty and morality, an idea rooted in the male chauvinism that became synonymous with black cultural nationalism. In *A Black Mass,* Jones would repeat this sexist trope of a more complicit black female, but in many respects, this one-act departs from his earlier experiments with whiting up. Larry Neal once identified *A Black Mass* as Jones's "most important play mainly because it is informed by a mythology that is wholly the creation of the Afro-American sensibility."[107] The core proposition of this play is that whiteness was created by an ancient black scientist or magician. However, while staging and propagating this African-centered mythology, Jones critiques the "god complex" resident in Africans and Europeans.

LeRoi Jones started writing *A Black Mass* in 1965, as he fought to make BARTS work in the midst of hellacious internal conflicts and power struggles. The play did not premiere until 1966, when a reinvented Jones left Harlem and reconstituted his Black Arts efforts in Newark, New Jersey, with a new institution called Spirit House. During Jones/Baraka's nationalist period, both Islam and the Yoruba religion influenced his evolving spiritual philosophy, but he did not get serious about his faith until he moved back to Newark and came under the influence of Sunni Muslims. *A Black Mass* premiered at Proctor's Theatre, a partially renovated movie theater in Newark, as a collaborative effort with jazz legend Sun Ra and his Myth Science Arkestra. Sun Ra's distinctive sound led the audience into a world of original, ancient black arts, with "music of eternal concentration and wisdom."[108]

Jacoub, the black magician at the center of Jones's ritual drama, is an overreaching, maniacal creationist who invents the "plague of time," accidentally produces animals spewing time, and intentionally forms a soulless, neutral creature antithetical to humanity. Why infect the world with such creations? *A Black Mass* suggests this reckless black magician/pseudoscientist suffers from an inner crisis related to a defective conception of "self." In a 1994 essay in which he reconsiders black aesthetics, Baraka reflects on what the movement, past and present, is trying to accomplish. He explains that "fundamentally we must pursue what DuBois called the True Self Consciousness and defeat its reverse the Double Consciousness."[109] In *Souls of Black Folk*, DuBois barely defines "true self-consciousness" and primarily references this identity concept in relation to double consciousness. As previously stated, DuBois argued that, in America, Negroes are born with a powerful veil that only allows them to see themselves through the eyes of others, which leads to a problematic double consciousness.[110] For Baraka, a true self-consciousness meant a grounded, unified sense of self liberated from white influence.

At BARTS and Spirit House, Jones was committed to moving Afro-America beyond that debilitating duality, the internally warring whiteness and blackness staged in Kennedy's horrific *Funnyhouse of a Negro*. Unlike Kennedy, Jones was committed to rapidly developing, staging, and propagating a triumphantly unified black self at war with internal white terror and external symbols of white oppression. Jacoub, the irresponsible scientist, suffers from a dualistic or fractured way of thinking and fails to accept the wholeness of black humanity. In *A Black Mass*, he is exposed, deconstructed, and sacrificed as a cautionary tale for Afro-America.

When Larry Neal used the term "Afro-American sensibility" to praise *A Black Mass*, he was referring to Jones's use of a creation myth borrowed from the Nation of Islam, a Black Muslim sect. The original Yakub story dates back to the 1930s during the formation of the Nation of Islam, and it is predicated on the belief that black people were not just the original inhabitants of the earth but the world's first scientists.[111] Yakub was literally and figuratively a "bigheaded" scientist who lived in an Edenlike Mecca among a harmonious black people. Yet Yakub was too ambitious and prideful to be satisfied with paradise on earth. He wanted to create a race of people completely opposite of his righteous black brothers and sisters, a colorless, white race that Yakub could control and reign over. Yakub's unsanctioned experiments with genetic engineering resulted in his banishment to an isolated island, along with his 59,999 followers. On this island, the relentless scientist continued breeding his new race, and along the way, Yakub created red, brown, and yellow peoples. Ultimately, his experiments yielded an entirely white race that, because of their lack of righteousness, became unmanageable and warlike. Yakub's white beasts soon devised a diabolical plan to conquer the original black people, and the rest is history.[112]

Alondra Nelson, in an essay on *A Black Mass*, explains how Jones philosophically diverged from the Nation of Islam's theology/mythology. The Nation's Yakub story is pro-science and embraces experimentation in the biosciences as an inherently black practice, but Jones rejects this idea and instead depicts Yakub's scientific inquiries as "anathema to authentic black creative expression."[113] While the Nation of Islam uncritically embraced "racialized experimental science, including eugenics," Jones's drama renounces any scientific experimentation that is "without human sanction." He even replaces the scientist protagonists in the original Nation myth with three black magicians. According to Nelson, Jones's version of this black mythology treats Yakub's "relentless rationalization of life" as antithetical to the traditional black cultural values Afro-America needed to rediscover.

As for the dramatic backstory of Jones's *A Black Mass*, Jacoub's first foray into whiteness was conceptual; he created the notion of time which has mutated into a disease. As the ritual drama opens, magicians Tanzil and Nasafi are working on a potion, a remedy for time, and Nasafi explains that "all who taste it will dance mad rhythms of the eternal universe until time is a weak thing."[114] Tanzil calls time "white madness" and inaccurately talks of destroying the animals "who bring it into the world." Nasafi, the wisest of the magicians and the authorial voice, explains to Tanzil that "we have made animals full of time to haunt us," meaning time has turned their black brothers and sisters into beasts. Nasafi uses the corporate "we" to take the blame for creating time and debasing their people, but it is really Jacoub who has hurt black humanity by creating this concept.

An unrepentant Jacoub admits he created time, and he claims he informed his fellow magicians about his "unsanctioned" experiments, but they conveniently forgot or ignored him. Jacoub also reminds them that he explained what time meant, but Tanzil still demonstrates his lack of understanding when he claims that "time is an animal thing." In terms of audience reception, Jones skillfully establishes Tanzil as the slightly lost spectator or reader, who, as the drama opens, is desperately trying to piece together the relationships between time, whiteness, and those strange animals. Back to the magician's conversation, Jacoub protests that time "is a human thing. A new quality for our minds." The always clarifying Nasafi again steps in to explain how time has turned human beings into animals who are "forced across the planet. With demon time in mad pursuit." Here we see Jones's brilliance, as he manipulates his audience to view the concept of time with fresh eyes. Through this subtle Afro-alienation act, he reestablishes time as a driving, terrorizing force rather than an ordering or productive tool. The animals who "hiss time madness in the air, and into our lives" are not new creatures like Tanzil and the audience might imagine; they are citizens of Mecca who have fallen prey to this destructive new invention and must be healed.

In Jacoub's larger plan, this "demon time" is just a metonymic precursor to the next level of whiteness, an actual creature or "being in love with time. A being for whom time will be good and strength." Beyond this preoccupation with time, the mad magician Jacoub envisions the following, more ominous traits for his "neutral" man: "a supernatural being . . . who will not respond to the world of humanity," "someone who will make its own will and direction," and "a being like us but completely separate." When Jacoub finally unveils his willful, solitary, neutral creation, this Beast is horrifying: "*A crouched figure is seen covered in red flowing skins like capes. He shoots up, leaping straight off the stage screaming, Sun-Ra music of shattering dimension. The figure is absolutely cold white with red lizard-devil mask which covers the whole head and ends up as a lizard spine cape. The figure screams, leaping and slobber laughing through the audience.*"[115] Jacoub's deathly cold white Beast is a thing of terror, an unmanageable menace from its inception. Although the Beast tries to articulate sounds beyond a sporadic screaming, the best it can muster is "White," as it vomits and licks the vomit off its body. This slobbering white Beast is a less subtle Afro-alienation act, through which Jones distills centuries of "horrific historical memory" into a single, fear-inducing embodiment of unbridled whiteness.[116]

Jones directed the debut of *A Black Mass* in Newark, and fellow playwright Ben Caldwell designed the Beast's attire. The body of a black actor was covered in white greasepaint, and a red devil mask extended down his back into a dinosaurlike tail.[117] This costumed creation sounds strikingly similar to the oyinbo or white man character from the Yoruba Apidan Theatre of early nineteenth-century Nigeria.[118] Apidan, which means "one who kills or performs tricks," was originally performed as part of Yoruba Egungun masquerades, typically at the end of these ancestral parades. In the early nineteenth century, secular, professional Apidan troupes started forming throughout Yorubaland, under the patronage of various local rulers. Over the years, oyinbo became a favorite Apidan performance, often used to impersonate and ridicule European explorers, colonial officials, missionaries, and tourists.

In 1826, before the British formally colonized what is now Nigeria, the Alafin of Katunga staged an Apidan performance for the explorer Hugh Clapperton and his assistant Richard Lander. The third act featured an actor who dropped his "ago," or full body costume, to reveal "a white head, at which all the crowd gave a shout that rent the air; they appeared indeed to enjoy this sight, as the perfection of the actor's art. The whole body was at last cleared of the encumbrance of the sack, when it exhibited the appearance of a human figure cast in white wax, of the middle size, miserably thin, and starved with cold."[119] From the coldness to the full body wax, Jones's Beast resembles this oyinbo figure, but the Yoruba stage European and his movements are far less horrifying and more realistic. Clapperton continues: "It frequently went through the motion of taking snuff, and rubbing its hands; when it walked, it was with the most awkward gait, treading as the most tender-footed white man would do in walking barefooted, for the first time, over new frozen ground." Typically in Apidan dramas, characters express themselves through dance, but oyinbo is the rare Apidan figure who does not dance, because Europeans are supposedly incapable of dancing. Yet this outsider does have distinctive gestures, like taking snuff or rubbing his hands. One signature action of oyinbo's is his repeated looking at his watch, an indication that oyinbo is a human being ruled by time. This Nigerian representation of a white man overly invested in the "goodness and strength" of time mirrors Jones's correlation between the Beast and "demon time."

Apidan Theatre's oyinbo is used primarily for parodic and celebratory purposes. Jones's goal with his Beast, this Afro-alienation act, however, was to defamiliarize whiteness and recast this racial construct as a malignancy. Jacoub's latest creation is not some harmless European caricature but a diseased white terror with the power to infect the citizens of Mecca on physical and psychological levels. The unleashed Beast first leaps at Jacoub, who stops him by conjuring an invisible wall. So instead of immediately infecting his maker, the white creature attacks a group of women in the lab, "grabbing throats or trying to throw open their robes and stick the head in."[120] With its "bite-caress," the Beast contaminates a woman named Tiila, and the changes start immediately: "*The Woman stumbles toward Jacoub, her face draining of color. Her voice grows coarse, she screams, covering herself with her robes. She emerges, slowly, from within the folds of the garment, her entire body shuddering, and beginning to do the small hop the beast did. Suddenly she throws back the robes, and she is white, or white blotches streak her face and hair. She laughs and weeps in a deadly cross between white and black. Her words have turned to grunts, and she moves like an animal robot.*"

Physically, Tiila's body shudders as the Beast transforms her into a white-speckled, incomplete copy of itself. She screams, grunts, and hops like the Beast, but her movements are a mixture of the animalistic and robotic. The psychological damage is strikingly apparent as Tiila slips into this paralyzing in-between place, what Jones calls "a deadly cross between white and black." Reminiscent of Adrienne Kennedy's *Funnyhouse*, Tiila's "blotchy" infection externalizes what whiteness does to the black psyche and stages how assimilation works or fails to work in Afro-America. Sandra Shannon, in her work on *A Black Mass*, explains how Tiila's incomplete transformation proves that "the effects of assimilation for blacks are never absolute"; in other words, as much as they embrace the dominant culture, they can never fully embody it.[121] This "crossed" and now permanently liminal Tiila devastatingly illustrates DuBois's malignant double consciousness, which Jones and the Black Arts movement sought to cleanse.

But why would Jacoub invent a "neutral" being with such malevolent power? Contented black magicians Nasafi and Tanzil view their black world as harmonious and, therefore, think it foolish "to invent what does not need to be invented."[122] In contrast, Jacoub believes "creation is its own end," and he boasts, "I will crowd the universe with my creations." The short answer is Jacoub created time and the white Beast because he could, and herein lies his grievous error. For Jones, Jacoub and his Beast represent the apolitical, communally disconnected artist fully invested in a self-indulgent idea of art. Sandra Shannon explains it best when she identifies the Beast as "a tangible production of art for art's sake."[123] In September 1999, Baraka explained how *A Black Mass* pursues "the premise, which I have long held, that Art is creation and that we must oppose the 'creation of what does not need to be created.'"[124]

Jacoub's creationist flaw goes deeper than a purely aesthetic impulse to create unnecessarily; there is an anti- or extrahuman impulse behind his desires, as he exhibits the same "anti-human" sensibility Larry Neal ascribed to whiteness and Euro-American aesthetics. When Nasafi accuses Jacoub of creating a soulless monster and doing so "without human sanction," Jacoub aligns himself with a "knowledge that is beyond the human mind."[125] In essence, Jacoub has ceased being human, and even after admitting he created an "inhuman" thing, he still hopes to benefit from its existence. Yet before he can explain how humans might benefit from this inhuman thing, Tiila starts to convulse into a horrifically crisscrossed condition, which prompts Jacoub to finally acknowledge his error. A now stricken and repentant Jacoub exclaims, "Izm-el-Azam,"—"May God have mercy"—and he asks Nasafi to explain his mistake.

Always obliging, Nasafi identifies Jacoub's grave mistake as "the substitution of thought for feeling . . . and a curiosity for anti-life." Here Jones departs from the Nation's pro-science position, as he depicts scientific inquiry as filled with temptations to choose cold facts and formulas over living, breathing, feeling humanity. Jones also uses whiting up as a political tool to align Jacoub's error with the white man's alienating "god complex." A foreign, infectious, greater-than-human pride has tempted this black magician to drift apart from his community. Even after acknowledging the terror he has unleashed, Jacoub still takes selfish pride in this product, which he brought into the world "by myself." But Nasafi informs Jacoub that this thing he so proudly created "is not ourselves. But the hatred of ourselves. Our wholeness." Jacoub erred because he failed to accept and embrace the completeness of the original people, because at his core, he despised his own kind and their wholeness.

The Beast and Jacoub are inextricably linked, so it is fitting that the man constantly creating something more is destroyed by his progeny. But before Jacoub gets devoured by his creations, he banishes the Beast and Tiila to the "diseased caves of the cold," a reference to Europe. And as was the convention for Jones's ritual theater, a Narrator then closes the drama by identifying what the audience must do once they leave: "There are beasts in our world, Brothers and Sisters. There are beasts in our world. Let us find them and slay them. Let us lock them in their caves. Let us declare the Holy War. The Jihad. Or we cannot deserve to live."[126] So how literal was this call for jihad in 1966 Newark? Were Jones's black actors and audiences expected to leave Proctor's Theatre and "slay" white beasts? What should we make of this call for jihad, in light of the fact that earlier in the text the three black magicians claim they cannot kill? Are we dealing with a contradiction in Jones's universe, or is there another explanation?

One might conclude that Jones's call to exterminate white people was not literal but figurative, and the determining factor is how broadly we interpret jihad. In the Qur'an, jihadists are described as "those who believe, emigrate and fight in the path of Allah."[127] Jihad is largely represented as militant, physical warfare with some support for a spiritual or strictly nonviolent component. In the ninth century, an ascetic movement within Islam and certain Sufi warriors started to distinguish between "greater" and "lesser" jihads. The supposedly greater jihad was defined as spiritual warfare against inner passions or the ego; this inner struggle involved confronting personal issues such as rebelliousness and hubris. Granted, in 1966, Jones was not fully immersed in Islam, but this notion of greater jihad appears to resolve the potential contradiction in *A Black Mass*. The black magicians and the community they serve cannot literally kill human beings, but they can wage jihad on the hubris within. Also by the end of the drama, Jones identifies Jacoub's "god complex," his aimless creativity, his antihuman science, and his self-hatred as the core problems African Americans need to address and repair. As exemplified by Tiila's incomplete yet devastating transformation, Afro-America's fractured sense of self is the result of constant exposure to a metaphoric white beast. The enemy was never the beast in the caves of Europe, but the beast residing inside each African American. So the greater jihad for the Spirit House audience was to fight this deadly whiteness within, the destructive passions and egos raging on the inside.

In 1972, *A Black Mass* was restaged as part of the Imamu Amiri Baraka theater festival in Harlem, and Mel Gussow summed up the one-act this way: "Black man creates white man—definitely not in his own image—and then ridicules him. A portentous ritual suddenly turns into a clown show, a notion that seemed to delight the almost all black audience opening night."[128] Gussow misread *A Black Mass*; Jones's mission was never to ridicule time, white people, or whiteness but to reveal the pernicious impacts of whiteness on the bodies, minds, and spirits of African Americans. For Gussow and some black patrons, this mythological cautionary tale may have devolved into a "clown show," but unlike Genet's well-received stage European production, *A Black Mass* was never designed to play as a dualistic production for white consumption.

Genet constructed a highly metaphoric onstage charade designed to occupy the white spectators while a more portentous trial transpired offstage, away from white surveillance. Once the verdict is handed down offstage and the imperative to balance the parallel worlds is removed, a character named Newport News comes onstage to explain the relationship between public and private transcripts:

> *Newport News:* . . . Our aim is not only to corrode and dissolve the idea they'd like us to have of them, we must also fight them in their actual persons, in their flesh and blood. As for you, you were present only for display. Behind . . .
>
> *The one who played the valet (curtly):* We know. Thanks to us, they've sensed nothing of what's going on elsewhere.[129]

Unlike Genet, Jones was unconcerned with dissolving the idea of whiteness or diverting white spectators; his project was to mythologize the birth of whiteness for an African American community in the process of reinventing itself. For both Genet and Jones, the next step is warfare, but in the offstage world of *The Blacks*, Genet envisions a "flesh and blood" fight with actual white persons. By contrast, Jones's *A Black Mass* stages an opening salvo in Afro-America's internal, greater jihad against a virulent whiteness, a fight that begins as his audience exits the theatrical space.

Although Jones, Ward, and Kennedy all developed theatrical careers partly through the patronage and media coverage of white producers, critics, and spectators, Euro-America was never the primary audience for their dramatic experiments. So, unlike Genet, who wrote for and imagined a white spectatorship, these black dramatists dispensed with veiled satire or coded language because it was no longer necessary to dissemble for a majority public. In terms of veils and masks, the stage Europeans from the Black Arts era have little in common with Paul Laurence Dunbar's famous "mask that grins and lies." In the 1960s, black dramatists are no longer interested in letting the "world dream otherwise." Ironically, Kennedy, Ward, and Jones use the mask of whiteness, not blackness, to reveal the internal bleeding hearts and suppressed cries that both Paul Laurence

Dunbar and W. E. B. DuBois identified as uniquely Negro conditions at the dawn of the twentieth century.[130]

At the close of Genet's *The Blacks*, two characters named Village and Virtue, the play's romantic couple, emerge triumphant as they share a private moment that affirms the real over the artificial. In particular, Virtue expresses what sounds like "true self-consciousness" when she informs Village that the illusion is over and he will no longer be running his fingers through her "long golden hair."[131] So at the end of their comparatively shorter dramatic journeys, have Kennedy, Ward, or Jones arrived at similar victories or triumphs? Based on the anxiety-inducing centrality of whiteness in 1960s black America, I specifically define victory as helping African American audiences achieve a level of core wholeness by cleansing or containing a whiteness that has defined and devalued blackness.

There are two steps to the potential victories for an African American public. The first step happens onstage with three very different kinds of white masking. While Euro-Americans are invited to watch, each playwright strategically deploys the mask of whiteness to speak directly to different segments and situations in Afro-America. Kennedy's stark white, alabaster, or yellowish white masks coupled with snakelike tresses externalize a terrifying yet highly personal interiority, a new expressionistic terrain for the 1960s as she ventures inside the American Negro psyche like never before. Inside Sarah's inside, Kennedy does not purport to represent all Negroes; rather, she stages an "unwieldy third space" where some African Americans can watch their DuBoisian "twoness" played out to a horrific conclusion. Now Ward's clownish reverse minstrel masks and blonde wigs, with bare black hands visible to show the slippages, highlight the artifice of racial performance so we always read and appreciate the interdependence of whiteness layered onto blackness. His whiteface mask speaks directly to the Negro workers laboring everywhere and allows them a serious laugh at the racial hierarchy and occupational stratification their labor supports. Finally, Jones's full-body, all-consuming mask of whiteness imagines the threat and consequence of Afro-America's complete immersion or absorption in a dehumanizing whiteness. In addition, the equally terrifying incomplete whiteness of the victimized Tiila, that "deadly cross of black and white," expresses the failure of Negro assimilation and acculturation. Jones's white beasts, fully or partially smeared in whiteness, speak to the cultural nationalists, confirming what they already know: Emulating whiteness has proven self-destructive, and this sickness must be contained and cleansed.

All three spectacular acts of masking estrange whiteness and its impacts on Afro-America, so black audiences can see their situations with fresh eyes and prepare for the next active step in their transcendent process. Using Jacoub as a cautionary tale, Jones activates willing warriors in his nationalist public, and these "jihadists" are now expected to engage in potentially physical but more likely spiritual warfare to fully defeat the double consciousness within themselves and other blacks. As Ward announced in his 1966 *New York Times* article, he was targeting an experienced and committed black public ready to process, debate, and perhaps act on his economic and cultural conclusions. Through a deceptively simple satire, Ward incites black New Yorkers, workers, and future generations of college students to strike, protest, and demonstrate economic power through their absence. Finally, even the fractured and seemingly apolitical Adrienne Kennedy anticipates and to some extent creates a small black public ready to process the monstrous impact of whiteness on the black imagination. But for Kennedy's public, those individuals working through very personal and complex relationships to whiteness, their active step toward some semblance of triumph may be delayed for awhile. To advance the cleansing process, Kennedy asks her wounded few to keep repeating the first step, continually perform and share their interiority—their personal rituals of crisscrossing, interlocked Euro and Afro selves—until the white ghosts vanish utterly.

Chapter 6 **White People Be Like . . .**

Black Solo and Racial Difference

At an April 2008 NAACP annual Freedom Fund dinner in Detroit, Michigan, the Reverend Jeremiah Wright, retired senior pastor of Chicago's Trinity United Church of Christ, delivered a keynote address on the theme "different but not deficient."[1] Wright explained how "in the past," Americans were conditioned to view people who were different from us as somehow deficient; for example, people who did not worship like us were perceived as lacking in spirituality or even culture. To stage the worship differences, Wright's rich voice leaped into a high-toned, hypercorrect cantata, singing "comfort ye in the glory, the glory of the Lord." He then explained how those "lovers of European cantatas saw lovers of common meter—'I love the Lord, He heard my cry'—they saw them as deficient." For the common meter, Wright rolled seamlessly into a visceral, lower register and literally moaned a black congregational hymn.

With this praise comparison designed to illustrate that different is not deficient, Wright participated in what some have termed "white people be like" comedy, a form of whiteface minstrelsy rooted in perceived racial difference. Media scholar Bambi Haggins typifies this observational humor as a low-brow subgenre of black comedy popularized through programs like Russell Simmons's *Def Comedy Jam*.[2] For decades, this somewhat reductive brand of humor, rooted in the performance of social perceptions, has circulated in stand-up comedy clubs, recorded albums, and taped "live" performances. These comedic comparisons appear in the repertoire of nearly every black comic from Eddie Murphy to Monique to Kat Williams.

Wright manipulated body and voice to catalog several distinctions between European and African cultures, and he was at his most vivid when comparing black and white marching bands. Out of respect for his current location, Wright launched his racial comparison with the University of Michigan and Michigan State marching bands, describing how they hit the field with "excellent European precision." Wright embodied this precision with a very controlled, focused, and forceful march, in place, directly behind the podium. But then Wright suggested we "go to a Florida A&M and Grambling Band," and he broke into a highly percussive beat-box and lost himself in a whirling, twirling march that took him away from the podium.[3] At the Freedom Fund dinner, Wright's unexpected and passionate reenactment of black marching bands elicited recognition, laughter, and applause from the NAACP crowd and even brought some dignitaries on the dais to their feet. However, the outspoken minister delivered this illuminating speech in the wake of presidential candidate Barack Obama's "Reverend Wright controversy," so his impromptu beat-boxing and stylized marching probably disturbed or embarrassed some in attendance. On cable news, his inspired performance of racial difference was constantly replayed, but it was also dismissed as more racist rants from the problematic minister who would not "go away."

Through his incisive performance, the Reverend Jeremiah Wright delivered an important national reminder: Americans once "established arbitrary norms and then determined that anybody not like us was abnormal." Fortunately in this new day, Wright was seeing an erosion of such norms that divide and denigrate. Intoning a "change" mantra suggestive of candidate Obama, Wright proclaimed, "I believe that a change is going to come because many of us are committed to changing how we see others who are different." His cross-racially playful, never malicious marching band performance embodied that change. Admittedly, the gyrating black band was visually more engaging than the crisp white band, but Wright's point was clear: One is not superior to the other; they are simply different kinds of cultural expression. Pleased with his staged comparison, Wright confidently proclaimed, "You can't put that in no book," meaning the comparative truth he just physically embodied reaches far beyond any academic understanding of cultural difference.

In this chapter I attempt to put that truth in a book by returning to whiteface minstrelsy, the more improvisational, free-form mode of whiting up. I place black stand-up comics such as Jackie "Moms" Mabley, Dick Gregory, Richard Pryor, and Dave Chappelle in conversation with black performance artists/actors like Whoopi Goldberg, Anna Deavere Smith, and Sarah Jones to explore the perception and performance of cultural difference. Despite the low-brow connotations of stand-up and the highbrow patina of performance art, there is a shared emphasis on theatricality and self-reflexivity circulating among these solo artists. The fictional characters improvised by Pryor were just as compelling as the studied, mimicry-based re-creations of Smith and Jones. In the 1970s, as Pryor perfected his comedic voice, critics defined his work as "a new type of realistic theater" or "theater of the routine" because Pryor staged ordinary white and black folks in everyday situations.[4] Although Pryor and Smith never shared the same artistic process or venues, they were both committed to fostering dialogues between multiracial publics in fully integrated spaces. In this chapter I examine how solo black artists molded receptive audiences for their performances of difference, how they manipulated voice and body to control and exchange stereotypic notions of whiteness and blackness, and how they integrated a traditionally divisive whiteness into productive play and friendly relations with an equal and hardly deficient blackness.

From Moms Mabley to Sarah Jones, my selected comics and solo performers share an ethnographic approach in their onstage investigations of racial, class, and gender difference. Historian James Clifford generically defines modern ethnography as "simply diverse ways of thinking and writing about culture from a standpoint of participant observation."[5] He also identifies an artistic impulse in ethnography, claiming this investigative mode is about the invention of culture, not just reportage.[6] Finally, Clifford expands the definition of ethnography by bringing "native informants" into this process of simultaneously studying and inventing culture. He describes "native informants" as "indigenous ethnographers" studying their own cultures and offering "new angles of vision and depths of understanding."[7] Based on this expanded definition, stand-up comics and solo performers who observe and report on their own cultures can be considered ethnographers.

Additionally, the late ethnographer Dwight Conquergood has theorized and demonstrated in his own fieldwork the moral and ethical responsibilities of ethnography. For Conquergood, the "performance stance" in ethnographic fieldwork "struggles to bring together different voices, world views, value systems, and beliefs so that they can have a conversation with one another." He calls this conversation a "dialogical performance" with the aim of bringing "self and other together." The responsible performance ethnographer "must continuously play the oppositions between identity and difference" and "affirm cross-cultural accessibility without glossing very real differences." For Conquergood, the "dialogical performance" of a moral ethnographer involves an "intimate conversation with other people and cultures, instead of speaking about them, one speaks to and with them."[8] More recently, performer-scholar Joni Jones fine-tuned the definition of performance ethnography to include not just speaking to and with cultures but speaking physically through them. Like Conquergood, Joni Jones considers performance ethnography a form of dialogical, cultural exchange, but she believes the key is exploring "how culture is done in the body."[9]

Treating comedians of color as performance ethnographers is not a new concept. In the late 1970s, linguistic and cultural anthropologist Keith Basso revealed how Western Apache jokers functioned as performance ethnographers by sharing their "findings" about "the whiteman" through living models or physical and vocal imitations of Anglo-Americans.[10] But bear in mind, the "indigenous ethnographers" covered in this chapter are not necessarily permanent insiders in one discrete culture; some even consider themselves "outsiders" moving between and creating "dialogical performances" with various racial, class, and gender communities. For many of these artists, their shared ethnographic agendas were to advance understanding between multiple cultures and to revolutionize who defines cultural discourse in America.

During the civil rights movement, Black Power struggles, and our current postsoul moment, these artists have functioned as fluid informants reporting to all sides on any cultural or political issue. As strategic conduits, artists like Dick Gregory and Sarah Jones used the solo stage to demand a truly democratized public discourse in America, and they articulated this integrationist desire while asserting a representational command historically denied black performers. Cultural critic Michael Eric Dyson notes how many artists and intellectuals of color "are deeply invested in reversing the terror of ethnography" and are no longer interested in "being the disciplined subject of an often intellectually poisonous white anthropological scrutiny." Today, African Americans, Native Americans, Latinos, and Asians "yearn to return the favor of interrogation," but their motives are not malicious; rather, they "simply seek to unveil the myths of universality and invisibility that have informed the ideological strata of white supremacy."[11] At various points in history, black solo performers, free of overt hostility, interrogated the myths and realities of white supremacy and developed cross-racial performances to make more of America vocal and visible.

The solo performers in this chapter are not merely telling jokes with punch lines predicated on difference; they are physically embodying cultural markers to stretch and test their reliability and relevance. They play with identity oppositions, confront real and imagined differences between black and white America, and occasionally create avenues for cross-cultural, interracial connection. Interconnections always sound promising, but Joni Jones reminds us that performance ethnography is also driven by the idea "that identity and daily interactions are a series of conscious and unconscious choices improvised within culturally and socially specific guidelines."[12] The keen participant observations and comedic embodiments of Dave Chappelle or Whoopi Goldberg, as well as the reality-based character reconstructions of Anna Deavere Smith and Sarah Jones, seek not only to perform our conscious and unconscious choices but to expose those cultural and social expectations shaping our identities.

Integrationist Solo: Creating an Interracial Public

How exactly did African Americans in the mid-twentieth century understand integration? What were the terms of American citizenship and inclusion from the perspective of black activists, artists, and intellectuals, and how did they express their integrationist desires? Looking at the "long civil rights era," which spans many decades, Nikhil Pal Singh found that answers to such questions changed over time and varied depending on the specific black subjects. For some, integration meant assimilation, and the term or price of acceptance in the American nation-state was the erasure of black identity. For others, integrationist desire comprised two separate steps or stages: first, the development of "self-constituting feelings of racial pride" and, second, "uncompromising demands for national equality."[13] Far from favoring assimilation, which might ignore centuries of black cultural formation, this two-step integrationist desire fully acknowledged what African Americans were bringing to the national project and demanded that others do so as well.

Writing about the cultural and social guidelines governing integration in America, novelist and essayist Ralph Ellison claims that much of this nation's discourse on difference is rooted in "the white American's Manichaean fascination with the symbolism of blackness and whiteness."[14] Driven by this fascination, the "white folk mind" shackled black America with all the derogatory traits Euro-America determined it was not, and onstage, that symbolism fully manifested itself with the breakaway, national popularity of blackface minstrelsy. Journalist Mel Watkins, in his research on black comedy, found that Euro-America's Manichaean fascination has defined much of black American humor, including "white people be like" comedy. Like most African Americans, black comedians were conditioned to see themselves through the Euro-American imagination; however, Watkins argues these perceptive humorists still managed to scrutinize and challenge white American claims of superiority.[15]

As black comics and other solo artists integrated into mainstream American entertainment, they persistently worked toward an equal performative playing field, onstage and offstage. In the midst of a civil rights struggle that redefined America, the mainstreaming black comic's challenge was to craft an "integrated joke" that allowed white and black audiences to laugh at themselves, at one another, and with one another. They had to defuse an always-simmering racial hostility, what Mel Watkins calls an "entrenched 'us' versus 'them' syndrome" typical for most white-black relationships in the civil rights era. Patricia J. Williams describes this syndrome as a "crisis of community" where "whites fear blacks, blacks fear whites. Each is the enemy against whom authorities will not act."[16]

To address America's crisis of community, black solo performers first had to adjust how they interacted with white audiences. When comics worked the white vaudeville circuits or the black Theatre Owners Booking Association (TOBA) circuit, they were circumscribed by the legacy of blackface minstrelsy. They were not allowed to communicate directly with the public; in fact, performers were specifically instructed not to address the audience.[17] Within the blackface tradition there were solo "stump speeches" involving Negro dialect orations designed to satirize black preachers or other Negro intellectuals. But truly audience-directed, conversational comic monologues did not emerge until the early 1930s when Jewish comics like Jack Benny and Milton Berle began directly addressing their publics.

Black comedians working in white venues did not start talking directly to audiences until the 1950s. So why did black comedians lag behind in embracing this new mode of comic delivery? Expanding on Ellison's assessment of the cultural guidelines, Watkins explains that white audiences believed the onstage buffoonery executed between black comic personae was an accurate reflection of black life. By breaking the fourth wall and intelligently addressing whites, black comics would have disrupted the clown illusion and the fantasy of white superiority. Also, allowing a black comic to converse casually with a white public would have acknowledged a level of equality many Euro-Americans were not ready to accept or promote. Some Negro comics on the TOBA, euphemistically called the "chitlin' circuit," did adopt a direct style with their largely black audiences, but those pioneers were virtually ignored by white producers and theatrical bookers.

Loretta Mary Aiken, later Jackie "Moms" Mabley, was a pioneering performer whom Mel Watkins identifies as one of the first black comics to perform direct-address monologue humor.[18] A young Loretta Aiken entered show business as a blues singer and dancer in the 1910s, and when she began touring with her boyfriend Jack Mabley, she adopted the name Jackie Mabley. In the 1930s, after an ugly break with her performative and life partner, Mabley created a new solo act consisting of an old, matronly character—costumed in a floppy hat, work shoes, and housedress—who ambled onstage and "schooled" the audience, "her children," in a raspy but wise voice. Watkins believes Mabley constructed this elderly comic persona and maternal relationship with her audiences to soften any potential resistance to a woman appearing as a solo performer and speaking directly to her public. In the mid-1930s, Jackie "Moms" Mabley became the first comedienne to perform alone at the Apollo Theater in Harlem, and for the next three decades, she remained a fixture at this legendary black venue.

In her study of black comic personae, Bambi Haggins astutely reads Moms as perfecting a motherly image for her black and white children that "operated within a stone's throw of the mammy, thus supplying some degree of comfort to audiences to whom the minstrel archetypes still appealed."[19] With her dualistic onstage attitude, Moms fashioned a "revisionist mammy" who reassured and nurtured her initially black and eventually white patrons while also exploiting "masculine forms of black humor." By masculine, Haggins refers to how, like many male comedic acts on the TOBA, Mabley's material was "blue," meaning highly sexualized and laced with strong language. Mabley's trademark shtick was a lecherous older woman sexually disinterested in old men and constantly searching for a young one.

"Masculine forms of black humor" also indicates that Moms Mabley was not content with critiquing mainstream America through coded messages or indirection. Haggins argues that Moms embraced "a new form of direct comedic sociopolitical discourse" that highlighted white bigotry and stupidity whenever possible. This more aggressive, confident, masculine style, which Mabley mastered, would become the signature delivery mode for "white people be like" comedy. Mel Watkins traces this confrontational brand of black stand-up back to the slave era, to the satiric humor produced by enslaved Africans at the expense of the master class and "poor white trash." In the antebellum era, enslaved and free blacks proved especially adept at producing Irish brogues and making comic sport of "green horn" immigrants. This black humor remained vibrant throughout the blackface minstrel era and resurfaced in pioneering solo acts like Moms Mabley.[20]

Moms was an important transitional figure for black comics interested in developing direct-address social commentary on racial difference in front of white audiences. One of Mabley's most-cited examples of sociopolitical humor is a story about two bank robbers, one white and one black, who kill three bank tellers and two policemen during a horribly botched bank heist. After the partners in crime are sentenced to hang, Moms voices the terrified white robber who pleads, "I don't want to be hung." The black robber responds coolly and calmly to his white accomplice, "We done killed up all them people and you talk about you don't want to be hung. . . . They gonna hang you, so why don't you face it like a man?" Still incredulous at his death sentence, the white robber says to the black robber, "That's easy for you to say, you're used to it."[21] In this progressive tale of crime and punishment, Mabley first exposes the history of legal inequality in the United States, which the white robber hopes will still work in his favor. Yet, in the end, Mabley's egalitarian joke depicts an American judicial system that is capable of doling out equal punishment for equal crimes regardless of color.

A significant moment in Mabley's career came in August 1961, when she tested her interracial jokes at Hugh Hefner's Playboy Club, a somewhat integrated venue in downtown Chicago. I say somewhat integrated because Hefner's hip establishment welcomed black performers onstage and in the audience, but the club was not frequented by comparable numbers of whites and nonwhites. On her recording *"Moms" Mabley at the Playboy Club*, Mabley combines material from her debut Playboy appearance with segments from a performance at the black Uptown Theatre in Philadelphia. As an introduction to track 3, which contains strictly Playboy Club material, Moms explains how "half of this record was made for my other children because mom is color-blind, thank God."[22] A comparison of the recorded material from the white Playboy Club and the black Uptown reveals that Mabley's act received very different responses from the two audiences. At the Playboy, she offered her signature shtick, an old woman hunting young men, but the white patrons appeared unfamiliar with her act and barely responded. Moms tried to sell her multifaceted "revisionist mammy," but the sexually licentious bits failed to win white converts. By contrast, with the majority-black Philadelphia audience, her stock material went over big, as the crowd howled in full recognition of Moms and her famously lecherous ways.

After the blue material bombed at the Playboy Club, Mabley tried to connect with the progressive white hipsters by aligning herself with the civil rights movement. During the Playboy section of *"Moms" Mabley*, she slips into a slightly "cool" but still Moms voice to explain how she was "too hip" for the South and how Alabama and Mississippi were foreign countries that she did not wish to visit.[23] Her political posturing seemed to generate a connection with her audience, so Mabley next pivots to integrationist efforts. Mabley suggests the civil rights leadership should "lay off" bus boycotts and lunch-counter protests and, instead, focus on integrating the funny papers. By selecting an easy target for desegregation, and an area a humorist should know something about, Moms discovered the "integrated joke" around which an older black comedienne and this young, predominantly white crowd could coalesce.

Mabley helped open the door but failed to dominate in white venues. A new breed of young New Negro intellectual comics—Dick Gregory, Bill Cosby, and Godfrey Cambridge—would continue building dialogical performances with white America. Richard Claxton Gregory, a track star turned comic and political activist from St. Louis, Missouri, was the very embodiment of the New Negro comic ready to defuse any racial or representational crisis. On NBC's *Steve Allen Show* in 1964, Gregory explained this new breed of black entertainer: "You see us everyday: *Wall Street Journal* under one arm, *New York Times* under the other and *Jet* and *Ebony* tucked in between them."[24] Gregory characterizes the New Negro comic as a bicultural performer who is very connected to what happens in the dominant culture. Early in his career, Gregory made a calculated decision to avoid the blue material associated with many Negro comics and focus on topical material drawn from mainstream newspapers and magazines.[25] The black monthlies folded within the white journals signify that Gregory and his fellow black social commentators also remained committed to African American culture. As bicultural native informants, this new breed of black comic kept tabs on two worlds and reported their "findings" to an interracial public. More than any other New Negro stand-up artist, Gregory exhibited that balanced, two-step integrationist desire, where he exuded racial pride and demanded racial equality.

To ensure success in front of interracial audiences, Gregory devised a strategy based on the challenges of an older comic, Nipsey Russell. Gregory noticed how when Russell performed his routine at white versus black clubs, the results were noticeably different. He observed how a white patron arrives at a black club "so hung up in this race problem, so nervous and afraid of the neighborhood and the people that anything the comic says to relieve his tension will absolutely knock him out."[26] The harder the white customer laughs, the more he feels alright, and the less he is filled with guilt and fear. By contrast, when Russell played white clubs, "he was in the white man's house and the white man felt comfortable and secure. He didn't have to laugh at racial material that he really didn't want to hear." So in order to work comfortably and regularly at white clubs, Gregory had to persuade whites to laugh at racial material, including themselves, and prevent whites from hating, feeling sorry for, or condescending to this young Negro comic.

Despite the "us versus them" climate outside the club, Gregory believed "comedy is friendly relations," and as a gesture of friendship, he understood he had to "make jokes about myself, before I can make jokes about them and their society—that way, they can't hate me." Gregory admitted at one point in his career that "what I like most about my type of humor—it's easy."[27] The product may have felt easy, after Gregory's work on himself and his audience, but for this comedy of racial difference to foster ease and community, Gregory had to establish a baseline equitable relationship between the races. He had to create a rare, truly democratized space in American culture where the black/white hierarchy was leveled and a dialogical performance could truly happen.

After practice runs in small white clubs throughout the Midwest, a witty and facile Dick Gregory was ready to defuse racial hostility and flatten the hierarchy at the Playboy Club in Chicago. In January 1961, months before Mabley played this interracial venue, Gregory tested his observations on whiteness and blackness in front of a potentially hostile crowd of white frozen food executives from the South.[28] Gregory recorded most of his Playboy set on *In Living Black and White*; the title of this album concisely articulates his bicultural position as Negro comic operating in a Manichaean universe.

On the opening track, "Congo Daily Tribune," Gregory quickly and deftly molds his majority-white audience: "Say, I wish you would read all the papers, you know, you've been reading these local papers, you know, calling me the Negro Mort Sahl. You have to read the Congo papers, and see where they call Mort Sahl the white Dick Gregory. . . . I'm trying to find out who I am, okay, they called me Bob Newhart, Shelly Berman, Mort Sahl, and a couple others—I'm so confused being three white boys and myself, I don't know—[laughter]."[29] Immediately, an erudite, newspaper-reading Gregory playfully casts his audience as provincial white Americans and gently challenges them to realize the world is much larger than they might imagine. In the newly independent Republic of the Congo, black comics are the originals and white performers like Newhart and Berman are considered imitators.

Yet, in this shrewd opening, Gregory still aligns himself with the "three white boys." After all, his audience was probably more familiar with known commodities like Mort Sahl, and furthermore, those white comics represented the kind of artist Gregory aspired to be. In 1961, Newhart, Berman, and Sahl all had major comedy albums and were associated with an intellectual style of comedy, especially Mort Sahl, who was considered the "father" of topical, observation-based stand-up. As a young artist finding his voice, Gregory may have suffered from a hint of identity confusion, but this media association with comedic heavyweights was more energizing than debilitating. Reminiscent of the imitative relationship between opera singers Matilda Jones and Adelina Patti, Gregory worked press comparisons to get his foot in the door and to speak as freely as those "white boys."

The approving group laughter, which stopped Gregory's introduction, confirmed he had successfully connected with his interracial public, much better than Moms Mabley would at the Playboy in August 1961. But the evening was young, and the white patrons were not yet fully convinced or inebriated. In his biographical writing, Gregory recalls how the audience on that snowy night in January fought him with "dirty, little, insulting statements," but he was quicker and wittier than their constant chatter.[30] Before playing the Playboy Club, Gregory anticipated his biggest problem would be drunk and loose-lipped hecklers, whom he would have to deal with quickly but not too harshly for fear of losing the white crowd.

On the track "Not Poor—Just Busted," Gregory demonstrates how to shut down a drunken heckler. He begins with mock concern, "How are you?" but then rapidly attacks with "Trying to get you to shut up is like trying to explain integration to a lynch mob."[31] The audience erupts with laughter, clearly on Gregory's side, and he wins this exchange, maintaining control. Gregory successfully stopped this one white heckler and other potential troublemakers by releasing an incredibly loaded signifier, "lynch mob," into a room filled with white southerners. For the rest of the evening, the "mob" subsided and listened intently; his fifty-minute set grew to nearly two hours, and when he left the stage, the initially hostile crowd endorsed him with a standing ovation. During the Uptown gig in Philadelphia, Mabley related a similar but probably apocryphal story of how she performed for the KKK in Miami. She boasted that she made them laugh so hard "they forgot what they come from."[32] Whether real or imagined, both Mabley and Gregory believed humor predicated on racial difference could produce unity through laughter.

In *Jokes and Their Relation to the Unconscious*, Sigmund Freud claims that "every joke calls for a public of its own and laughing at the same jokes is evidence of a far-reaching psychical conformity."[33] Playboy owner Hugh Hefner lauded Gregory as the first black comic to achieve that conformity, to gain acceptance in "first-rate" nightclubs, thus opening the doors for other black performers. Thanks to his calm and calculated wit, Gregory could defuse any situation and turn a potential crisis into laughter.[34] Hefner's assessment speaks to Gregory's integrationist desire for interracial intimacies not only in nightclub spaces but beyond. As a nationally respected civil rights activist, Gregory was also working daily, in dangerous places, to bring these intimate "friendly relations" to American neighborhoods and lunch counters. The communal laughter Gregory generated at the Playboy Club did suggest a "psychical conformity" and that this particular audience endorsed his activist vision of America.

Gregory understood how to disarm his audience with humorous, lighthearted responses to the racism afflicting not only the South but, potentially, Hefner's somewhat integrated club. To continue building support for his integrationist vision, Gregory playfully signified on the constructed nature of racial, ethnic, and regional differences while still respecting their resonances in the real worlds of his audience. In a humorous story about the "Deep South," Gregory explains how he got himself into a potentially dangerous situation.[35] Gregory first admits that when he gets drunk, he thinks he is Polish, and as a pretend Pole filled with liquid courage, he wandered into a white diner and ordered fried chicken. To be historically accurate, we must note that real courage, not alcohol, often placed activist Dick Gregory in such racially charged locations, and so he was inventing and rearranging circumstances purely to sell this joke. To contextualize the joke and make fun of himself as well as white people, Gregory combines ethnic humor about Poles with a stereotypic association between blacks and fried chicken. While he waits for this racially marked meal order, Gregory is confronted by "three cousins" named "Klu, Kluck, and Klan." After the chicken is delivered, the Klan members snarl at Gregory in a thick southern drawl, "Boy, we're givin' you fair warnin'. Anything you do to that chicken, we're gonna do to you." Gregory coolly describes how he put down his knife and fork, said "Y'all line up," and then kissed the chicken.

With a regional twang, heavy usage of "boy," and a mocking, directed use of "y'all," Gregory develops an intriguing conflict and transference between white and black speech. Regarding the vocal embodiment of whiteness and blackness, Moms Mabley rarely explored a distinctively "white sound" and, instead, used her signature slow, raspy speech, reminiscent of vaudeville or the TOBA circuit, for all of her characters. By contrast, Gregory's coolly intellectual voice and crisp diction produced a cosmopolitan New Negro sound that forced his audience to reconsider what "educated" sounds and looks like. On most tracks from *In Living Black and White*, Gregory intermingles hip phrasing with Black English grammatical structure—for example, "All them cats be outta work." When opportunities arise to slip into nonstandard words like "cain't," Gregory refuses to embrace that diction as part of his onstage black persona. Instead, he opts to say "can't," which sounds like Standard English and which traditionally reads as more "white" than "black." By flipping the racial script to make his Klansmen sound uneducated and the Negro comic sound milky smooth and erudite, Gregory effectively disconnects whiteness from "educated" and associates a stylish Standard English with his blackness. It is also interesting where Gregory elects not to slip from his learned black sound into a countrified "white voice." For instance, when he briefly assumes the role of the southern white waitress, who actually serves him in this Jim Crow diner, his diction, inflection, and rhythm remain unaltered. With that subtle vocal choice, Gregory suggests the potential for commonality between himself and some whites.

We can also see Gregory working toward his integrationist vision in a comedic observation on Miami, color, Jewishness, and lunch-counter demonstrations. Gregory opens with a complaint: "People keep talking about the white race and the black race and it really doesn't make sense."[36] He is questioning the entire basis for segregation and Jim Crow laws, highlighting how racial categories rooted in biology are really just social constructions designed to separate and punish. Then Gregory recalls how he was playing a date in Miami and met a "fella two shades darker than me—and his name was Ginsberg." Here Gregory signifies on the prevalence of especially tanned Jews in Miami, the cultural dilemma of black Jews like his colleague Sammy Davis Jr., and the tension between ethnic and religious categories. Gregory brings the joke home when he explains how this Ginsberg "fella," because he was so dark, participated in a couple of lunch-counter demonstrations racially passing as black. But when they tried to conquer a third lunch counter, Ginsberg "blew the whole bit. Asked for blintzes." To allow his audience their tension-releasing, psychically conforming laughter, Gregory again relies on culinary stereotyping. A dark-skinned, Jewish, and politically active Ginsberg blows his cross-racial impersonation because he cannot resist an ethnic comfort food like blintzes.

Moms Mabley and Dick Gregory created a foundation for the solo performance of racial difference by confronting, mastering, and potentially transforming unwieldy racial imagery. A second wave of black solo artists, specifically Whoopi Goldberg and Anna Deavere Smith, would continue building dialogical relationships between whiteness and blackness, male and female, insider and outsider. These two gifted actors would carve out a uniquely universalized space where their black female bodies could move fluidly back and forth between the competing yet conversing cultures represented in their ethnographic performances.

During the early 1980s, actress Caryn Johnson worked in theater and improvisational comedy on the West Coast and developed her distinctive stage persona. Over the years, naming has proven especially important for this singular artist. First, Johnson has famously and violently resisted the name "African American" because she believes this particular identity and other hyphenated "Americans" "divides us, as a nation and as people." She believes this historically grounded yet imagined ethnic moniker, African American, effectively cuts her off from "everything plain old regular Americans are entitled to."[37] Second, Johnson has always resisted the labels "comedienne" or "actress" because of the gender and occupational distinctions and, instead, identifies herself as an actor.[38] Finally, there is her current enigmatic stage name, Whoopi Goldberg, which sounds like a transformative stage European performance in itself, but is not even close. She was called "Whoopi" by her friends when she was in her twenties, because Johnson used to "fart up a storm" due to ulcers; she subsequently settled on "Whoopi Cushion" as an early stage name. The actor would later adopt "Goldberg" and claim it was an homage to her Jewish ancestry, or in an alternative version, a name suggested to her by a "burning bush." In reality, her mother thought the name "Whoopi Cushion" was too sophomoric, and so they settled on "Whoopi Goldberg."[39]

In 1982, Goldberg wrote and codirected, with David Schein, her first one-person project, *The Spook Show*. Starting with the provocative title, Goldberg and Schein were interested in breaking expectations and showcasing Goldberg's range as an actor, with characters as divergent as a black male drug addict and a pregnant white teenage surfer girl. *Spook Show* debuted in Berkeley, California, toured Europe, and reached Broadway in 1984 under a new title, *Whoopi Goldberg, Live on Broadway*.[40] With her hard-won commercial success, Goldberg would became a poster child for crossover artists, in terms of the multiple communities she sought to embody in her solo performances and the insider-outsider position she fiercely maintained with the American entertainment industry. As a performer on Broadway and in Hollywood, Goldberg refused to be "niched" by audiences or producers and always insisted on defining herself artistically. In an interview for her Broadway debut, Goldberg explained that "she likes people to come without expectations."[41] However, Goldberg fully expected audiences to participate, as we shall see shortly.

Goldberg's richly ambivalent, body-centered, one-person shows place her in as many positions in the dialogical conversation as possible: white and black, male and female, physically challenged, privileged and poor. Bambi Haggins describes her body as a "sort of tabula rasa on which she detailed the characters she embodied, with her dark-skinned, dreadlocked androgyny acting as their counterpoint."[42] Her physically distinct features effectively clash with those of most of her subjects, whether she is playing a seemingly carefree white girl or a dispossessed, recovering black male addict. Through this counterpoint, through her mismatched body, Goldberg places disparate cultures in conversation with one another.

For her Broadway debut, Goldberg resurrected two contrasting characters from *The Spook Show*, "Surfer Girl" and "Little Girl with the Long Luxurious Blonde Hair." Both identities explore whiteness and interact with each other through Goldberg, the "tabula rasa." In performance, Goldberg tears into Surfer Girl at full bubble, with her then-small dreadlocks bouncing around as if they were long blonde tresses. Like Robert Norwood from Langston Hughes's *Mulatto*, Goldberg mastered the multi-signifying white hair flip. She also fully absorbed Surfer Girl speech, with "so like," "okay, okay," "you know," "totally," and "really" serving as her verbal staples. This linguistically loose character may sound like the stereotypic Valley Girl, but Surfer Girl makes it plain that she is no Valley Girl, because before there was a mall there was an ocean and she is "aesthetically connected to the ocean." The dramatic issue in Surfer Girl's monologue: she is "totally PG," meaning pregnant, after having sex with a random guy on the beach. Scared and confused, she looks to adults for help, but she only finds miscommunication and rejection. As she reaches out, using the immediate audience as her adults, another recurring Surfer Girl phrase dominates: "Do you get it." She confesses to the priest and nuns at her church, but they "totally don't get it." The major blow comes when she tells her mother, who is "totally her best friend," but she also does not "get it" and kicks her daughter out of the house, into the street.

Instantly, this cruel turn tilts the performance and the audience in a new and darker direction. We thought we were getting a story about a carefree and irresponsible surfer "chick"; but that bubble has burst, and Goldberg moves us toward empathy for a deeply troubled little girl. The monologue's conclusion comes rapidly and is quite jarring. Surfer Girl casually describes how she stopped by a Jiffy Cleaners on her way to the beach; she straightened a hanger into one long piece and pulled down on her uterus. Surfer Girl claims she is not "freaked out," but she clearly is. Goldberg tries to lighten the mood with a laugh line: "I'm turning fourteen next week, God, you know, I mean there's so much I want to do." But finding out how young she is only makes the moment more unbearable and heartbreaking.

In his review of Goldberg's Broadway debut, *New York Times* critic Frank Rich incorrectly describes Surfer Girl as "a whiter-than-white 12-year-old Los Angeles Valley Girl."[43] With Goldberg's voice inflections, vernacular choices, and idiosyncratic hair flips, as well as the prevalence of white Valley Girls in the 1980s, it is easy to see how Rich came away with this particular misreading. But as previously mentioned, Surfer Girl disassociates herself from the Valley. Also, in the recorded video performance, Goldberg never actually mentions the young girl's color. She never nails down her racial location; so Surfer Girl could be a young black girl in this predicament, but most of Goldberg's gestural and vocal signifiers do suggest "whiter-than-white." By leaving the racial possibility somewhat open, Goldberg continues to play with our expectations of whiteness and blackness.

Yet what truly justifies Rich's presumption of performed whiteness is the next character. Following the "freaked out" and now homeless Surfer Girl, Goldberg immediately morphs into Little Girl with the Long Luxurious Blonde Hair, a seven-year-old black girl who desperately wants to flip her long blonde tresses and perform her unique version of televisual whiteness. On a racial level, these two characters work in tandem, as the little girl's tortured blackness makes Surfer Girl's whiteness more visible.

In terms of social and communal healing, the pair also works together by foregrounding an integrationist desire to embrace all children, regardless of race. The devastation the audience feels after experiencing Surfer Girl cannot be salved, but Goldberg brings the audience to some catharsis with this next, equally troubled young woman.

This seven-year-old black girl has resolutely announced to her mother, "I don't want to be black no more," and she is upset that her hair does not blow in the wind or cascade down her back. To compensate, she wears a shirt on her head and pretends to have "long luxurious blonde hair." When she grows up, she wants to be blonde, blue-eyed, and white; live with Barbie and Ken; and make an appearance on *The Love Boat*. But to be on that television program, she needs to have long hair. This black child's self-image has been shaped or warped by American television, what LeRoi Jones once called "a steady deadly whiteness beaming forth."[44] But in a truly dialogical conversation with her audience, Goldberg enlists their help to deconstruct and defuse this little girl's desire to be white.

The audience-interactive transformation begins when Goldberg, as the seven-year-old, peeks past the fourth wall and notices a black male in the audience who has hair just like hers, but to her surprise he does not have a shirt on his head. Goldberg then completely obliterates the fourth wall and asks to touch his "Afro," and she has him touch her hair. Both are soft. In this integrated audience, two white women are sitting on either side of the black man, so the little girl asks them, "Y'all don't care he doesn't have his shirt on his head?" They both acknowledge that they do not care, and the young girl is amazed. Goldberg next singles out a white lady a few rows back. The cameras pan to the woman, whose hair is a little frizzy, and the seven-year-old asks, "Somebody in your family look like me?" The audience roars with laughter, proof that they are connecting across racial lines, and that Goldberg is progressing toward her ultimate objective. Emboldened, the little girl now identifies other audience members without shirts and with hair just like hers, and she has an epiphany. Goldberg's little black girl realizes she no longer has to wear the shirt because the black man with the soft Afro said she could be cute without "long luxurious blonde hair." Unlike the lost, white Surfer Girl, this seven-year-old emerges on the other end of her story healed, or at least on her way to healing. But with a nod to how unstable self-image can be, the little girl reserves the right to hold on to her shirt, just in case the nice black man in the audience lied to her.

Like Goldberg, Anna Deavere Smith is a universalizing black female artist who defies categorization to broker dialogical performances between multiple communities. As a solo performer, Smith seems to share a theatrical heritage with Charles Mathews, the globetrotting English one-man show and James Hewlett role model featured in Chapter 2. Mathews observed and mastered unique national characters from Ireland to America and staged these treasures of local specificity in his famously polyphonic "at homes." But in a 1993 interview, Smith asserted, "I don't think I'm placed squarely in any tradition. I've always been on the outside, and have been an observer who steps in and the steps back out." Smith concedes her work is theater, but for her it is more than that; "It's also community work in some ways. It's a kind of low anthropology, low journalism; it's a bit documentary." Consistent with Smith's embrace of anthropology and theater, bell hooks has called her work "critical ethnography" that uses "polyphonic strategies to convey specific aspects of black experience."[45] To expand hooks's description, Smith's multivocal mimicry stages the experiences of not just black people but many different cultural communities.

Smith grew up in Baltimore, Maryland, during the 1950s, when racial segregation was the norm, but her particular community attempted to integrate. In interviews, Smith remembers her upbringing as "an experiment," a courageous commingling of black and white people with no established rules or structure. Looking back, Smith wonders if integration was a failed experiment. While some citizens fought and died for this worthy cause, most Americans were not fully committed to seeing it through, were not "willing to sacrifice their lives for the experiment."[46] In later years, Smith grew to mistrust idyllic notions of a multicultural America because she believes "there are too many contradictions, problems, and lies in American society about the melting pot. You're invited to jump into the hot stew but you're not wanted." In the early 1990s, as she reevaluated her performance ethnography, Smith was inspired by artists and theorists who talked about "negotiating boundaries." They inspired her to start thinking "about difference as a very active negotiation rather than an image of all of us holding hands."[47]

As a classically trained actor conversant with Shakespearean texts, Smith learned to appreciate the relationship between word and character, especially how language was the "locus of identity." Later, as an acting teacher looking for new ways to train her students, Smith started focusing on patterns and rhythms in everyday speech and on television talk shows. She began her ethnographic research by walking up to people on the street and offering to interview and perform them. Her emphasis eventually shifted from re-creating individuals to interviewing and performing whole communities, as Smith sought "to capture the personality of a place by attempting to embody its varied population and varied points of view in one person—myself."[48]

In the late 1970s, Smith's exploration of place and individual identities, as mediated through her solo body, developed into the "On the Road" series, a search for American character. During her travels to observe and perform in communities across the country, Smith would interview subjects and then edit and stage their words verbatim, while mimicking their vocal and physical idiosyncrasies almost exactly. Smith's process is about discovering her interviewees not from what they tell her, but from "how" they tell her. She is specifically interested in what details or issues her subjects verbally struggle with as they try to project themselves. For Smith, those struggles with language and the attendant unselfconscious gestures reveal a person's core identity, and that is the true self Smith wants to recognize and stage. Smith's process may sound objective, but as she selects, edits, and re-creates her interviewees for performance, she produces a highly subjective commentary around her subjects.[49] In short, Smith's carefully crafted one-person shows are about the core "selves" in conflict that Smith decides to bring to the stage.

This focus on the "personality of a place" intensified when Smith brought her ethnographic work to Brooklyn to document the multiple tragedies of Crown Heights. In August 1991, a Hasidic driver struck and killed a Guyanese American child; this act inflamed racial, ethnic, and religious tensions in this diverse neighborhood. What drew Smith to this crisis were the "graphic differences." She was struck by how in Crown Heights "everyone wears their beliefs on their bodies—their costumes. You can't pass. Crown is no melting pot and I really respect that."[50] The resulting performative intervention, *Fires in the Mirror*, debuted at New York's Public Theatre in May 1992. Smith's staged dialogical performance was by no means a closed conversation between Jews and blacks in Crown Heights, but a much broader conversation about how Americans struggle with conceptions of personal identity and community. As an artist, Smith intervened in the internal and external reactions to Crown Heights with the goal of empowering this unmelted community to reflect and move forward. Although she respects the "graphic differences," Smith still views gender, religious, and other identities as performative; therefore, she is drawn to moments when her subjects question the community-defined "scripts" they have learned to embrace and perform. Ultimately, Smith hopes to inspire her interviewees and audiences to realize their ability to author their own scripts.[51]

In one segment of *Fires in the Mirror*, Anna Deavere Smith embodies a Lubavitch woman named Rivkah Siegal, and through this particular Hasidic identity, Smith locates and universalizes herself as performer. For the Public Broadcasting Service (PBS) film version of *Fires*, Smith and director George Wolfe incorporated costume changes, introductory music, and photo montages to produce a highly subjective commentary on her interview subjects. In a segment titled "Wigs," Smith features Siegal, an unremarkable graphic artist, contrasted against the larger-than-life political activist Reverend Al Sharpton.[52] The Sharpton monologue is a "hot" scene featuring the boisterous minister in his signature James Brown–inspired, processed hairdo. By contrast, Siegal's scene is a "cool" moment, with the subject seated behind a desk calmly delivering a very unselfconscious story about identity and hair. This intentional juxtaposition of "hot" blackness and "cool" whiteness encapsulates Smith and Wolfe's very subtle contribution to "white people be like" performance, with whiteness or Jewishness receiving the more serious exploration.

At one key moment fairly early in the Siegal monologue, the Lubavitch woman attempts to draw in Smith. As she describes *mikveh*, a ritual immersion in water, and how the person and his or her hair must be completely submerged, Siegal interrupts herself to say to Smith, "Maybe you know." Based on how Smith incorporated this interjection into the Siegal performance, it would appear that during the original interview the two women connected. Siegal noticed a flash of recognition from Smith and attempted to establish a deeper connection with this seeming outsider who might know something about her faith. Some semblance of recognition might have registered on Smith's face because, in her integrationist past or performance research, she may have had contact with Lubavitch women. Also, from Siegal's perspective, Smith could have been Jewish, which speaks to how mutable this religious and ethnic identity can be, with various bodies having the potential to "read" as Jewish.

The "Maybe you know" interjection appears in the filmed version of *Fires* and not the published text, but this scene is where Smith begins to assert her mutability as a performer. Her spot-on performance of Siegal not only reinforces the expansive potential of Jewishness but allows Smith to affirm her unique talents as a universal performative vessel. Smith's racial body is an undeniable asset that allows her to move between very different ethnic and racial positions. Janelle Reinelt has remarked that "it probably helps that she is a light-skinned black woman: her light skin makes her specularly mobile."[53] Her mobility harkens back to Sam T. Jack's "Creole beauties" who morphed into various exotic images of colonial desire. More accurately, Smith's combination of visual ambiguity and virtuosity reminds us of earlier fair-skinned black female performers like the Whitman Sisters, Evelyn Preer, and Fredi Washington. However, in re-creating Siegal, Smith is not only visually mobile; her performance is cross-culturally empathetic.

In the recorded performance, Rivkah Siegal encounters her unique linguistic struggle when she talks about marrying late. Siegal reveals that she did not grow up Lubavitch but married into this faith, and she was so excited about finally getting married that she was willing to cut her hair down to two inches according to Lubavitch custom. She imagines her issues with hair might have developed differently if she had been raised Lubavitch and cut her hair after marriage. In Siegal's moments of verbal difficulty, the virtuoso and empathetic Smith comes alive, as she balances Siegal's great joy over matrimony with an identity crisis.

Siegal explains how before, with her natural hair, she could "keep it very simple" or experiment with various styles. Now with her real hair gone, she has to rely on wigs to achieve any versatility, and the wigs feel "like it's not me." It bothers her that she seems to be "fooling the world," when she is simply trying "to be as much of myself as I can." Eventually Siegal felt compelled to inform coworkers that a new wig was not her real hair, and fluctuating between "wearing wigs and not wearing wigs" became a major issue for her.[54] By the end of her narrative, you sense Siegal has worked through her hair issues and has stopped experimenting with misleading wigs. As a performed identity, Siegal is questioning and self-effacing yet fully committed to a religious faith and its values, and Smith leaves us with a complicated image of a woman grounded in a delicate balance of joy and regret.

Janelle Reinelt claims Smith can reproduce these kinds of nuances because she is committed to the process of "bridging difference, seeking information and understanding, and finessing questions of identity." Also, Smith is totally embraced as a Lubavitch woman, the Reverend Al Sharpton, or a Guyanese American because under the guise of documentary reportage, she creates the perception that she is presenting the "truth" about a real-life social drama. Functioning as both compassionate artist-activist and trusted journalist, Smith positions herself as a "privileged voice who may speak for others across race, class, and gender boundaries." But ultimately Smith's authority to speak for and represent multiple identities is not just about her "ethical and political credentials"; it is also about her virtuosity as a talented actor.[55]

The key ingredient in Smith's highly skilled mimicry is her ability to be a simultaneously visible and invisible interlocutor. As she performs the personal struggles of Rivkah Siegal, Smith concedes, "I'm probably also leaving myself room as a performer to struggle and come through." The repetition of the language and gestures of her interview subjects leaves a deep impression on Smith's body and psyche, and in performance, she fully interfaces with and "becomes" these people. The imitative relationship between Smith and her subjects is "difference and inspiration," whereby a Lubavitch woman inspires a universal black female performer to temporarily lose or collapse herself into this particular white identity.[56] But in the final analysis, this expansive dialogical performance of what "white people be like" is about Smith's capacity to question, recognize, absorb, personally connect with, and technically execute her interviewees' core selves.

Black Power Solo; or, The Melancholic Revolutionary

Psychologist and postcolonial theorist Frantz Fanon attributes black interest in and perhaps aspirations toward whiteness to a "racialization of thought" engendered by European colonizers. After being force-fed white cultural and social values for years, decolonizing Africans throughout the Diaspora responded to "racialization" with a series of cultural and social revolutions. The New Negro movement and Harlem Renaissance of the 1920s, Negritude in the 1930s, and the Black Arts movement in the 1960s all emerged to demonstrate that African cultures existed and mattered. Yet in the process of reestablishing "what black people be like," Afro-Diasporic intellectuals and artists also naturally redefined what "white people be like."

According to Fanon, Negritude poets promulgated powerful dichotomies: "an old Europe to a young Africa, tiresome reasoning to lyricism, oppressive logic to high-stepping nature, and on one side stiffness, ceremony, etiquette, and skepticism, while on the other frankness, liveliness, liberty."[57] Remarkably, in the twentieth and twenty-first centuries, many African American comics have promoted this "racialization of thought," as they developed stand-up comedy sets rooted in the very same racial dichotomies, especially white stiffness versus black liveliness. "White people be like" comedy is predicated on conflicting verbal and physical markers of racial style, as well as on anecdotal or historically grounded differences in black and white worldviews on everything from child rearing to bungee jumping.

If you are unfamiliar with what "white people be like" comedy looks and sounds like, comedian Tracy Morgan, in his November 2010 Home Box Office (HBO) special recorded at the Apollo Theater, indulges in some racial dichotomies.[58] Morgan opens with how black and white people have different "medical terminologies for shit"; for example, white people use the appropriate term "diabetes," while black people simply call it "that sugar." Next, he comments on the divergent parenting approaches between blacks and whites, claiming that white people will allow their sixteen-year-old child to sail around the world, while Morgan will only "allow" his teenage daughter to "sail her ass" into the kitchen and help her mother make lasagna with six cheeses. Finally, Morgan informs his Apollo audience, a largely black crowd, that "white rage, white boy mad" is worse than black anger because white boys, like Mel Gibson, turn colors and make noise. If white men are especially incensed, white women come up missing and the husbands pretend like nothing happened. According to Morgan's "white people be like" scorecard, whiteness is medically informed, overly liberal or solicitous with white children, but more dangerous than the angriest black man.

Performer and performance theorist Coco Fusco cautions against buying into this Manichaean universe, these "dynamics of objectification" ultimately produced by the white imagination. Fusco laments that instead of pursuing an "imaginative retrieval of 'original' cultural forms" from non-European sources or the creation of "entirely new paradigms devoid of historical traces," many postcolonial artists of color have opted to rework inherited stereotypes and risk "the danger of inadvertently recapitulating the scenarios they seek to subvert."[59] Hortense Spillers claims this narrow, racialized mind-set, which hampered Negritude and other black artists, will not be overcome until "the culture worker breaks through the 'perceptual cramp' that focuses his/her eyeball on 'The Man.'" Instead, artists and academics should break down the "dynamics of structure that impact individual psyches and social-political-administrative institutions."[60] Fusco's reservations and Spillers's redirection raise an important question: Can black solo performers develop productive relationships between racial difference and stereotype?

Whiteness scholar Richard Dyer claims it is possible. In his study of whiteness and representation, *The Matter of Images*, Dyer takes the strong position that "it is not stereotypes, as an aspect of human thought and representations, that are wrong, but who controls and defines them, what interests they serve."[61] Glenda R. Carpio, in her study of black humor and slavery, concedes that stereotypes may be marked by history—as Fanon, and Fusco suggest—but they are not necessarily owned by anyone, even the white imagination. True, working with this deeply racist material is a "volatile artistic gambit," but Carpio believes the performative risk can open up an audience. By appropriating and reworking stereotypes, an artist can investigate "the fetishistic force of stereotype in American culture."[62]

During the civil rights era, Moms Mabley helped establish the Negro comic's right to speak to white audiences, and Dick Gregory skillfully manipulated and reversed regional, ethnic, and racial stereotypes. A few years later, amidst the cultural and political emergence of Black Power, Richard Pryor further developed comedy of racial difference by redefining and reshaping not only stereotypes but the audiences that define and deploy cultural assumptions. It would take a young Pryor several years to fully command the performance space, including his physical presence, resonating imagery, and his audience. During his years of comedic experimentation, Pryor operated in what Hortense Spillers calls the "African-American personality situated in the crossroads of conflicting motivations."[63] This means Pryor was working in a performative terrain where differences in black and white styles were not always as clearly delineated as one might think. As his act matured, Pryor learned to punctuate certain differences in blackness and whiteness, while allowing other racial markers to remain shared or ambiguous.

After dropping out of high school and serving a short stint in the army, Pryor entered the world of stand-up comedy as an emcee at Harold's Club, a "black and tan," or integrated, establishment in his hometown of Peoria, Illinois. Pryor's early act consisted of jokes and impressions of major white stars like Dean Martin, Jerry Lewis, and pioneering black entertainer Sammy Davis Jr.[64] Davis is an instructive figure who represents where Pryor's career might have landed if he had not, on some level, resolved his "crossroads of conflicting motivations." Sammy Davis Jr. broke into show business as a child singer and dancer performing with his father, Sammy Davis Sr., and Will Mastin in the Will Mastin Trio. The much younger Davis truly discovered his performative niche when he started impersonating white stars that he and other Americans adored. Adopting the imitative rhythm of "difference and inspiration," Davis found he could lose himself inside personalities like Jimmy Cagney, Boris Karloff, and Frank Sinatra. His white role models drove Davis, empowered him, made him a headliner, and earned him a place in the hugely influential "Rat Pack" alongside Dean Martin and Frank Sinatra. Davis biographer Will Haygood wrote that "white Sammy could do whatever he wanted to do."[65]

However, unlike some performers in this whiting up study, who worked with whiteness and other markers of difference to create empowered black performative identities, "white Sammy" never mastered his "crossroads." Davis mentioned in a 1966 *Playboy Magazine* interview that to win the approval of predominantly white nightclub audiences, he had to "rob them of what they're sitting there thinking: NEGRO."[66] At first glance, Davis's approach sounds similar to Dick Gregory's strategy to prevent white audiences from hating or feeling sorry for the Negro comic. Yet unlike Gregory, Davis never solved the integrationist dilemma of assimilation as erasure. In an insightful article on Davis, cultural critic John McWhorter places this ultimate entertainer in a pre–civil rights context, where he had to erase or downplay his blackness and mimic white stars in order to survive professionally. McWhorter presents Davis as a pioneer, one of the first black artists to directly address whites while most black comedians simply talked to the other performers onstage.[67] But sadly, Davis never fully cultivated the power of imitation, like James Hewlett or Anna Deavere Smith; instead, he settled for a "copycat essence" that "prevented him from passing from personality to artist." The core problem was the absence of a real or substantive Sammy underneath his dead-on mimicry of Sinatra or Cagney. Davis lacked that distinctive being or presence necessary to become his own star, and to survive, he simply morphed into whatever mainstream audiences needed or wanted him to be.

Returning to Pryor's career path, the young comic graduated from imitating celebrities in small clubs to doing the same act in larger integrated but majority-white venues. Pryor also worked black clubs on the "Blackbelt" circuit, joining the ranks of numerous black comics who honed their comedic and improvisational skills before a demanding black public. While maturing in these two very different contexts, Pryor attracted enough attention to move to New York, where he made a reputation in downtown, interracial clubs and appeared on television shows like *Merv Griffin* and *Ed Sullivan*. To engineer this steady climb through the standup ranks, Pryor heeded the counsel of a fellow comedian who advised him to stay away from the "nigger" background of his childhood and be a "Negro." In the politically charged 1960s, many whites mistrusted Dick Gregory's civil rights–inspired comedic commentary and wanted to be entertained by "colorless" Negro comics like Bill Cosby.

"Colorless" definitely suited Pryor's childhood self-conception. Growing up in Peoria, in a whorehouse on the questionable side of town, Pryor created a raceless alter ego: "I called myself Sun, the Secret Prince. As Sun the Secret Prince, I was colorless. I was just light and energy, caroming off the planets. No boundaries. Simply alive."[68] In negotiating his "crossroads of conflicting motivations," a young Pryor experienced what Anne Cheng calls racial melancholia, which refers to how a "racially impugned person processes the experience of denigration" and also how he or she deals with the "dynamic of rejection and internalization."[69] Racial melancholia can serve as a "theoretical model of identity" to help us understand how grief plays a role in forming racial or ethnic identities like Sun, the Secret Prince. Pryor created his border-transcending, colorless alter ego to cope with the stigma of growing up in a whorehouse and the rejection he experienced from white peers at school.

As for the institutional and social racism Pryor internalized and then externalized, Nikhil Pal Singh characterizes the black American dilemma in the 1960s as "subjects proscribed from participating" in society and subjects whose relationship to civic life is always in "radical doubt."[70] For years, Pryor tried to erase the doubt by cultivating and protecting his colorless Secret Prince persona. He made a conscious decision to ignore his personal story, ignore the social stigmas and racial divisions, and pursue a nonthreatening style of stand-up. Pryor developed a Bill Cosby imitation that proved lucrative, advanced his career, but also earned him the label "copyist." Even Cosby gave Pryor some friendly advice: "Find your own thing."

One night, Cosby's sage advice sunk in dramatically. Onstage during a Las Vegas performance in September 1967, Pryor said to a sold-out crowd, "What the fuck am I doing here?" He left the stage, stepped away from a promising career in mainstream comedy, and committed to discovering what he was "doing." A fellow comic, friend, and eventual writing partner Paul Mooney would help Pryor find his comedic voice. Unlike Pryor, Mooney was strongly hooked into the black comedy scene, and he was also much clearer on his role as a performer. Mooney once explained, "My job is to make white people mad. They have to learn how to laugh at themselves." Under Mooney's influence, Pryor would adopt this more aggressive comedic approach.[71] Working in black comedy venues, such as Redd

Foxx's club in Los Angeles, Pryor developed a more biographical yet experimental stand-up comedy unapologetically rooted in racial difference.

As Pryor figured out who he was as a person and an artist, Mooney was not the only influence in his transformation, especially in terms of his expanding relationship to black culture. The high school dropout actually went to "college" when he relocated to Berkeley, California, and spent time with black intellectuals, artists, and activists such as Angela Davis, Ishmael Reed, and Claude Brown. In his autobiography, Pryor described this community as "smart, proud, committed, and uncompromisingly black."[72] They contributed to Pryor's cultural and artistic awakening by shifting his imagination back home to his upbringing in a Peoria whorehouse surrounded by hustlers, winos, and other addicts. These were not the most progressive black images, but Pryor learned to respect and value urban folk culture, thanks, in part, to Berkeley's black intelligentsia.

Compared with this culturally immersed, even nationalist crowd in northern California, an always honest Pryor admitted there were limits to his revolutionary potential. Pryor humorously explained, "I could be a revolutionary, but I like white women. I have a white-women disease."[73] This personal weakness for white women, which Pryor jokes about in print and various stand-up performances, supposedly precluded him from being a pro-black activist in the Dick Gregory mold. Admittedly Pryor would never earn a leadership role in any black political organization, but onstage, he did understand how his stand-up could be revolutionary. First, he recognized that the comedy club stage, where he interacted with all kinds of people, was a powerful platform for generating significant trouble. Second, Pryor understood how his behind-the-scenes interactions with certain aspects of whiteness, including white women, afforded him the license to speak as a cultural informant on whiteness. Gradually Pryor would work through the impact of racism on his young psyche and quiet the doubts about his place in American society to become a melancholic revolutionary positioned to reshape interracial audiences and their stereotypic assumptions.

Pryor experienced a major transitional moment in April 1971 when he appeared at the Improv Comedy Club, a small but important New York stand-up venue. Armed with his new, aggressive, highly personal material, Pryor struggled through a painfully awkward set of raw racial difference comedy. The performance was captured on film as *Richard Pryor: Live & Smokin'*, and at the start of the film, director Michael Blum makes their intentions clear with a tight shot of Pryor's handwritten set list.[74]

The list includes bits like "black cat w/neat hair," "eating w/white friends," and "white folks don't come." The opening, "black cat w/neat hair," offers a window into Pryor's conflicted feelings on blackness and whiteness. An unsteady Pryor describes how there were few Puerto Ricans around when he was growing up in the Midwest, so he pretended to be one and relaxed his hair to sell the ethnic deception. He explains his motivation: "I never wanted to be white. I always wanted to be something different than a nigger, because niggers had it so rough. I tried to be a black cat with neat hair. I thought that was the problem—the hair."[75] Pryor thought manageable hair would resolve his feelings of not fitting in at the integrated and segregated schools he attended. Instead of embracing blackness or aspiring toward whiteness, Pryor longed for an in-between, third space. Eventually he would learn how to cultivate and manipulate that strategic middle position, but not in April 1971.

Unlike Dick Gregory's "friendly" comic relations, Pryor's early experiment in "white people be like" comedy moved aggressively, rapidly dividing his white and black patrons along physical and vocal lines. The first half of *Live & Smokin'* is almost a steady stream of racial dichotomies. On black versus white families, Pryor recalls how politely the white families of his friends ate, while his black family broke bread with sound and fury, every man, woman, and child for him- or herself. On a political level, Pryor did a bit on how white neighborhoods have all the banks, while black communities have all the liquor stores. Pryor attempted to use this economic and health disparity to awaken his integrated but largely white Improv audience to the two Americas emerging outside this club.

But the majority of Pryor's observations on white versus black culture revolved around sex and the sex trade, areas in which Pryor was quite conversant. Bravely working through his childhood, Pryor recalls how polite white guys would come to his neighborhood and his house looking for sex. He specifically recalls very real encounters with white "tricks" looking to sleep with his mother—interracial interactions that had the potential to embitter a young Pryor. As a calculated reversal, Pryor imagines what it would be like for a swaggering brother to "roll" into a white neighborhood and tell a young white boy he is here to get a blow job from his mother. The psychic pain for Pryor is undeniable. Extending the sexual comparisons, Pryor takes us inside the whorehouse and re-creates a bedroom scene where an excited "hillbilly john" gets off, while a laid-back black hooker merely puts in work. Demonstrating that racial difference is often situational, Pryor later performs a reversal of this contrast in which a businesslike, polite white couple have quiet intercourse, while black lovers engage in loud, belligerent lovemaking.

The predominant stereotypic relationship underlying all of Pryor's racial comparisons is this colorful, uninhibited, and boisterous blackness contrasted against a plain, polite, and restrained whiteness. In *Live & Smokin'*, Pryor tries to sell the authenticity of his racial imagery by claiming he gathered these "findings" from firsthand experience. His act suggests he had dinner with his white friends and studied how the other half lives; however, in his autobiography, Pryor admits he learned what white families were like by watching television shows like *Father Knows Best*. In part, Pryor's whiteness was mediated, a product of the white world he saw on television, a world that did not at all resemble his own and contributed to his "radical doubts" about his place in American culture. Pryor also explains that he developed material on white sex practices by listening and watching through keyholes in his whorehouse home and, later, from his sexual conquests of white women. But again, Pryor admits he learned some things about white sex from watching movies, and he even concedes that both film and television "fucked me up."[76] Maybe Pryor was not the most ethical ethnographer, but his "research" on whiteness proves to be a somewhat credible and effective combination of debilitating media images, voyeuristic encounters, and real-life experiences.

While Pryor performs and relives some of his experiences, the pain rests just beneath the surface. He openly admits the "white johns" invading his neighborhood could have made him hate white people, but he rationalizes that those encounters merely exposed him to whiteness on an intimate and uncomfortable level. Anne Cheng explains that "when it comes to facing discrimination, we need to understand subjective agency as a convoluted, ongoing, generative, and at times self-contradicting negotiation with pain."[77] Pryor needed to work out the pain and grief he experienced growing up in a whorehouse, where his mother was sexually available to random white men. Pryor's performative emphasis on sex was a way of turning his childhood suffering and shame into a public airing of grievances with the majority culture. Pryor was developing what Cheng calls a "psychic strategy in response" to rejection by the dominant culture.[78] In April 1971, Pryor's fresh and unwieldy "white people be like" comedy explored years of rejection and suffering, but unfortunately, he was never in full command of the performance, especially his physical presence.

During the aforementioned political *Live & Smokin'* bit about banks versus liquor stores in white and black neighborhoods, Pryor displays an intriguing slippage in his embodiment of racial difference. He starts with an observation on how "niggers can get liquor, just walk out of their house"; but as he represents this black person walking out of his home, Pryor slips into a nasally constricted "white voice" and says, "Oh, here's a liquor store." Even as Pryor attempts to highlight a very real economic disparity between two communities, he vocally and perhaps unconsciously conflates whiteness and blackness. Throughout the performance, Pryor indiscriminately uses his white voice for both black and white characters, as if he cannot keep his racial styles straight. He also drops into his white voice to transition between failed bits, a tactic that reads like a nervous black performer relying on white authority to segue out of trouble. One possible explanation for this uneven and erratic set was the mind-altering drugs often associated with Richard Pryor. His notorious drug use would surface in his material for most of his career, and in April 1971, Pryor's "using" may have directly impaired his performance.

Another illustration of Pryor's nervous, uncontrolled energy flashes in the opening minutes of *Live & Smokin'*, during the "neat hair" segment. Pryor explains how he always wanted to do the hair flip, like white "cats" coming out of the shower after gym class. They would flip their hair as if saying to the "nappy-headed" Negro, "Hey Dick, can you do that?" In performance, a short-haired Pryor executes this taunting white hair flip to perfection, which evokes Robert Norwood's "'fay" hair toss from Langston Hughes's *Mulatto*. In the high school locker room, Pryor's slightly intimidated, internal response to this white challenge is "not yet motherfucker, but I will tomorrow." Later in the set, Pryor reveals that he actually got a "process" or perm so he could flip his hair like the white boys. Pryor's admitted desire for a white standard of beauty exposes feelings of inadequacy shared by many young blacks who straightened their hair to chase whiteness. But Pryor's flip plays another role in the 1971 Improv performance. During a moment of uncomfortable silence, after an awkward story about "rough," retaliatory sex with white women, Pryor deploys this nervous hair flip to change the subject, to use white biological privilege to again segue out of trouble.

Pryor's entire Improv performance was convoluted and uncontrolled, rendering his ambiguous white voice and nervous hair flip difficult to read. Did these uneven appropriations simply indicate an anxious, slightly high black performer in trouble? Were the fused markers of racial style part of a brilliant commentary on the fluidity of racial signification? Or were these idiosyncratic physical and vocal gestures manifestations of Pryor's desire for whiteness? An otherwise unremarkable *Live & Smokin'* is fascinating because this filmed document leaves us with these kinds of questions. I do not want to push too far into Pryor's early 1970s psyche, but struggling with personal demons and deficiencies is central to the work of the best stand-up comics. Reading into his racial comparisons, we could surmise that Pryor was longing for "what white people be like": the quiet and nurturing family dinners, the compliant white girls, the bank on every corner, and the tossable hair. In Pryor's first major experiment with comedy of racial difference, there are signs of deficiency, and blackness appears to be losing in this comedic comparison.

Throughout *Live & Smokin'* Pryor struggles mightily onstage, and during one of the many lulls in this brutal set, he asks if the audience has any requests. Several times Pryor blames his profound uneasiness on the artificiality of the filming process, which was perhaps a minor factor. But why was Pryor really so nervous and unsure? Possible drug effects aside, he probably understood how large the stakes were. Pryor was picking up the dialogical performance where Mabley and Gregory had left off, and his solo work was moving into taboo areas, like interracial sex and economic disparities. Breaking new ground was exciting, but it was also nerve-racking, which might explain why Pryor chain smokes throughout the entire set.[79] I also suspect that Pryor did not yet trust this comedy predicated on difference and was unsure about presenting such broad racial contrasts. Even as he crafts extreme, Manichaean dichotomies, Pryor also questions the presumed differences with recurring phrases such as "so they say" or "so they tell us." At one point he explains why he is content with being black: "I'm glad to be black, hate to be white. Cuz y'all got to go to the moon." He then suggests there are no black people qualified to join a space mission, but he quickly adds "so they tell us," which contests whether this racial limitation is indeed an accurate reflection of "what black people be like." In this small club in New York City, a jittery, insecure Richard Pryor appears to question and even undermine his innovative exploration of race and cultural style.

With years of work, Pryor would discover how to confidently perform this admittedly dangerous material in interracial spaces, learn to harness his vocal and physical markers, and finally realize his revolutionary potential as a comic. We can witness the revolutionary yet still melancholic Pryor in 1979, when, at the height of his comedic powers, he filmed a stand-up concert in Long Beach, California, released as *Richard Pryor: Live in Concert*.[80] Taking a cue from Dick Gregory, Pryor realized he had to do a better job of defining and controlling his interracial audience. And a couple factors were now working in his favor. His Long Beach audience was larger and more racially diverse than the somewhat hostile, majority-white crowd at the 1971 Improv date, so Pryor was dealing with a very different public. Also, Pryor was now a bona fide star with major comedy albums, films, and television appearances to his credit.

In 1979, Pryor hit the Long Beach stage fully confident and firing on all cylinders. As the room settled after intermission, Pryor spent the first few minutes of his set "casting" his audience, especially the white patrons. He explains how he takes great joy in watching—more likely imagining—the public confrontations when whites return to their good seats to find "niggers" have taken their places. To embody the surprised white couple, Pryor finds his high-pitched, timid white voice and whines, "We were sitting here"; a deep, self-assured black voice coolly fires back, "You ain't sitting here now motherfucker."

According to stand-up comedy theorist John Limon, Pryor's opening attack on his audience was a dangerous gambit, a move even the notorious Lenny Bruce would never attempt. In the first ten minutes of his set, Pryor effectively divides his audience into black and white and challenges them to "live as a division but laugh as a unity." But literary theorist Glenda Carpio explains what Pryor was up to: "Even as Pryor repeatedly invokes a divisive past, he also works toward the creation of community."[81] This divisive past is synonymous with a stereotypic present where Pryor seems to reinforce certain cultural assumptions about whiteness and blackness—for example, the timid, hypercorrect white voice. In 1971, Pryor's audience was unwilling to play with this divisiveness probably because they did not trust an insecure, uneven performer. The stereotypes were clearly controlling Pryor as opposed to him controlling them. Conversely, in 1979, his interracial public had confidence in Pryor; they acquiesced to the intentional division because they believed he could and would ultimately resolve the fissures and produce a new version of community.

So how does Pryor break and remake community? Combining two whiting up modes, Pryor's whiteface minstrelsy first estranges whiteness and blackness and then encourages his interracial public to identity with and against their presumed racial positions. Limon describes it as triangulation, where Pryor divides his audience into black and white constituents while he assumes a third space between the halves. He then functions as a powerful half-white/half-black facilitator who maneuvers both camps into laughing at themselves and others from the outside. In other words,

Pryor positions both groups to experience their blackness or whiteness from a critical distance. He facilitates this estranged, disidentifying cross-racial laughter by appearing to jump from one team to the other in an ongoing white-folk-versus-black-folk comedic showdown. For instance, to balance the aforementioned fearful white patrons returning to their stolen seats, Pryor also imagines a no-nonsense white dude, a crazy white "cat" who will not back down if you take his seat or cut in front of him in line. Pryor illustrates this fearlessness by improvising an upset, head-bobbing, yet still nasal white voice that unleashes a torrent of invective aimed at blacks: "Cut the crapola. . . . Come on pecker wood, come on you fucking jerk-off, son-of-a-bitch, come on." Although Pryor is obviously mocking how whites curse, this brave and enraged version of whiteness must be taken seriously because he is ready to rumble.

Still actively casting and triangulating his audience, Pryor explains that such white audacity is a product of Caucasians being more comfortable on their own turf, such as a predominately white Long Beach, California. He even asks the audience if they have ever noticed how whites are more cautious and cordial in a room full of black people, constantly checking the temperature of the room by nervously asking, "How are you doing?" But when there are only a few black people around, he claims white folks "be funky." To demonstrate, Pryor stiffens his walk and bursts through imaginary black bodies, nasally screaming, "Taking up all the fucking area, Jesus Christ!" Pryor's observations on white attitudes are consistent with Gregory's assessment of white attitudes in white versus black clubs, but Pryor physically incorporated this particular "finding" into the many contextual behaviors that comprised his performed whiteness.

In fact, one hallmark of Pryor's mocking, or "marking," of white people is his variety, especially his range of white voicing. Sociolinguist Jacquelyn Rahman has studied various Pryor performances and noted the different linguistic features and attitudes of his white impersonations. Specifically, Pryor draws distinctions between country white characters, corporate or middle-class white authority figures, and a menacing but ultimately engaging white Mafia/Italian presence. By breaking or estranging whiteness into different social, geographic, and ethnic groups, Pryor is making the important performative point that his "white people be like" comedy is not monolithic.[82]

With the filming of *Live in Concert*, Pryor arrived as a commanding black solo persona, and that sense of presence shows through his signature onstage prowl, a confident strut later replicated by stand-up stars like

Eddie Murphy and Chris Rock. Unlike *Live & Smokin'*, where Pryor was glued to the microphone stand, in the Long Beach concert, he moves up and down, physically dominating a fairly large performance space. As the audience retakes their seats, Pryor punctuates his blackness and representational control not only with his supremely confident prowl but with a soulful "What's happening, blood" to a black man finding his seat. Pryor also physically affirms a stereotypic blackness with a bit on black men holding their dicks, which he proceeds to do onstage. As far as controlling this racial imagery, by 1979 Pryor had full command of his racialized body, and he was not bound or determined by the divisive past and stereotypic present he performed. Freed from that racial tension, Pryor functioned, according to Carpio, as a "conduit for a laughter that releases that tension in a play that celebrates the body's freedom to *perform* rather than be defined by stereotypes."[83]

As early as 1975, Richard Pryor understood his role as a conduit. He describes in a *New York Times* interview that "I be listening to dudes talking, all over. . . . No matter what city you go to it's the same feeling, a universal feeling."[84] Pryor is specifically referencing the black people he meets, but in his mind, he is tapping into something more general or collective. He contends his audiences, black or white, are laughing because "they see themselves when I do a character." Similar to Anna Deavere Smith, Pryor claims he can become "possessed" by his characters.[85] The channeling is so complete and convincing that even white hillbillies see themselves in Pryor's whiteface minstrelsy. During the 1975 *Times* interview, Pryor slipped into a print version of his hillbilly whiteness to explain that whites come up to him after a show and admit, "I know a guy just like that."

Times interviewer James McPherson believed Pryor triggered recognition in multiple audiences because he "presents them with such thoroughness and fidelity to their speech, gestures, flaws and style in general that the same characters are recognizable to audiences in all parts of the country."[86] Without a single costume or trace of makeup and using only posture, voice, and gestures, Pryor re-created the minutest details of black and white Americans across the nation. Physically, Pryor developed what Carpio calls a "humor of incongruity" in which a dualistic yet confident Pryor effortlessly embodied opposing ideologies, cultural styles, and worldviews.[87]

In *Live in Concert*, Pryor uses this incongruity to demonstrate why black people do not get bitten by snakes as they stroll through the woods, but white people do. The specific estrangement here is that blacks, not normally associated with outdoor activities like hiking, turn out to be more attuned to nature due to their relaxed cultural style.[88] Pryor opens this bit by portraying a black man strolling through the woods, utterly cool and self-possessed yet still hyperaware of his surroundings. As he walks he spies a snake, nonchalantly says "snake," and subtly shifts out of its striking zone. Next, Pryor demonstrates how white people have a very different, more erratic rhythm when they walk, which does not help as they navigate dangerous spaces like the woods. Pryor transforms into a white body, painfully awkward, visibly nervous, yet oblivious to his environment. Not surprisingly, he steps on a snake and gets bitten.

Pryor's performative contrast highlights how white and black bodies in motion express different cultural attitudes. The black Pryor's stroll is not about where he is headed but about how he is getting there; this black body is not just walking but swaggering through space in rhythmic harmony with his surroundings, enjoying the journey. Conversely, the white Pryor fumbles through the woods, uncomfortable and out of place, because he is thoroughly distracted by where he is headed. With this latest comedic comparison, Pryor no longer mediates between the camps but clearly takes a side. He establishes a noticeable difference between blackness and whiteness and even stages a noticeable deficiency; however, in this case, Pryor positions blackness as the more desirable or advantageous cultural style.

After he abandoned his derivative "colorless" stand-up homage to Bill Cosby, Pryor, the melancholic revolutionary, devised a psychic strategy to deal with years of rejection and doubt through a comedy predicated on racial difference. Pryor was hardly the architect of these perceived and clearly constructed racial differences; he was merely the conduit through which stereotypes could flow and perhaps signify in new directions. Through hard work over several years, Pryor realized Paul Mooney's difficult agenda: making white folks laugh at themselves. This is the revolution in Pryor's performance ethnography; his research and reportage eventually produced an interracial public that could laugh at itself and rearrange its cultural assumptions. By the end of his 1979 Long Beach performance, Pryor, as a facilitator, effectively reunited the two halves of his public "on a new principle of identification," a new nation based on "the model of a stand-up audience."[89] Some things may have changed within this "new principle of identification." In Pryor's comedic universe, white dudes can be assertive in certain contexts, but even in the great outdoors, urban black "cool" is better than white awkwardness and preoccupation.

Postsoul Solo; or, Code-Switching Kids

Solo performers like Sarah Jones and Dave Chappelle are part of that young generation in which civil rights "lion" the Reverend Jeremiah Wright sees great promise. Over the past twenty years, some have labeled this generation postsoul, postblack, post–civil rights, maybe even postracial. This last descriptor, "postracial," is difficult to define, but in its most basic sense it signals the declining significance of race. Looking at Internet blogs and newspaper editorials, one might think "postracial" first emerged during Barack Obama's 2008 presidential campaign, but this concept has been a topic in public and academic discourses since the mid-1990s. In academic and art circles, cultural critic Kobena Mercer's *Welcome to the Jungle* (1994) introduced post-identity and potentially postblack approaches to analyzing Afro-Diasporic art in a postmodern context. In 1995, conservative critic Dinesh D'Souza's *End of Racism* attempted to expose the American obsession with race as unproductive and move the national discourse beyond racism. Debra Dickerson's *End of Blackness* (2004) proclaimed the final days of "blackness" as a reliable descriptor for African American cultural, social, and political behavior, and Leon Wynter's *American Skin* (2002) did virtually the same for whiteness and white America.

I am not convinced the term "postracial" applies to solo artists like Jones and Chappelle and the onstage personae they package and project. Unlike Anne Cheng's melancholic African American, they hardly view themselves as deficient in their representational work; they are not determined or paralyzed by old ideas about race but work with and through the divisions. Far from postracial, both performers are supremely conscious of race in America and do not show a compulsion to transcend cultural difference or embrace color blindness. In fact, that would be bad for business. Based on their crossover fan base, Jones and Chappelle draw and engage black, white, brown, and yellow worlds, as their dialogical performances seek to embrace as many different cultural communities as possible. And their appeal or niche requires that their diverse audiences see and celebrate the fact that artists with brown skin or cornrows are bringing all these people together. The visible disjunction between black bodies performing nonblack characters showcases these artists' versatility and universality.

"Postsoul" is a better descriptor for how Jones and Chappelle engage their multiple publics and explore what "white people be like." In the early 1990s, while writing for the *Village Voice*, cultural critic Nelson George introduced "postsoul" to his readership and further defined the concept in his 2004 cultural memoir of the 1980s. George temporally places "the post-soul nation" as emerging from the "troubling" and "terrific years since the mid-seventies when black America moved into a new phase of its history."[90] In terms of cultural hierarchy, this new phase of African American history witnessed "the unprecedented acceptance of black people in the public life of America." From art to politics to business, African Americans moved from the margins into the center and were "to a remarkable degree considering this country's brutal history" embraced as vital American citizens. For George, journalist Greg Tate, and novelist Trey Ellis, post-soul artists are the products of attempted integration in the suburbs and graduates of majority-white colleges. They tend to be disconnected from a black cultural past, especially the Black Arts movement, and choose to explore multiple significations of blackness. Finally, this generation of artists tends to be unconcerned with overt forms of racism.[91]

Further theorizing postsoul, literary scholar Mark Anthony Neal agrees the term refers to a historical break or political shift away from the civil rights and Black Power movements of the 1960s and early 1970s. Those earlier cultural and political movements definitely made this younger generation of artists possible, but now they feel liberated enough to take their explorations of blackness, or "blaxplorations," in new and different directions. As he worked through these blaxplorations in the classroom and in his scholarship, Neal needed the proper language to "critique the postmodern realities that confront the African-American 'community,'" and so he arrived at "post-soul aesthetic." Yet Neal and other postsoul proponents caution that we should not exclude older artists from this postmodern conversation, artists who were exhibiting postsoul sensibilities before journalists and theorists officially arrived at this new label.[92]

Media scholar Bambi Haggins has applied the label to performance and argues the most significant voices in contemporary black comedy, including Dave Chappelle, are "post-soul babies" whose "complex tastes and cultural practices" emerged after the civil rights era. Their performance practices are predicated on "individual and communal experiences of the African American condition," yet those black experiences are mediated, meaning the "post-soul babies are media babies."[93] Similar to Richard Pryor's imaginative contact with whiteness through television and film, Jones and Chappelle's conceptions of multiple cultures are shaped by and sometimes against sound, film, television, and new media. According to performance theorist Philip Auslander, all of these mediatized performance modes borrow from one another and constantly compete with live performance for audiences in our current cultural economy.[94] So it is no surprise that old and new media would exert a significant influence on Jones, Chappelle, and their live performances.

In a roundtable session on the dynamics of a postsoul aesthetic, Alexander Weheliye remarked how Dave Chappelle and his short-lived television program *Chappelle's Show* engendered a different way of thinking about identity and race that resonated with the postsoul generation. Mark Anthony Neal pointed out how Chappelle's comedy depended on generating sensationalized, "water cooler" buzz in order to remain on air, but like the best postsoul literary texts, Chappelle's work still managed to transmit "this deeper thing" on multiple levels.[95] While developing their "deeper thing," both Chappelle and Jones exhibited the fourth function of whiting up, identifying with and slightly against the majority culture. On one level, these two unique artists appear driven by a shared integrationist desire that says to the majority culture, "I am one of you, I know whiteness, I have been there." As two of the best racial informants in this chapter, their ethnographic potential is unlimited. Yet on another level, and with a nod to Pryor's revolutionary restructuring of audiences and stereotypes, Jones and Chappelle also project themselves as the transracial, fixity-defying personae the world has been waiting for in order to move beyond racial division.

Sarah Jones reads as a universal black female performer positioned to build on Smith's studied mimicry and Goldberg's crossover appeal. This slam-poet-turned-performance-artist differs from Smith in that she openly embraces the subjective nature of her creative process and rarely claims any documentarian or journalistic bona fides. Her performances evince more of that "we are the world" quality Anna Deavere Smith distrusts, but Jones is by no means naive and brings a political awareness to her work. For *Village Voice* critic James Hannaham, what distinguishes Jones from other performance poets is "her mastery of the mix" and an embrace of "human contradiction, particularly the irony of searching for politics of identity in a realm where identity and image whirl in an unstable pas de deux."[96] The unstable performative mix Jones masters is not nearly as dramatic as Smith's interventions into communal crises like Crown Heights in 1991 or Los Angeles in 1992. Yet her performance ethnography does share Smith's and Goldberg's affinity for moments in which individuals question or subvert identity expectations.

According to Bertram Ashe, one key component of the postsoul aesthetic or artist is a self-aware "cultural mulatto archetype" that feels at home operating between worlds. It is in these in-between spaces, the "wobbly interstices" barely separating categories like whiteness and blackness, where the postsoul artist lives and is most comfortable.[97] As the biracial daughter of an African American father and a Euro-Caribbean mother, Jones has always resided between and within racial categories. Growing up in the District of Columbia, Jones often oscillated between "D.C. Bama slang" and "whitey-white Sarah," depending on the moment or the circumstances. She spoke to her father one way and another way with her mother. Initially, this constant linguistic slippage was not necessarily empowering for Sarah; it led to her being called "zebra," a metaphor for a black-white girl, by classmates, or "fake," because her peers did not trust someone who triangulates so naturally.

Jones would later learn to embrace the power of her "cultural mulatto" position and understand that for most of her life she had been "code switching."[98] Dwight Conquergood describes this concept as "a commonplace ethnographic term used to describe the complex shifts minority people deftly and continuously negotiate between the communication styles of dominant culture and subculture."[99] Within the D.C. mix of her youth, Jones constantly adopted or embodied different racial and class styles. When her family moved to New York City and she began attending the United Nations School, Jones started to impersonate her friends from all over the globe, mastering their accents and intonations. She even learned to reproduce the speech patterns and rhythms of their parents, which made evading various responsibilities and punishments much easier.[100]

During an appearance on the *Charlie Rose Show* with guest interviewer *New York Times* critic Charles Isherwood, a more mature Jones articulated her mission as a solo artist. She wants to stage a "fully democratized American culture," not as a melting pot but as a stew where ingredients "flavor one another."[101] Sarah Jones first experienced this richly flavored democratized culture at the Nuyorican Poets Café on New York's Lower East Side, where anyone could step to the microphone and speak their truth. At the Nuyorican in 1998, Jones debuted her first solo work, *Surface Transit*, a series of interconnected monologues in which she inhabits various racial and ethnic New Yorkers.[102] Jones features four stage Europeans in *Surface Transit*: a Russian woman raising a biracial girl in the "hood," an elderly Jewish woman who is upset with her gay son, an Italian cop who must undergo counseling for his abuse of homosexuals, and a white southerner who belongs to the CWM (Civil Whites Movement), a more "enlightened" version of the Klan.

Critic Charles Isherwood noted how Jones often demonstrated great empathy for her characters, even modern-day racists.[103] As a performer, Sarah Jones rivals both Goldberg and Smith in her ability to personally connect with divergent identities and bridge differences. During the Isherwood interview, as she explains where her unique skills originated, Jones slips into Lorraine Levine, the Jewish mother from *Surface Transit* with the gay son. In a dead-on Long Island Jewish accent, Lorraine describes how a young Sarah was around so many different sorts of people growing up, especially in her mixed-heritage family. All she had to do was listen and collect characters. Slipping back into Sarah Jones, the artist tells Isherwood that it all started with Lorraine, who was based on an older relative. This Jewish alter ego also makes an appearance in Jones's follow-up 2004 solo piece *Bridge and Tunnel.* But despite her familial connections and empathy with her characters, a postsoul Jones understands race, ethnicity, and other markers of difference as mediated and always performative. Her solo pieces treat blackness and whiteness as commodities created for others to consume, and any resemblances to lived experiences of racial, gendered, or class dichotomies are secondary.

In *Surface Transit*, Jones's most geographically distant yet still empathetic character is Pasha, a Russian immigrant mother raising a biracial child. Although Pasha's situation is not necessarily unique in a heterogeneous city like New York, how Jones handles Pasha is remarkable. Unlike Anna Deavere Smith, who draws a stark contrast between the hair stories of Rivkah Siegal and the Reverend Al Sharpton, Jones's virtuosity shows in her subtle merger of a Russian woman and her black daughter. Through a heavy Russian accent, Jones recounts how Pasha came to be the lone Russian in an all-black neighborhood and how she navigates being an immigrant in America. As she narrates, Pasha is putting cornrows in her daughter's hair, miming the dexterity of this West African hairstyle. The presence of the daughter, whose voice is never heard, is felt through the loving act of a mother doing her child's hair. At the performance I witnessed, Jones wore cornrows, so as the audience is drawn in by Jones's precise mimicry of Russianness and Pasha's absorbing narrative, we visually experience Pasha's little black-white girl through Jones's braided hair.

Solo performers like Sarah Jones and Anna Deavere Smith share the imitative rhythm of "difference and inspiration," and at some point both artists have explained how they "become" the characters they study and re-create onstage. Their models or subjects transmit inspiration or core aspects of character that allow these universalizing female artists to lose themselves in these appropriated identities. However, when Jones becomes Pasha or Smith becomes Rivkah, they are not possessed in the sense that the white entities take over their bodies. More accurately, neither the model Pasha nor the mimic Sarah Jones is in control. Within this imitative rhythm, explains rhetorician John Muckelbauer, the distinction between imitator and model virtually disappears as both become "responsiveness itself" and an "affirmative rhythm of transformation."[104] Jones, Smith, and their performative subjects are transformed by this dialogical conversation with one another. In addition, by witnessing this unique process onstage, their audiences are afforded an opportunity to take a similarly transgressive journey.

Jones and Smith also share strong ideas on what a democratized American theater should look like onstage and offstage. Anna Deavere Smith argues that paralyzing representational debates over "Who has the right to speak for whom?" have arrested the development of a fully participatory American theater. If only men can perform men and only whites can perform whites, then Smith believes we are inhibiting "the spirit of the theater." Dwight Conquergood takes a similar position when he claims ethnographers and audiences need to abandon this notion that only blacks can understand and perform black literature and only whites, white literature.[105] A mature American theater means actors of all colors should have access to every race, ethnicity, gender, and class in the performative spectrum. Smith and Jones, two universal minority artists skilled at mimicry and cross-cultural empathy, perfectly embody this representational revolution.

From his first comedy set in the late 1980s, at the tender age of fourteen, Dave Chappelle has focused on racial material in his stand-up, with jokes about Jesse Jackson becoming president and a spaceship landing in the "hood."[106] Growing up in a race-obsessed culture and with parents who encouraged him to listen to political artists like Dick Gregory and the Last Poets, Chappelle had no choice but to grapple with America's political and cultural hierarchies. Yet his preparation to personify blackness and whiteness onstage is rooted in geographic diversity as much as in racial consciousness. Chappelle's parents divorced when he was young. His mother was concerned about a young Dave running "wild" in Washington, D.C., so she sent him and his brother to live with their father in Yellow Springs, Ohio. Chappelle spent his middle school years in this "hippie" town, surrounded by rural white kids. Apparently, this unincorporated Ohio community left such an impression on Chappelle that he would later purchase a farm in Yellow Springs where he and his family would settle.

After several bucolic years in Ohio, around age thirteen or fourteen, Chappelle returned to a drug-infested D.C. nearly devastated by a national crack epidemic. Chappelle's friends were selling product and dying daily, while racial inequities in the nation's capital were worsening. The racial and class disparities left a lasting impression on the young comic, but Chappelle is quick to point out how his comedy of racial difference was never designed to be malicious or accusatory. Unlike his friends from rural Ohio or inner-city Washington, Chappelle had the benefit of direct contact with many different types of people. His "white people be like" ethnography is rooted in sympathetic composites of white people he has actually encountered. Due to his exposure to widely divergent environments and populations, Chappelle became a versatile, perhaps even objective racial informant who could work across class, race, and geography to report from virtually any position in America's cultural and political landscape.

So not surprisingly, after starring in stoner classics like *Half-Baked* (1998) and black cult comedies like *Undercover Brother* (2003), Dave Chappelle became the ultimate crossover artist with credibility in what Bambi Haggins calls the "Afrocentrism of black hip hop intelligentsia and the skater/slacker/stoner ethos of suburban life."[107] Part of Chappelle's cross-racial dynamism stems from his geographic diversity, but some of his representational fluidity can be attributed to a once-productive working relationship with his white writing partner Neal Brennan. Bambi Haggins claims that as a writing team, Chappelle and Brennan modeled a "comedic social discourse where the unspoken is spoken—and the absurdities and hypocrisies that often inform 'polite' conversations about race relations are laid bare."[108] Starting in their teenage years when Chappelle was doing stand-up in D.C., he and Brennan collaborated on a variety of projects, most of which were frank dialogical conversations on racial difference between Chappelle/Brennan and a diverse public. They co-wrote *Half-Baked*, but after that stoner comedy failed to live up to expectations, the duo temporarily parted ways. But while "wasting away" on his Ohio farm, Chappelle called up Brennan, and they started brainstorming on a new sketch comedy show that would become the groundbreaking but short-lived *Chappelle's Show*.

Much has been made of Richard Pryor metaphorically passing the comedic "torch" to Chappelle, which the younger stand-up comic has accepted but with understandable trepidation.[109] One Pryor legacy Chappelle has fully embraced is building an interracial public willing to confront a divisive past and racially obsessed present. In his 2000 comedy special *Killin' Them Softly*, filmed at the Lincoln Theater in Washington, D.C., we can see how Chappelle deftly flirts with invidiousness while still uniting his multilayered audience.[110] Chappelle opens his stand-up set by establishing his racial credibility on both sides of the divide. He first positions himself as a black man returning home to D.C., only to find his city has changed dramatically. In his signature edgy yet confident style, Chappelle glances sideways at his integrated audience and quips to the black patrons, "lots of white people walking around." The D.C. he left in his late teens for New York and Hollywood was rapidly declining into the murder capital of America. In his act, Chappelle recalls how white people over in Virginia would never venture into the district; they would peer over the Potomac and declare "that looks dangerous, not yet." White Virginians were biding their time, waiting for the right opportunity to gentrify Washington, D.C., and apparently that time was now; they were infiltrating in droves.

As he remembers and embodies those white Virginians patiently waiting out the crack and crime issues, Chappelle subtly aligns himself with this cautious, privileged whiteness. Several minutes into *Killin' Them Softly*, Chappelle introduces a bit where he takes a limousine ride through the "hood" and feels uncomfortable. On *Inside the Actor's Studio*, host James Lipton noted how "just like a honky" peering at D.C. from that safe distance in Virginia, Chappelle seemed afraid of the inner city.[111] Chappelle was impressed and not the least bit offended by Lipton's "honky" analysis. Lipton astutely registered the subtle cross-racial identification Chappelle was making, how as a black man riding in a limousine, which introduces the element of class privilege, he was also concerned about his person and possessions being threatened by a still-dangerous District of Columbia.

In terms of performance, Chappelle's embodied and vocalized whiteness is not nearly as elastic, empathetic, or transformative as Sarah Jones's, but he has developed his hypercorrect white voice with some attention to detail. In an NPR *Fresh Air* interview with Terry Gross, Chappelle explains how he achieves this white sound by "taking all the rhythm out of my voice and speaking as monotone as possible." During his *Inside the Actor's Studio* interview, James Lipton remarked on how Chappelle and Martin Lawrence play "white dudes." Lipton praised Chappelle's white speech, claiming it is "so pitch perfect" the comic could speak this way all the time.[112] To be precise, Sarah Jones's multiple white voices are "pitch perfect," while Chappelle's intentionally monotone whiteness is designed as respectful but satiric commentary on white authority.

Lipton probably meant that Chappelle's white voice sounds like an integral part of the comedian's core identity; it comes from a real and connected place that suggests this black comic is identifying with whiteness. In the interview, Chappelle embraces and expands on Lipton's insinuation and explains how all black Americans are bilingual; out of necessity they have learned to code-switch between "street vernacular" and "job interview." Chappelle's explanation is not entirely accurate. Historically, many blacks have been compelled to speak differently in different contexts, but not all African Americans have cultivated this pseudo-bilingualism. Chappelle acknowledges in his *Fresh Air* interview that many African Americans have not had extended, intimate contact with whites, but he is an exception. Thanks to their diverse histories and experiences, both Jones and Chappelle have been positioned to study and master whiteness, and more importantly, they have consciously embraced code-switching. He explains in his *Fresh Air* interview how he speaks street vernacular in contexts where he is comfortable and in control, like onstage at a comedy club. By contrast, he speaks job interview in a Hollywood meeting as he tries to get a project "green-lit" by a studio.[113] Chappelle understands he must "sound white" to gain access to certain opportunities, but not all African Americans are equipped and willing to channel whiteness.

Chappelle further explains how many of his black friends in Washington, D.C., only knew whiteness from television or authority figures such as teachers or cops. They never developed personal connections with average Euro-Americans, so for them, "those people" remained thoroughly stereotyped. On this point, the monotone white voice Chappelle typically adopts throughout his stand-up is not a pitch-perfect white voicing fully representative of his intimate experiences with a diversified whiteness. Rather, the white voice Chappelle presents onstage is the stereotypic sound of "The Man," which many African Americans might hear or imagine in their heads. He is basically exploiting a comedic recognition among the black and brown segment of his interracial public, but Chappelle is also tapping into something deeper with this voice of hegemonic authority.

Throughout *Killin' Them Softly*, the predominant white sound is associated with the police, but if you listen closely to Chappelle's white cop, his voice is not necessarily the bland, monotone Chappelle described in his *Fresh Air* interview. This cop carries a little flavor, even rhythm in his voice, and most distinctive, Chappelle's white cop has that booming sound of confidence and unquestioned authority, a kind of "superman" or heroic bass that Chappelle claims makes black folks just fall apart. In fact, he informs his interracial audience at the Lincoln Theatre in D.C. that all black people, not just a paranoid Chappelle, are afraid of this particular white sound, especially when it comes from the police. He hypothesizes that this fear of police authority is a learned element of black culture because cops have historically treated blacks differently and harshly.

Chappelle admits he did not realize this intense fear of the police was a cultural or racially specific thing until he started hanging out with his white friend Chip, who, ironically enough, projects the same coplike air of dominance and entitlement. In fact, Chip's sound is a version of Chappelle's cop voice, but even more booming and commanding; Chip exudes hegemonic white privilege. During one stretch of his set, Chappelle recalls how he was absolutely incredulous when a fearless and completely trashed Chip walked up to a cop, admitted he was high, and asked the cop for directions. Chappelle was stunned by Chip's audacity and the cop's casual reaction.

To further establish his point on the different treatment blacks receive from cops, Chappelle asks a young white lady in attendance what cops say to her when they pull her over. He assumes they say, "Let me see your license and registration." He informs her and other white patrons that they would not believe what cops say to black motorists: "Spread your butt cheeks and lift your sack." This hyperbolic take on a policing double standard redirects Chappelle into an inventive "mock exposé" on police brutality. Chappelle imaginatively re-creates what happens when a white cop accidentally knocks out a black suspect. The immediate reaction is to cover up the incident, as Chappelle's white police officer, in his cool and confident deep bass, advises, "No, no paper work, just sprinkle some crack on him and let's get out of here." For the rest of *Killin' Them Softly*, white cops sprinkling crack on unconscious black "perps" becomes a running joke.

Richard Pryor, in his 1979 *Live in Concert*, introduced equally brutal white cops who administer illegal choke holds that put black suspects to sleep. Pryor slips into a squeaky-voiced, seemingly harmless white cop who whines, "I think I broke the nigger," and he then consults his manual to see if he followed proper procedure and discovers it is perfectly acceptable to "break a nigger." Without a hint of malice, Pryor jokes that his white fans have no idea what he is talking about: "choke hold, what choke hold?" For black fans, these abusive white cops reincarnated the "Angry Saxon," that rapacious, marauding symbol of colonialism and slavery. While white patrons may have been unaware of or oblivious to this hegemonic, historically rooted white terror, Chappelle's booming yet satiric white voice and Pryor's timid but still-sadistic white sound surely sent chills through their black audiences.

Another episode with Dave's bodacious white friend Chip further confirms that this fear of the police is indeed a "black" thing and that excessive white privilege is alive and well in law enforcement. One evening, Dave is out riding shotgun and "half-baked" with Chip, who happens to be driving drunk. Uninhibited and unafraid, the inebriated Chip impulsively decides to race another car. A hazy, weed-impaired Dave knows he should talk Chip out of this risky move, but he only manages to endorse Chip's impromptu drag race with "Well nigger, sometimes you just gotta race, I don't know." When the duo is pulled over by a patrol car, Dave starts to freak out, but in his ultra-deep, authoritative white voice, Chip commands Dave to relax. Without even turning down his radio, which is blaring Twisted Sister's quintessential white-angst anthem "We're Not Gonna Take It," Chip deals coolly and calmly with the police. He explains to the officer that he is sorry about the misunderstanding and "he did not realize he couldn't do that." Much to Chappelle's surprise, Chip is released without a ticket, and as he drives off, an unrepentant Chip lets out a maniacal laugh and informs Dave "he did know he couldn't do that."

Now out of whiteface mode and reflecting on what just happened, Chappelle marvels at Chip's incredible composure and nerve with the policeman. But throughout these two Chip tales, Chappelle's satiric target was never his white friend or even the cops. In fact, Chappelle admits he likes cops; he is just afraid of them. Rather, his target is an American legal system that affords white skin noticeable advantages and requires that African Americans be hypervigilant when dealing with law enforcement. Chappelle explains that unlike his white friend Chip, every black man he knows would never assume such ease and amity with a cop—not because they are guilty but because their criminality is assumed or suspected until proven otherwise. Based on his whiteness, Chip is allowed to perpetrate and get away with serious offenses, and based on his confident laughter and commanding voice, Chip is supremely aware of his protected status.

With issues like police brutality and cop paranoia in Afro-America, cross-racial understanding may not be possible. Legal scholar Patricia

J. Williams recalls numerous situations and issues involving race where whites claim ignorance; they "just didn't know" or "never thought about it." On a daily basis, blacks are forced to deal with certain social realities and anxieties, and she questions why whites are not encouraged to ponder such things. Williams also wonders why, when whites are challenged to do so, the potential conversation on racial disparities is viewed as a "burdensome" imposition from which nothing good can come.[114] Dwight Conquergood explains that any dialogical performance is about bringing "self and other together so they can question, debate, and challenge one another."[115] As a responsible and ethical ethnographer, Chappelle does not allow his audience to plead ignorance and tries to comically convince his public that white privilege, police brutality, and evidence planting still exist. This is common knowledge for blacks, but Chappelle jokes that whites are just learning about and perhaps believing this legal disparity because *Newsweek*, a reputable white magazine, recently ran a story.

Chappelle's "white people be like" comedy is never static and refuses to dwell on a single issue like abusive white authority. Extending Richard Pryor's revolutionary work with racial stereotypes and transference, Chappelle warns his D.C. audience, especially his black friends, that twenty-first-century Caucasians are different. You cannot scare them as in years past. Chappelle admits he has tried, but the response he now gets from whites, which he delivers in his signature white voice, is a belligerent "What the hell is wrong with you? Those days are over." Far from antagonistic, Chappelle has already positioned himself as an insider, intimately conversant with all varieties of whiteness. He knows white people, hangs out with them, and smokes marijuana with them, and therefore he feels a responsibility to report a significant finding: Contrary to Richard Pryor, he has discovered that white folks can be dangerous even when they are in the minority. Chappelle recommends that his audience pay close attention to the solitary white guy socializing in a group of young black males. Those lone white guys are typically "the most dangerous motherfuckers in them groups," because they have done some unspeakably "thuggish" things to gain the respect of their black friends. Of course Chappelle's warning reinforces a stereotypic image of threatening black youth, but he also displaces some of that menace onto twentieth-first-century whiteness, which is, after all, a prime objective of his dialogical performance.

The ambitious agenda of Chappelle's mutually embedded racial reportage, Jones's fully democratized mimicry, Pryor's triangulation, Smith's critical ethnography, Goldberg's audience-interactive transformations,

Gregory's "friendly" comedic relations, and Mabley's "revisionist mammy" was to break and remake American society. Such dividing and recombining can be messy. Patricia J. Williams explains that creating true community "involves this most difficult work of negotiating real divisions, of considering boundaries before we go crashing through, and of pondering our differences before we can ever agree on the terms of sameness."[116] At its best, "white people be like" solo performance negotiates the divisions without flattening or denying difference, without acquiescing to a "we are the world" sameness before this serious cross-racial play is allowed to perform its cultural work.

At its worst, this kind of whiting up performance can be reductive and reactionary, trapped in a received racialism that ossifies blackness and whiteness. After intervening in crisis moments in Crown Heights and, later, Los Angeles, Anna Deavere Smith learned firsthand how entrenched ethnic, racial, class, and religious boundaries can be. She discovered that Americans reside in "safe houses of identity" or "little identity camps."[117] Smith saw these camps when young black kids in Los Angeles burned Korean stores, or in her own generation, which talked about integration but never developed substantive efforts to facilitate racial intermixture. So today, as an ethnographic performer, Smith is no longer interested in those "graphic differences" and intransigent locations where people wear their identities on their sleeves. She now encourages young artists to step outside their "safe houses of identity," never look back, and operate in the "crossroads of ambiguity" where some truly fascinating things can happen. Smith's advice is tailor-made for postsoul solo performers like Jones and Chappelle; her vision looks like an older generation longing for a radically different playing field and calling the next generation of performers into action.

Conclusion

Problems and Possibilities of Whiting Up

Suzan-Lori Parks, one of America's most innovative playwrights, has experimented with stage Europeans on at least two occasions. In *The America Play* (1994) and *Topdog/Underdog* (2001), Parks features black men impersonating President Abraham Lincoln, complete with his iconic stovepipe hat, a black or sometimes blonde beard, and sometimes whiteface makeup. Parks has been asked why she keeps returning to President Lincoln, and she claims, "I don't choose Lincoln. Lincoln chooses me. It's a continual choosing, and I'm not sure why, but here I am."[1] *The America Play* is about a black man who so strongly resembles the sixteenth president of the United States that he finds work at an amusement park, the Great Hole of History, where he dresses up as Honest Abe and allows customers to assassinate him, just like the infamous John Wilkes Booth. Parks recalls her first encounter with this black Lincoln: It "was literally as if he walked into the room. Not the historical Lincoln. This other guy, this black guy who looked just like him walked into the room, sat down." Her Lincoln started talking, and "all I was doing was just writing down what he said. It was trippy." Later, with her Pulitzer Prize–winning *Topdog/Underdog* and second black Lincoln, Parks recalls how she was thinking about the first Lincoln when this new impersonator, whose named just happened to be Lincoln, stepped into her imagination. However, this time Parks decided to focus on Lincoln's home life, the offstage or backstage world he inhabited with his brother, ominously named Booth.

Parks's playful appropriations of historical whiteness place her dramaturgy in the tradition of whiting up and provide more avenues for black bodies to complicate race onstage. In an explanatory and exploratory essay titled "An Equation for Black People Onstage," Parks articulates a unique predicament for black characters and actors: "As African-Americans we have a history, a future, and a daily reality in which a confrontation with a White ruling class is a central feature. This reality makes life difficult." In this brief assessment, Parks captures the basic tension between America's racial hierarchies, African American performance, and stage Europeans. Yet she warns that insisting "'Whitey' has to be present in Black drama because Whitey is an inextricable aspect of Black reality is like saying that every play has to have a murder in it."[2] "Whitey" or whiteness was a defining preoccupation for black cultural production in the 1960s, but as an essentially postsoul, maybe even postracial artist, Parks rejects the presumption that the only way to explore black experiences is in relation to a dominant, oppressive whiteness. Parks concedes white hegemonic power is a central feature in the daily lives of black people, but much like Sarah Jones or Dave Chappelle, Parks approaches race as always mediated, always commodified, always performative. Whiteness, now a fully estranged cultural and social construction, is formidable but no longer normative in Parks's imagination, and unlike the Black Arts generation, cleansing whiteness is not central to her aesthetic or cultural agendas.

With her first Lincoln, known as the Foundling Father in *The America Play*, Parks subtly downplays race while chronicling how her central character struggles with the weight of historical whiteness. Although the Foundling Father is typically played by an African American actor, Parks makes few if any direct references to race. One possible racial marker surfaces in the second act, when the Foundling Father has died and Lucy and Brazil, his wife and son, have come to collect his remains. Their language is scripted in Parks's signature phonetic style, which suggests black speech but not unequivocally.[3] At the same time, in her text Parks calls for her first Lincoln impersonator to experiment with visual signifiers of whiteness, like an estranging blonde beard instead of Abe Lincoln's iconic black beard. Beyond racial similarity or dissimilarity, the Foundling Father's strongest visual connection to Lincoln is his thin build, long legs, and similar gait. But ultimately, the impersonator understands and expresses the core relationship between model and imitator as more than physical, as he tries "somehow to equal the Great Man in stature, word and deed going forward."[4] In the end, the burden of daily comparisons to the "greater" Lincoln wears the "lesser" Lincoln down and leads to an early death. Presumably the black Lincoln cannot measure up to or ever match the white original.

In a very different, more detached expression of performed whiteness, *Topdog/Underdog* treats this entire Lincoln impersonation as mere fakery, artifice that the new Lincoln can pick up and put down at any time. *Topdog/Underdog* takes us inside a black carnival performer's personal life, and the dramatic focus is hardly the historical Lincoln but, rather, an archetypal battle between two brothers, Lincoln and Booth. The brothers are defined by their birth order, their damaged relationships with now-absent parents, and the urban con game of three-card monte. In this second Lincoln drama, Parks is more explicit about Lincoln's and Booth's blackness and their underclass status. Also, to draw more attention to the performativity of whiteness, and race in general, Parks makes it plain that Lincoln's only resemblance to the assassinated president is the name. Therefore, this desperate black actor is forced to wear whiteface as part of his carnival act, where he sits in a replica of Ford's Theatre and is shot in the head by customers. As recognition of painfully real racial inequities, this underclass Lincoln complains that the carnival pays him less money than it would pay a real white actor.

In the opening scene, Lincoln returns home from work in full whiteface makeup and costume because he did not want to miss his bus. His brother, Booth, strenuously objects, claims Lincoln looks like "a spook," and tells him to take the costume "off at work and leave it there."[5] Lincoln coolly explains that he does leave it at work, and this performed whiteness has very little to do with his core identity; in short, wearing whiteface, a fake beard, and a stovepipe hat "don't make me into no Lincoln. I was Lincoln on my own before any of that." This is a job he simply makes "a living at. . . . But it don't make me." Later, when Lincoln is worried that he might be replaced by a wax dummy, he dresses up in his "full Lincoln Regalia," including the whiteface, to practice some new modifications in his performance. He admits to Booth that a "brother" playing Lincoln is a stretch "for anyone's imagination," so at work, he must leave his own issues, "my own shit at the door," to make the illusion work.[6] The work is hard, but this second Lincoln partly succeeds because, unlike Parks's Foundling Father, he compartmentalizes, constructs a buffer between his actual life and his profession. With both forays into performed whiteness, Parks reveals how struggling to master, overcome, or cleanse "Whitey" can be a pointless trap.[7] The first Lincoln perishes under the weight of trying to match a national icon, while the second Lincoln treats his appropriation of historic whiteness as purely performative; but he is ultimately still stuck in a dead-end job where he is paid less than a white actor.

So is whiting up ultimately a similar kind of trap waiting to ensnare black actors? For postsoul artists like Parks, are its cultural and political functions no longer relevant or effective? As the nation and its theater appear to embrace less-graphic differences and intransigent identities, have stage Europeans and whiteface minstrels run their course? I have been thinking about the death of whiting up since the end of Chapter 4, when we began to see, thanks to Evelyn Preer and Canada Lee, major industry breakthroughs for black actors in the 1950s. But the final word on whiting up's relevance or effectiveness is directly tied to how younger generations view race in the twenty-first century. Is race a wounded attachment that we need to transcend, or can race function as a productive signifier in a theater artist's representational toolbox? These competing questions lead us back to the seemingly contradictory possibilities for whiting up, which I briefly mention in the introduction to this study: racially transcendent or racially deconstructive performances. I believe there is room for both manifestations of performed whiteness to flourish in American theatrical practice, but first the objections.

From my whiting up seminars for graduate and undergraduate students, I have learned younger generations increasingly view themselves as postracial, meaning race plays a diminished role in their lives.[8] But it is a misnomer to say they do not see color; most students are willing to see difference, but they feel racial assumptions have less cachet with their generation. The "millennial" generation—those born between 1980 and 2000—understand that racism and forms of segregation still exist, but they do not believe racial hierarchy operates on institutional or systematic levels.[9] Essentially, this generation believes they have overcome or transcended race and, therefore, do not have inherited racial biases and hegemonic structures to contend with or dismantle.[10]

A couple graduate students, who actually did acknowledge racial hierarchies, made the compelling argument that performed whiteness was not particularly effective at dismantling racial structures, because even within the tradition, whiteness remained normative. Specifically, students pointed out that when Bob Cole created Willie Wayside, he sought to master allegedly white artistic forms in order to embody the full measure of humanity. Thus Cole's very agenda reinforced the notion of whiteness as universal. Furthermore, one student claimed that when a white figure like Wayside is placed in the outsider role, he does not necessarily feel marginalized or inferior because racial and cultural hierarchies confirm his sense of supremacy. This student comment echoes what postcolonial theorist Frantz Fanon discovered years ago: The white man never feels inferior in a colonial context, even when he is the clear minority.[11] This particular reading of *A Trip to Coontown* is born out not just by Wayside's status as a white hero in a black musical, but by the most popular song in the musical, "No Coons Allowed," in which low-class whiteness triumphs over middle-class blackness. Furthermore, certain whiting up acts such as whiteface minstrel cakewalks may have repositioned black performers, but this tradition did not fully dislodge whiteness from the center of the representational and political universe.

One persistent postracial objection, typically from white undergraduates, was that performing difference keeps racial wounds open. And their integrationist desire was to move beyond race, put this tired construct to rest once and for all. As I discussed in Chapter 6, Richard Pryor, Dave Chappelle, and Patricia J. Williams all contend that many white Americans are allowed to avoid race in most parts of their daily lives, so any effort to seriously consider its impacts is often perceived as an imposition. As we examined racial impacts through black performance, some white undergraduates mistrusted the integrated laughter produced by whiteface minstrels and stage Europeans. In 1975, in his interview with Richard Pryor, critic James McPherson expressed a similar distrust. He wrote that in America, "we tend to laugh because laughter creates the illusion of unity and ease, when in fact we have never been unified or at ease."[12] For McPherson and some of my white students, the seemingly unifying laughter produced at a Richard Pryor concert or feelings of cross-cultural, transnational connection engendered by a nineteenth-century James Hewlett performance were temporary at best and deceptive at worst.

Some white undergraduates also mistrusted the laughter because they sensed a lack of equality or core fairness in how race was used as a representational tool. Much like colonial South Carolina's Stranger, who determined that Negro country dances were not designed for the benefit of whites, these students believed something nefarious was happening within whiting up. They decried a double standard that allowed black artists more rhetorical room for racial commentary than their white counterparts. They wanted to know why black comics like Eddie Murphy or Richard Pryor were free to satirize white people, while white comics could not return the favor. I would like to think these suspicious white students simply wanted a fully democratized performance arena, but I suspect their concern was that blacks were now dominating cross-racial theatrics due to representational affirmative action.

I understand this concern from white students because for centuries Euro-American artists dominated cross-racial play; they controlled most signifiers of difference and how they were deployed. Also, today's black artists do have greater latitude with racial signifiers, while many white artists are encouraged to steer clear of this representational third rail. In his 1971 film *Richard Pryor: Live & Smokin'*, Pryor offers a possible explanation for the double standard: the persistent position of blackness at the bottom of America's political and cultural hierarchies. Pryor slyly admits he has fun being black because Caucasians cannot say or get away with as much as black people. As a test case, he suggests to a white audience member that he try to curse out his boss the next time he is at work.[13] In Pryor's 1970s, post–civil rights America, an "Angry Saxon" could never pull off such belligerence, while an "Angry Negro" is allowed his justifiable outrage. The implication here is that black performers are free to speak the unspeakable not because blacks are inherently hostile but because they are persistently oppressed by figures and symbols of white authority.

However, it is not completely accurate to say racial impersonation has swung completely in one direction. Even though the minstrel monster nearly ruined cross-racial play for the majority culture, white actors have continued to "brown up." In terms of popular, "mediatized performance," on *Saturday Night Live*, white comedian Darrell Hammond has been browning up for years with his pitch-perfect impersonation of Jessie Jackson. Also, the fearless comedian Sarah Silverman blacked up for an episode of her show *The Sarah Silverman Project*, comedic actor Jane Krakowski has appeared in brownface on NBC's *Thirty Rock*, and film star Robert Downey Jr. browned up in the major motion picture *Tropic Thunder* (2008).[14]

As for live performance, since the early 1990s, white solo artist, actor, and hip hop theater pioneer Danny Hoch has engaged in emotionally connected, socially committed, and racially deconstructive cross-racial play. Not surprisingly, when responsible, historically aware critics review Hoch's work, they often reference blackface minstrelsy, pointing back to America's long and troubled history of white representational domination. These critics and other solo performers raise understandable questions of image control and cultural ownership when Hoch "talks black" or embodies the Cuban, Nuyorican, and African American characters that he sees as part of his immediate community.[15] With pieces like *Some People* (1994) and *Jails, Hospitals & Hip Hop* (1998), Hoch has managed to unravel the assumed connections between skin color and how and where we culturally identify, while still working to expose the persistent impacts of class and racial hierarchies on all Americans. With his most recent work, *Tak-*

ing Over (2008), Hoch continues to bounce skillfully between blackness, whiteness, brownness, maleness, and femaleness.[16] In particular, Hoch shape-shifts gender and race to realize a middle-aged black woman in Williamsburg, Brooklyn, Hoch's own community, who resents the fancy French pastry shops moving into her neighborhood but just cannot resist their baked goods.

Perhaps black artists have earned somewhat protected status when it comes to playing with race because they have proven, in general, to be better architects and stewards of cross-racial performance. According to Patricia J. Williams, when the dominant culture develops performances around dispossessed groups, the racial signifiers become so fixed and ingrained that even sincere efforts to fully explore other cultures degenerate into fetishizing "the primitive."[17] Few African American artists have developed a fixed or fetishistic relationship to performed whiteness, perhaps because they have always had more to gain from a progressive and consistent democratization of American performance. Daphne Brooks encapsulates the problem with white cross-racial performance when she explains how blackface minstrelsy "conserves the performance of 'whiteness' and 'blackness' holding them in tension with one another," while still acknowledging that these contrasting cultural signifiers are mutually constitutive.[18]

Performances about cultural difference or sameness are ultimately more successful when there is not just mutual constitution but mutual respect between the cultures. In his cross-racial play, nineteenth-century entertainer James Hewlett respectfully appropriated Scottish folk material and, as a result, resolved some of the tensions between early national blackness and whiteness in America. Gifted performers Anna Deavere Smith, Whoopi Goldberg, and Sarah Jones worked across race, class, ethnicity, and gender to produce new universals and generate beneficial cross-cultural recognitions. Similar to Danny Hoch, these black solo artists crafted moral and ethical performance ethnographies that speak to and with other cultures, rather than merely about them. But for performance scholar Coco Fusco, performance is "as much concerned with what we can control about our identities as what we cannot."[19] In this swirl of interacting cultures and new meanings, there is always the threat of losing representational control.

To appreciate the difficulty of maintaining representational control, we should revisit the cakewalk, a whiteface minstrel dance initially created by Negroes in the antebellum South but then refigured by Euro-

American blackface minstrel artists. White performers transformed this African-European hybrid dance expressive of African American identity into crudely comical prancing, and by the late 1890s, concerned black citizens were disturbed and speaking out. In a letter to the editor of the *Republican Progress* in Bloomington, Indiana, a proud representative "of the colored race" warned that this cakewalk "fad" was leading Negroes down a path of irredeemable social death and destruction.[20] Without the slightest regard for colored people and their public image, whites perpetuated these "monkefied contortions" and then expected theatrical and musical "coons" to entertain white America with this denigrating imagery.

George L. Knox, editor of the *Indianapolis Freeman*, reprinted this concerned citizen's entire letter and added his own denunciation of the cakewalk. Knox agreed the cakewalk had become a detriment to the African American image, but he did not solely blame white Americans. He targeted Negro artists and audiences: "If 'cake walks' are to become a characteristic feature of Negro life then the clamoring for elevation in the social scale should cease." Knox reasoned cakewalks "and higher life are not compatible or synonymous by any means, and if the race is to be seduced by these mazy gyrations that so readily bespeak an easy virtue, then the race will be set down according to the sign it wears."[21] Knox's position echoes Bob Cole's objection to the cakewalk and his eventual disavowal of the word "coon." As cultural critics, both Knox and Cole read this appropriated and now uncontrollable dance form as severely detrimental to racial uplift.

This ongoing struggle over racial imagery continues with the current generation of postsoul black artists. Dave Chappelle experienced a crisis of representational control in 2004 while taping a sketch for the third season of *Chappelle's Show*. This problematic sketch featured a blackface "Nigger Pixie" character—the minstrel monster dies hard—and during the taping, a white staffer let out a prolonged laugh that made Chappelle uneasy. On his own set, where he wielded significant power as a producer, Chappelle felt like his "inner coon" was creeping out and that he was endorsing as opposed to defusing stereotypes.[22] As black artists like Pryor or Chappelle triangulated interracial audiences, played with the divisive "fire" of stereotypes, and searched for the perfect "integrated joke," they enjoyed some command of their satiric targets. But how long could this last? Given the unpredictability and mutability of performance, the operative question may not be whether this dual tradition has lost its relevance in our current moment. The key question may be How can whiting up transform to meet the needs of American theater and social performance in the twenty-first century?

To answer this question, I turn to my second potential future for whiting up: more innovative artists and academics exploring satiric, imitative, terrifying, and disidentifying performances of whiteness, blackness, brownness, and yellowness. Moving forward, studies of extra-theatrical whiteface minstrelsy may prove more illuminating and productive when they directly address and perhaps resolve the sociological phenomenon of "acting white." Here I am referring to the pathological classroom taunts and fixed racial notions that I attempted to distinguish from whiting up at the beginning of this study. Since I am not a trained sociologist or psychologist, I have refrained from wading into the dynamics of "acting white" accusations. At most, I have dissected cross-racial informants like Sarah Jones and Dave Chappelle, who have developed their code-switching skills with an innate ability to know when and where to "sound white."

But recent sociological and linguistic investigations into the subject have revealed how institutionalized racism in certain closed cultures continues to privilege whiteness and require nonwhites to "act white" in order to advance. British ex–soccer player Colin King has studied the predicament of former black footballers who want to become managers and how they must master a constantly changing whiteness to advance through the ranks of English football.[23] In addition, John McWhorter's work on Sammy Davis Jr. places this iconic, triple-threat entertainer within a historical and representational environment where Davis was expected to "act white" to ensure his own professional survival.[24] Finally, in her important work on stylized mocking among high school students, linguist Elaine Chun explores how "acting white" has expanded to include parodies of "hyper-feminine" white "preppy" kids.[25] Chun examines how this social performance of a "waspy" whiteness, deftly executed by Asian American students, negotiates race, class, and gender. Her sociolinguistic work should prove fertile ground for understanding how younger generations of minority and majority students identify with and against whiteness, and the broader impacts of their social experiments on identity construction and deconstruction. Such sociological investigations of cross-racial play have the potential to defuse and perhaps dismantle the paralyzing racial assumptions behind "acting white" taunts.

As for stage Europeans in the twenty-first century, the quantity and quality of incisive, racially deconstructive white characters designed for black performers have diminished over the years. We can see a poor remnant of this once proud tradition in Shawn and Marlon Wayans's *White Chicks* (2006), a Hollywood studio film about two black government agents who go undercover as rich white society girls. Movie critic Robert Wolinsky attempted to place *White Chicks* within a whiting up tradition by drawing connections to Eddie Murphy and Andy Breckman's 1984 *Saturday Night Live* short film *White Like Me*. In that earlier, masterful whiting up act, Murphy disguises himself in whiteface and a greeting-card vocabulary to infiltrate white society. Wolinsky hoped *White Chicks* would be an extension of Murphy and Breckman's shrewd and studied satire, but he was profoundly disappointed and predicted *White Chicks* "will disappear from theaters long before it can raise a ruckus among black filmmakers and filmgoers who will damn it as a thousand steps in the wrong direction."[26]

More recently, actor-producer Halle Berry crafted an incredible whiting up act for the 2010 film *Frankie and Alice* which does move in the right direction. In this passion project, which was inspired by a true story, Berry plays a black woman named Frankie Murdoch with dissociative identity disorder.[27] One of her personalities is a racist and privileged white woman named Alice, a character drawn from Frankie's formative years in Georgia. Frankie carries this white woman with her and unleashes this curious identity in various social contexts, including at the wedding of Frankie's childhood friend and in the lobby of a fancy hotel. Without resorting to whiteface masks or blonde wigs, Halle Barry and her production team take the interiority of Adrienne Kennedy's *Funnyhouse of a Negro* to another level. The film *Frankie and Alice* realistically externalizes Frankie's childhood trauma and psychic damage through a stunningly horrific stage European rooted in racial animus.

As for productive, racially deconstructive stage Europeans in live, theatrical performance, we can look at older works like Marcia L. Leslie's *The Trial of One Short-Sighted Black Woman vs. Mammy Louise and Safreeta Mae* (1995) or Syl Jones's 1998 adaptation of George Schuyler's *Black No More* (see Chapter 5). Both of these stage comedies position black actors to engage in well-designed cross-racial theatrics. In the twenty-first century, longtime *New Yorker* cartoonist William Hamilton scripted *White Chocolate* (2004), a high-society satire that proves stage Europeans can still expose white privilege while moving audiences toward unifying laughter.[28] *White Chocolate* is about two Caucasian socialites who mysteriously turn black and must deal with the consequences of this devastating status change. Produced by The Culture Project, a politically conscious theater company in New York City, Hamilton's live stage Europeans afforded veteran black actors Reg G. Cathey and Lynn Whitfield full access to a veritable buffet of excessive white privilege and pretension.

Even Broadway has rediscovered the rich tradition of whiting up thanks to Kander and Ebb's innovative musical *The Scottsboro Boys* (2010). For years, the writing team of composer John Kander and lyricist Fred Ebb wrestled with setting the infamous 1930s Scottsboro rape case to music. If the subject matter was not challenging enough, their production concept embraced the blackface minstrel semicircle, complete with a white interlocutor and the notorious blackface endmen Mr. Tambo and Mr. Bones. After Ebb's death in 2004, the project was shelved until director Susan Stroman and writer David Thompson stepped in to complete Kander and Ebb's musical. Working with and against the blackface tradition, Stroman and Thompson allow their archetypal endmen to do much more than caricature blackness. In their current version, Tambo and Bones satirize and expose the major white figures in this legal farce: incompetent white lawyers, lying white female witnesses, and sadistic white prison guards.[29] We should note that in this case, the stage Europeans were crafted not by black playwrights but by white musical theater artists, thus proving any skilled practitioner can contribute to twenty-first-century whiting up. In October 2010, Stroman and Thompson's version debuted on Broadway, where it stunned mainstream audiences yet reaffirmed the commercial potential of well-executed, penetrating, and elastic stage Europeans.

Admittedly, the *Scottsboro* brand of racially provocative stage Europeans has become less common in the twenty-first century. This noticeable decline in one aspect of whiting up is partly due to the rise of "color-blind" and nontraditional casting, professional practices that have broadened the performative playing field and truly democratized American theater. Which brings us to the other potential future for whiting up in American theatrical practice: expanding the pool of white roles available to actors of color without altering the original material. Black British actor Idris Elba was recently cast in the major motion picture *Thor* (2011) as Heimdall, the Norse "god of light" and the "whitest" of all the Nordic deities. Elba correctly identified this racially transcendent, nontraditional production decision as "a sign of the times for the future" and as an example of "multilevel casting."[30]

As might be expected, news of this courageous casting decision generated vehement reactions, protests from cultural advocacy groups such as the Council of Conservative Citizens. This white supremacist group denounced Elba's Heimdall as a vicious attack on European heritage and an example of social engineering forced on Nordic mythology.[31] Such protests are nothing new. Earlier "trespassing" black performers like Evelyn Preer and Canada Lee braved black and white critical opposition to eliminate representational barriers. Due to their pioneering efforts, CCH Pounder and Denzel Washington could assume racially transcendent roles in Ibsen or Shakespeare with the focus primarily on their talent and not their color. The original objective of color-blind and nontraditional casting was to place gifted black, brown, and yellow bodies into roles written by dead white playwrights who never dreamed of such living, breathing diversity inhabiting their work. Today, living white screenwriters, producers, and musical theaters have taken this next gigantic step of strategically placing black bodies into white narratives without whiteface and without altering the original. I imagine these are the very conditions under which Canada Lee would have preferred to play Daniel de Bosola on Broadway back in 1946, performing this Spaniard free of face paint in a cast of white actors. Lee's forced experiment and the long history of performed whiteness has made Elba's contested trespass on Nordic cultural property a fairly common occurrence, and I wholeheartedly endorse this new generation of brave new representational realities.

Clear progress in casting practices has moved American theater, film, and television toward the representational meritocracy Earle Hyman and Anna Deavere Smith envisioned years ago. In theory, recognizing an actor's talent more than his or her color is a commendable goal that I fully support; however, in theatrical practice, the notion of not seeing color or not using race as a powerful signifier seems counterintuitive. The literal meaning of the Greek *theatron* is "the seeing place," so surely theater practitioners understand that ignoring how bodies read onstage—how difference amplifies, complicates, and enriches—leads to incomplete and disengaged theatrical experiences. Consequently, there is a significant difference between racially transcendent and racially deconstructive whiting up, between stage Europeans who seek to "get beyond" race and whiteface minstrels and stage Europeans who directly address racial representation onstage and identity construction offstage.

Cartoonist William Hamilton's off-Broadway stage Europeans from *White Chocolate* and the Broadway minstrel endmen from Stroman and Thompson's *Scottsboro Boys* force hip New Yorkers and Broadway tourists to confront the colors of their characters and their actors. These productions challenge an interracial public to read the broader class and racial implications of a sometimes terrifying white privilege, while still recognizing the gifts of the skilled actors engaged in cross-racial play. Both objectives can be accomplished in the same production. Cole and Johnson's performative crisscrossing of race and class in *A Trip to Coontown,* LeRoi Jones's white beast spawned by an anticommunal black magician, and Sarah Jones's hair-braiding Russian immigrant all initiate complex conversations around race and representation in American culture. At the same time, some nontraditional stage European roles simply provide broadening, professionalizing opportunities for African American, Latino, and Asian American artists without advancing national discourses on color, culture, and power, which is perfectly acceptable and understandable.

After operating in four different centuries, often right beneath America's representational radar screen, whiting up still has the potential to cultivate a less racially charged, less suspicious, and more dialogical performance environment where it is acceptable to see color and laugh at difference. According to historian Nikhil Pal Singh, black freedom struggles in the United States have never been just about "market access, equal citizenship, or integrating black people into common national subjectivity." The ultimate agendas of Afro-America's resistant acts and counterstatements have been to widen the "circle of common humanity" and generate "new universals."[32] Whiting up has produced "new universals" with trend-setting fashionable black promenaders, convention-defying actors like Evelyn Preer and Canada Lee, and multisignifying black solo artists like Whoopi Goldberg, Anna Deavere Smith, and Sarah Jones. When these black artists engage in cross-racial play, the results are transnational alliances, new identity models, perceptive critiques of racial hegemony, and ultimately more performance options for all actors. Because when we learn from whiteface minstrels and stage Europeans, specifically how to perform race without fixing race, the nation's performative playing field can become virtually unlimited.

Playwright David Henry Hwang has learned, explored, and illustrated this lesson with his play *Yellowface* (2007), which uses the theater, both stage and industry, to interrogate race as one of many performative "faces."[33] Hwang's 2007 meta-theatrical drama refers to and builds on his earlier 1990s play *Face Value,* which failed on Broadway but, more importantly, featured two Asian actors performing in whiteface. In the fearlessly self-reflexive *Yellowface,* character/producer/playwright David Henry Hwang mistakenly casts a white actor as one of his Asian stars in the Broadway-bound *Face Value*. Through this instance of color-conscious casting gone horribly wrong, *Yellowface* questions how we read race onstage and offstage. But so does the miscast white actor who, in the dramatic narrative of *Yellowface*, settles into his accidental "yellowness" to become an Asian American activist. Hwang imagines an American theater and broader culture where sociocultural constructs like blackness, brownness, whiteness, or yellowness are not troublesome signifiers of invidiousness but cultural tools to be noticed, deployed, explored, and challenged by everyone.

Anthropologist-turned-dramaturg Dorinne Kondo has explained how race operates as such a debilitating, power-laden construct that the supposedly progressive liberal humanist solution is to transcend race in all representations.[34] However, she argues pretending to be postracial or color-blind in casting, theatrical practice, or cultural discourse does not lead to universality or a greater appreciation for a performer's humanity. Ignoring or pretending to ignore race only limits creative options and causes us to succumb to an irrational fear that if we notice racial difference, we cannot help but respond with a host of negative cultural assumptions. The key audience question is How does an interracial public in the twenty-first century process difference? Surely we can "see" and handle visual distinctions, release the historical baggage that automatically reads different as deficient, and realize that any performer can embody multiple colors, cultures, sexualities, and genders. Based on this logic, a radically restructured theatrical playing field and audience would embrace not only a black actor playing Heimdall in *Thor* but a white actor dropped into the middle of August Wilson's *Piano Lesson*.

For centuries, whiting up has proven that theatrical and extra-theatrical audiences can and will learn to process difference differently, as they agree to constantly shifting cultural assumptions about what black, brown, yellow, and white represent. As sociolinguist Elaine Chun has shown, in contemporary American high schools, this kind of cross-racial, cross-gender cultural mind-set is operating in everyday, teenage social performance. When American theater catches up to David Henry Hwang and high school students, the cross-racial theatrics could prove explosive: dark Latinas playing white figures, Asian actors playing Hispanic roles, and Euro-American actors confidently and respectfully playing black characters. Well beyond academia, I hope to see comedians, playwrights, composers, filmmakers, television writers, and actors expanding, not limiting, their representational palates. I look forward to analyzing even more acts of performed whiteness that engage race, gender, and other identity constructs.

To close, I want to introduce a final and perhaps improbable possibility of whiting up. Abolitionist Frederick Douglass and comic-activist Dick Gregory both concluded that diversions like cakewalks and stand-up comedy are nothing more than "safety valves" or "narcotics" designed to distract black communities.[35] Other artists examined in these pages, including Dave Chappelle, Anna Deavere Smith, Jean Genet, and Evelyn Preer, have also contemplated their level of responsibility for how blackness and whiteness are represented, received, and recirculated by their audiences. Perhaps whiting up is another opiate for the masses, and the representational powers that be—indulgent slave masters, Broadway producers, comedy club owners—have allowed this artistic commentary from below because they recognized the significant difference between representing race and combating racism. But what if whiting up could resolve racism?

When cultural critics and political scientists assess race relations or contemplate the end of racism, they tend to arrive at well-worn clichés like "we have come a long way but we are not there yet." Rarely do they describe what "there" looks like or the actions necessary to get "there." However, legal theorist Patricia J. Williams has defined "there" as a world where "we could all wake up and see all of ourselves reflected in the world, not merely in a territorial sense but with a kind of non-exclusive entitlement that grants not so much possession as investment."[36] Instead of possessive investments in whiteness as privilege or in blackness as territory, "there" looks like an "investment that envisions each of us in each other."

As for how we get there, Williams believes we can cure social ills like racism, anti-Semitism, and xenophobia by creating "a livable space between the poles of other people's imagination and the nice calm center of oneself where dignity resides."[37] For centuries, whiting up artists have worked to create those livable in-between spaces, but with varying degrees of success because realizing or restoring dignity under hostile conditions takes time. Nevertheless, whiteface minstrels and stage Europeans perform the "us in each other," first, by appropriating products of the white imagination and, second, by fashioning new black identities through those white forms. Granted, some works of performed whiteness are about psychic terror and the impossibility of sustaining a livable space amidst blackness and whiteness. With her externalization of a troubled African American psyche, Adrienne Kennedy stages an ultimately tragic "third space." But Whoopi Goldberg's beautifully improvised negotiation between a hair-flipping white Surfer Girl, a little black girl longing for blonde tresses, and an interracial Broadway audience offers an antidote to racism. The outcome of Goldberg's dialogical performance is the calming of a little black girl's center and the potential beginning of a dignified life less scarred by a deadly, debilitating, televisual whiteness.

In answering a series of rhetorical questions on cross-racial representations, performance theorist and practitioner E. Patrick Johnson concludes that "some sites of cross-cultural appropriation provide fertile ground on which to formulate new epistemologies of self and other."[38] Whiting up has proven to be a fertile ground where black artists, and more recently white artists, can formulate a collective understanding of themselves and others. As a site of cross-racial play, whiteface minstrels and stage Europeans have succeeded where blackface minstrelsy failed precisely because these acts reject a top-down, exclusionary performance model. The best and brightest of this dual tradition continue to demonstrate that when we respectfully appropriate whiteness, blackness, yellowness, or brownness, we can transform our social deconstructions and reconstructions into new universals. We can create cross-cultural commodities that ethically reflect and thoroughly entertain a fully democratized nation, a nation where difference is celebrated and racism is a problem vigilantly relegated to the past.

Notes

Introduction

1. I arrived at the term "stage European" while working on my dissertation on William Brown's early nineteenth-century Manhattan entertainments. During this exciting period in American theater history, white artists were performing stage Africans and stage Indians created by white dramatists. Brown's Negro company was doing something slightly different with black actors performing white characters, so to describe their cross-racial performances in the context of this dynamic theatrical landscape, I adopted the name "stage European." See McAllister, "'White People Do Not Know How to Behave.'"

2. The following studies theorize or historicize performed whiteness: Roach, *Cities of the Dead*; Cockrell, *Demons of Disorder*; Krasner, *Resistance, Parody, and Double Consciousness*; George-Graves, *Royalty of Negro Vaudeville*; Brown, *Babylon Girls*; Muñoz, *Disidentifications*; and Rahman, "It's Serious Business."

3. See Thompson, "Practicing Theory/Theorizing a Practice."

4. Wilson, "Ground on Which I Stand," 499.

5. Hyman was interviewed by Laura Winer for the *New York Times*, March 24, 1991. Glenda E. Gill excerpts some of this *Times* interview in Gill, "Triumphs and Struggles of Earle Hyman," 71.

6. Smith is quoted in Reinelt, "Performing Race," 614.

7. Michael Phillips, "Globe Puts Fiery Spin on Ibsen's 'Gabler,'" *San Diego Union-Tribune*, May 8, 1995, D1.

8. I am referring to the 2007 Broadway production of *Cat on a Hot Tin Roof*, starring James Earl Jones, Phylicia Rashad, and Terrence Howard, and the 2009 Yale Repertory Theatre and Broadway production of Arthur Miller's *Death of a Salesman*, featuring Charles Dutton as Willy Loman.

9. In terms of racial and ethnic descriptors for people of African descent in the United States, I use a combination of "colored," "Negro," "black," and "African American" throughout this study, depending on historical context and the terminology preferred by a particular artist.

10. See Riis, "Black Musical Theatre in New York," 56 n. 44.

11. The single "Dangerous" can be found on Busta Rhymes's September 1997 album *When Disaster Strikes*. The video is included on a video compilation *Party Over Here* (1998). The Mountain Dew commercial aired frequently between 1997 and 1998 as part of a national advertising campaign.

12. Brooks, *Bodies in Dissent*, 58, 65.

13. Johnson, *Appropriating Blackness*, 6.

14. Dick Hebdige relies on Matthew Arnold and Raymond Williams to delineate these two basic conceptions of culture. See Hebdige, *Subculture*, 6.

15. Babcock, "Introduction," 24–25, 29.

16. In her analysis of David F. Dorr's nineteenth-century travel novel *A Colored Man Round the World* (1858), Malini Johar Schueller poses similar questions concerning Dorr's act of literary whiteface. Responding to Judith Butler and Eric Lott, Schueller applauds their work on the performativity of race and gender, which question the fixity of identity categories, but she points out how these conversations often overlook questions of "access and power." See Schueller, "Performing Whiteness, Performing Blackness."

17. Haggins, *Laughing Mad*, 5.

18. As for how identities are constructed onstage and offstage, I adopt a post-positivist realist approach to identity that embraces fluidity but also accounts for the potential fixity wrought by historically rooted power structures, material conditions, and representational conventions. See Moya and Hames-Garcia, *Reclaiming Identity*.

19. Brown, *Babylon Girls*, 105

20. Jacobson, *Whiteness of a Different Color*, 9.

21. Cheng, *Melancholy of Race*, 10.

22. Early reactions to America's increasingly troublesome ethnic and racial diversity can be found in Thomas Jefferson's *Notes on Virginia* and Timothy Dwight's *Travels in New England and New York*, vol. 1. For a more balanced historical perspective, see Singh, *Black Is a Country*.

23. Jacobson, *Whiteness of a Different Color*, 13, 22.

24. On the historical construction of America's racial hierarchy, see Jordan, *White over Black*; Asim, *The N Word*; and Harris, "Whiteness as Property."

25. Noel Ignatiev's *How the Irish Became White* traces Irish assimilation into white America in the mid-nineteenth century. David Roediger's *Working toward Whiteness* deals with a variety of white ethnics and their march toward whiteness. George Lipsitz's *The Possessive Investment in Whiteness* examines how whiteness, as a valuable and protected commodity, affects African Americans, Asian Americans, Native Americans, and Latinos. Lisa Tessman and Bat-Ami Bar On, in "The Other Colors of Whiteness," write about how Israeli nationals are encouraged by U.S. immigration officials to declare themselves Caucasian.

26. For more on the agendas of whiteness studies, see Dyer, *White*; Newitz and Wray, *White Trash*; McLaren, "Whiteness Is"; and Kincheloe, Steinberg, Rodriguez, and Chennault, *White Reign*.

27. Lipsitz, *Possessive Investment in Whiteness*, 3; Roediger, *Wages of Whiteness*, 59–60.

28. Harris, "Whiteness as Property," 281.

29. See Herskovits, *Myth of the Negro Past.*

30. Fanon, *Black Skin, White Masks,* 12. For more on this Manichaean opposition of the superior colonizer and the inferior colonized, see JanMohamed, *Manichean Aesthetics.*

31. Spillers, "'All the Things You Could Be by Now,'" 390.

32. For theories on passing, see Robinson, "Forms of Appearance of Value"; Ginsberg, "Introduction"; and Piper, "Passing for White, Passing for Black."

33. Smith, *Not Just Race, Not Just Gender,* 40.

34. By "false consciousness" I am referring to how culturally and economically dominant groups indoctrinate subalterns into a distorted and inferior mind-set that prevents them from breaking free of their subordinate position. False consciousness is a Marxist concept used to explain the failure of ordinary citizens to understand the economic causes of their positions in society. Political theorist and activist Antonio Gramsci explains that through ideas and symbolism, subordinated groups are taught to internalize as natural a value system that justifies their domination. According to Gramsci, this kind of hegemonic power is not universal; it has to be maintained and reproduced. It is a "moving equilibrium" affected by various forces. Since these hegemonic forms and practices are by nature unstable, they can be demystified and deconstructed. The masses can resist false consciousness with the help of activists, artists, and educators committed to radical cultural change. See Gramsci, *Selections from the Prison Notebooks*; Genovese, *Roll, Jordan, Roll*; Scott, *Weapons of the Weak* and *Domination and the Arts of Resistance*; and Hebdige, *Subculture.*

35. See Roland Fryer's 2006 article "Acting White," an abridged version of a larger empirical study. Fryer found that motivated black students, as well as other minorities, were more likely to be stigmatized in integrated public schools as opposed to predominantly minority public schools or private institutions. The issue of "acting white" was major news in the mid-1980s when daily newspapers from the *Washington Post* to the *Atlanta Journal-Constitution* published articles about this pathology in urban classrooms. In 1986, Signithia Fordham and John Ogbu published a well-researched sociological study of the issue titled "Black Students' School Success: Coping with the Burden of 'Acting White.'" In 2000, John H. McWhorter published a personal memoir, *Losing the Race: Self-Sabotage in Black America,* in which he shares his experiences with the "acting white" problem and its impact on black academic performance.

36. Roach, *Cities of the Dead,* 236.

37. Plessy's calculated actions remind me of the work of conceptual and contemporary performance artist Adrian Piper, a light-skinned African American woman who, in the 1980s, "passed" as white in social situations. When whites in these public gatherings would assume no racial difference between themselves and Piper, maybe drop some racist or insensitive remark, she would distribute cards announcing her racial identity. See Phelan, *Unmarked,* 97–98, and Piper, "Passing for White, Passing for Black."

38. Some revisionist minstrel texts include Wilentz, *Chants Democratic*; Saxton, *Rise and Fall of the White Republic*; Roediger, *Wages of Whiteness*; Lott, *Love and*

Theft; Cockrell, *Demons of Disorder*; Lhamon, *Raising Cain*; Mahar, *Behind the Burnt Cork Mask*; and Bean, Hatch, and McNamara, *Inside the Minstrel Mask*.

39. Hartman, *Scenes of Subjection*, 29–32.

40. Gaines, *Uplifting the Race*, 67.

41. See Lott, *Love and Theft*; Wilentz, *Chants Democratic*; Saxton, *Rise and Fall of the White Republic*; and Roediger, *Wages of Whiteness*.

42. See *Saturday Night Live: The Best of Eddie Murphy*.

43. I have taught undergraduate and graduate courses on whiting up at the University of California–Berkeley, the Catholic University of America in Washington, D.C., and the City University of New York's Graduate Center. Based on my experiences in these courses, I chose to narrow my project. Some good work on whiteface on small and large screens is being done by media scholars, theorists, and critics; see, for example, Bambi Haggins's *Laughing Mad*. Performance scholar Annemarie Bean is working on a manuscript titled "Transperformance: Almost Crossing America," which looks at cross-dressed and cross-raced performance onstage and on television.

Also, when I first began researching performed whiteness, I envisioned a transnational project that tracked whiting up in three different Afro-Diasporic locations: the United States, Jamaica, and Nigeria. But I quickly realized each Afro-Diasporic location deserves its own fully immersed history of performed whiteness. For example, to write effectively about oyinbo or "white man" figures in Nigerian theater, a scholar needs a firm handle on precolonial, colonial, and postcolonial conceptions of race and representation in Nigeria. Kacke Götrick's *Apidan Theatre and Modern Drama* does a fully contextualized job of explaining Nigerian oyinbo performance. I cannot claim expertise on racial and cultural histories in Nigeria or Jamaica; therefore, I decided to limit my project to whiting up in the United States. Although the project is confined by the national borders, I embrace the idea of African Diaspora as both a political and analytical concept, and I trust some insights from my national project can resonate with other Afro-Diasporic communities. See Brock, Kelley, and Sotiropoulos, "Transnational Black Studies."

44. Auslander, *Liveness*, 5–6.

45. See Dyer and McDonald, *Stars*, and Burns, *Theatricality*.

46. Abram L. Harris, "The Ethiopian Art Players and the Nordic Complex," *Messenger* 5, no. 7 (July 1923): 775.

47. See Bay, *White Image in the Black Mind*.

48. Jameson, *Brecht and Method*, 39; Brooks, *Bodies in Dissent*, 5.

49. Cheng, *Melancholy of Race*, 7.

50. Muñoz, *Disidentifications*, 4–8.

51. Dyer and McDonald, *Stars*, 200. Also, Helen Gilbert, in her work on whiteface performance among indigenous performers in Canada and Australia, claims acts of whiting up constitute "activist work," because they expose the fixity of race and reveal identity as malleable while also "exposing the very real consequences of racism" in specific geographic and historical contexts. See Gilbert, "Black and White and Re(a)d All Over Again," 696.

52. Auslander, *Liveness*, 55–57.

Chapter 1

1. *New York Evening Post*, August 24, 1820, 2. For more on black promenaders in New York City and their version of whiteface minstrelsy, see McAllister, *White People Do Not Know How to Behave*, and White and White, *Stylin'*.

2. M. M. Noah, "Blacks," *National Advocate*, July 9, 1822, 2.

3. Scott, *Domination and the Arts of Resistance*, 2–15.

4. Genovese, *Roll, Jordan, Roll*, 5–7.

5. The comments of former slaves Mom Ryer Emmanual, Mary Frances Brown, and Dinah Cunningham can be found in Rawick, *American Slave*, vol. 2, pt. 1, pp. 11–12, 131, 235.

6. Bay, *White Image in the Black Mind*, 119, 136–37. Due to the sometimes coercive nature of the WPA interview process, Bay and other historians have suggested that these ex-slave interviews are not always the most reliable records of enslaved experience.

7. Gomez, *Exchanging Our Country Marks*, 9–10, 299 n. 18. In addition, anthropologist Jean Muteba Rahier argues that Melville Herskovits's acculturation model, as applied throughout the African Diaspora, was not comprehensive enough because it was "spaceless"; it lacked a full appreciation for the local or an "awareness of the spatial constitution of societies." See Rahier, *Representations of Blackness and the Performance of Identities*, xix.

8. The following discussion of colonial and antebellum South Carolina history is based on Wood, *Black Majority*; Littlefield, *Rice and Slaves*; and Klingberg, *Appraisal of the Negro in Colonial South Carolina.*

9. In *Rice and Slaves*, historian Daniel Littlefield makes this argument about a dependent economic relationship and the benefits for enslaved Africans.

10. This economic and population history of the city of Charleston draws on Wood, *Black Majority*; Powers, *Black Charlestonians*; and Goldin, *Urban Slavery in the American South.*

11. For more on hiring out in Charleston and other southern municipalities, see Wade, *Slavery in the Cities*, 39–52.

12. Ibid., 52.

13. *Digest of the Ordinances of the City Council of Charleston*, 185–86.

14. For more on living out, see Wade, *Slavery in the Cities*, and Goldin, *Urban Slavery in the American South.*

15. Wade, *Slavery in the Cities*, 74–75.

16. Ibid., 4.

17. Hartman, *Scenes of Subjection*, 67–69.

18. See Olmsted, *Journey in the Seaboard Slave States*, and Rawick, *American Slave*, vol. 2, pt. 1, pp. 1, 169.

19. *South Carolina Gazette*, August 13, 1772, 1–2. I first read about The Stranger in Cohen, "Negro 'Folk Game' in Colonial South Carolina."

20. *South Carolina Gazette*, August 27, 1772, 1. The Stranger remarked that upon seeing the incredible numbers of Negroes in Charleston, he felt like he had arrived

in "Lucifer's court," a stereotypic characterization that played on a racist linkage between blackness and evil.

21. Brooks, *Bodies in Dissent*, 9–10; Hartman, *Scenes of Subjection*, 10–11.

22. *South Carolina Gazette*, September 17, 1772, 1. All subsequent descriptions of the country dance come from this Stranger article.

23. Hartman, *Scenes of Subjection*, 59–60.

24. Hutcheon, *Theory of Parody*, 26, 37.

25. Gilroy, "'To Be Real,'" 14–15.

26. Goldin, *Urban Slavery in the American South*, 133–34; *Digest of the Ordinances of the City Council of Charleston*, 180.

27. Hartman, *Scenes of Subjection*, 60. Hartman's question echoes Anne Cheng's query about the political agency for racial others who have been tagged as deficient; see Cheng, *Melancholy of Race*, 7.

28. Nyong'o, *Amalgamation Waltz*, 13–14.

29. Lipsitz, *Time Passages*, 16.

30. This discussion of plantation parties relies on Genovese, *Roll, Jordan, Roll*; Abrahams, *Singing the Master*; Littlefield, *Rice and Slaves*; and Wood, *Black Majority*.

31. Rawick, *American Slave*, vol. 2, pt. 1, p. 16.

32. Genovese quotes Douglass in *Roll, Jordan, Roll*, 577–78; also see Douglass, *Life and Times*, 147–48.

33. For cakewalk histories, see Baldwin, "Cakewalk"; Desmond, "Embodying Difference"; Stearns and Stearns, *Jazz Dance*; and Cook, "Change the Joke and Slip the Yoke."

34. Quoted in Baldwin, "Cakewalk," 208.

35. Desmond, "Embodying Difference," 40–41.

36. See Cook, "Change the Joke and Slip the Yoke," and Baldwin, "Cakewalk."

37. Many cakewalk scholars concentrate on the European origins of this dance, but dance historian Brooke Baldwin identifies anthropologists and artists who argue that the cakewalk, with its polyrhythmic structures, was strikingly similar to dances from Ghana and Nigeria. For more on the African and European influences in the cakewalk, see Gottschild, *Digging the Africanist Presence in American Performance*; Baldwin, "Cakewalk"; and Stearns and Stearns, *Jazz Dance*.

38. Rose, *Parody*, 36–46, 81–82.

39. Thompson, "Aesthetic of the Cool," 109.

40. Brooks, *Bodies in Dissent*, 272–73.

41. See Nyong'o, *Amalgamation Waltz*, and Muñoz, *Disidentifications*.

42. For typical reactions from masters, see Abrahams, *Afro-American Folktales*, 12.

43. This famous slave informant has been quoted in various secondary sources, including Stearns and Stearns, *Jazz Dance*, 22; Piersen, *Black Legacy*, 64; and Blesh and Janis, *They All Played Ragtime*, 95–96.

44. Genovese, *Roll, Jordan, Roll*; Sundquist, *To Wake the Nations*; Stearns and Stearns, *Jazz Dance*.

45. Miller, *Slaves to Fashion*, 48–49.

46. Ibid., 1.

47. *South Carolina Gazette*, August 27, 1772, 1, and September 24, 1772, 1.

48. Ibid., September 24, 1772, 2.

49. For an extensive discussion of this 1735 act, see Wood, *Black Majority*, 232. Also, for ex-slave commentary, see Sam Polite and Mom Louisa Collier in Rawick, *American Slave*, vol. 2, pt. 1, p. 221, and vol. 3, pt. 3, p. 272.

50. Miller, *Slaves to Fashion*, 81.

51. *Southern Patriot and Commercial Advertiser*, September, 12, 1822, 2. All subsequent Rusticus quotes refer to this letter.

52. Elijah Green in Rawick, *American Slave*, vol. 2, pt. 1, p. 195.

53. The *South Carolina Gazette* published advertisements from merchants such as Brian Cape and Mansell & Corbett announcing the latest articles arriving from Europe and India. See p. 3 of the June 6 and June 13, 1771, issues for typical examples.

54. See White and White, *Stylin'*, 9, and Rawick, *American Slave*, vol. 2, pt. 2, p. 46.

55. Powers, *Black Charlestonians*, 22.

56. Miller, *Slaves to Fashion*, 1, 10.

57. This phenomenon was by no means limited to South Carolina. From the early 1700s on, stylish urban blacks dominated in major New World cities from Charleston to Manhattan to Kingston, setting trends for national and international fashion. Shane White and Graham White make this argument in *Stylin'*, and Frederick Law Olmsted reported seeing fashionable promenaders in Richmond, Virginia; see Olmsted, *Journey in the Seaboard Slave States*. Also, Orlando Patterson records Kingston, Jamaica, promenaders in *Sociology of Slavery*. More recently, Shane White has written about the proliferation of fashionable African American balls in northern cities, especially New York and Philadelphia, which attracted the attention of white citizens, critics, and artists; see *Stories of Freedom in Black New York*.

58. Hebdige, *Subculture*, 18–19.

59. Ibid., 102.

60. Gates, *Signifying Monkey*, 88, 124.

61. *Southern Patriot and Commercial Advertiser*, September, 12, 1822, 2.

62. Harris, "Whiteness as Property," 282.

63. Powers, *Black Charlestonians*, 22.

64. In an anthology on "white trash" in the United States, whiteness scholars Annalee Newitz and Matt Wray trace the origins of this class-marked racial identity. Although their search was inconclusive, they found sources that attributed the term's origins to enslaved Africans. But even if this class and racial slur was not coined by enslaved Africans, they definitely exploited this distinction between different classes of whites. See Newitz and Wray, *White Trash*, 2.

65. Miller, *Slaves to Fashion*, 3, 98. For more on this white artistic reaction to whiteface minstrelsy, see chap. 5 of McAllister, *White People Do Not Know How to Behave*. Also, Shane White, in his chapter titled "Imitation" in *Stories of Freedom in Black New York*, mentions the unprecedented numbers of whites who began imitating and parodying increasingly visible free blacks.

66. Hartman, *Scenes of Subjection*, 47.

67. See Killens, *Trial Record of Denmark Vesey*.

68. Gilroy, *Black Atlantic*; Linebaugh, "All the Atlantic Mountains Shook."

69. Killens, *Trial Record of Denmark Vesey*, 25.

70. Ibid., 27–28.

71. See Davis, "Women on Top."

72. Ex-slaves Henry Brown of Charleston, Charles Davis of Columbia, and Samuel Boulware of Columbia all mention these lower-class white patrols; see Rawick, *American Slave*, vol. 2, pt. 1, pp. 69, 124, 252.

73. For the reactions of white Charlestonians, see Goldin, *Urban Slavery in the American South*, 33, 142 n. 13.

74. Brooks, *Bodies in Dissent*, 65

Chapter 2

1. Bolster, *Black Jacks*, 102–21.

2. See Edwards and Walvin, *Black Personalities in the Era of the Slave Trade*; McAllister, *White People Do Not Know How to Behave*; and Lindfors, "'Mislike Me Not for My Complexion.'"

3. Using court records and articles published in newspapers such as the *National Advocate* and the *American*, archivist George Thompson synthesized the story behind Taft's fondness for *Richard III*, as well as his larceny and subsequent incarceration. See Thompson, *Documentary History of the African Theatre.*

4. Emerson, *Essays*, 259.

5. *National Advocate*, April 18, 1821, 3.

6. Dyer and McDonald, *Stars*, 91; Burns, *Theatricality*, 170–71.

7. Mathews is quoted in Davis, "Representing the Comic Actor at Work," 10.

8. Ibid., 8–9.

9. Muckelbauer, *Future of Invention*, 56–57, 72.

10. This discussion of the various interpretations of *Richard III* is based on Wood, *Stage History of Shakespeare's King Richard the Third.*

11. *New York Evening Post*, October 8, 1821, 2.

12. Muckelbauer, *Future of Invention*, 72–75.

13. *American Monthly Magazine and Critical Review* 1, no. 4 (August 1817): 322.

14. Herskovits, *Myth of the Negro Past*, 141–42.

15. *National Advocate*, August 3, 1821, 2; critic Leigh Hunt is quoted in Davis, "Representing the Comic Actor at Work," 11.

16. Hurston, "Characteristics of Negro Expression," 28. Also, historian Shane White briefly comments on the role of imitation in nineteenth-century African performance; see *Stories of Freedom in Black New York*, 186–87.

17. See Cibber, *Tragical History of King Richard III.* Cibber's version was the most popular acting edition of *Richard III* during this time period.

18. The Hewlett biography was originally published in the *Brooklyn Star* and reprinted in the *National Advocate*, December 30, 1825, 2. The next series of quotes comes from that piece.

19. Two of Hewlett's *Richard III* playbills are included in Thompson, *Documentary History of the African Theatre*, 83, 127.

20. See Roach, *Cities of the Dead*, and Cheng, *Melancholy of Race.*

21. Hartman, *Scenes of Subjection*, 31–32, 212 n. 53.

22. In theorizing cross-cultural performance, Helen Gilbert and Jacqueline Lo identify a specific subset of cross-cultural theater, called transcultural performance, that attempts to "transcend culture-specific codification to reach a more universal human condition." See Gilbert and Lo, "Toward a Topography of Cross-Cultural Theatre Praxis," 8.

23. Brown's Minor Theatre advertisement was included in the *National Advocate*, August 9, 1822, 3. Samuel Hay, in *African-American Theatre*, chronicles the company's imprisonment for performing Shakespeare and theorizes who was behind these arrests. I also deal with this incident in *White People Do Not Know How to Behave*. The term "minor" is a reference to England's 1737 Licensing Act that created a cultural hierarchy of patent and nonpatent theaters restricted to specific kinds of material. Patent or "major" houses, like London's Drury Lane and Covent Garden, were authorized to perform "legitimate" dramas and comedies, while nonpatent or "minor" theaters were relegated to "illegitimate" pantomimes, musicals, and ballad operas. See Connolly, *Censorship of English Drama*.

24. Blake's rendering of the Don Juan legend is not a conventional pantomime; in fact, for his August 1822 production, Brown announced Blake's version as a farce.

25. For the March 1823 benefit playbill, see Thompson, *Documentary History of the African Theatre*, 127.

26. Connor, *Dumbstruck*, 266–79.

27. See *Memoirs of Charles Mathews* and Hodge, "Charles Mathews Reports on America."

28. Connor, *Dumbstruck*, 279–80.

29. The following commentary and references are based on an online version of "La Diligence" that can be found at http://www.bbk.ac.uk/english/skc/dumbstruck/archive/dilig.htm.

30. See Thompson, *Documentary History of the African Theatre*, 127.

31. The January 1824 benefit playbill can be found in Thompson, *Documentary History of the African Theatre*, 144. For more on Mathews's creations and his process, see *Memoirs of Charles Mathews*.

32. Hewlett's biography is documented in Thompson, *Documentary History of the African Theatre*, and White, *Stories of Freedom in Black New York*.

33. For these benefit playbills, see Odell, *Annals of the New York Stage*, vol. 3, facing p. 35, and Thompson, *Documentary History of the African Theatre*, 82–83.

34. William Brown's production of *Douglas* is mentioned in Peter Nielsen's *Recollections of a Six-Years' Residence in the United States of America*.

35. Advertisements for these intertextual evenings can be found in the *American*, June 18, 1821, 3, and June 29, 1821, 3. Morton's *The Slave* was a musical version of Thomas Southerne's *Oroonoko* (1695/1696), adapted from Aphra Behn's short novel *Oroonoko: or The Royal Slave* (1688). Davy and Bishop's *Rob Roy* musical was adapted from Sir Walter Scott's 1817 novel *Rob Roy*. Scott's novel was inspired by Rob Roy MacGregor, a clan leader and folk hero widely recognized as the Scottish Robin Hood.

36. *African Repository and Colonial Journal*, March 1825, 31.

37. Hamm, *Yesterdays*, 110–12.

38. Tobin, *Plays by Scots*, 37, 164–65. Apparently Home did not sanitize the story enough, because after the Edinburgh debut and a London production, controversy over the national drama forced Home to resign his ministerial position.

39. Nielsen, *Recollections of a Six-Years' Residence in the United States of America*, 20.

40. Lewis, *Journal of a West India Proprietor*, 56. Jonkonnu is an Afro-Diasporic holiday that originated in Jamaica and spread throughout the Caribbean. In its original form, Jonkonnu featured an array of street performers including a Jonkonnu king, Actor Boys, and Set Girls. The observance of Jonkonnu typically began on December 26, Boxing Day, and continued into the new year.

41. See Gale, "Archibald MacLaren's 'The Negro Slaves,'" 78–79. In this article, Gale also points out that Scottish dramatist Archibald MacLaren was so inspired by his countrymen's intellectual and political stance against slavery that he composed *The Negro Slaves; or, The Blackman and Blackbird* (1799). In this sentimental stage African drama, white and black characters eloquently advocate for the end of slavery.

42. Bold, *Burns Companion*, 340–41.

43. For the entire Burns ballad, see Cole, *The Minstrel*, 120–21. All subsequent excerpts come from the Cole collection.

44. This brief history of Wallace and Bruce is rooted in MacLean, *Scotland and Highlanders*, and Mitchison, *History of Scotland*.

45. McCants, *Patrick Henry*, 57–58.

46. Both Henry and Burns were by no means fervent antislavery advocates; to the contrary, their histories reveal conflicted relationships to New World slavery. Although Burns wrote the famous "The Slave's Lament" (1792), he also considered working as a bookkeeper on a Jamaican plantation. See Crawford, *The Bard*.

47. Crawford, *The Bard*, 124–25.

48. Thompson, *Documentary History of the African Theatre*, 58–59, 61–62.

49. In 1799 and 1817, the New York state legislature passed gradual manumission acts. See Litwack, *North of Slavery*, and White, *Somewhat More Independent*.

50. Bay, *White Image in the Black Mind*, 40–41. Bay quotes Walker in her work.

51. Lipsitz, *Time Passages*, 16.

Chapter 3

1. Patricia Herrera, a former student at the City University of New York's Graduate Center, researched Gillam as part of a project for my whiting up course in the fall of 2000. And I want to thank Patricia again for her contributions to this study. These details on Harry Gillam and his sister Bessie come from the *Freeman*, an Indianapolis-based colored arts magazine. See the following issues: November 6, 1897, 5; January 15, 1898, 5; April 23, 1898, 5; February 11, 1899, 5; and February 25, 1899, 5.

2. Playbills, press clippings, and advertisements on Gillam can be found in "George & Hart's Up to Date Minstrels" Scrapbook, 1900–1901, Collection 576, Box 2, Archives Center, National Museum of American History, Washington, D.C.

3. Roediger, *Wages of Whiteness*, 117–18; Williams, *Seeing a Color-Blind Future*, 56; Morrison, *Playing in the Dark*, 51–52.

4. See Jacobson, *Whiteness of a Different Color.*

5. Ibid., 222.

6. Singh, *Black Is a Country*, 24–29; Brown, *Babylon Girls*, 103. Both historians link the codification of racial segregation at home with increased U.S. imperialism abroad.

7. Blesh and Janis, *They All Played Ragtime*, 92–93.

8. See Snyder, *Voice of the City*, and McLean, *American Vaudeville as Ritual.*

9. Dyer, *Matter of Images*, 3–4; Jacobson, *Whiteness of a Different Color*, 9.

10. See Rogin, *Blackface, White Noise.*

11. Dyson and Chennault, "Giving Whiteness a Black Eye," 320. Based on my reading of *The Matter of Images*, I suspect Richard Dyer would disagree with Dyson that the fracturing of whiteness into specific ethnic groups is a positive development. Dyer argues that the diversification of whiteness into subcategories of Irishness, Jewishness, or Russianness only makes "white" appear like the measure of all humanity. Robyn Wiegman further grapples with this question on the varieties of whiteness in her article "Whiteness Studies and the Paradox of Particularity." Contemporary debates on whiteness and reinscription notwithstanding, William Brown's early nineteenth-century entertainments and Cole and Johnson's turn-of-the-century *Coontown* specialties were productively separating whiteness into ethnically particular stage Europeans.

12. Brown, *Babylon Girls*, 124.

13. African American performers like Anna Madah and Emma Louise Hyers were the true pioneers of the colored road shows. They opened up alternative entertainment possibilities for performers of color and demonstrated that Negro artists, free of most minstrel elements, could attract audiences. For more on the Hyers Sisters, see Southern, *African American Theater*, and for more on colored road shows, see Watkins, *On the Real Side*, chap. 4.

14. Brown, *Babylon Girls*, 96, 104.

15. Fletcher, *100 Years of the Negro in Show Business*, 41–53; Brown, *Babylon Girls*, 92–93; Abbott and Seroff, *Out of Sight*, 151–56. Florence Hines was a well-known male impersonator who marketed herself as the "American Vesta Tilley." Her stage moniker was an homage to British actress Matilda Alice Powles, who rose through the ranks of English and American popular entertainment by impersonating foppish boys and dashing English gentlemen.

16. Sotiropoulos, *Staging Race*, 3–10.

17. Waldo is quoted in Krasner, *Resistance, Parody, and Double Consciousness*, 72–73. Poet, playwright, and politico LeRoi Jones (later Amiri Baraka) posed an interesting question relative to the cakewalk's transformation: "If it is a Negro dance caricaturing white customs, what is that dance when a white theater company tries to satirize it as a Negro dance?" Jones found it ironic how whites were satirizing a dance originally designed to satirize them; see Jones, *Blues People*, 86.

18. Blesh and Janis, *They All Played Ragtime*, 97; Abbott and Seroff, *Out of Sight*, 214; "The Death of Bob Cole," *New York Age*, August 10, 1911, 6.

19. For Matilda Sissieretta Jones's history, I am relying on Fletcher, *100 Years of the Negro in Show Business*; Blesh and Janis, *They All Played Ragtime*; Sampson,

Blacks in Blackface; Johnson, *Black Manhattan*; Riis, *Just before Jazz*; and Abbott and Seroff, *Out of Sight*. For an excellent discussion of the sobriquet "Black Patti," see Graziano, "Early Life and Career of the 'Black Patti,'" 566–67.

20. There is an excellent front-page biographical article on the two *Coontown* creators in a special Christmas edition of the *Freeman*, December 30, 1899, 1. Also, for more on Bob Cole and Billy Johnson's stints with colored road shows and minstrel troupes, see Abbott and Seroff, *Out of Sight*.

21. Much of this Black Patti Troubadours and *Coontown* production history has been covered in Thomas Riis's extensive musical research; Woll, *Black Musical Theatre*; Krasner, *Resistance, Parody, and Double Consciousness*; and Abbott and Seroff, *Ragged but Right*.

22. Frazier, *Black Bourgeoisie*, 124–25.

23. Gaines, *Uplifting the Race*, 3.

24. Abbott and Seroff, *Ragged but Right*, 69; *Freeman*, June 19, 1897, 6.

25. Lewis, "Pioneers of the Stage," 48.

26. *Freeman*, July 10, 1897, 5.

27. *New York Clipper*, September 18, 1897, 6.

28. Ibid., March 5, 1898, 5.

29. The *Freeman's* "On the Road" column tracked *Coontown*'s first tour in the following issues: November 13, 1897, 5; November 27, 1897, 5; January 8, 1898, 5; March 12, 1898, 5. Also, *Coontown*'s out-of-town announcements can be found under "Variety" listings in the *New York Clipper* for January 15 and 22 and March 5 and 19, 1898.

30. *New York Clipper*, April 9, 1898, 6; April 16, 1898, 4; April 24, 1898, 8. Also see "The Death of Bob Cole," *New York Age*, August 10, 1911, 6, and *Freeman*, October 22, 1898, 6. After a triumphant return to Broadway, *Coontown* went on a tour of Nova Scotia, New Brunswick, and Prince Edward Island.

31. Johnson, *Black Manhattan*, 102; Sampson, *Blacks in Blackface*, 9.

32. See the reprint of this *New York Sun* review in the *Freeman*, April 16, 1898, 5.

33. I have previously worked through some of these ideas on *A Trip to Coontown* in my article "Bob Cole's Willie Wayside."

34. *Freeman*, October 20, 1900, 5.

35. Ibid.

36. Krasner, *Resistance, Parody, and Double Consciousness*, 27.

37. This brief treatment of opera in the United States, primarily New York, is based on Dizikes, *Opera in America*.

38. My information on Gibbs and other operatic specialties comes from two Canadian programs for *Coontown* performances at the Grand Opera House in London, Ontario, dated February 12, 1898, and January 24, 1900. Both programs are available on microfiche as part of the Pre-1900 and Early Canadiana Research Collection, Folger Library, University of Maine, Orono.

39. Brooks, *Bodies in Dissent*, 312–15.

40. Abbott and Seroff, *Ragged but Right*, 71; *Freeman*, October 10, 1896, 5; March 11, 1899, 5; March 14, 1899, 5; and October 20, 1900, 5.

41. See the February 12, 1898, Grand Opera House program and a review in the *Dramatic Mirror*, April 9, 1898, 3.

42. *New York Clipper*, January 30, 1897, 5. Camille Casselle was not the only young singer using the sobriquet "Mme Calve"; other aspiring divas similarly aligned themselves with this French opera star. One description of performances at Miner's Bowery Theatre mentions two separate singers, Nellie Seymour and Edna Aug, who both performed variety/vaudeville specialty acts titled "Mme Calve." See *New York Clipper*, April 16, 1898, 6.

43. Reprint of the *New York Sun* review in *Freeman*, April 16, 1898, 5.

44. See the February 12, 1898, Grand Opera House program, London, Ontario, Pre-1900 and Early Canadiana Research Collection, Folger Library, University of Maine, Orono; *Dramatic Mirror*, April 9, 1898, 3; and *New York Clipper*, April 9, 1898, 6. I assume Brown's "Rube" referred to a new migrant from the countryside to the city, but in playbills and reviews there was never any specific indication of this "Rube's" race.

45. Reprint of the *New York Sun* review in *Freeman*, April 16, 1898, 5.

46. Schechter, *History of Negro Humor in America*, 72.

47. See Brown, *Babylon Girls*, 93, 115. As far as we know, *Tolosa* was never produced.

48. See the January 24, 1900, Grand Opera House program, London, Ontario, Pre-1900 and Early Canadiana Research Collection, Folger Library, University of Maine, Orono.

49. Allen, *City in Slang*, 66–67.

50. Burk, *Theatre Culture in America*, 85–91.

51. Stansell, *City of Women*, 218.

52. Ibid., 87–89; Peiss, *Cheap Amusements*, 14

53. See Burk, *Theatre Culture in America*, 86–88. Also, in March 1895, at Proctor's Theatre, a white comic duo named Lawrence and Harrington billed themselves as the original "Bowery Spielers." See *New York Times*, March 19, 1895, 5.

54. Brown, *Babylon Girls*, 120–24.

55. Unidentified Boston newspaper clipping, February 6, 1900, Grand Opera House, Harvard Theatre Collection, Theatrical Clippings File, Houghton Library, Harvard University, Cambridge, Mass.

56. See Fletcher, *100 Years of the Negro in Show Business*, 41. Also, during their 1900–1901 tour through the Great Plains, the innovative George and Hart's Up to Date Minstrels introduced a Negro woman named Carrie B. Wood as their interlocutor. Wood preferred the name "conversationalist," as it was her responsibility to keep the conversation flowing between the male comedians onstage. See "George & Hart's Up to Date Minstrels" Scrapbook, 1900–1901, Collection 576, Box 2, Archives Center, National Museum of American History, Washington, D.C.

57. Former CUNY Graduate Center student Carmelina Cartei researched various theatrical representations of Bowery Gals, and she noticed how proactive and forceful Jennie Hillman's Bowery Gal was in comparison with earlier versions. The original Lize and a later incarnation named Kittie were more interested in chasing status than chasing cops.

58. Burk, *Theatre Culture in America*, 90.

59. See Lott, *Love and Theft*; Cockrell, *Demons of Disorder*; Lhamon, *Raising Cain*; and Mahar, *Behind the Burnt Cork Mask*.

60. Lyrics from this signature Flimflammer melody can be found in Riis, *More Than Just Minstrel Shows*, 16–19.

61. See Abbott and Seroff, *Out of Sight*, 134. For his popular tunes, including "All Coons Look Alike to Me," Hogan was collecting nearly $400 a month in royalties, according to the *Freeman*, September 11, 1897, 5. Although Hogan has long been associated with "coon" songs, he was a talented composer capable of venturing into other musical traditions. In July 1897, Hogan advertised a "real" Irish melody for purchase, titled "Sit Down, Brophy," about a rich Irishman who becomes a prizefighter. See *New York Clipper*, July 31, 1897, 15.

62. *Freeman*, April 30, 1898, 5. Another interesting detail laced into this Chicago review was that Voelckel and Nolan's road show, originally structured around the operatic selections of Black Patti, was now featuring a cakewalk competition with the audience deciding the winner.

63. Krasner, *Resistance, Parody, and Double Consciousness*, 32–33.

64. Watkins, *On the Real Side*, 169.

65. Krasner, *Resistance, Parody, and Double Consciousness*, 32.

66. Ibid., 37.

67. Watkins, *On the Real Side*, 169. Other musical theater performers, such as black blackface artists Tom McIntosh and Bert Williams, have experimented with similar down-and-out tramps. Most notable is Williams's "Jonah Man" routine, which he created while performing with Florenz Ziegfeld's *Follies* in the 1910s.

68. See Riis, *Just before Jazz* and *More Than Just Minstrel Shows*, and *New York Clipper*, September 24, 1898, 18. Additional chicken numbers appeared on the *Coontown* playlist, like "When the Chickens Go to Sleep" (1898).

69. Blesh and Janis, *They All Played Ragtime*, 88; Abbott and Seroff, *Out of Sight* 455.

70. Deas and Wilson, "All I Wants Is Ma Chickens," 2–4. This sheet music can be found in the Arthur B. Spingarn Sheet Music Collection, Moorland-Spingarn Research Center, Howard University, Washington, D.C.

71. Cole, Johnson, and Accooe, "Chicken," 3. This music can be found in the Sheet Music Collection, Music Department, Performing Arts Division, Library of Congress, Washington, D.C.

72. Cole and Johnson, "Pickin' on a Chicken Bone."

73. Frazier, *Black Bourgeoisie*, 70–71.

74. The sheet music for "Mr. Coon You're All Right in Your Place" can be found in the Arthur B. Spingarn Sheet Music Collection, Moorland-Spingarn Research Center, Howard University, Washington, D.C.

75. During the 1890s, antilynching activist and journalist Ida B. Wells drew compelling connections between Anglo-Saxon barbarism, lynching, and colonialism. See Bay, *White Image in the Black Mind*, 102–3.

76. Gaines, *Uplifting the Race*, 2–4, 68, 74–75.

77. Brown, *Babylon Girls*, 97.

78. Muñoz, *Disidentifications*, 4.

79. Dyer, *White*, 35.

80. Newitz and Wray, *White Trash*, 136.

81. Ibid., 149.

82. Writing about cross-racial joking among the Western Apache, Keith Basso discusses how their white characters were often given personal and social characteristics that were not necessarily indicative of all white people. See Basso, *Portraits of "The Whiteman,"* 42.

83. Riis, *More Than Just Minstrel Shows*, 17.

84. Ibid., 18.

85. Reprint of the *New York Sun* review in the *Freeman*, April 16, 1898, 5.

86. *Freeman*, October 10, 1898, 5.

87. Riis, "Black Musical Theatre in New York," 56 n. 44.

88. Cole's sympathetic white clown may have been the prototype for later tramp characters such as Charlie Chaplin's "Little Tramp," popularized in silent films of the 1910s and 1920s; Emmett Kelly's "Weary Willie," from the Ringling Bros. and Barnum & Bailey Circus of the 1930s, 1940s, and 1950s; Red Skelton's "Willy Lump Lump" on 1950s and 1960s television; and singer Lecil Martin's "Boxcar Willie," popularized in 1970s country music. See Jenkins, *Subversive Laughter.*

89. *Freeman*, October 2, 1897, 5.

90. Gilje, *Road to Mobocracy*, 153–55; Lapsanksy, "Since They Got Those Separate Churches."

91. David Krasner discusses *Coontown* in relation to the *Plessy* case and Jim Crow segregation, in *Resistance, Parody, and Double Consciousness*, 37–38.

92. Bob Cole and Billy Johnson's "No Coons Allowed" can be found in the Arthur B. Spingarn Sheet Music Collection, Moorland-Spingarn Research Center, Howard University, Washington, D.C.

93. Krasner, *Resistance, Parody, and Double Consciousness*, 168 n. 37; Abbott and Seroff, *Ragged but Right*, 35.

94. *Dramatic Mirror*, April 9, 1898; reprint of the *New York Sun* review in the *Freeman*, April 16, 1898, 5.

95. "The Death of Bob Cole," *New York Age*, August 10, 1911, 6.

Chapter 4

1. Hughes, *Mulatto*, 13.

2. For more on performers of color and disidentification, see Muñoz, *Disidentifications*, and Olaniyan, *Scars of Conquest/Masks of Resistance.*

3. Elam and Elam, "Reparations in Langston Hughes's *Mulatto*," 95–98.

4. Ibid.

5. Lester A. Walton, "A Long Step Forward," *New York Age*, January 13, 1916, 6.

6. Abram L. Harris, "The Ethiopian Art Players and the Nordic Complex," *Messenger* 5, no. 7 (July 1923): 775.

7. This brief history of the Anita Bush Stock Company and Lafayette Players is based on Sister Francesca Thompson's "Evelyn Preer" biography and her article "The Lafayette Players, 1915–1932"; Lester A. Walton, "Over the Footlights," *New York Age*, December 30, 1915, 6; and Theophilus Lewis, "Magic Hours in the Theatre," *Pittsburgh Courier*, March 12, 1927, sec. 2, p. 1.

8. See Lester A. Walton, "Over the Footlights," *New York Age*, December 30, 1915, 6. Today, we might perceive Walton's dual roles as drama critic and Lafayette comanager as a conflict of interest, but in the late 1910s, his wearing of two hats barely raised an eyebrow. Walton as manager and cultural critic was an effective catalyst for advancing Negro theater in America. He functioned as both an insider positioned to make informed production choices and an outsider objective enough to criticize the results.

9. Lester A. Walton, "A Long Step Forward," *New York Age*, January 13, 1916, 6. The next series of quotes on the *Octoroon* production comes from this article.

10. For more on whiteface at the Lafayette, see Thompson, "Lafayette Players"; Monroe, "Harlem Little Theatre Movement," 63; and B. J. Mason, "The Grand Old Man of Good Hope Valley," *Ebony Magazine*, September 1972, 53.

11. Lester A. Walton, "Passing for White," *New York Age*, January 6, 1916, 6.

12. Lester A. Walton, "Over the Footlights," *New York Age*, December 30, 1915, 6.

13. George-Graves, *Royalty of Negro Vaudeville*, 68–70.

14. See ibid., 70. The Whitman Sisters booked their own performances without relying on "the usual white male representative." Writing about passing, race, and gender, Valerie Smith adds that black women, among other dispossessed groups, have had to "masquerade to protect themselves and exercise power"; see her *Not Just Race, Not Just Gender*, 54. Also, John W. Isham, a fair-skinned African American theatrical producer, would often pass for white to secure certain benefits and job opportunities; see Abbott and Seroff, *Out of Sight*, 156.

15. George-Graves, *Royalty of Negro Vaudeville*, 68.

16. Robinson, "Forms of Appearance of Value," 237.

17. *Freeman*, April 16, 1898, 5.

18. For an example of these advertisements, see the *New York Amsterdam News*, August 24, 1946, 9.

19. These comments come from Harrison's October 3, 1917, *Voice* article, "Negro Society and the Negro Stage." The article was reprinted in the *Hubert Harrison Reader*, 373. Harrison founded the *Voice* in 1917 and later became the managing editor of *Negro World*, the official publication of Marcus Garvey's Universal Negro Improvement Association.

20. Harrison, *Hubert Harrison Reader*, 376; Gaines, *Uplifting the Race*, 234–36.

21. Ginsberg, "Introduction," 2.

22. Smith, *Not Just Race, Not Just Gender*, 60.

23. Lester A. Walton, "Passing for White," *New York Age*, January 6, 1916, 6. Walton was writing about the issue a decade before Nella Larsen published her novella *Passing* (1929), in which she depicted a range of passing individuals. Also, onstage, the Williams and Walker Company created a song and dance number for their musical *In Dahomey* (1902–4) titled "Vassar Girl." This musical specialty capitalized on a real-life situation where a black woman attempted to pass as white and matriculate at Vassar College. See Brooks, *Bodies in Dissent*, 326.

24. See Hutchinson, "Mediating 'Race' and 'Nation.'" Hutchinson describes A. Philip Randolph as a proud integrationist who preferred classical music to jazz or blues and helped establish a Harlem-based amateur theater group devoted to performing Shakespeare.

25. As for the politics of the *Messenger*, union organizer Randolph maintained a strong socialist position that attributed racial prejudice to capitalism and advocated worker solidarity across the color line.

26. See Hutchinson, "Mediating 'Race' and 'Nation,'" 535–38, and George Schuyler, "The Negro-Art Hokum," *Nation*, June 16, 1926, 662.

27. Abram L. Harris, "The Ethiopian Art Players and the Nordic Complex," *Messenger* 5, no. 7 (July 1923): 775. Subsequent quotes refer to this article.

28. George Schuyler also frequently addressed the "Nordics," and through heavy satire, he attempted to debunk the myth of white superiority. His finest articulation of the "Nordic" problem came in a six-page *Messenger* article called "The Negro and Nordic Civilization"; see *Messenger* 7, no. 5 (May 1925): 198–201, 207–8.

29. The following profile of Evelyn Preer is based on Thompson, "Evelyn Preer"; Cripps, *Slow Fade to Black*; Scott, "Negroes as Actors in Serious Plays"; Floyd Calvin, "Evelyn Preer Ranks First as Stage and Movie Star," *Pittsburgh Courier*, April 16, 1927, sec. 2, p. 1; and Clarence Muse, "December 8, 1932, Preer Eulogy," *Pittsburgh Courier*, December 10, 1932, sec. 2, p. 6.

30. This history of the Ethiopian Art Theatre draws primarily on two theater history articles: Anderson, "Ethiopian Art Theatre," and Peterson, "Pride and Prejudice."

31. O'Neil's "training" statement comes from a May 23, 1923, Frazee Theatre Broadway program for *Salomé* and *Chip Woman's Fortune*. His comments were first reprinted in Fanin Belcher Jr.'s groundbreaking dissertation "The Place of the Negro in the Evolution of the American Theatre." I encountered O'Neil's statement in Anderson's and Peterson's articles on the Ethiopian Art Theatre. O'Neil was not alone in seeing a potential marriage between Negro "gifts" and European art theater. Howard philosophy professor and a progenitor of the Harlem Renaissance Alain Locke interviewed German director Max Reinhardt, who saw wonderful aesthetic possibilities for Negro performers if they exploited the "primitive" art of pantomime. Locke wrote an article publicizing Reinhardt's insights and even quotes Raymond O'Neil on the "freshness and vigor" of the Ethiopian Art Theatre. See Locke, "Negro and the American Stage," 114–16.

32. Scott, "Negroes as Actors in Serious Plays," 21.

33. *Chicago Tribune*, January 30, 1923, 27; *Chicago Defender*, February 3, 1923, 6; *Chicago Daily News*, January 30, 1923, 14.

34. My Wilde history draws on Ellman, *Oscar Wilde*, and Raby, *Oscar Wilde*.

35. Wilde, *Salomé*, 319–22.

36. Raymond O'Neil, "A Negro Theatre," *Crisis* 25 (April 1923): 251.

37. Wilde, *Salomé*, 319–23, 335, 343.

38. Ibid., 326–28.

39. Richard Dyer, "Colour of Virtue," 2–3.

40. John Corbin, "Jewels in Ethiope's Ear," *New York Times*, May 20, 1923, 11. The following quotes come from this article.

41. Alexander Woollcott, "Black Art," *New York Herald and Tribune*, May 9, 1923, 12; Percy Hammond, "The Ethiopian Art Theater," *New York Tribune*, May 13, 1923, sec. 6, p. 1.

42. Roediger, *Working toward Whiteness*, 98–99, 125–27.

43. Jacobson, *Whiteness of a Different Color*, 6, 177, 199.

44. Lerner and West, *Jews and Blacks*, 67, 70.

45. Scott, "Negroes as Actors in Serious Plays," 20.

46. Wilde, *Salomé*, 347.

47. For this American conception and reception of *Salomé*, see Dizikes, *Opera in America*, 315, and Krasner, *Beautiful Pageant*, 64–65.

48. John Corbin, "Jewels in Ethiope's Ear," *New York Times*, May 20, 1923, 11, and "'Salome' Again Barred," *New York Times*, October 19, 1923, 17.

49. *New York Age*, April 23, 1923, 6.

50. See Krasner, *Beautiful Pageant*, 63–70.

51. Brooks, *Bodies in Dissent*, 326–32.

52. Ibid., 334–36. Brooks includes an image of Walker from the Billy Rose Theatre Collection that shows her glittering and somewhat seductive Salome costume.

53. Putnam is quoted in Scott, "Negroes as Actors in Serious Plays," 23.

54. Metcalfe, "The Theatre: Oscar Wilde Might Protest," *Wall Street Journal*, May 10, 1923.

55. Harrison's Broadway article was never published in the early 1920s, but it is included in *Hubert Harrison Reader*, 384–86.

56. Daphne Brooks quotes cultural critic Susan Glenn, who has written about male critical responses to *Salomé*; see Brooks, *Bodies in Dissent*, 333.

57. Gaines, *Uplifting the Race*, 12–13, 243.

58. John Corbin, "Jewels in Ethiope's Ear," *New York Times*, May 20, 1923, 11.

59. John Corbin, "Ethiopians Act 'Salome': Art Theatre Gives a Performance Not Entirely Art," *New York Times*, May 8, 1923, 22. The following quotes come from this article.

60. Brooks, *Bodies in Dissent*, 331.

61. Spillers, "Interstices," 166–67.

62. Ibid., 174.

63. Putnam is quoted in Scott, "Negroes as Actors in Serious Plays," 23.

64. Stevens is quoted in ibid.

65. Sheppard Butler, "Oscar Wilde at Thirty-First and Indiana," *Chicago Tribune*, February 4, 1923, pt. 7, p. 1.

66. Percy Hammond, "The Ethiopian Art Theater," *New York Tribune*, May 13, 1923, sec. 6, p. 1. The next series of quotes comes from this article.

67. Dizikes, *Opera in America*, 313–15.

68. Peterson, "Pride and Prejudice," 146.

69. Abram L. Harris, "The Ethiopian Art Players and the Nordic Complex," *Messenger* 5, no. 7 (July 1923): 775; John Corbin, "Ethiopians Act 'Salome': Art Theatre Gives a Performance Not Entirely Art," *New York Times*, May 8, 1923, 22.

70. *New York Herald*, May 16, 1923, 10.

71. Sheppard Butler, "Oscar Wilde at Thirty-First and Indiana," *Chicago Tribune*, February 4, 1923, pt. 7, p. 1; W. E. Clark, "Harlem Audiences Spoil Strong Drama Given by Chicago Colored Players," *New York Age*, April 28, 1923, 6.

72. Theophilus Lewis, "Primer Lesson for Harlem Critics," *Messenger* 7, no. 6 (June 1925): 230. The next series of quotes comes from this article.

73. Theophilus Lewis, "Dogday Blues," *Messenger* 6, no. 9 (September 1924): 291, and "Survey of the Negro Theatre III," *Messenger* 8, no. 10 (October 1926): 301–2. Beyond critiquing the Lafayette Players, Lewis decried the tendency of many Negro theatrical ventures to rely on the leadership of white producers and directors. He directly cited the Ethiopian Art Theatre, which depended on white director Raymond O'Neil. Another attempt to build a Negro theater, the National Ethiopian Art Theatre, was headed by a white female producer named Anne Wolter. Lewis and the *Messenger* actually supported and offered constructive criticism on Wolter's well-meaning efforts until 1925, when Wolter lost most of her talented acting company to David Belasco's Broadway production of *Lulu Belle*.

74. Harrison, *Hubert Harrison Reader*, 384.

75. See John Corbin, "Ethiopians Act 'Salome': Art Theatre Gives a Performance Not Entirely Art," *New York Times*, May 8, 1923, 22, and Alexander Woollcott, "Black Art," *New York Herald and Tribune*, May 9, 1923, 12.

76. Peterson, "Pride and Prejudice," 145; Anderson, "Ethiopian Art Theatre," 143, 147. When the company first introduced their eclectic repertory in Chicago, critic Sheppard Butler wrote that "the enterprise is to be conducted on a straight forward commercial basis," but he thought the choice of plays—Wilde, Molière, Shakespeare—was "unusual" for a commercial venture, meaning the company risked financial failure. See Sheppard Butler, "Oscar Wilde at Thirty-First and Indiana," *Chicago Tribune*, February 4, 1923, pt. 7, p. 1.

77. Scott, "Negroes as Actors in Serious Plays," 21.

78. "The Ethiopian Art Theatre," *Crisis* 26, no. 3 (July 1923): 103–4. Subsequent quotes refer to this article.

79. See Black, "Looking White, Acting Black." As with Evelyn Preer, some critics did not believe Washington was truly a Negro and wanted proof of her racial heritage.

80. John Corbin, "Jazzed Shakespeare," *New York Times*, May 16, 1923, 22.

81. Watson, *Preparing for Saints*, 6.

82. See Hill, *Shakespeare in Sable*, and Hill and Hatch, *History of African American Theatre*. Since *Anna Lucasta*, there have been many highly acclaimed "blackened" productions of white dramatic material, such as *Gospel at Colonus*, Mambo Mine's 1985 gospel version of Sophocles's *Oedipus at Colonus*, featuring the Blind Boys of Alabama as Oedipus. Also, since the 1950s, Tennessee Williams has been the most popular playwright for all-black productions of white dramas. A recent example is the 2007 Broadway production of *Cat on a Hot Tin Roof* starring James Earl Jones, Phylicia Rashad, and Terrence Howard. Philip Kolin has written extensively about black performances of Williams and the "essential" American Negro presence in Williams's dramatic oeuvre; see Kolin, "Williams in Ebony." More recently, in 2009, Charles Dutton starred as Willy Loman in an all-black version of Arthur Miller's *Death of a Salesman*.

83. The following profile of Canada Lee relies heavily on Mona Z. Smith's wonderful biography *Becoming Something*.

84. For this casting story, see ibid., 217; Elliot Norton, "Dearth of Actors Gave Opportunity to Canada Lee," *Boston Post*, September 29, 1946, A7; and Sam Zolotow, "Canada Lee to Act White Role in Play," *New York Times*, September 16, 1946, 10.

85. See Smith, *Becoming Something*, 218. Elliot Norton published a similar statement, and he even claimed he did his research; see Norton, "Dearth of Actors Gave Opportunity to Canada Lee," *Boston Post*, September 29, 1946, A7.

86. "Canada Lee in 'Malfi,'" *Daily Worker*, September 25, 1946, 11.

87. Lee's comments can be found in Smith, *Becoming Something*, 223. Also see Langston Hughes, "The Negro Artist and the Racial Mountain," *Nation*, June 23, 1926, 692, 694. In this famous essay, Hughes interprets a young Negro poet's comment that he wants to be seen as simply a poet as a desire to be a white writer and abandon his racial resources.

88. "Canada Lee in 'Malfi,'" *Daily Worker*, September 25, 1946, 11.

89. Elliot Norton, "Actor Canada Lee Has Great Chance in White Role," *Boston Post*, September 22, 1946, A7. Norton's article is also quoted extensively in Smith, *Becoming Something*, 221.

90. Swan's article, "Negro Star to Portray White Man in Play Here," was published in the *Providence Bulletin*, September 20, 1946, and is quoted in Smith, *Becoming Something*, 219.

91. Bill Chase, "All Ears," *New York Amsterdam News*, September 21, 1946, 8.

92. Robert Garland, "'Duchess of Malfi' at the Barrymore," *New York Journal-American*, October 16, 1946, 14.

93. Bill Chase, "Canada Lee Makes 'White Man' Debut," *New York Amsterdam News*, October 5, 1946, 1, 25; "Lee Makes Stage History as He Plays White Role," *New York Times*, September 26, 1946, 40.

94. Bill Chase, "Canada Lee Makes 'White Man' Debut," *New York Amsterdam News*, October 5, 1946, 1, 25. Chase's hopeful remarks on the potential of white greasepaint remind me of Eddie Murphy's 1985 short film *White Like Me* broadcast on *Saturday Night Live*. Murphy's mock exposé plays with assumed white privilege, black paranoia, and the color line, but by the end of the short film, he threatens white viewers with the possibility that his "groovy" black friends have more makeup and may be passing into their personal lives soon. See *Saturday Night Live: The Best of Eddie Murphy*.

95. Elliot Norton, "Makes History on Stage in Hub: Colored Man Takes White's Role and Result Is Interesting and Good Performance," *Boston Post*, September 26, 1946, 1, 4.

96. "Lee Makes Stage History as He Plays White Role," *New York Times*, September 26, 1946, 40.

97. Elliot Norton, "Makes History on Stage in Hub: Colored Man Takes White's Role and Result Is Interesting and Good Performance," *Boston Post*, September 26, 1946, 1, 4.

98. Webster, *Duchess of Malfi*, 42.

99. Ibid., 25. For more on dysthymia, see Vontress, Woodland, and Epp, "Cultural Dysthymia."

100. Webster, *Duchess of Malfi*, 24, 33.

101. Robert Garland, "'Duchess of Malfi' at the Barrymore," *New York Journal-American*, October 16, 1946, 14. The following quotes come from this article.

102. Wolcott Gibbs, "Out of the Library," *New Yorker*, October 26, 1946, 52; Brooks Atkinson, "The Play," *New York Times*, October 16, 1946, 35.

103. Smith, *Becoming Something*, 220, 223.

104. Washington is quoted in Black, "'New Negro' Performance in Art and Life," 62. Black draws on Fredi Washington's November 16, 1946, column in the *People's Voice*.

105. The following discussion of Lee's political activities draws on Smith, *Becoming Something*, 102–6, 189, 283.

106. Singh, *Black Is a Country*, 116.

107. See Smith, *Becoming Something*, 291–93.

108. Kelley, *Freedom Dreams*, 51.

109. Twenty years earlier, as a young aspiring actor, Robeson expressed his hope that one day in American and European theater he would be able to play any role. See Paul Robeson, "An Actor's Wandering and Hopes," *Messenger* 7, no. 1 (January 1925): 32.

110. "Negro in American Theatre Discussed," *Daily Worker*, September 21, 1946, 11.

111. Samuel Sillen, "A Significant Dent in Jimcrow Theatre Tradition," *Daily Worker*, September 20, 1946, 11.

112. Perhaps to remind his public how prescient he was, Sillen interjected large portions of his February 1945 article into his September 1946 article on Lee's theatrical breakthrough.

113. George Jean Nathan, "Black Up, You-All, and Get a Job," *New York Journal-American*, October 28, 1946, 12. The following Nathan quotes come from this article.

114. Westbrook Pegler, "Professionals Promote Most of U.S. Intolerance," *New York Journal-American*, May 7, 1947, 3; Smith, *Becoming Something*, 225.

115. Westbrook Pegler, "Comments on Trends of Movie Red Probe," *New York Journal-American*, December 18, 1947, 3.

116. See Smith, *Becoming Something*, 227–33, 238.

117. See the two Elliot Norton articles: "Actor Canada Lee Has Great Chance in White Role," *Boston Post*, September 22, 1946, A7, and "Dearth of Actors Gave Opportunity to Canada Lee," *Boston Post*, September 29, 1946, A7.

118. Cohen, "Guild Seminar," 12.

119. Gill, "Triumphs and Struggles of Earle Hyman," 53.

120. Ibid., 60–61. Gill quotes *New York Times* critic Brooks Atkinson and a review by Miles Jefferson published in *Phylon*.

Chapter 5

1. Taubes, "White Mask Falls," 91.

2. See Hill and Hatch, *History of African American Theatre*; Savona, *Jean Genet*; and Schechter, *History of Negro Humor in America*. Genet's *The Blacks* would launch stand-up comic and actor Godfrey Cambridge into Hollywood stardom. Cambridge would move on to play the title role in Melvin Van Peebles's *Watermelon Man* (1970), a film about a white man who mysteriously turns black. For the first fifteen minutes of this film you can see the impact of Genet's reverse minstrel show on Hollywood. In full white paste, Cambridge opens the movie as an overbearing white businessman, but in the closing moments of *Watermelon Man*, Cambridge's once-white character, now fully adjusted to his blackness, trains as a black nationalist.

3. Bruce Webber, "Race Peers out of Masks," *New York Times*, February 13, 2003, E1.

4. Sandarg, "Jean Genet and the Black Panther Party," 270. Genet was not delusional. He realized he was not biologically or culturally black, but to affirm his metaphoric and political "blackness," Genet abandoned literature and theater to get involved in radical politics. In the 1970s, he was invited to live, work with, and speak on behalf of the Black Panthers as they tried to free Bobby Seale from a New Haven, Connecticut, jail.

5. See Mkapa, "What Black Is Black?"

6. Jameson, *Brecht and Method*, 39.

7. Brooks, *Bodies in Dissent*, 5.

8. Genet, *The Blacks*, 7–8.

9. Lane, "Voided Role," 887.

10. DuBois, *Souls of Black Folk*, 3

11. Fabre, *Drumbeats, Masks, and Metaphor*, 56.

12. De Grazia and Genet, "Interview," 316.

13. Nyong'o, *Amalgamation Waltz*, 13–14.

14. *Kerner Report*, 1.

15. Ibid., 383. Also, LeRoi Jones is quoted in Collins and Crawford, "Introduction," 8.

16. Collins and Crawford, "Introduction," 5.

17. *Kerner Report*, 110–11.

18. Ibid., 11–12.

19. Ibid., 110.

20. Neal, "Black Arts Movement," 29.

21. Ibid., 30.

22. Ibid., 39.

23. Collins and Crawford, "Introduction," 9–12.

24. Bernard, "Familiar Strangeness," 268–69.

25. For excellent analyses of this play, see Kolin, *Understanding Adrienne Kennedy*; Thompson, "Reversing Blackface Minstrelsy"; and Wood, "Weight of the Mask."

26. Cohn, *New American Dramatists*, 108.

27. Kaufman, "Delicate World of Reprobation," 208.

28. Quoted in Kolin, *Understanding Adrienne Kennedy*, 24–26.

29. Moten, *In the Break*, 241.

30. See Thompson, "Reversing Blackface Minstrelsy," 14–17, 20, 30, and Kolin, *Understanding Adrienne Kennedy*, 39.

31. Wood is building on Homi Bhabha's conception of third space as a "terrain for elaborating strategies of selfhood—singular or communal—that initiate new signs of identity, and innovative sites of collaboration and contestation." See Wood, "Weight of the Mask," 5, 12.

32. Barnett, "Prison of Object Relations," 379. Kennedy has used this kind of ventriloquist projection in other work, specifically in *A Movie Star Has to Star in Black and White* (1976).

33. Howard Taubman, "The Theater: 'Funnyhouse of a Negro,'" *New York Times*, January 15, 1964, 25.

34. Michael Smith, "Theatre: Funnyhouse of a Negro," *Village Voice*, January 23, 1964, 11.

35. Kolin, *Understanding Adrienne Kennedy*, 41.

36. This student production was directed by Beth Coleman and produced by Heritage Theatre Ensemble of Yale University in November/December 1988.

37. DuBois, *Souls of Black Folk*, 3–4.

38. Genet, *The Blacks*, 24.

39. Kennedy, *Funnyhouse of a Negro*, 6.

40. Ibid., 5.

41. Michael Smith, "Theatre: Funnyhouse of a Negro," *Village Voice*, January 23, 1964, 11.

42. Kennedy, "On the Writing of *Funnyhouse of a Negro*," 27–28. While her husband conducted business in Nigeria, Kennedy and her son Joe settled in Rome, where Kennedy spent her afternoons walking through ancient ruins of the famous Forum. In a small room not far from this once-vibrant center of Roman civic culture, she placed the final touches on her one-act drama.

43. Kennedy, *People Who Led to My Plays*, 118; Wood, "Weight of the Mask," 17.

44. See Barnett, "Prison of Object Relations," 379, and Kennedy, *People Who Led to My Plays*, 96. In 1957, Kennedy and her husband visited the Habsburg's Chapultepec Palace in Mexico, which further ingrained the Duchess in her active imagination. Jacqueline Wood suggests Kennedy may have also been referencing a Duchess Maria Theresa of the eighteenth-century Habsburgs. See Wood, "Weight of the Mask," 18.

45. Bryant-Jackson and Overbeck, "Adrienne Kennedy," 4.

46. Kennedy, "On the Writing of *Funnyhouse of a Negro*," 27–28; Singh, *Black Is a Country*, 184–87.

47. Singh, *Black Is a Country*, 174.

48. Kennedy, *Funnyhouse of a Negro*, 13.

49. Ibid., 5.

50. Ibid., 2–3.

51. Kennedy, "On the Writing of *Funnyhouse of a Negro*," 27.

52. Kennedy, *Funnyhouse of a Negro*, 6, 13.

53. Ibid., 17.

54. Ibid., 3.

55. Ibid.

56. Ibid., 9–11.

57. Ibid., 7.

58. Ibid., 17.

59. Ibid., 19.

60. Ibid., 19–20.

61. Ibid., 20. Also, in *People Who Led to My Plays*, Kennedy reveals that while she was in Accra, Ghana, Patrice Lumumba was assassinated, and rumors spread that the U.S. Central Intelligence Agency and the Belgian government were behind his murder because both feared a truly independent leader in the Congo.

62. Kennedy, *Funnyhouse of a Negro*, 20–22.

63. Ibid., 22.

64. Ibid., 5.

65. Hooks, "Representations of Whiteness in the Black Imagination," 39.

66. Margo Jefferson, "A Family's Story Merges with the Nation's," *New York Times*, October 8, 1995, 43.

67. Genet, *The Blacks*, 103.

68. See Binder and Kennedy, "*MELUS* Interview," 108, and Kolin, *Understanding Adrienne Kennedy*, 43.

69. Ward, *Day of Absence*, 266.

70. Bigsby, "Three Black Playwrights," 162.

71. For reviews of *Day of Absence*, see Howard Taubman, "Theatre: Satiric Twin Bill," *New York Times*, November 16, 1965, 56; Michael Smith, "Theatre Journal," *Village Voice*, November 18, 1965, 11; and Alvin Klein, "'Day of Absence' Offers Fantasy on Prejudice," *New York Times*, October 17, 1993, WC19.

72. Hay, *African American Theatre*, 161–62.

73. Douglas Turner Ward "American Theater: For Whites Only?," *New York Times*, August 14, 1966, D1.

74. Ward, *Day of Absence*, 272–75.

75. Ibid., 275–77. This next series of play quotes comes from Mayor Lee's speech.

76. See Howard Taubman, "Theatre: Satiric Twin Bill," *New York Times*, November 16, 1965, 56, and Michael Smith, "Theatre Journal," *Village Voice*, November 18, 1965, 11

77. Michael Smith, "Theatre Journal," *Village Voice*, November 18, 1965, 11. Although the other patrons were fully invested in this broadly satirical comedy, Smith admits he did not understand why they enjoyed it; in fact, he did not find the play funny at all.

78. Ward, *Day of Absence*, 269.

79. Ibid., 270–71.

80. Ibid., 269–70.

81. Ibid., 271.

82. Ibid., 269.

83. Ibid., 273.

84. For the different uses of parody and satire, see Piersen, *Black Legacy*; Abrahams, *Singing the Master*; and Rose, *Parody*.

85. Ward, *Day of Absence*, 276.

86. Ibid.

87. Ibid., 276–77.

88. Ibid., 279.

89. Ferguson, *Sage of Sugar Hill*, 217.

90. If this scenario sounds familiar, for the first season of their sketch comedy *Chappelle's Show*, Dave Chappelle and his then-writing partner Neal Brennan created Clayton Bigsby, a black and blind white supremacist. In a hilarious *Frontline* "mockumentary," Bigsby explains how he learned to be white and to hate black people, thus proving racial categories are pure constructions that can be interchanged

or transferred. White supremacy proves lucrative for Bigsby, as his well-honed racial hatred makes him a very popular writer of white supremacist literature until his fellow Klansmen discover Clayton's biological identity. See Carpio, *Laughing Fit to Kill*, 27–28, and *Chappelle's Show: Season One, Uncensored.*

91. Bob Mondello, "Black and Whitewash," *Washington City Paper*, May 15–21, 1998, theater section.

92. Howard Taubman, "Theatre: Satiric Twin Bill," *New York Times*, November 16, 1965, 56.

93. Ferguson, *Sage of Sugar Hill*, 216.

94. Ward, *Day of Absence*, 276–77.

95. Ibid., 280.

96. Wood, "Weight of the Mask," 10.

97. Fabre, *Drumbeats, Masks, and Metaphor*, 70–71.

98. Bigsby, "Three Black Playwrights," 162. Historians James Hatch and Ted Shine mention the creation of the "Day of Absence" protest in their introduction to *Day of Absence* in *Black Theatre USA: The Recent Period, 1935–Today.* I had not heard of "Day of Absence" until I was a first-year student in college and participated in this public protest on the campus of Yale University. We asserted our presence in two ways: first, by being absent from class and, second, by engaging in public demonstrations on campus, such as a rally in front of Sterling Memorial Library and a large black student dinner at the Commons. This annual demonstration may have brought greater awareness to our "ten-percent" presence at a privileged, majority-white institution, but this protest was never linked to a concrete set of issues or actions. More recently, immigration activists have been inspired by Ward's 1965 satire to shoot a documentary, titled *Day of Absence*, about the importance of immigrant labor to the national economy. See http://www.dayofabsence.com/.

99. Foreman, "Negro Ensemble Company," 279.

100. Roberts, "Healing Myths from the Ethnic Community," 150.

101. Ibid., 154.

102. Catanese, "Teaching *A Day of Absence*," 36. Over the last decade, *Day of Absence* has been produced at the College of William and Mary, the University of California–Berkeley, and the University of Virginia. When I was an undergraduate at Yale University, in the early 1990s, our African American theater association, Heritage Theatre Ensemble, also produced *Day of Absence.*

103. My brief introduction to LeRoi Jones in Harlem draws on Baraka, *Autobiography of LeRoi Jones.*

104. See *Experimental Death Unit #1* in Baraka, *Four Black Revolutionary Plays.*

105. Baraka, *Autobiography of LeRoi Jones*, 203; Mel Gussow, "'Junkies,' Most Adept, Hits at Drug Evils," *New York Times*, September 20, 1972, 41.

106. See *Madheart* in Baraka, *Four Black Revolutionary Plays.*

107. Neal, "Black Arts Movement," 36.

108. See X and Faruk, "Islam and Black Art," and Baraka, *Autobiography of LeRoi Jones*, 210, 238. *A Black Mass* can also be found in *Four Black Revolutionary Plays*, along with *Madheart* and *Experimental Death Unit #1.* There is also an audio record-

ing of *A Black Mass*, first recorded in 1968 and reissued on CD in 1999. I want to thank Carmelina Cartei, a student in my whiting up course at the CUNY Graduate Center, for introducing me to this CD reissue.

109. Baraka, "Black Arts Movement," 503.

110. DuBois, *Souls of Black Folk*, 3.

111. My brief reiteration of "Yakub's History" relies on Nelson, "*A Black Mass* as Black Gothic," 138–41.

112. In a 1968 interview, Baraka explained how he was first introduced to Islam through Malcolm X, or Hajj Malik, and he initially associated the Nation of Islam with progressive social thought. He also originally viewed the Nation's theology on Yakub as "an expression of truth on many levels about man, Black man, spiritual man's subjugation by anti-spiritual forces." See X and Faruk, "Islam and Black Art," 51.

113. Nelson, "*A Black Mass* as Black Gothic," 138, 147.

114. This conversation and the next series of quotes come from Baraka, *A Black Mass*, 22–23.

115. Ibid., 30.

116. Brooks, *Bodies in Dissent*, 5.

117. Shannon, "Amiri Baraka on Directing," 233.

118. For more on Nigeria's Apidan Theatre and oyinbo, see Clapperton, *Journal of a Second Expedition*, 53–56; Götrick, *Apidan Theatre and Modern Drama*, 31–41, 92–95; and Adedeji, "Traditional Yoruba Theater." Jones was influenced by Yoruba religion, but there is no evidence that he was familiar with this Yoruba performance of whiteness while composing *A Black Mass*.

119. Clapperton, *Journal of a Second Expedition*, 55–56.

120. This and the following quotes come from Baraka, *A Black Mass*, 32–33.

121. Shannon, "Manipulating Myth, Magic, and Legend," 366.

122. These philosophical exchanges between the three magicians come from Baraka, *A Black Mass*, 24–31.

123. Shannon, "Manipulating Myth, Magic, and Legend," 365.

124. See the liner notes for *A Black Mass* audio CD.

125. Baraka, *A Black Mass*, 25–26. The next series of quotes comes from this section.

126. Ibid., 39.

127. This conversation on greater and lesser jihad relies on Cook, *Understanding Jihad*, 32–48. Cook argues that the notion of "greater jihad" as a nonviolent jihad is largely an "advertisement" and an attempt to radically alter tradition. He claims the term has little "historical depth or universal acceptance in classical or even in contemporary Islam." The concept is primarily dealt with in Western scholarly interpretations of jihad, and the texts are largely written in European languages for non-Muslim audiences. Cook also stresses that the ninth-century ascetic and Sufi groups who initially advocated jihad as spiritual warfare promoted it as a supplement or preparation for the more militant and supposedly "lesser" jihad.

128. Mel Gussow, "'Madheart' and 'Black Mass' Are Staged," *New York Times*, September 30, 1972, 18.

129. Genet, *The Blacks*, 112.

130. See Dunbar's poem "We Wear the Mask," from *Lyrics of Lowly Life* (1896), and DuBois, *Souls of Black Folk* (1903).

131. Genet, *The Blacks*, 128.

Chapter 6

1. A transcript of Wright's speech can be found on the CNN website, http://www.cnn.com/2008/POLITICS/04/28/wright.transcript/index.html. For a video of the NAACP speech, see http://www.mlive.com/news/index.ssf/2008/04/watch_rev_jeremiah_wrights_spe.html.

2. Haggins, *Laughing Mad*, 192, 194.

3. Wright was not the first black solo performer to exploit this comparison between black and white marching bands. During the mid-1990s, at the height of his stand-up career, comedian Sinbad worked the same racialized contrast. See Limon, *Stand-Up Comedy in Theory*, 85.

4. James McPherson, "The New Comic Style of Richard Pryor," *New York Times*, April 27, 1975, 20.

5. Clifford, *Predicament of Culture*, 9.

6. The intersection between performance and anthropology is nothing new for theater scholars and practitioners. Since the early 1970s, anthropologist Victor Turner and performance theorist/director Richard Schechner have engaged in a very productive interdisciplinary conversation. See Turner, *Anthropology of Performance*, and Schechner, *Between Theater and Anthropology*.

7. See Clifford, "Introduction," 5–7.

8. Conquergood, "Performing as a Moral Act," 9–10.

9. Jones, "Performance Ethnography," 7.

10. Basso, *Portraits of "The Whiteman,"* 17–18.

11. Dyson and Chennault, "Giving Whiteness a Black Eye," 303.

12. Jones, "Performance Ethnography," 7.

13. Singh, *Black Is a Country*, 52, 127–28.

14. Ellison, "Change the Joke and Slip the Yoke," 102.

15. Watkins, *On the Real Side*, 567–68.

16. Ibid., 494–95, 527–28; Williams, *Seeing a Color-Blind Future*, 12.

17. Watkins, *On the Real Side*, 394.

18. This brief history of Jackie "Moms" Mabley relies on Watkins, *On the Real Side*, 390–93, and Bill Dahl's liner notes included with her comedy album *"Moms" Mabley: Comedy Ain't Pretty* (2004).

19. Haggins, *Laughing Mad*, 150.

20. In addition to Watkins's *On the Real Side*, see Lawrence Levine's "Laughing at the Man" section in *Black Culture and Black Consciousness*, 300–320.

21. This Mabley joke is quoted in Watkins, *On the Real Side*, 392.

22. The following discussion of the Playboy Club and Uptown Theatre appearances is based on the *"Moms" Mabley at the Playboy Club* compilation CD (2003).

23. See track 3 of ibid.

24. His appearance on the *Steve Allen Show* is quoted in Haggins, *Laughing Mad*, 20.

25. This background on Gregory's early career and research process relies on Gregory and Lipsyte, *Nigger*, 121–28, and Gregory and Moses, *Callus on My Soul*, 31–32.

26. Gregory and Lipsyte, *Nigger*, 147–48.

27. Ibid., 148, and Gregory, *From the Back of the Bus*, 17.

28. Gregory and Lipsyte, *Nigger*, 158–59.

29. See Gregory, *In Living Black and White.*

30. Gregory and Lipsyte, *Nigger*, 149, 160–61.

31. See Gregory, *In Living Black and White.*

32. See track 1 of *"Moms" Mabley at the Playboy Club.*

33. Freud is quoted in Carpio, *Laughing Fit to Kill*, 14, and Watkins, *On the Real Side*, 527.

34. See Hefner's introduction to Gregory, *From the Back of the Bus*, 18.

35. Part of this KKK material is reprinted in Gregory and Lipsyte, *Nigger*, 160. You can also hear it on the "Comedians of the 1960s" track from Gregory, *In Living Black and White.*

36. This comedic bit was published in Gregory, *From the Back of the Bus*, 46.

37. Goldberg, *Book*, 105.

38. Enid Nemy, "Whoopi's Ready, but Is Broadway?," *New York Times*, October 21, 1984, H1.

39. Goldberg, *Book*, 10; Nemy, "Whoopi's Ready, but Is Broadway?," *New York Times*, October 21, 1984, H4.

40. My descriptions of Goldberg's one-person show come from a recording of the 1984 Broadway performance *Whoopi Goldberg*, which originally aired on HBO. In 2004, Goldberg returned to the Lyceum Theatre to film a twentieth anniversary of her Broadway debut; that stand-up film is titled *Whoopi: Back to Broadway.*

41. Haggins, *Laughing Mad*, 148; Nemy, "Whoopi's Ready, but Is Broadway?," *New York Times*, October 21, 1984, H1.

42. Haggins, *Laughing Mad*, 133, 135–36.

43. Frank Rich, "Stage: *Whoopi Goldberg* Opens," *New York Times*, October 26, 1984, C17.

44. LeRoi Jones is quoted in Collins and Crawford, "Introduction," 8.

45. Lewis and Smith, "Circle of Confusion," 56; hooks, "Performance Practice as a Site of Opposition," 214.

46. See Lewis and Smith, "Circle of Confusion," 62.

47. Martin and Smith, "Anna Deavere Smith," 52–55.

48. Ibid., 47.

49. See Richards, "Caught in the Act of Social Definition." Richards does an excellent job of revealing the subjective nature of Smith's work and its potential impacts on the communities Smith selects for her dialogical conversations.

50. Hooks, "Performance Practice as a Site of Opposition," 214; Cornel West's foreword in Smith, *Fires in the Mirror*, xix.

51. Thompson, "Is Race a Trope?," 132; Smith, *Fires in the Mirror*, xxxi. In another insightful critique of Anna Deavere Smith's On the Road series, Sandra L. Richards

claims that interventionist performance ethnography can help a community see its problems in new and different ways, but identifying issues is only part of a longer process. Communities want artist-activists like Smith to help them "explore difference and attempt to eradicate its invidiousness" but also to help them formulate solutions to their problems. See Richards, "Caught in the Act of Social Definition," 50–51.

52. This discussion of *Fires in the Mirror* is based on Smith, *Fires in the Mirror*, 19–25, and the *Fires in the Mirror* April 1993 PBS *American Playhouse* production directed by George Wolfe.

53. Reinelt, "Performing Race," 614.

54. It is interesting to note that in the stage directions in the published version, Siegal is described as wearing a wig during the interview, while her neighbor, another Lubavitch woman at the interview, is not. See Smith, *Fire in the Mirror*, 23

55. Reinelt, "Performing Race," 609, 615.

56. Martin and Smith, "Anna Deavere Smith," 51–52, 57; Muckelbauer, *Future of Invention*, 72–75.

57. Fanon, *Wretched of the Earth*, 212–13.

58. *Tracy Morgan: Black and Blue*, directed by John Moffitt, originally aired on HBO on November 15, 2010.

59. Fusco, "Performance and the Power of the Popular," 161.

60. Spillers, "'All the Things You Could Be by Now,'" 390–91.

61. Dyer, *Matter of Images*, 11–12.

62. Carpio, *Laughing Fit to Kill*, 14.

63. Spillers, "All the Things You Could Be by Now," 390.

64. My biographical information on Pryor draws on Pryor and Gold, *Pryor Convictions*.

65. Muckelbauer, *Future of Invention*, 72–75; Haygood, *In Black and White*, 116.

66. Haygood, *In Black and White*, 379.

67. McWhorter, "Mr. Mimic."

68. Pryor and Gold, *Pryor Convictions*, 16.

69. Cheng, *Melancholy of Race*, x–xi.

70. Singh, *Black Is a Country*, 22.

71. Mooney is quoted in Watkins, *On the Real Side*, 579.

72. Pryor and Gold, *Pryor Convictions*, 117.

73. Ibid., 121.

74. All subsequent references to the recorded April 1971 Improv performance come from Pryor, *Richard Pryor: Live & Smokin'*. Some of these humorous observations are also published in Pryor and Gold, *Pryor Convictions*.

75. Pryor and Gold, *Pryor Convictions*, 16.

76. Ibid.

77. Cheng, *Melancholy of Race*, 15.

78. Ibid., 20.

79. Pryor and Gold, *Pryor Convictions*, 128; Watkins, *On the Real Side*, 544.

80. This and all subsequent descriptions of the 1979 Long Beach filmed concert are based on Pryor, *Richard Pryor: Live in Concert*.

81. Limon, *Stand-Up Comedy in Theory*, 84–85; Carpio, *Laughing Fit to Kill*, 79.

82. Rahman, "It's Serious Business," 102–3.

83. Carpio, *Laughing Fit to Kill*, 87.

84. James McPherson, "The New Comic Style of Richard Pryor," *New York Times*, April 27, 1975, 32.

85. Carpio, *Laughing Fit to Kill*, 75.

86. James McPherson, "The New Comic Style of Richard Pryor," *New York Times*, April 27, 1975, 32.

87. Carpio, *Laughing Fit to Kill*, 87.

88. During the early 1970s, sociologists, linguists, and theatrical theorists were interested in the different verbal and nonverbal styles cultivated in black and white communities. See Kochman, *Black and White Styles in Conflict*; Harrison, *Drama of Nommo*; and Johnson, "Black Kinesics."

89. Limon, *Stand-Up Comedy in Theory*, 102–3.

90. George, *Post-Soul Nation*, ix. Also see his other work that deals with postsoul culture: "The Complete History of Post-Soul Culture," *Village Voice*, March 17, 1992, and *Buppies, B-Boys, Baps & Bohos*.

91. Also see the early postsoul theorizing of Greg Tate, "Cult Nats Meet the Freaky Deke: The Return of the Black Aesthetic," *Village Voice*, literary supplement, December 9, 1986, 5–8, and Ellis, "New Black Aesthetic."

92. Neal, *Soul Babies*, 2–3; Ashe, Anderson, and Neal, "These—Are—the 'Breaks'"; Ashe, "Theorizing the Post-Soul Aesthetic."

93. Haggins, *Laughing Mad*, 5.

94. See Auslander, *Liveness*.

95. Ashe, Anderson, and Neal, "These—Are—the 'Breaks,'" 791, 798.

96. James Hannaham, "Zebra Lives: Sarah Jones—Awhirl in Race's Unstable Dance," *Village Voice*, January 5, 1999, 108.

97. The other key components of Ashe's triangular postsoul matrix are "the execution of an exploration of blackness" and "allusion-disruption gestures." See Ashe, "Theorizing the Post-Soul Aesthetic," 609, 613–14.

98. James Hannaham, "Zebra Lives: Sarah Jones—Awhirl in Race's Unstable Dance," *Village Voice*, January 5, 1999, 108.

99. Conquergood, "Performing as a Moral Act," 8.

100. "A Conversation with Guest Host Charles Isherwood and Playwright Sarah Jones," *Charlie Rose*, May 26, 2006, http://www.charlierose.com/view/interview/388.

101. Ibid. Sarah Jones's comments echo another biracial Ms. Jones, journalist and author Lisa Jones. Lisa Jones writes about embracing "difference as one of the rich facts of one's life" and as a kind of personal "pleasure" that can provide "more power, and more flavor." See Jones, *Bulletproof Diva*, 33.

102. My discussion of this solo piece is based on a performance of *Surface Transit* that I personally witnessed at San Francisco's Theatre Artaud in September 1999.

103. See "A Conversation with Guest Host Charles Isherwood and Playwright Sarah Jones," *Charlie Rose*, May 26, 2006, http://www.charlierose.com/view/interview/388.

104. Muckelbauer, *Future of Invention*, 74–75.

105. Reinelt, "Performing Race," 614; Conquergood, "Performing as a Moral Act," 8.

106. Chappelle's personal and professional biography comes from two interviews:

"Dave Chappelle Interview with James Lipton" and "Diversions: Comedian Dave Chappelle."

107. Haggins, *Laughing Mad*, 179. Gregory developed a similar dual identity as civil rights satirist and hip, young comic well-versed in "reefer" jokes. See McCandlish Phillips, "Dick Gregory in an Hour at Carnegie," *New York Times*, November, 27, 1969, 51.

108. Haggins, *Laughing Mad*, 207. These kinds of collaborations between white and black writers have been especially productive for black comedians. Dick Gregory teamed with white writer Ed Wineberger, who often traveled with Gregory during his civil rights work in the South. See Gregory, *Callus on My Soul*, 50. Also, Eddie Murphy and white writer Andy Breckman cowrote the *Saturday Night Live* short film *White Like Me* (1985).

109. Chappelle discusses the passing of this "Pryor mantle" in "Dave Chappelle Interview with James Lipton"; also see Carpio, *Laughing Fit to Kill*, 116.

110. My description of Chappelle's stand-up is based on a video recording of this 2000 HBO comedy special. I have also written about this performance previously; see McAllister, "Dave Chappelle, Whiteface Minstrelsy, and 'Irresponsible' Satire."

111. Chapelle, "Dave Chappelle Interview with James Lipton."

112. Chapelle, "Diversions: Comedian Dave Chappelle" and "Dave Chappelle Interview with James Lipton."

113. Chapelle, "Diversions: Comedian Dave Chappelle."

114. Williams, *Seeing a Color-Blind Future*, 27–28.

115. Conquergood, "Performing as a Moral Act," 9.

116. Williams, *Seeing a Color-Blind Future*, 6.

117. "Anna Deavere Smith interview with David Brancaccio," PBS *Now*, August 11, 2006, http://www.pbs.org/now/transcript/232.html.

Conclusion

1. Suzan-Lori Parks online interview, June 22, 2007, Academy of Achievement website, http://www.achievement.org/autodoc/page/par1int-6. The next two quotes come from this interview. Parks has even more Lincoln characters sprinkled throughout her *365 Days/365 Plays* (2006) anthology, in which the playwright set out to write a play a day for an entire year.

2. Parks, *America Play*, 19–20.

3. For the 1993 workshop productions of *The America Play* at Arena Stage and the Dallas Theater Center, and the official premiere at the Public Theatre in 1994, the role of the Foundling Father was played by black actors. Even on the back cover of the published anthology, a black Abe Lincoln is pictured. In the text there is only one brief reference to race, when the Foundling Father's wife, Lucy, states that one of her "favorite pages" from the book of Lincoln was "of course where he frees all thuh slaves." This line subtly hints at Lucy's race. See Parks, *America Play*, 190.

4. Ibid., 171.

5. Parks, *Topdog/Underdog*, 15.

6. Ibid., 57.

7. Parks, *America Play*, 21–22. In her introductory essay for this anthology, Parks actually calls this preoccupation with "Whitey" a "fucked up trap."

8. As I mentioned in the Introduction, I have taught versions of this course at the University of California–Berkeley, the Catholic University of America in Washington, D.C., and the City University of New York's Graduate Center.

9. Twenge, *Generation Me*, 182.

10. This is the case until an outrageous racial incident, usually on a college campus, brings personal and institutional racism front and center for this generation. One such incident surfaced in early 2010 with the University of California–San Diego's "Compton Cookout," a fraternity-sponsored party designed to ridicule Black History Month. See Eleanor Yang Su, "Outrage Expressed over Party; UCSD Students Mock Black Culture," *San Diego Union-Tribune*, February 17, 2010, B1. Apparently this was just the beginning of a series of racist or racially tinged incidents on campus, but UC–San Diego is hardly an exception. These kinds of race-conscious yet insensitive parties happen on campuses all across the country, which suggests this millennial generation may have a problem fully processing racial and ethnic differences.

11. See Fanon, *Black Skin, White Masks*, 92.

12. James McPherson, "The New Comic Style of Richard Pryor," *New York Times*, April 27, 1975, 32.

13. This discussion is based on the video recording of Pryor's 1971 New York City Improv performance, *Richard Pryor: Live & Smokin'*.

14. In *Tropic Thunder*, Robert Downey Jr. plays a white Australian actor named Kirk Lazarus who is cast as Osiris, a hard-core black soldier in a Vietnam War film. As the consummate five-time Oscar-winning, method actor, Lazarus undergoes a pigment procedure to darken his skin, and he is so committed to the role that he stays in character even on breaks. On its face, *Tropic Thunder* is about a range of representations, from race to sexuality to body image, but the movie is also about how deeply actors submerge themselves in roles. During a conversation with the lone black actor cast in the film within this film, Kirk Lazarus admits he is in too deep. His brownface embodiment of 1960s blackness has been overwhelmed by a confluence of cultural stereotypes from film, television, music, and soul food. He openly admits he cannot dig out from under the layers of racial signification; the cross-racial play has gotten the better of him.

15. See Strand, "*Jails, Hospitals & Hip Hop* Review," and Somini Sengupta, "A Multicultural Chameleon: Actor's Experience Spawns Polyglot Cast of Characters," *New York Times*, October 9, 1999, B1, B7.

16. Kate Taylor, "Assault on the Gentrifiers, and the Audience," *New York Times*, November 14, 2008.

17. Williams, *Seeing a Color-Blind Future*, 25–26. The late ethnographer Dwight Conquergood takes a similar position; see his "Performing as a Moral Act."

18. Brooks, *Bodies in Dissent*, 29.

19. Fusco, "Performance and the Power of the Popular," 174–75.

20. The letter was reprinted in the *Freeman*, April 2, 1898, 4.

21. Ibid.

22. Chappelle first told this story in print and later on the *Oprah* show. See "David Chappelle Interview with Oprah Winfrey," *Oprah*, February 3, 2006, and Christopher John Farley, "Dave Speaks," *Time*, March 23, 2005, 68–73.

23. See King, *Offside Racism*.

24. McWhorter, "Mr. Mimic."

25. See Elaine Chun's dissertation, "The Meaning of Mocking." Related to Chun's work is the earlier linguistic study by ethnographer Keith Basso, *Portraits of "The Whiteman,"* which looks at how Apaches mock Anglo-Americans for social and interpretive purposes.

26. Robert Wolinsky, "Wrong Wayans, Do the Right Thing: Avoid White Chicks in Bad Masks," *Houston Press*, June 24, 2006, http://www.houstonpress.com/2004-06-24/film/wrong-wayans/.

27. Peter Debruge, "*Frankie and Alice* Review," *Variety*, November 18, 2010, http://www.variety.com/review/VE1117944069?refcatid=31. I want to thank my sister Gina McAllister for informing me about this film before its official release in February 2011.

28. See John Lahr, "The Laughing Cure," *New Yorker*, October 18, 2004, 211–12.

29. Patrick Healy, "Blackface and Bigotry, Finely Tuned," *New York Times*, October 17, 2010, AR4.

30. Sam Jones, "Idris Elba Defends Thor Film Role," *guardian.co.uk*, April 27, 2010, http://www.guardian.co.uk/culture/2010/apr/27/idris-elba-thor-race-debate.

31. Zaki Hasan, "*Thor* Is Unfair to White People? Seriously?," December 17, 2010, Huffington Post website, http://www.huffingtonpost.com/zaki-hasan/thor-movie-unfair-to-whit_b_798365.html. I want to thank Scott Trafton, my friend and colleague at the University of South Carolina, for bringing this *Thor* film and the controversy to my attention.

32. Singh, *Black Is a Country*, 44.

33. Hwang's somewhat autobiographical *Yellowface* debuted in December 2007 at the Public Theatre in New York City.

34. Kondo has worked on and written about cross-racial performances flowing in multiple directions. She rejects the liberal humanist idea that race is an identity that must be transcended or ignored. Kondo believes the racial, gender, class, and sexual identities represented by performers of color, like Anna Deavere Smith, are the products of "axes of power and inequality." But these cross-racial and cross-gender performances create opportunities to reconsider political inequities and to forge progressive political alliances between different minority communities. See Kondo, "(Re)Visions of Race."

35. See Douglass, *Life and Times*, 147–48. Dick Gregory is quoted as saying comedy is a "narcotic" for the oppressed, in Schechter, *History of Negro Humor in America*, 186.

36. Williams, *Seeing a Color-Blind Future*, 16.

37. Ibid., 73.

38. Johnson, *Appropriating Blackness*, 6.

Bibliography

Manuscript Collections

Cambridge, Mass.
  Houghton Library, Harvard University
    Harvard Theatre Collection, Theatrical Clippings Files
New York, N.Y.
  Rare Books and Manuscript Library, Columbia University
    Brander Mathews Dramatic Museum Portraits
Orono, Maine
  Folger Library, University of Maine
    Pre-1900 and Early Canadiana Research Collection
      (CIHM/ICMH Microfiche Series)
Washington, D.C.
  Archives Center, National Museum of American History
    "George & Hart's Up to Date Minstrels" Scrapbook, 1900–1901,
      Collection 576
  Folger Shakespeare Library
    Art Collection: Portraits, 19th Century Male
  Library of Congress, Performing Arts Division
    Music Department, Sheet Music Collection
  Moorland-Spingarn Research Center, Howard University
    Arthur B. Spingarn Sheet Music Collection
  Channing Pollock Theatre Collection, Howard University
    Photograph Files

Newspapers and Magazines

African Repository and Colonial Journal, 1825
American (New York), 1820–21
American Monthly Magazine and Critical Review, 1817
Boston Post, 1946
Brooklyn Star, 1825
Charleston Courier, 1822
Chicago Daily News, 1923
Chicago Defender, 1923

Chicago Tribune, 1923
Crisis Magazine, 1915–26
Daily Worker, 1945–46
Dramatic Mirror (New York), 1898
Ebony Magazine (Chicago), 1972
Freedom's Journal (New York), 1827
Freeman (Indianapolis), 1898–1900
Harper's Weekly, 1861–65
Houston Press, 2006
Messenger (New York), 1923–26
Nation (New York), 1926
National Advocate (New York), 1820–25
New York Age, 1916–32
New York American, 1821
New York Amsterdam News, 1946
New York Clipper, 1897–1900
New Yorker, 1946–2004
New York Evening Post, 1820–24
New York Herald and Tribune, 1923
New York Journal-American, 1946–47
New York Times, 1895–2010
New York Tribune, 1923–24
Opportunity Magazine, 1923
Pittsburgh Courier, 1927–32
Progressive (New York), 2004
San Diego Herald-Tribune, 1995
Soil (New York), 1916
South Carolina Gazette (Charleston), 1771–73
Southern Patriot and Commercial Advertiser (Charleston), 1822
Spectator (New York), 1821–29
Variety, 2010
Village Voice (New York), 1965–99
Wall Street Journal, 1923
Washington City Paper, 1998

Books, Articles, Dissertations, Interviews, Plays, Recordings, Sheet Music, and Websites

Abbott, Lynn, and Doug Seroff. *Out of Sight: The Rise of African American Popular Music, 1889–1895*. Jackson: University of Mississippi Press, 2002.
———. *Ragged but Right: Black Traveling Shows, "Coon Songs," and the Dark Pathway to Blues and Jazz*. Jackson: University of Mississippi Press, 2007.
Abrahams, Roger D. *Afro-American Folktales: Stories from Black Traditions in the New World*. New York: Pantheon, 1985.
———. *Singing the Master: The Emergence of African American Culture in the Plantation South*. New York: Pantheon, 1992.
Adedeji, Joel. "Traditional Yoruba Theater." *African Arts* 3, no. 1 (1969): 60–63.
Aldridge, Ira. *Memoir and Theatrical Career of Ira Aldridge, the African Roscius*. London: J. Onuhyn, 1849.
Allen, Irving Lewis. *City in Slang: New York Life and Popular Speech*. New York: Oxford University Press, 1993.
Anderson, Addell Austin. "The Ethiopian Art Theatre." *Theatre Survey* 33, no. 2 (November 1992): 132–43.
Armstead-Johnson, Helen. "Themes and Values in Afro-American Librettos and Book Musicals, 1898–1930." In *Musical Theatre in America: Papers and Proceeding of the Conference on the Musical Theatre in America*, edited by Glenn Loney, 133–42. Westport, Conn.: Greenwood, 1984.
Arnold, Samuel J. *The Devil's Bridge: An Opera in Three Acts*. New York: Longworth, 1817.

Ashe, Bertram D. "Theorizing the Post-Soul Aesthetic: An Introduction." *African American Review* 41, no. 4 (Winter 2007): 609–23.

Ashe, Bertram D., Crystal Anderson, and Mark Anthony Neal. "These—Are—the 'Breaks': A Roundtable Discussion on Teaching the Post-Soul Aesthetic." *African American Review* 41, no. 4 (Winter 2007): 787–803.

Asim, Jabari. *The N Word: Who Can Say It, Who Shouldn't, and Why*. New York: Houghton Mifflin, 2007.

Auslander, Philip. *Liveness: Performance in a Mediatized Culture*. London: Routledge, 1999.

Awkward, Michael. *Negotiating Difference: Race, Gender, and the Politics of Positionality*. Chicago: University of Chicago Press, 1995.

Babcock, Barbara A. "Introduction." In *The Reversible World: Symbolic Inversion in Art and Society*, edited by Barbara A. Babcock, 13–36. Ithaca, N.Y.: Cornell University Press, 1978.

Baldwin, Brooke. "The Cakewalk: A Study in Stereotype and Reality." *Journal of Social History* 15, no. 2 (Winter 1981): 205–18.

Baraka, Amiri. *The Autobiography of LeRoi Jones*. Chicago: Lawrence Hill Books, 1984.

———. "The Black Arts Movement." In *The LeRoi Jones/Amiri Baraka Reader*, edited by William J. Harris and Amiri Baraka, 495–506. New York: Thunder Mouth's Press, 1999.

———. *A Black Mass*. Audio CD. Produced by Amiri Baraka and Sun Ra & the Myth Science Arkestra. Washington, D.C.: Son Boy Records, 1999.

———. *Four Black Revolutionary Plays: All Praises to the Black Man: Experimental Death Unit #1; A Black Mass; Great Goodness of Life; Madheart*. Indianapolis: Bobbs Merrill, 1969.

Barnett, Claudia. "A Prison of Object Relations: Adrienne Kennedy's *Funnyhouse of a Negro*." *Modern Drama* 40, no. 3 (1997): 374–84.

Barton, Andrew. *The Disappointment, or the Force of Credulity*. 1767. Reprint, Gainesville: University of Florida Press, 1976.

Basso, Keith H. *Portraits of "The Whiteman": Linguistic Play and Cultural Symbols among the Western Apache*. New York: Cambridge University Press, 1979.

Bay, Mia. *White Image in the Black Mind: African-American Ideas about White People, 1830–1925*. New York: Oxford University Press, 2000.

Bean, Annemarie, James V. Hatch, and Brooks McNamara, eds. *Inside the Minstrel Mask: Readings in Nineteenth-Century Blackface Minstrelsy*. Hanover, N.H.: Wesleyan University Press, 1996.

Belcher, Fanin, Jr. "The Place of the Negro in the Evolution of the American Theatre, 1767-1940." Unpublished dissertation, Yale University, 1945.

Berlin, Ira. "The Structure of the Free Negro Caste in the Antebellum United States." *Journal of Social History* 9, no. 3 (Spring 1976): 297–318.

Bernard, Emily. "A Familiar Strangeness: The Spectre of Whiteness in the Harlem Renaissance and the Black Arts Movement." In *New Thoughts on the Black Arts Movement*, edited by Lisa Gail Collins and Margo Natalie Crawford, 255–72. New Brunswick, N.J.: Rutgers University Press, 2006.

Bigsby, C. W. E. "Three Black Playwrights: Lofton Mitchell, Ossie Davis, Douglas Turner Ward." In *The Theatre of Black Americans: A Collection of Critical Essays*, edited by Errol Hill, 148–67. New York: Applause, 1987.
Binder, Wolfgang, and Adrienne Kennedy. "A *MELUS* Interview: Adrienne Kennedy." *MELUS* 12, no. 3 (Fall 1985): 99–108.
Black, Cheryl. "Looking White, Acting Black: Cast(e)ing Fredi Washington." *Theatre Survey* 45, no. 1 (May 2004): 19–40.
———. "'New Negro' Performance in Art and Life: Fredi Washington and the Theatrical Columns of *The People's Voice*, 1943–47." *Theatre History Studies* 24 (June 2004): 57–72.
Blake, William. *Don Juan; or, The Libertine Destroy'd, a Tragic Pantomimical Entertainment, in Two Acts*. 1795. Reprint, London: J. Roach, 1820.
Blesh, Rudi, and Harriet Janis. *They All Played Ragtime*. 1950. Reprint, New York: Oak Publications, 1971.
Bold, Alan. *A Burns Companion*. New York: St. Martin's, 1991.
Bolster, Jeffrey W. *Black Jacks: African-American Seamen in the Age of Sail*. Cambridge, Mass.: Harvard University Press, 1997.
Brock, Lisa, Robin D. G. Kelley, and Karen Sotiropoulos. "Transnational Black Studies: Editor's Introduction." *Radical History Review* 87 (Fall 2003): 1–3.
Brooks, Daphne A. *Bodies in Dissent: Spectacular Performances of Race and Freedom, 1850–1910*. Durham, N.C.: Duke University Press, 2006.
Brown, Jayna. *Babylon Girls: Black Women Performers and the Shaping of the Modern*. Durham, N.C.: Duke University Press, 2008.
Brustein, Robert S. *Reimagining American Theatre*. New York: Hill and Wang, 1991.
Bryant-Jackson, Paul K. "Kennedy's Travelers in the American and African Continuum." In *Intersecting Boundaries: The Theatre of Adrienne Kennedy*, edited by Paul K. Bryant-Jackson and Lois More Overbeck, 45–57. Minneapolis: University of Minnesota Press, 1992.
Bryant-Jackson, Paul K., and Lois More Overbeck. "Adrienne Kennedy: An Interview." In *Intersecting Boundaries: The Theatre of Adrienne Kennedy*, edited by Paul K. Bryant-Jackson and Lois More Overbeck, 3–12. Minneapolis: University of Minnesota Press, 1992.
Burk, Rosemarie K. *Theatre Culture in America, 1825–1860*. New York: Cambridge University Press, 1997.
Burma, John H. "Humor as a Technique in Race Conflict." *American Sociological Review* 11, no. 6 (December 1946): 710–15.
Burns, Elizabeth. *Theatricality: A Study of Convention in the Theatre and Social Life*. New York: Harper & Row, 1972.
Carpio, Glenda R. *Laughing Fit to Kill: Black Humor in the Fictions of Slavery*. New York: Oxford University Press, 2008.
Catanese, Brandi Wilkins. "Teaching *A Day of Absence* 'at [your] own risk.'" *Theatre Topics* 19, no. 1 (March 2009): 29–38.
Chappelle, Dave. *Chappelle's Show: Season One, Uncensored*. DVD. Hollywood, Calif.: Paramount Pictures, 2004.

———. "Dave Chappelle Interview with James Lipton." *Inside the Actor's Studio*, February 12, 2006.
———. "Diversions: Comedian Dave Chappelle." Interview with Terry Gross. NPR's *Fresh Air*, September 2, 2004, http://www.npr.org/templates/story/story.php?storyId=3886000.
Cheng, Anne Anlin. *The Melancholy of Race*. New York: Oxford University Press, 2000.
Chun, Elaine. "The Meaning of Mocking: Stylizations of Asians and Preps at a U.S. High School." Unpublished dissertation, University of Texas–Austin, 2007.
Cibber, Colley. *The Tragical History of King Richard III*. In *Five Restoration Adaptations of Shakespeare*, edited by Christopher Spencer, 275–344. Urbana: University of Illinois Press, 1965.
Clapperton, Hugh. *Journal of a Second Expedition into the Interior of Africa, from the Bight of Benin to Soccatoo; to which is added the Journal of Richard Lander from Kano to the Sea-Coast, Partly by a More Eastern Route*. 1829. Reprint, London: F. Cass, 1966.
Clifford, James. "Introduction: Partial Truths." In *Writing Culture: The Poetics and Politics of Ethnography*, edited by James Clifford and George E. Marcus, 1–26. Berkeley: University of California Press, 1986.
———. *The Predicament of Culture: Twentieth-Century Ethnography, Literature, and Art*. Cambridge, Mass.: Harvard University Press, 1988.
Cockrell, Dale. *Demons of Disorder: Early Blackface Minstrels and Their World*. New York: Cambridge University Press, 1997.
Cohen, Hennig. "A Negro 'Folk Game' in Colonial South Carolina." *Southern Folklore Quarterly* 16 (September 1952): 183–85.
Cohen, Patricia. "Guild Seminar: Race and Politics in Theater." *Dramatist: The Journal of the Dramatists Guild of America, Inc.* 7, no. 4 (March/April 2005): 6–15.
Cohn, Ruby. *New American Dramatists, 1960–1980*. New York: Grove Press, 1982.
Cole, Bob, and Billy Johnson. "Mr. Coon You're All Right in Your Place." New York: Haviland & Co., 1899.
———. "No Coons Allowed." New York: Howley, Haviland & Co., 1897.
Cole, Bob, and Rosmand Johnson. "Pickin' on a Chicken Bone." 1900. Levy Sheet Music Collection Online, Johns Hopkins University, https://jscholarship.library.jhu.edu/handle/1774.2/9571 (accessed August 27, 2010).
Cole, Bob, Billy Johnson, and Will Accooe. "Chicken." New York: Howley, Haviland & Co., 189?.
Cole, John. *The Minstrel: A Collection of Celebrated Songs*. Baltimore: F. Lucas, 1812.
Collins, Lisa Gail, and Margo Natalie Crawford. "Introduction: Power to the People! The Art of Black Power." In *New Thoughts on the Black Arts Movement*, edited by Lisa Gail Collins and Margo Natalie Crawford, 1–19. New Brunswick, N.J.: Rutgers University Press, 2006.
Connolly, L. W. *The Censorship of English Drama, 1737–1824*. San Marino, Calif.: Huntington Library, 1974.

Connor, Steven. *Dumbstruck: A Cultural History of Ventriloquism*. Oxford: Oxford University Press, 2000.
Conquergood, Dwight. "Performing as a Moral Act: Ethical Dimensions of the Ethnography of Performance." *Literature in Performance* 5, no. 2 (1985): 1–13.
Cook, David. *Understanding Jihad*. Berkeley: University of California Press, 2005.
Cook, William W. "Change the Joke and Slip the Yoke: Traditions of Afro-American Satire." *Journal of Ethnic Studies* 13, no. 1 (Spring 1985): 109–34.
Crawford, Robert. *The Bard: Robert Burns, a Biography*. London: Jonathan Cape, 2009.
Cripps, Thomas. *Slow Fade to Black: The Negro in American Film, 1900–1942*. New York: Oxford University Press, 1977.
Curry, Leonard P. *The Free Black in Urban America, 1800–1850: The Shadow of the Dream*. Chicago: University of Chicago Press, 1983.
Davis, Jim. "Representing the Comic Actor at Work: The Harlow Portrait of Charles Mathews." *Nineteenth-Century Theatre and Film* 31, no. 2 (Winter 2004): 3–15.
Davis, Natalie Zemon. "Women on Top." In *Society and Culture in Early Modern France: Eight Essays by Natalie Zemon Davis*, 124–51. Palo Alto: Stanford University Press, 1975.
Deas, Laurence, and Jack Wilson. "All I Wants Is Ma Chickens." New York: Jos. W. Stern & Co., 1899.
de Grazia, Edward, and Jean Genet. "An Interview with Jean Genet." *Cardozo Studies in Law and Literature* 5, no. 2 (Autumn 1993): 307–24.
Dennison, Sam. *Scandalize My Name: Black Images in American Popular Music*. New York: Oxford University Press, 1982.
Desmond, Jane C. "Embodying Difference: Issues in Dance and Cultural Studies." *Cultural Critique* 26 (Winter 1993–94): 33–63.
Dickerson, Debra. *The End of Blackness*. New York: Pantheon, 2004.
Dickerson, Glenda. "The Cult of True Womanhood: Toward a Womanist Attitude in African American Theatre." In *Performing Feminisms: Feminist Critical Theory and Theatre*, edited by Sue Ellen Case, 109–18. Baltimore: Johns Hopkins University Press, 1990.
Digest of the Ordinances of the City Council of Charleston, from the year 1783 to July 1818; to which are annexed, extracts from the acts of the legislature which relate to the city of Charleston. Charleston: A. E. Miller, 1818.
Dizikes, John. *Opera in America: A Cultural History*. New Haven: Yale University Press, 1993.
Donohue, Joseph. "Distance, Death and Desire in *Salome*." In *The Cambridge Companion to Oscar Wilde*, edited by Peter Raby, 118–42. Cambridge: Cambridge University Press, 1997.
Douglass, Frederick. *Life and Times of Frederick Douglass*. 1892. Reprint, New York: Collier, 1962.
D'Souza, Dinesh. *The End of Racism: Principles for a Multicultural Society*. New York: Free Press, 1995.
DuBois, W. E. B. *The Souls of Black Folk*. 1903. Reprint, New York: Penguin, 1989.

Dunbar, Paul Laurence. *Lyrics of Lowly Life*. 1896. Reprint, New York: Arno, 1969.
Dwight, Timothy. *Travels in New England and New York*. Vol. 3. 1822. Reprint, Cambridge, Mass.: Harvard University Press, 1969.
Dyer, Richard. "The Colour of Virtue: Lillian Gish, Whiteness, and Femininity." In *Women and Film: A Sight and Sound Reader*, edited by Pam Cook and Philip Dodd, 1–9. Philadelphia: Temple University Press, 1993.
———. *Heavenly Bodies: Film Stars and Society*. 1986. Reprint, London: Routledge, 2004.
———. *The Matter of Images: Essays on Representations*. London: Routledge, 1993.
———. *White*. London: Routledge, 1997.
Dyer, Richard, and Paul McDonald. *Stars: New Edition*. London: British Film Institute, 1998.
Dyson, Michael, and Ronald Chennault. "Giving Whiteness a Black Eye: An Interview with Michael Eric Dyson." In *White Reign: Deploying Whiteness in America*, edited by Joe L. Kincheloe, Shirley R. Steinberg, Nelson M. Rodriguez, and Ronald E. Chennault, 299–328. New York: St. Martin's, 1998.
Edwards, Paul, and James Walvin. *Black Personalities in the Era of the Slave Trade*. Baton Rouge: Louisiana State University Press, 1983.
Elam, Harry J., Jr., and Michele Elam. "Blood Debt: Reparations in Langston Hughes's *Mulatto*." *Theatre Journal* 61, no. 1 (March 2009): 85–103.
Ellis, David Maldwyn. *New York, State and City*. Ithaca, N.Y.: Cornell University Press, 1979.
Ellis, Trey. "The New Black Aesthetic." *Callaloo* 12, no. 38 (Winter 1989): 233–43.
Ellison, Ralph. "Change the Joke and Slip the Yoke." In *Collected Essays of Ralph Ellison*, edited by John F. Callahan, 100–112. New York: Modern Library, 1995.
Ellman, Richard. *Oscar Wilde*. New York: Random House, 1988.
Emerson, Ralph Waldo. *Essays: First Series*. 1841. http://etext.virginia.edu/toc/modeng/public/EmeEssF.html (accessed April 1, 2011).
Encyclopedia of the Harlem Renaissance. Edited by Cary D. Wintz and Paul Finkelman. New York: Routledge, 2004.
Fabre, Geneviève. "African-American Commemorative Celebrations in the 19th Century." In *History and Memory in African-American Culture*, edited by Geneviève Fabre and Robert O'Meally, 72–91. New York: Oxford University Press, 1994.
———. *Drumbeats, Masks, and Metaphor*. Translated by Melvin Dixon. Cambridge, Mass.: Harvard University Press, 1983.
Fairchild, Henry Pratt. *The Melting-Pot Mistake*. Boston: Little, Brown, 1926.
Fanon, Frantz. *Black Skin, White Masks*. 1952. Translated by Charles Lam Markmann. Reprint, New York: Grove Press, 1967.
———. *The Wretched of the Earth*. 1961. Translated by Constance Farrington. Reprint, New York: Grove Press, 1963.
Faulkner, Howard J. "A Vanishing Race." *CLA Journal* 37, no. 3 (March 1994): 274–92.
Ferguson, Jeffrey B. *The Sage of Sugar Hill: George Schuyler and the Harlem Renaissance*. New Haven: Yale University Press, 2005.
Fischer, Michael M. J. "Ethnicity and the Post-Modern Arts of Memory." In *Writing*

Culture: The Poetics and Politics of Ethnography, edited by James Clifford and George E. Marcus, 194–233. Berkeley: University of California Press, 1986.

Fletcher, Tom. *100 Years of the Negro in Show Business*. 1954. Reprint, New York: Da Capo, 1984.

Fordham, Signithia, and John Ogbu. "Black Students' School Success: Coping with the Burden of 'Acting White.'" *Urban Review* 18, no. 3 (1986): 176–206.

Foreman, Ellen. "The Negro Ensemble Company: A Transcendent Vision." In *The Theatre of Black Americans: A Collection of Critical Essays*, edited by Errol Hill, 270–82. New York: Applause, 1987.

Fox, Dixon Ryan. "The Negro Vote in Old New York." *Political Science Quarterly* 32 (February 1917): 252–75.

Frazier, E. Franklin. *Black Bourgeoisie: The Rise of a New Middle Class in the United States*. New York: Collier, 1962.

Freeman, Rhoda Golden. *The Free Negro in New York City in the Era before the Civil War*. New York: Garland, 1994.

Fryer, Roland G. "Acting White: The Social Price Paid by the Best and Brightest Minority Students." *Education Next* 6, no. 1 (Winter 2006): 52–59. http://educationnext.org/actingwhite/ (accessed August 27, 2010).

Fusco, Coco. "Performance and the Power of the Popular." In *Let's Get It On: Politics of Black Performance*, edited by Catherine Ugwu, 158–75. Seattle: Bay Press, 1995.

Gaines, Kevin K. *Uplifting the Race: Black Leadership, Politics, and Culture in the Twentieth Century*. Chapel Hill: University of North Carolina Press, 1996.

Gale, Richard. "Archibald MacLaren's *The Negro Slaves* and the Scottish Response to British Colonialism." *Theatre Survey* 35 (November 1994): 77–93.

Gates, Henry Louis, Jr. *The Signifying Monkey: A Theory of African-American Literary Criticism*. New York: Oxford University Press, 1988.

Genet, Jean. *The Blacks: A Clown Show*. 1960. Translated by Bernard Frechtman. Reprint, New York: Grove Press, 1994.

Genovese, Eugene. "'Rather Be a Nigger Than a Poor White Man': Slave Perceptions of Southern Yeomen and Poor Whites." In *Toward a New View of America: Essays in Honor of Arthur C. Cole*, edited by Hans L. Trefousse, 79–96. New York: Burt Franklin, 1977.

———. *Roll, Jordan, Roll: The World the Slaves Made*. New York: Vintage, 1976.

George, Nelson. *Buppies, B-Boys, Baps & Bohos: Notes on Post-Soul Culture*. New York: Da Capo, 2001.

———. *Post-Soul Nation: The Explosive, Contradictory, Triumphant and Tragic 1980s as Experienced by African Americans (Previously Known as Blacks and Before That Negroes)*. New York: Penguin Group, 2004.

George-Graves, Nadine. *The Royalty of Negro Vaudeville: The Whitman Sisters and the Negotiation of Race, Gender, and Class in African American Theater, 1900–1940*. New York: St. Martin's, 2000.

Gilbert, Helen. "Black and White and Re(a)d All Over Again: Indigenous Minstrelsy in Contemporary Canadian and Australian Theatre." *Theatre Journal* 55, no. 4 (December 2003): 679–98.

Gilbert, Helen, and Jacqueline Lo. "Toward a Topography of Cross-Cultural Theatre Praxis." *Drama Review* 46, no. 3 (Autumn 2002): 31–53.
Gilje, Paul A. *The Road to Mobocracy: Popular Disorder in New York City, 1763–1834*. Chapel Hill: University of North Carolina Press, 1987.
Gill, Glenda E. "The Triumphs and Struggles of Earle Hyman in Traditional and Non-Traditional Roles." *Journal of American Drama and Theatre* 13, no. 1 (Winter 2001): 52–72.
Gilroy, Paul. *The Black Atlantic: Modernity and Double Consciousness*. Cambridge, Mass.: Harvard University Press, 1993.
———. "'. . . To Be Real': The Dissident Forms of Black Expressive Culture." In *Let's Get It On: Politics of Black Performance*, edited by Catherine Ugwu, 12–33. Seattle: Bay Press, 1995.
Ginsberg, Elaine K. "Introduction: The Politics of Passing." In *Passing and the Fictions of Identity*, edited by Elaine K. Ginsberg, 1–18. Durham, N.C.: Duke University Press, 1996.
Goldberg, Whoopi. *Book*. New York: Avon, 1998.
———. *Whoopi: Back to Broadway*. DVD. Directed by Marty Callner. New York: HBO, 2005.
———. *Whoopi Goldberg*. VHS. Directed by Thomas Schlamme. 1984. Stamford, Conn.: Vestron Video, 1986.
Goldin, Claudia Dale. *Urban Slavery in the American South, 1820–1860: A Quantitative History*. Chicago: University of Chicago Press, 1976.
Gomez, Michael A. *Exchanging Our Country Marks: The Transformation of African Identities in the Colonial and Antebellum South*. Chapel Hill: University of North Carolina Press, 1998.
Götrick, Kacke. *Apidan Theatre and Modern Drama: A Study in a Traditional Yoruba Theatre and Its Influence on Modern Drama by Yoruba Playwrights*. Stockholm: Almqvist & Wiksell International, 1984.
Gottschild, Brenda Dixon. *Digging the Africanist Presence in American Performance: Dance and Other Contexts*. Westport, Conn.: Greenwood, 1996.
Gramsci, Antonio. *Selections from the Prison Notebooks of Antonio Gramsci*. 1971. Translated by Quintin Hoare and Geoffrey Nowell Smith. Reprint, New York: International Publishers, 1978.
Graziano, John. "The Early Life and Career of the 'Black Patti': The Odyssey of an African American Singer in the Late Nineteenth Century." *Journal of the American Musicological Society* 53, no. 3 (Autumn 2000): 543–96.
Gregory, Dick. *From the Back of the Bus*. Edited by Bob Orben. New York: Avon, 1962.
———. *In Living Black and White*. CD. Ithaca, Ill.: Collector's Choice Music, 2008.
Gregory, Dick, and Robert Lipsyte. *Nigger: An Autobiography by Dick Gregory*. New York: Dutton, 1964.
Gregory, Dick, and Shelia P. Moses. *Callus on My Soul: A Memoir*. New York: Kensington, 2000.
Grubar, Susan. *Racechanges: White Skin, Black Face in American Culture*. New York: Oxford University Press, 1997.

Haggins, Bambi. *Laughing Mad: The Black Comic Persona in Post-Soul America.* New Brunswick, N.J.: Rutgers University Press, 2007.
Hamm, Charles. *Yesterdays: Popular Song in America.* New York: Norton, 1979.
Harris, Cheryl I. "Whiteness as Property." In *Critical Race Theory: The Key Writings That Formed the Movement*, edited by Kimberle Crenshaw, Neil Gotanda, Gary Peller, and Kendall Thomas, 276–91. New York: New Press, 1996.
Harris, Leslie. "Creating the African-American Working Class: Black and White Workers, Abolitionists, Reformers in New York City, 1785–1863." Unpublished dissertation, Stanford University, 1994.
Harrison, Hubert. *A Hubert Harrison Reader.* Edited by Jeffrey B. Perry. Middleton, Conn.: Wesleyan University Press, 2001.
Harrison, Paul Carter. *The Drama of Nommo.* New York: Grove Press, 1972.
Hartman, Saidiya. *Scenes of Subjection: Terror, Slavery, and Self-Making in Nineteenth-Century America.* New York: Oxford University Press, 1997.
Hay, Samuel. *African-American Theatre: An Historical and Critical Analysis.* New York: Cambridge University Press, 1994.
Haygood, Will. *In Black and White: The Life of Sammy Davis Jr.* New York: Knopf, 2003.
Hebdige, Dick. *Subculture: Meaning of Style.* London: Routledge, 2002.
Herskovits, Melville J. *The Myth of the Negro Past.* 1941. Reprint, Boston: Beacon Press, 1990.
Hill, Errol G. *Shakespeare in Sable.* Amherst: University of Massachusetts Press, 1984.
Hill, Errol G., and James V. Hatch. *A History of African American Theatre.* New York: Cambridge University Press, 2003.
Hitchcock, Wiley H. *Music in the United States: A Historical Introduction.* Englewood Cliffs, N.J.: Prentice-Hall, 1974.
Hodge, Francis. "Charles Mathews Reports on America." *Quarterly Journal of Speech* 36 (December 1950): 492–99.
Home, John. *Douglas: A Tragedy.* 1771. In *English Plays, 1660–1820*, edited by A. E. Morgan, 715–47. New York: Harper & Brothers, 1955.
hooks, bell. "Critical Reflections: Adrienne Kennedy, the Writer, the Work." In *Intersecting Boundaries: The Theatre of Adrienne Kennedy*, edited by Paul K. Bryant-Jackson and Lois More Overbeck, 179–85. Minneapolis: University of Minnesota Press, 1992.
———. "Performance Practice as a Site of Opposition." In *Let's Get It On: Politics of Black Performance*, edited by Catherine Ugwu, 210–21. Seattle: Bay Press, 1995.
———. "Representations of Whiteness in the Black Imagination." In *Black on White: Black Writers on What It Means to Be White*, edited by David Roediger, 38–53. New York: Schocken, 1998.
Hughes, Langston. *Mulatto: A Tragedy of the Deep South.* In *Black Theatre USA: Plays by African Americans: The Recent Period, 1935–Today*, edited by James V. Hatch and Ted Shine, 4–23. New York: Free Press, 1996.
Hurston, Zora Neale. "Characteristics of Negro Expression." In *Negro: An Anthology*, edited by Nancy Cunard, 24–31. New York: Frederick Ungar, 1970.

Hutcheon, Linda. *A Theory of Parody*. New York: Methuen, 1985.
Hutchinson, George. "Mediating 'Race' and 'Nation': The Cultural Politics of the Messenger." *African American Review* 28, no. 4 (Winter 1994): 531–48.
Hwang, David Henry. *Yellowface*. *American Theatre* 25, no. 4 (April 2008): 59–79.
Idowu, E. Bolaji. *Olódùmarè: God in Yorùbá Belief*. Longman Nigeria, 1996.
Ignatiev, Noel. *How the Irish Became White*. New York: Routledge, 1995.
Jacobson, Matthew Frye. *Whiteness of a Different Color: European Immigrants and the Alchemy of Race*. Cambridge, Mass.: Harvard University Press, 1998.
Jameson, Frederic. *Brecht and Method*. London: Verso, 1998.
JanMohamed, Abdul. *Manichean Aesthetics: The Politics of Literature in Colonial Africa*. Amherst: University of Massachusetts Press, 1983.
Jefferson, Thomas. *The Complete Jefferson, Containing His Major Writings, Published and Unpublished, Except His Letters*. Edited by Saul K. Padover. New York: Tudor Publishing Company, 1943.
Jenkins, Ron. *Subversive Laughter: The Liberating Power of Comedy*. New York: Free Press, 1994.
Johnson, E. Patrick. *Appropriating Blackness: Performance and the Politics of Authenticity*. Durham, N.C.: Duke University Press, 2003.
Johnson, James Weldon. *Black Manhattan*. New York: Knopf, 1930.
Johnson, Kenneth R. "Black Kinesics: Some Non-Verbal Communication Patterns in the Black Culture." *Florida FL Reporter* 9 (Spring/Fall 1971): 17–20, 57.
Jones, Joni L. "Performance Ethnography: The Role of Embodiment in Cultural Authenticity." *Theatre Topics* 12, no. 1 (2002): 1–15.
Jones, LeRoi. *Blues People: Negro Music in White America*. New York: William Morrow, 1963.
Jones, Lisa. *Bulletproof Diva: Tales of Race, Sex and Hair*. New York: Anchor, 1994.
Jordan, Winthrop D. *White over Black: American Attitudes toward the Negro, 1550-1812*. Chapel Hill: University of North Carolina Press, 1968.
Kaufman, Michael W. "The Delicate World of Reprobation: A Note on the Black Revolutionary Theater." In *The Theatre of Black Americans: A Collection of Critical Essays*, edited by Errol Hill, 192–209. New York: Applause, 1987.
Kelley, Robin D. G. *Freedom Dreams: The Black Radical Imagination*. Boston: Beacon Press, 2002.
Kemble, Edward Windsor. *Coontown's 400*. New York: Life Publishing Company, 1899.
Kennedy, Adrienne. *Funnyhouse of a Negro*. 1964. In *Adrienne Kennedy in One Act*, 1–23. Minneapolis: University of Minnesota Press, 1988.
———. *A Movie Star Has to Star in Black and White*. In *Adrienne Kennedy in One Act*, 79–103. Minneapolis: University of Minnesota Press, 1988.
———. "On the Writing of *Funnyhouse of a Negro*." In *The Adrienne Kennedy Reader*, 27–28. Minneapolis: University of Minnesota Press, 2001.
———. *People Who Led to My Plays*. New York: Theatre Communications Group, 1987.
Kennedy, Randall. *Nigger: The Strange Career of a Troublesome Word*. New York: Pantheon, 2002.

The Kerner Report: The 1968 Report of the National Advisory Commission on Civil Disorders. 1968. Reprint, New York: Pantheon, 1988.

Killens, John Oliver, ed. *The Trial Record of Denmark Vesey*. 1822. Reprint, Boston: Beacon Press, 1970.

Killin' Them Softly. VHS. Directed by Stan Lathan. New York: HBO/Pilot Boy Productions/UrbanWorks, 2000.

Kincheloe, Joe L., Shirley R. Steinberg, Nelson M. Rodriguez, and Ronald E. Chennault, eds. *White Reign: Deploying Whiteness in America*. New York: St. Martin's, 1998.

King, Colin. *Offside Racism: Playing the White Man*. Oxford: Berg, 2004.

Klingberg, Frank J. *An Appraisal of the Negro in Colonial South Carolina: A Study in Americanization*. Philadelphia: Porcupine Press, 1975.

Knight, Christina. *Bridge and Tunnel* review. *Theatre Journal* 57, no. 4 (December 2005): 720–22.

Kochman, Thomas. *Black and White Styles in Conflict*. Chicago: University of Chicago Press, 1981.

Kolin, Philip C. "Williams in Ebony: Black and Multi-Racial Productions of *A Streetcar Named Desire*." *Black American Literature Forum* 25, no. 1 (Spring 1991): 147–81.

Kondo, Dorinne. "(Re)Visions of Race: Contemporary Race Theory and the Cultural Politics of Racial Crossover in Documentary Theatre." *Theatre Journal* 52, no. 1 (2000): 81–107.

Krasner, David. *A Beautiful Pageant: African American Theatre, Drama, and Performance in the Harlem Renaissance, 1910–1927*. New York: Palgrave Macmillan, 2002.

———. *Resistance, Parody, and Double Consciousness in African American Theatre, 1895–1910*. New York: St. Martin's, 1997.

Lane, Christopher. "Voided Role: On Genet." *MLN* 112, no. 5 (December 1997): 876–908.

Lapsanksy, Emma Jones. "Since They Got Those Separate Churches: Afro-Americans and Racism in Jacksonian Philadelphia." *American Quarterly* 32 (Spring 1980): 54–78.

Lawal, Babatunde. *The Gèlèdé Spectacle: Art, Gender, and Social Harmony in an African Culture*. Seattle: University of Washington Press, 1996.

Lerner, Michael, and Cornel West. *Jews and Blacks: Let the Healing Begin*. New York: G. P. Putnam's Sons, 1995.

Levine, Lawrence. *Black Culture and Black Consciousness*. London: Oxford University Press, 1977.

Lewis, Barbara, and Anna Deavere Smith. "The Circle of Confusion: A Conversation with Anna Deavere Smith." *Kenyon Review* 15, no. 4 (Fall 1993): 54–64.

Lewis, Matthew Gregory. *Journal of a West India Proprietor*. 1834. Reprint, New York: Houghton Mifflin, 1929.

Lewis, Theophilus, ed. "Pioneers of the Stage: Memoirs of William Foster." *The Official Theatrical World of Colored Artists, National Directory & Guide* 1 (April 1928): 40–49.

Lhamon, W. T., Jr. *Raising Cain: Blackface Performance from Jim Crow to Hip Hop.* Cambridge, Mass.: Harvard University Press, 1998.
Limon, John. *Stand-Up Comedy in Theory, or, Abjection in America.* Durham, N.C.: Duke University Press, 2000.
Lindfors, Bernth. "'Mislike Me Not for My Complexion . . .': Ira Aldridge in Whiteface." *African American Review* 33 (Summer 1999): 347–54.
Linebaugh, Peter. "All the Atlantic Mountains Shook." *Labour/Le Travailleur* 10 (Autumn 1982): 87–121.
Lipsitz, George. *The Possessive Investment in Whiteness: How White People Profit from Identity Politics.* Philadelphia: Temple University Press, 1998.
———. *Time Passages: Collective Memory and American Popular Culture.* Minneapolis: University of Minnesota Press, 1990.
Littlefield, Daniel C. *Rice and Slaves: Ethnicity and the Slave Trade in Colonial South Carolina.* Baton Rouge: Louisiana State University Press, 1981.
Litwack, Leon. *North of Slavery: The Negro in the Free States, 1790–1860.* Chicago: University of Chicago Press, 1961.
Locke, Alain. "The Negro and the American Stage." *Theatre Arts Monthly* 10 (February 1926): 112–20.
Lott, Eric. *Love and Theft: Blackface Minstrelsy and the American Working Class.* New York: Oxford University Press, 1993.
MacLean, Fitzroy. *Highlanders: A History of the Scottish Clans.* New York: Viking Studio Books, 1995.
———. *Scotland: A Concise History.* London: Thames & Hudson, 1993.
Mahar, William J. *Behind the Burnt Cork Mask: Early Blackface Minstrelsy and Antebellum American Popular Culture.* Urbana: University of Illinois Press, 1998.
Martin, Carol, and Anna Deavere Smith. "Anna Deavere Smith: The Word Becomes You, an Interview." *Drama Review* 37, no. 4 (Winter 1993): 45–62.
Mathews, Charles. "La Diligence." http://www.bbk.ac.uk/english/skc/dumbstruck/archive/dilig.htm (accessed December 30, 2008).
———. *Mr. Mathews's Trip to America.* Philadelphia: Simon Probasco, 1824.
McAllister, Marvin. "Bob Cole's Willie Wayside: Whiteface Hobo, Middle-Class Farmer, White Trash Hero." *Journal of American Drama and Theatre* 14, no. 1 (Winter 2002): 64–77.
———. "Dave Chappelle, Whiteface Minstrelsy, and 'Irresponsible' Satire." In *African American Humor, Irony, and Satire: Ishmael Reed, Satirically Speaking,* edited by Dana Williams, 118–30. Newcastle upon Tyne: Cambridge Scholars Publishing, 2007.
———. "'White People Do Not Know How to Behave at Entertainments Designed for Ladies and Gentlemen of Colour': A History of New York's African Grove/African Theatre." Unpublished dissertation, Northwestern University, 1997.
———. *White People Do Not Know How to Behave at Entertainments Designed for Ladies and Gentlemen of Colour: William Brown's African and American Theater.* Chapel Hill: University of North Carolina Press, 2003.
McCants, David A. *Patrick Henry, the Orator.* New York: Greenwood, 1990.

McLaren, Peter. "Whiteness Is . . . The Struggle for Postcolonial Hybridity." In *White Reign: Deploying Whiteness in America*, edited by Joe L. Kincheloe, Shirley R. Steinberg, Nelson M. Rodriguez, and Ronald E. Chennault, 63–76. New York: St. Martin's, 1998.

McLean, Albert F. *American Vaudeville as Ritual*. Lexington: University of Kentucky Press, 1965.

McManus, Edgar. *A History of Negro Slavery in New York*. Syracuse: Syracuse University Press, 1960.

McWhorter, John. *Losing the Race: Self-Sabotage in Black America*. New York: Perennial, 2001.

———. "Mr. Mimic: The Extraordinary Gifts and Fleeting Legacy of Sammy Davis, Jr." *City Journal* 20, no. 2 (Spring 2010). http://city-journal.org/2010/20_2_urb-sammy-davis-jr.html (accessed August 25, 2010).

Memoirs of Charles Mathews, Comedian. Vol. 3. Edited by Anne Jackson Mathews. London: R. Bentley, 1839.

Miller, Monica L. *Slaves to Fashion: Black Dandyism and the Styling of Black Diasporic Identity*. Durham, N.C.: Duke University Press, 2009.

Mitchison, Rosalind. *A History of Scotland*. 2nd ed. London: Routledge, 1990.

Mkapa, Ben W. "What Black Is Black? Thoughts on Jean Genet's *The Blacks*." *Transition* 1 (November 1961): 39–40.

"Moms" Mabley: Comedy Ain't Pretty. CD. Universal City, Calif.: Fuel 2000 Records, 2004.

"Moms" Mabley at the Playboy Club. CD. Tarzana, Calif.: Laugh.com and Universal Music Enterprises, 2003.

Monroe, John G. "The Harlem Little Theatre Movement, 1920–1929." *Journal of American Culture* 6, no. 4 (Winter 1983): 63–70.

Morrison, Toni. *Playing in the Dark: Whiteness and the Literary Imagination*. Cambridge, Mass.: Harvard University Press, 1992.

Moten, Fred. *In the Break: The Aesthetics of the Black Radical Tradition*. Minneapolis: University of Minnesota Press, 2003.

Moya, Paula, and Michael R. Hames-Garcia, eds. *Reclaiming Identity: Realist Theory and the Predicament of Postmodernism*. Berkeley: University of California Press, 2000.

Muckelbauer, John. *The Future of Invention: Rhetoric, Postmodernism, and the Problem of Change*. Albany: State University of New York Press, 2008.

Muñoz, José Esteban. *Disidentifications: Queers of Color and the Performance of Politics*. Minneapolis: University of Minnesota Press, 1999.

Neal, Larry. "The Black Arts Movement." *Drama Review* 12, no. 4 (Summer 1968): 28–39.

Neal, Mark Anthony. *Soul Babies: Black Popular Culture and the Post-Soul Aesthetic*. New York: Routledge, 2002.

Nelson, Alondra. "*A Black Mass* as Black Gothic: Myth and Bioscience in Black Cultural Nationalism." In *New Thoughts on the Black Arts Movement*, edited by Lisa Gail Collins and Margo Natalie Crawford, 137–53. New Brunswick, N.J.: Rutgers University Press, 2006.

Newitz, Annalee, and Matt Wray, eds. *White Trash: Race and Class in America.* New York: Routledge, 1997.
Nielsen, Peter. *Recollections of a Six-Years' Residence in the United States of America, Interspersed with Original Anecdotes.* Glasgow: D. Robertson, 1830.
Nyong'o, Tavia. *The Amalgamation Waltz: Race, Performance and the Ruses of Memory.* Minneapolis: University of Minnesota Press, 2009.
Odell, George C. D. *Annals of the New York Stage.* Vol. 3. New York: Columbia University Press, 1927.
O'Keeffe, John. *The Poor Soldier.* 1782. Reprinted in *The Plays of John O'Keeffe*, vol. 2, edited by Frederick M. Link, 265–311. New York: Garland, 1981.
Olaniyan, Tejumola. *Scars of Conquest/Masks of Resistance: The Invention of Cultural Identities in African, African-American, and Caribbean Drama.* New York: Oxford University Press, 1995.
Olmsted, Frederick Law. *A Journey in the Seaboard Slave States, With Remarks on Their Economy.* New York: Mason Brothers, 1859.
Ottley, Roi, and William J. Weatherby, eds. *Negro in New York: An Informal Social History.* New York: Oceana Publications, 1967.
Panton, Kenneth J., and Keith A. Cowland. *Historical Dictionary of the United Kingdom.* Vol. 2. London: Scarecrow, 1998.
Parks, Suzan-Lori. *The America Play and Other Works.* New York: Theatre Communications Group, 1995.
———. *Topdog/Underdog.* New York: Dramatist Play Service, 2002.
Patterson, Orlando. *The Sociology of Slavery: An Analysis of the Origins, Development, and Structure of Negro Slave Society in Jamaica.* Rutherford, N.J.: Fairleigh Dickinson University Press, 1969.
Paulin, Diana. "Representing Forbidden Desire: Interracial Unions, Surrogacy and Performance." *Theatre Journal* 49, no. 4 (1997): 417–39.
Payne, Aaron. "The Negro in New York prior to 1860." *Howard Review* 1 (June 1923): 1–64.
Peiss, Kathy. *Cheap Amusements: Working Women and Leisure in Turn-of-the-Century New York.* Philadelphia: Temple University Press, 1986.
Peterson, Jane T. "Pride and Prejudice: The Demise of the Ethiopian Art Theatre." *Theatre History Studies* 14 (June 1994): 141–49.
Phelan, Peggy. *Unmarked: The Politics of Performance.* London: Routledge, 1993.
Piersen, William. *Black Legacy: America's Hidden Heritage.* Amherst: University of Massachusetts Press, 1993.
Piper, Adrian. "Passing for White, Passing for Black." In *Passing and the Fictions of Identity*, edited by Elaine K. Ginsberg, 234–69. Durham, N.C.: Duke University Press, 1996.
Porter, Susan L. *With an Air Debonair: Musical Theatre in America, 1785–1815.* Washington, D.C.: Smithsonian Institution Press, 1991.
Powers, Bernard E., Jr. *Black Charlestonians: A Social History, 1832–1885.* Fayetteville: University of Arkansas Press, 1994.
Pratt, Mary Louise. "Fieldwork in Common Places." In *Writing Culture: The Poetics

and Politics of Ethnography, edited by James Clifford and George E. Marcus, 27–50. Berkeley: University of California Press, 1986.
Pryor, Richard. *Richard Pryor: Live & Smokin'*. VHS. Directed by Michael Blum. 1971. Orland Park, Ill.: MPI Home Video, 1997.
———. *Richard Pryor: Live in Concert*. VHS. Directed by Jeff Margolis. 1979. Orland Park, Ill.: MPI Home Video, 1996.
Pryor, Richard, and Todd Gold. *Pryor Convictions and Other Life Sentences*. New York: Pantheon, 1995.
Raby, Peter. *Oscar Wilde*. London: Cambridge University Press, 1988.
Rahier, Jean Muteba, ed. *Representations of Blackness and the Performance of Identities*. Westport, Conn.: Bergin & Garvey, 1999.
Rahman, Jacquelyn. "It's Serious Business: The Linguistic Construction of Middle-Class White Characters by African American Narrative Comedians." Unpublished dissertation, Stanford University, 2004.
Rawick, George, ed. *The American Slave: A Composite Autobiography*. Vols. 2 and 3. Westport, Conn.: Greenwood, 1978.
Reinelt, Janelle. "Performing Race: Anna Deavere Smith's *Fires in the Mirror*." *Modern Drama* 39, no. 4 (Winter 1996): 609–17.
Richards, Sandra L. "Caught in the Act of Social Definition: *On the Road* with Anna Deavere Smith." In *Acting Out: Feminist Performances*, edited by Lynda Hart and Peggy Phelan, 35–53. Ann Arbor: University of Michigan Press, 1993.
Riis, Thomas L. "Black Musical Theatre in New York, 1890–1915." Unpublished dissertation, University of Michigan, 1981.
———. "Bob Cole: His Life and His Legacy to Black Musical Theater." *Black Perspective in Music* 13, no. 2 (Fall 1985): 135–50.
———. *Just before Jazz: Black Musical Theatre in New York, 1890–1915*. Washington, D.C.: Smithsonian Institution Press, 1989.
———. *More Than Just Minstrel Shows: The Rise of Black Musical Theatre at the Turn of the Century*. Brooklyn: Brooklyn College Institute for Studies in American Music, 1992.
Roach, Joseph. *Cities of the Dead: Circum-Atlantic Performance*. New York: Columbia University Press, 1996.
Roberts, Jackie M. "Healing Myths from the Ethnic Community, or Why I Don't Teach August Wilson." *Theatre Topics* 20, no. 2 (September 2010): 147–56.
Robinson, Amy. "Forms of Appearance of Value: Homer Plessy and the Politics of Privacy." In *Performance and Cultural Politics*, edited by Elin Diamond, 237–61. London: Routledge, 1996.
Rodriguez, Richard. *Brown: The Last Discovery of America*. New York: Penguin Putnam, 2003.
Roediger, David R. *The Wages of Whiteness*. New York: Verso, 1991.
———. *Working toward Whiteness: How America's Immigrants Became White: The Strange Journey from Ellis Island to the Suburbs*. New York: Basic Books, 2005.
Rogin, Michael. *Blackface, White Noise: Jewish Immigrants in the Hollywood Melting Pot*. Berkeley: University of California Press, 1996.

Rose, Margaret. *Parody: Ancient, Modern, and Post-Modern.* New York: Cambridge University Press, 1993.
Sampson, Henry T. *Blacks in Blackface: A Sourcebook on Early Black Musical Shows.* Metuchen, N.J.: Scarecrow, 1980.
Sandarg, Robert. "Jean Genet and the Black Panther Party." *Journal of Black Studies* 16, no. 3 (March 1986): 269–82.
Sanders, Leslie Catherine. *The Development of Black Theater in America.* Baton Rouge: Louisiana State University Press, 1988.
Saturday Night Live: The Best of Eddie Murphy. VHS. New York: NBC Home Video, 1998.
Savona, Jeanette L. *Jean Genet.* London: Macmillan, 1983.
Saxton, Alexander. *The Rise and Fall of the White Republic: Class Politics and Mass Culture in Nineteenth-Century America.* 2nd ed. London: Verso, 2003.
Scales-Trent, Judy. "The American Celebration of Whiteness." In *Whiteness: Feminist Philosophical Reflections*, edited by Chris J. Cuomo and Kim Q. Hall, 56–57. Lanham, Md.: Rowman & Littlefield, 1999.
Schechner, Richard. *Between Theater and Anthropology.* Philadelphia: University of Pennsylvania Press, 1985.
Schechter, William. *The History of Negro Humor in America.* New York: Fleet Press, 1970.
Schueller, Malini Johar. "Performing Whiteness, Performing Blackness: Dorr's Cultural Capital and the Critique of Slavery." *Criticism* 41 (Spring 1999): 233–56.
Schuyler, George. *Black No More: Being an Account of the Strange and Wonderful Workings of Science in the Land of the Free, A.D. 1933–1940.* 1931. Reprint, New York: Negro Universities Press, 1969.
Scott, Esther Fulks. "Negroes as Actors in Serious Plays." *Opportunity Magazine* 1, no. 4 (April 1923): 20–23.
Scott, James C. *Domination and the Arts of Resistance: Hidden Transcripts.* New Haven: Yale University Press, 1990.
———. *Weapons of the Weak: Everyday Forms of Peasant Resistance.* New Haven: Yale University Press, 1985.
Shannon, Sandra G. "Amiri Baraka on Directing." In *Conversations with Amiri Baraka*, edited by Charlie Reilly, 230–38. Jackson: University Press of Mississippi, 1994.
———. "Manipulating Myth, Magic, and Legend: Amiri Baraka's *Black Mass.*" *CLA Journal* 39, no. 3 (March 1996): 357–68.
Singer, Armand E. "Don Juan in America." *Kentucky Foreign Language Quarterly* 7 (4th Quarter 1960): 226–32.
Singh, Nikhil Pal. *Black Is a Country: Race and the Unfinished Struggle for Democracy.* Cambridge, Mass.: Harvard University Press, 2004.
Smith, Anna Deavere. *Fires in the Mirror.* VHS. Directed by George Wolfe. Thousand Oaks, Calif.: Monterey Video, 2003.
———. *Fires in the Mirror: Crown Heights, Brooklyn and Other Identities.* New York: Anchor, 1993.

Smith, Mona Z. *Becoming Something: The Story of Canada Lee*. New York: Faber and Faber, 2004.

Smith, Valerie. *Not Just Race, Not Just Gender: Black Feminist Readings*. New York: Routledge, 1998.

Snipe, Simon. *Sports of New York: Containing a Peep at the Grand Military Ball, Hewlett at Home, Simon in Regimentals, etc*. New York, 1824.

Snyder, Robert W. *The Voice of the City: Vaudeville and Popular Culture in New York*. New York: Oxford University Press, 1989.

Sotiropoulos, Karen. *Staging Race: Black Performers in Turn of the Century America*. Cambridge, Mass.: Harvard University Press, 2006.

Southern, Eileen, ed. *African American Theater: Out of Bondage and Peculiar Sam, or, the Underground Railroad*. New York: Garland, 1994.

Spillers, Hortense J. "'All the Things You Could Be by Now, if Sigmund Freud's Wife Was Your Mother': Psychoanalysis and Race." In *Black, White, and in Color: Essays on American Literature and Culture*, 376–427. Chicago: University of Chicago Press, 2003.

———."The Idea of Black Culture." *CR: The New Centennial Review* 6, no. 3 (Winter 2006): 7–28.

———. "Interstices: A Small Drama of Words." In *Black, White, and in Color: Essays on American Literature and Culture*, 152–75. Chicago: University of Chicago Press, 2003.

Stansell, Christine. *City of Women: Sex and Class in New York, 1789–1860*. Urbana: University of Illinois Press, 1987.

Stearns, Marshall, and Jean Stearns. *Jazz Dance: The Story of American Vernacular Dance*. New York: Macmillan, 1968.

Strand, Ginger Gail. "*Jails, Hospitals & Hip Hop* Review." *Theatre Journal* 50, no. 4 (December 1998): 523–25.

Sundquist, Eric J. *To Wake the Nations: Race in the Making of American Literature*. Cambridge, Mass.: Harvard University Press, 1993.

Taubes, Susan. "The White Mask Falls." *Tulane Drama Review* 7, no. 3 (Spring 1963): 85–92.

Tessman, Lisa, and Bat-Ami Bar On. "The Other Colors of Whiteness: A Travelogue." In *Whiteness: Feminist Philosophical Reflections*, edited by Chris J. Cuomo and Kim Q. Hall, 108–14. Lanham, Md.: Rowman & Littlefield, 1999.

Thompson, Ayanna. "Practicing Theory/Theorizing a Practice: An Introduction to Shakespearean Colorblind Casting." In *Colorblind Shakespeare: New Perspectives on Race and Performance*, edited by Ayanna Thompson, 1–26. New York: Routledge, 2006.

Thompson, Debby. "Is Race a Trope? Anna Deavere and the Question of Racial Performativity." *African American Review* 37, no. 1 (2003) 127–39.

Thompson, Deborah. "Reversing Blackface Minstrelsy, Improvising Racial Identity: Adrienne Kennedy's 'Funnyhouse of a Negro.'" *Post Identity* 1, no. 1 (Fall 1997): 13–38.

Thompson, George A., Jr. *A Documentary History of the African Theatre*. Evanston, Ill.: Northwestern University Press, 1998.

Thompson, Robert Farris. "An Aesthetic of the Cool: West African Dance." In *The Theatre of Black Americans: A Collection of Critical Essays*, edited by Errol G. Hill, 99–111. New York: Applause, 1987.
Thompson, Sister Francesca. "Evelyn Preer." In *Notable Women in the American Theater: A Biographical Dictionary*, edited by Alice M. Robinson, Vera Mowry Roberts, and Milly S. Barranger, 731–35. New York: Greenwood, 1989.
———. "The Lafayette Players, 1915–1932." In *The Theatre of Black Americans: A Collection of Critical Essays*, edited by Errol G. Hill, 211–30. New York: Applause, 1987.
Tobin, Terrence. *Plays by Scots*. Iowa City: University of Iowa Press, 1974.
Toll, Robert. *Blacking Up: The Minstrel Show in Nineteenth Century America*. New York: Oxford University Press, 1974.
Turner, Victor W. *The Anthropology of Performance*. New York: PAJ Publications, 1988.
Tyler, Mois Coit. *Patrick Henry*. 1898. Reprint, Ithaca, N.Y.: Great Seal Books, 1962.
Twenge, Jean M. *Generation Me: Why Today's Young Americans Are More Confident, Assertive, Entitled and More Miserable Than Ever Before*. New York: Free Press, 2006.
Vontress, Clemmont E., Calvin E. Woodland, and Lawrence Epp. "Cultural Dysthymia: An Unrecognized Disorder among African Americans?" *Journal of Multicultural Counseling and Development* 35 (July 2007): 130–41.
Wade, Richard C. *Slavery in the Cities: The South, 1820–1860*. New York: Oxford University Press, 1964.
Ward, Douglas Turner. *Day of Absence*. In *Black Theatre USA: The Recent Period, 1935–Today*, edited by James V. Hatch and Ted Shine, 264–80. New York: Free Press, 1996.
Watermelon Man. VHS. Directed by Melvin Van Peebles. 1970. Burbank, Calif.: Columbia Tristar Home Video, 1987.
Watkins, Mel. *On the Real Side: A History of African-American Comedy*. Chicago: Lawrence Hill Books, 1999.
Watson, Steven. *Preparing for Saints: Gertrude Stein, Virgil Thomson, and the Mainstreaming of American Modernism*. Berkeley: University of California Press, 2000.
Webster, John. *The Duchess of Malfi*. 1614. Edited by Elizabeth M. Brennan. Reprint, New York: Hill and Wang, 1966.
Wemyss, Francis Courtney. *Wemyss' Chronology of the American Stage, from 1752 to 1852*. 1852. Reprint, New York: Benjamin Blom, 1968.
Wesley, Charles H. "The Negroes of New York in the Emancipation Movement." *Journal of Negro History* 24 (January 1939): 65–72.
White, Shane. *Somewhat More Independent*. Athens: University of Georgia Press, 1991.
———. *Stories of Freedom in Black New York*. Cambridge, Mass.: Harvard University Press, 2007.
White, Shane, and Graham J. White. *Stylin': African-American Expressive Culture from Its Beginnings to the Zoot Suit*. Ithaca, N.Y.: Cornell University Press, 1998.

Wiegman, Robyn. "Whiteness Studies and the Paradox of Particularity." *boundary 2* 26 (Autumn 1999): 115–50.

Wilde, Oscar. *Salomé.* 1891. Translated by Lord Alfred Douglas. In *Oscar Wilde: Plays*, 315–48. Baltimore: Penguin Plays, 1968.

Wilentz, Sean. *Chants Democratic: New York City and the Rise of the American Working Class, 1788–1850*. Oxford: Oxford University Press, 1984.

Williams, Patricia J. *Seeing a Color-Blind Future: The Paradox of Race.* New York: Noonday Press, 1998.

Wilson, August. "The Ground on Which I Stand." *Callaloo* 20, no. 3 (Summer 1997): 493–503.

Woll, Allen. *Black Musical Theatre: From Coontown to Dreamgirls.* Baton Rouge: Louisiana State University Press, 1989.

Wood, Alice. *The Stage History of Shakespeare's King Richard the Third.* New York: Columbia University Press, 1909.

Wood, Jacqueline. "Weight of the Mask: Parody and the Heritage of Minstrelsy in Adrienne Kennedy's *Funnyhouse of a Negro.*" *Journal of Dramatic Theory and Criticism* 17 (Spring 2003): 5–24.

Wood, Peter. *Black Majority: Negroes in Colonial South Carolina from 1670 through the Stono Rebellion.* New York: Norton, 1975.

Wright, Kai. "Reality Theater: A Profile of Performance Artist Sarah Jones." *Progressive* 68, no. 6 (June 2004). http://www.kaiwright.com/newmore.php?id=245_0_29_0_M (accessed August 27, 2010).

Wynter, Leon E. *American Skin: Pop Culture, Big Business, and the End of White America.* New York: Crown, 2002.

X, Marvin, and Faruk. "Islam and Black Art: An Interview with LeRoi Jones." In *Conversations with Amiri Baraka*, edited by Charlie Reilly, 51–61. Jackson: University Press of Mississippi, 1994.

Index

10/28/14